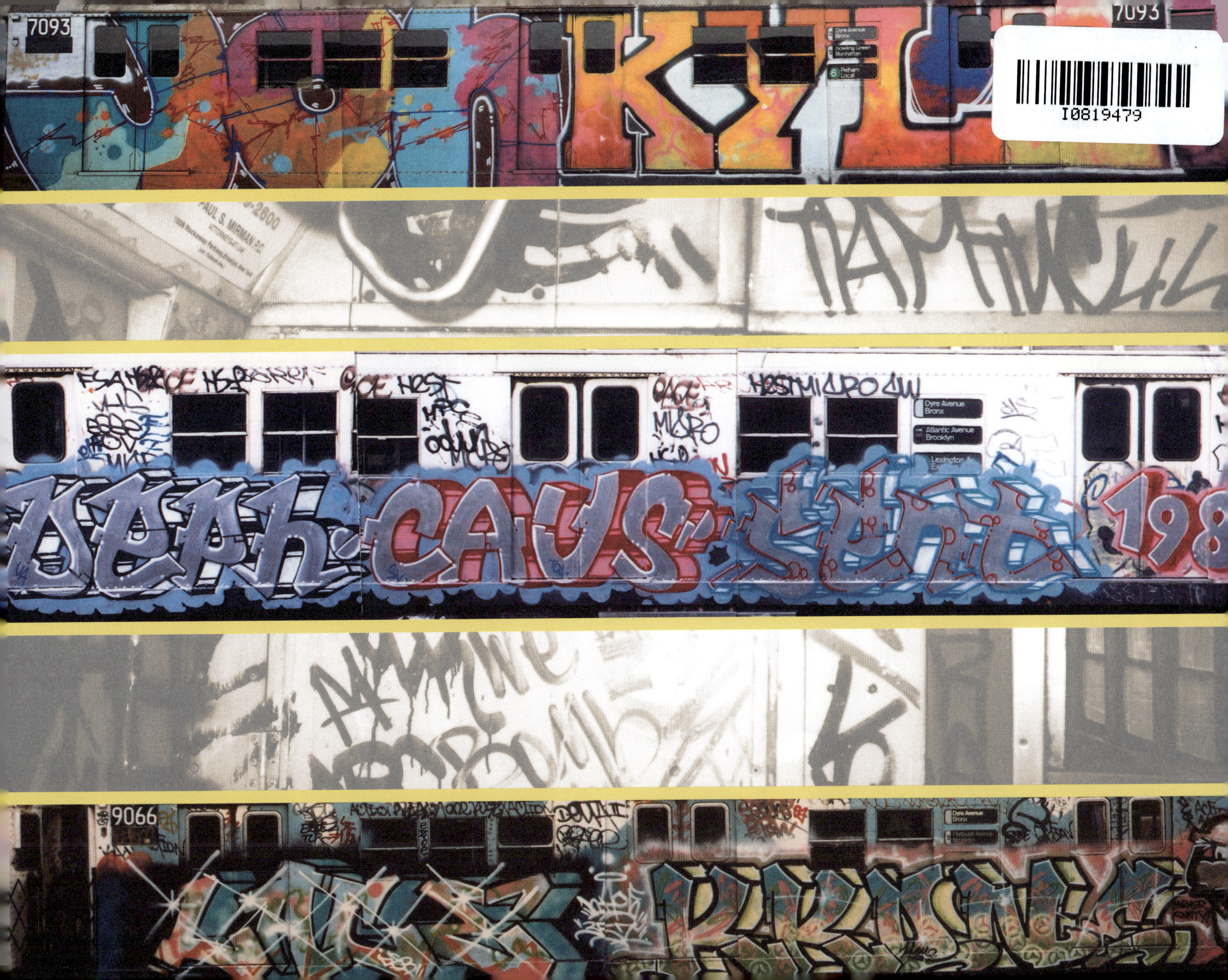
7093
7093
Dyre Avenue Bronx
Bowling Green Manhattan
6 Pelham Local
I0819479
Dyre Avenue Bronx
Atlantic Avenue Brooklyn
9066
Dyre Avenue Bronx

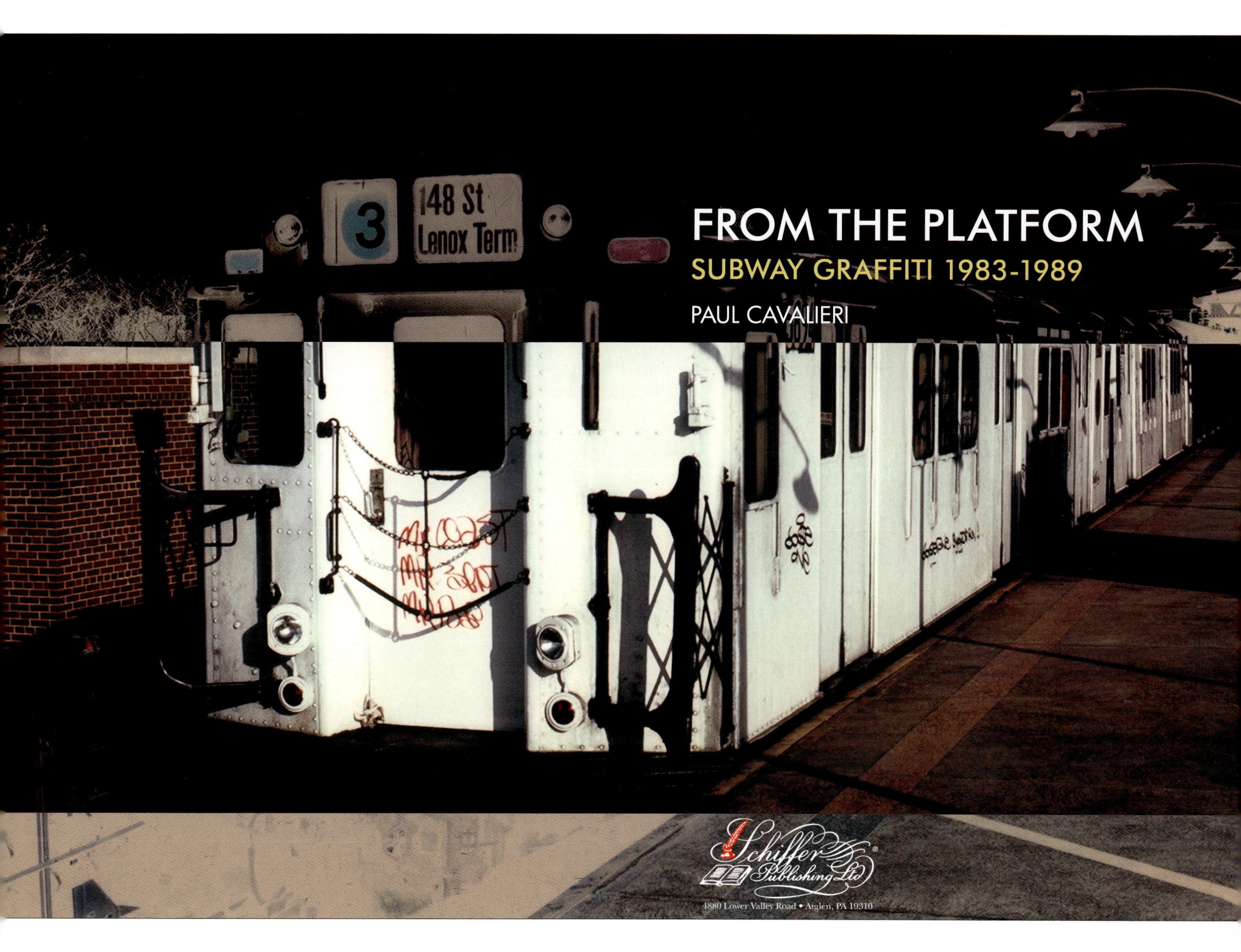
3
148 St
Lenox Term
FROM THE PLATFORM
SUBWAY GRAFFITI 1983-1989
PAUL CAVALIERI
Schiffer Publishing Ltd
4880 Lower Valley Road • Atglen, PA 19310

Schiffer Books are available at special discounts for bulk purchases for sales promotions or premiums. Special editions, including personalized covers, corporate imprints, and excerpts can be created in large quantities for special needs. For more information contact the publisher:

Published by Schiffer Publishing Ltd.
4880 Lower Valley Road
Atglen, PA 19310
Phone: (610) 593-1777; Fax: (610) 593-2002
E-mail: Info@schifferbooks.com

For the largest selection of fine reference books on this and related subjects, please visit our website at **www.schifferbooks.com**
We are always looking for people to write books on new and related subjects. If you have an idea for a book please contact us at the above address.

This book may be purchased from the publisher.
Please try your bookstore first.
You may write for a free catalog.

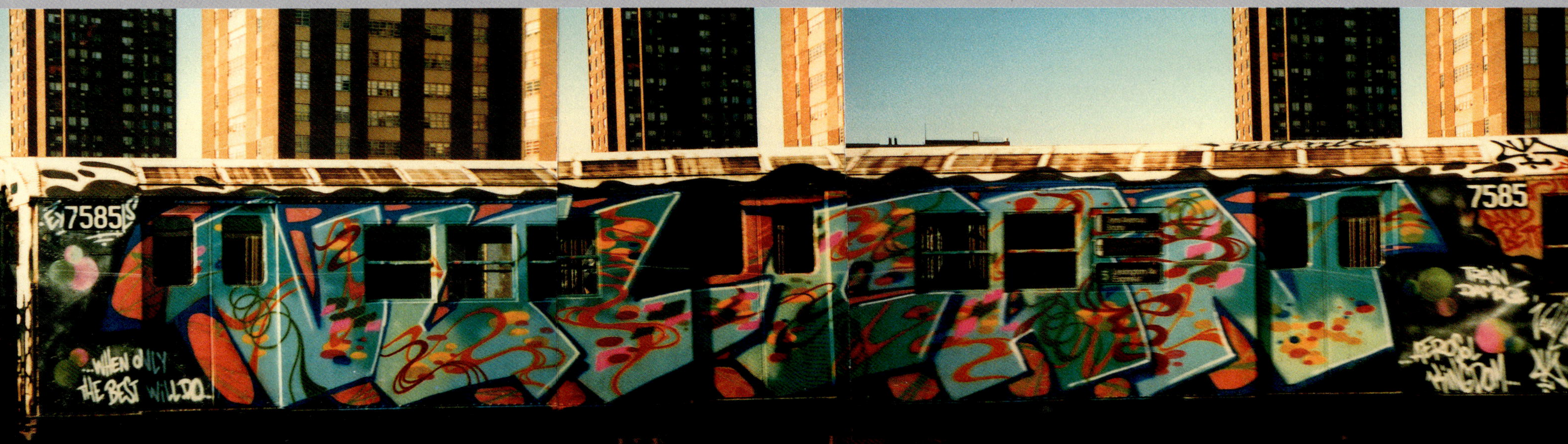

Title page:
3 Train at New Lots Ave. 1983

Other Schiffer Books By The Author:
Truck Art: A Decade of Graffiti, 978-0-7643-3493-1, $29.99

Other Schiffer Books on Related Subjects:
Fresh Paint: NYC, 978-0-7643-3495-5, $34.99
New York Subway Graffiti, 978-0-7643-3339-2, $29.99

Library of Congress Control Number: 2011920451

Designed by RoS
Type set in Futura Md BT/Alexon

ISBN: 978-0-7643-3723-9
Printed in China
6 5 4 3

I've had the name Cav ever since I was a young kid. The people in my neighborhood and at school gave me that name. "What's up Cav?" I would always hear. I became interested in graffiti back in 1982.

I started out by tagging the inside of the subway cars in 1983. The 2 line was my neighborhood line. I would go motion bombing (tagging up the inside of the train while the train was moving) whenever I got the chance. All I needed was a pilot marker in my pocket and I was good to go. It was a fun and easy way to get fame. While I was doing this I would look at all of the different tags in the car. Some of the tags would stick out more than others. Sometimes it was the amount of times I saw a particular name, and other times it was just the handstyle that someone had.

A short time later I became more interested in what was going on outside the trains. I would hang out with my younger brother who wrote, "Key," and together we would watch the trains as they pulled into the 238th street station. Key shared the same enthusiasm for writing as I did.

Watching all of these colorful names inspired me to take pictures of them. The first photos that I ever took of the trains was with my 126 camera. It was the first camera that I owned. I always had it out with me when we were on the block, or chilling in the neighborhood. Taking pictures was something that I enjoyed doing. It wasn't until 1984 that I was able to save up some loot and upgrade to a disk camera. By this time Key (armed with his trusty 110 camera) and I were familiarizing ourselves with the train schedules. If we missed something that we wanted pictures of we would just time it and wait for it to come back uptown. Once in a while our timing wasn't perfect, but for the most part we were usually on point. Even knowing the schedule was never a guarantee that we were going to get our photos. On numerous occasions we waited for a train to pull into the station, only to have another train come through on another track and cross directly in front of what we wanted to flick. That was always a big disappointment, but was just a part of the game.

Before I knew it, graffiti had consumed my life. I didn't take school seriously any more. As a matter of fact, I wound up getting kicked out of High School in my 3rd year. This just made my graffiti addiction worse. I was spending most of my time either writing on trains or loitering on subway platforms to take pictures. Back then East Tremont Ave on the 2 and 5 line was a big spot for writers to "bench" — gathering to either talk or take pictures of the trains. I spent countless hours and filled many rolls of film on that station alone. After a while I started to venture to other subway lines in the Bronx. I was benching the 2, 5, 3, 4, 6, and the 1 line. I was always aware of what was going on around me when I ventured out to other lines. New York City was a pretty rough place in the '80s. You always had to watch your back. If you didn't you could find yourself in a situation that you wouldn't want to be in.

In 1986 I got myself a 35mm camera. Those were the top of the line cameras for that time. By this time I was getting up on the 5 line for over a year with pieces. It wasn't until 1987 that I started to hit the BMT lines. I would go out there to take flicks of the stuff that I was doing. Through this I started to bench the B, J, L, and M line, as well as the Franklin Avenue Shuttle. I was even benching the C line out in Queens. I got to see a lot of different areas of Brooklyn, and familiarized myself with the writers that were getting up on those lines.

By the time I started going to the BMT lines, graffiti was disappearing from the trains. One by one each train line was getting clean. Once a line was clean the Transit Authority made sure that it stayed that way. If a clean car got painted it was taken out of service, and wasn't allowed to go back in until all of the graffiti was removed. I made it a point to not only do as many pieces as I could on the trains, but take as many photos also. I knew that it was only a matter of time before all of the lines were clean for good. I remember walking through the last bombed 5 train. Man, it was a really depressing feeling.

On May 12, 1989, the last train that had graffiti on it was cleaned and the entire fleet of the MTA subway was graffiti free. The trains that kids had painted for 20 years, and gave New York City its soul, were no more. The pieces that once attracted tourists from all over the world were either repainted burgundy or sent to Brooklyn to rot away or get scrapped.

As I look back on my years of painting subway trains, and photographing them, I feel fortunate that I was able to be a part of it. I went from doing tags on the insides of the trains to doing whole cars top to bottom. I was able to make a name for myself and become a part of New York City subway graffiti forever. This book is not about myself, but is a glimpse of what I saw in those years. Even though I was a part of this movement, I was also a fan. It took me years to amass such a collection of photos, and it's something that I want to share with the world. Where the book *Subway Art* leaves off, *From The Platform* begins. Straight from the Cavster and my brother Key's collection.

–Paul Cavalieri

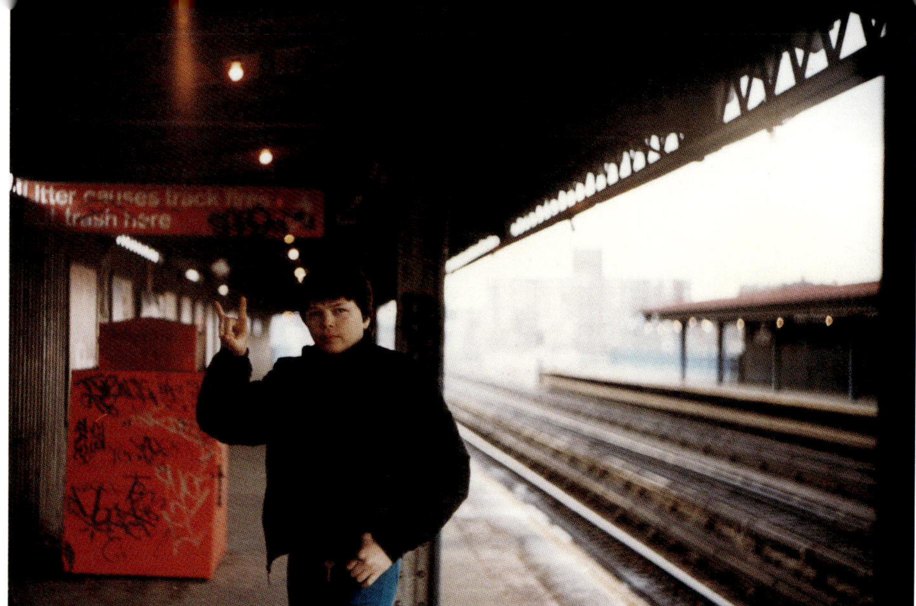

St. Lawrence Train Station, 1983

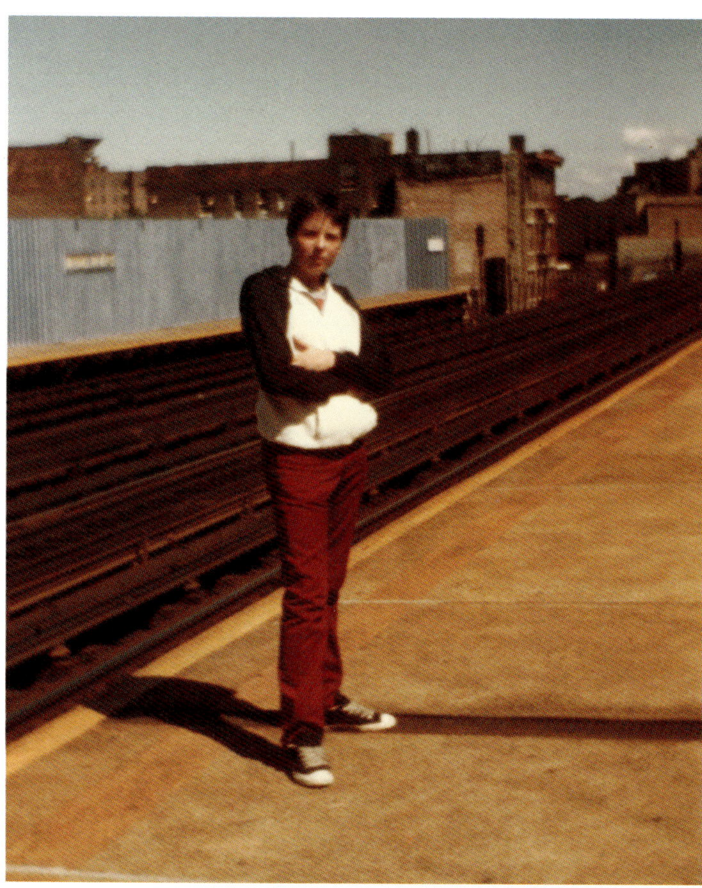

Key at Intervale train station, 1984

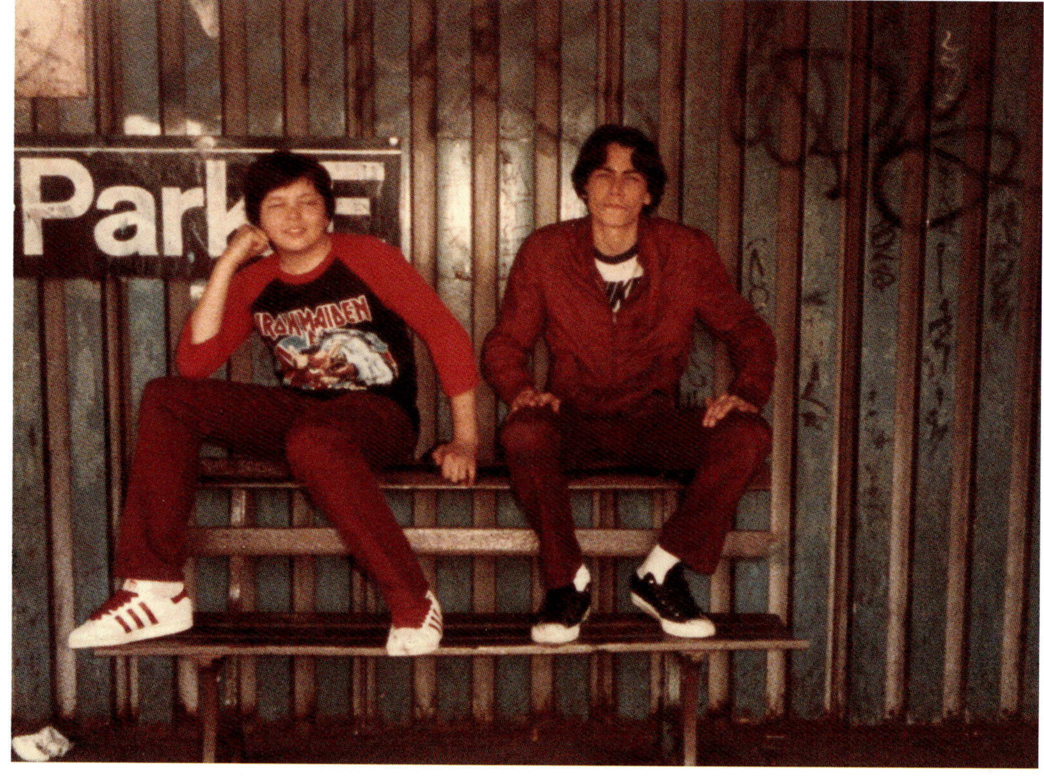

Cav & MK at Bronx Park East Train Station

In the early '80s I teamed up with Seen from the 6 IRT line. We went out to bomb the new white trains. We did around 500 each.

-Blade

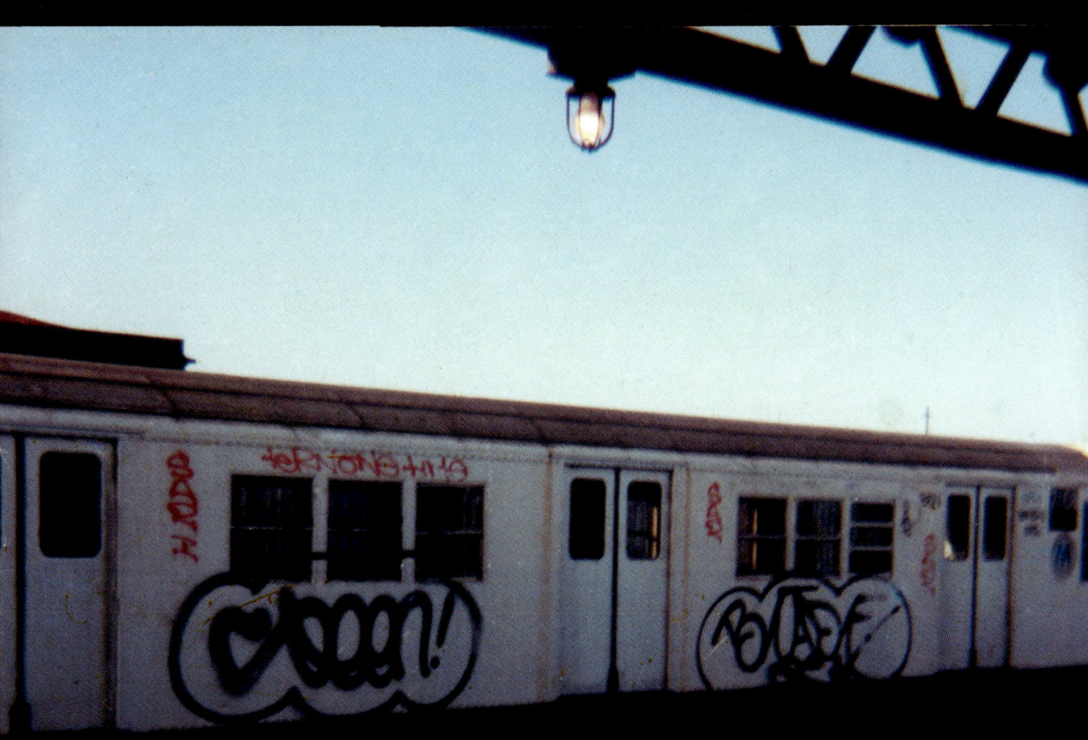

"Seen" & "Blade" on the 2 line.

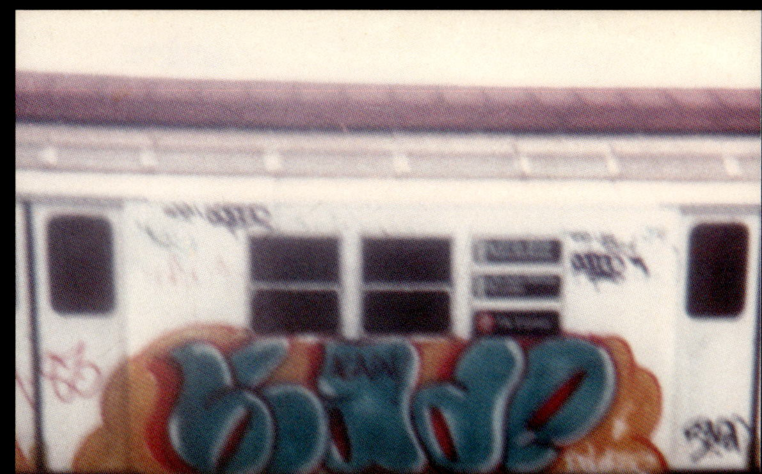

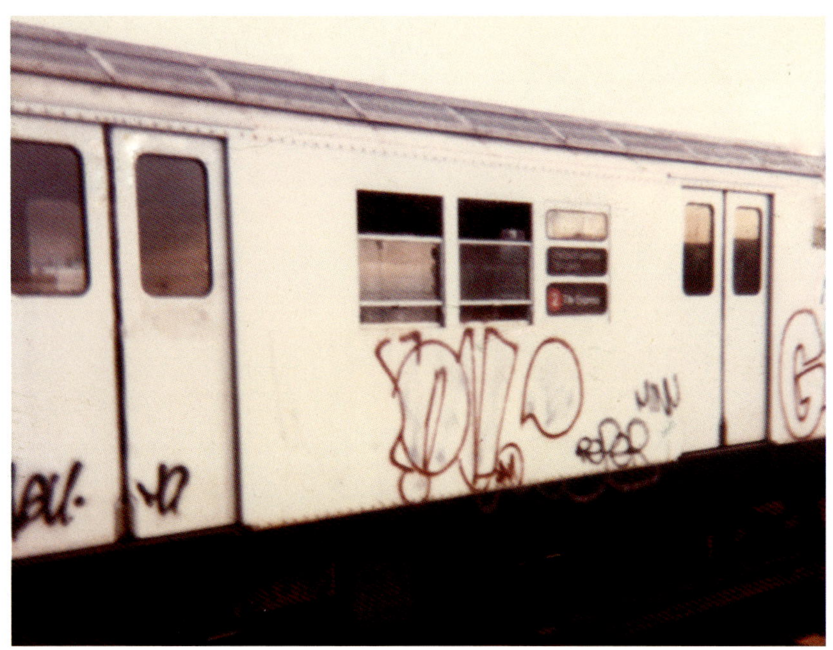

"PV," by Pove

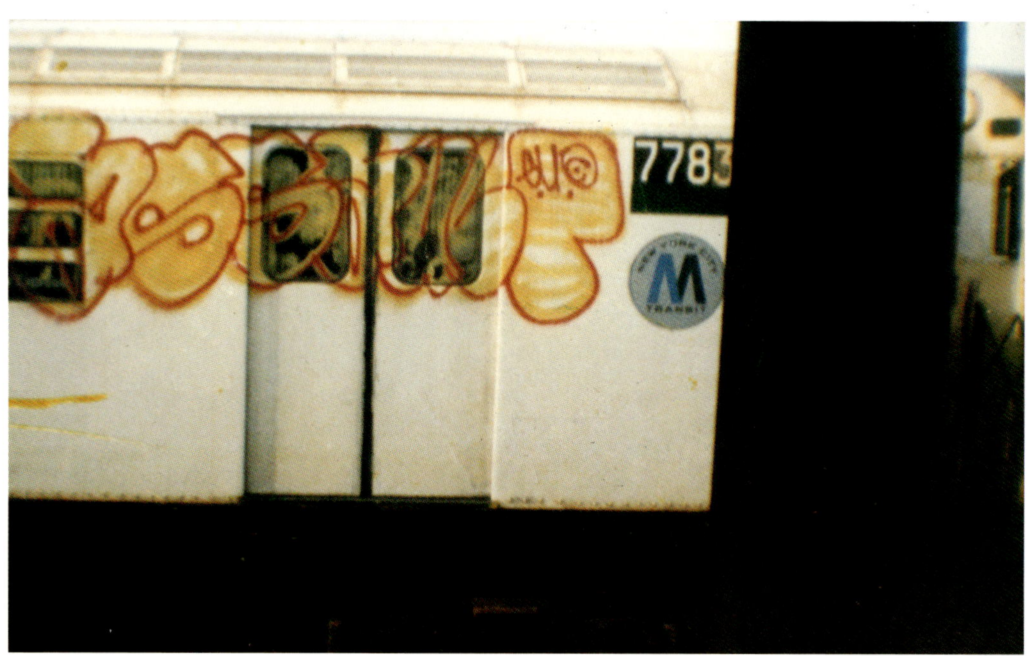

"Assault," by Pove

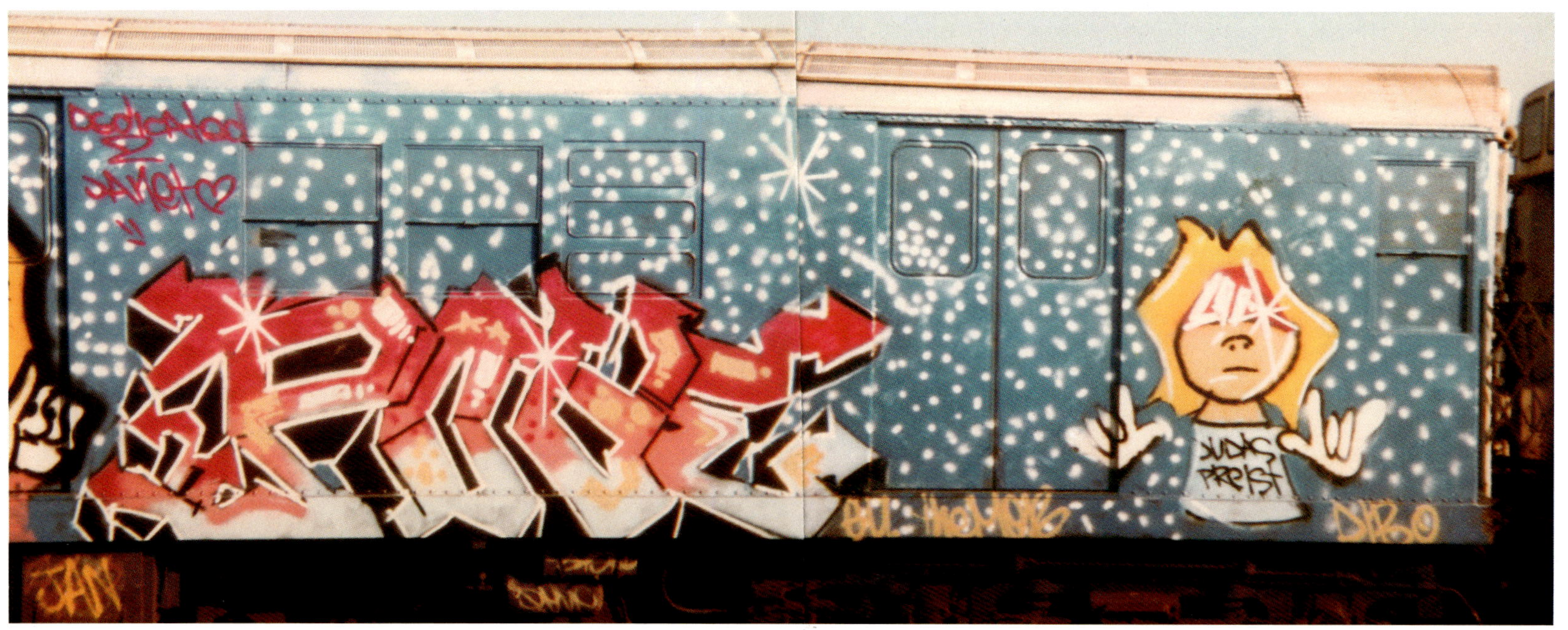

"Pove," 1983

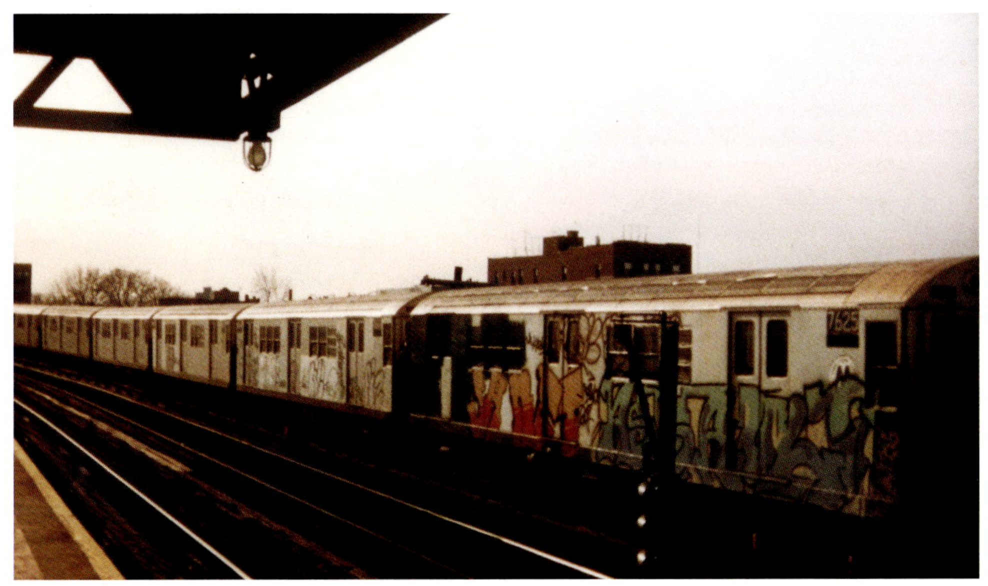

"Janet & Pove," 1983
This car also ran in the film *Beat Street*.

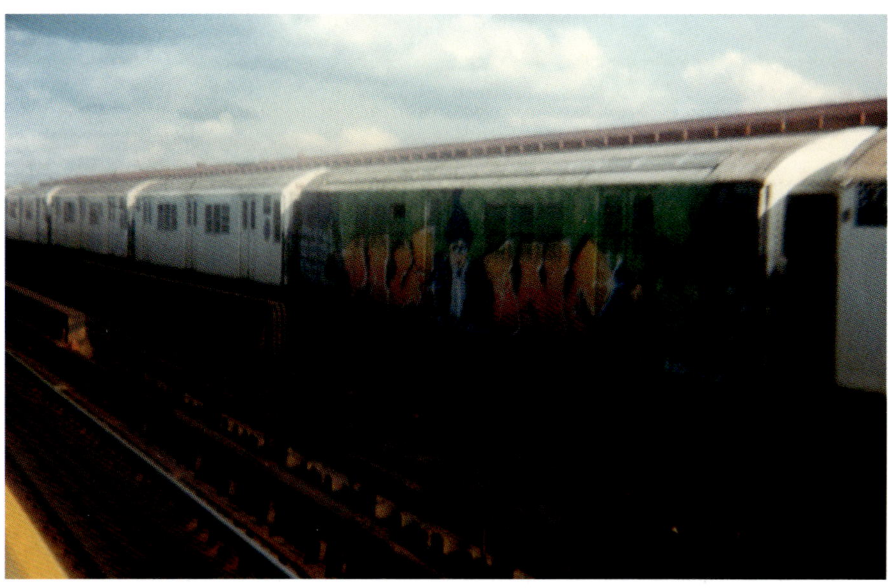

"Pove-One," 1983

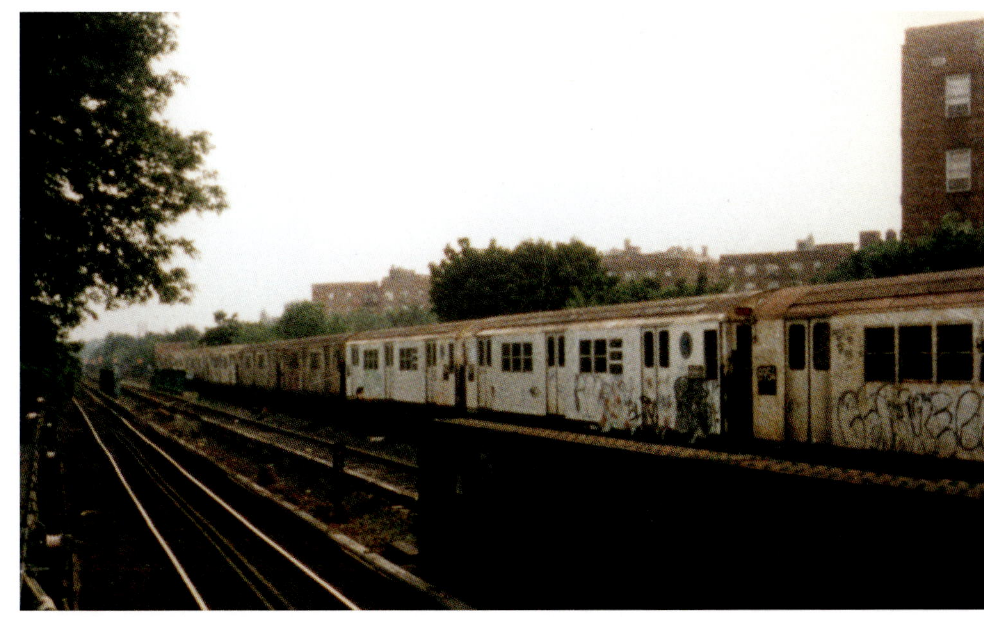

Esplanade lay up, 1983

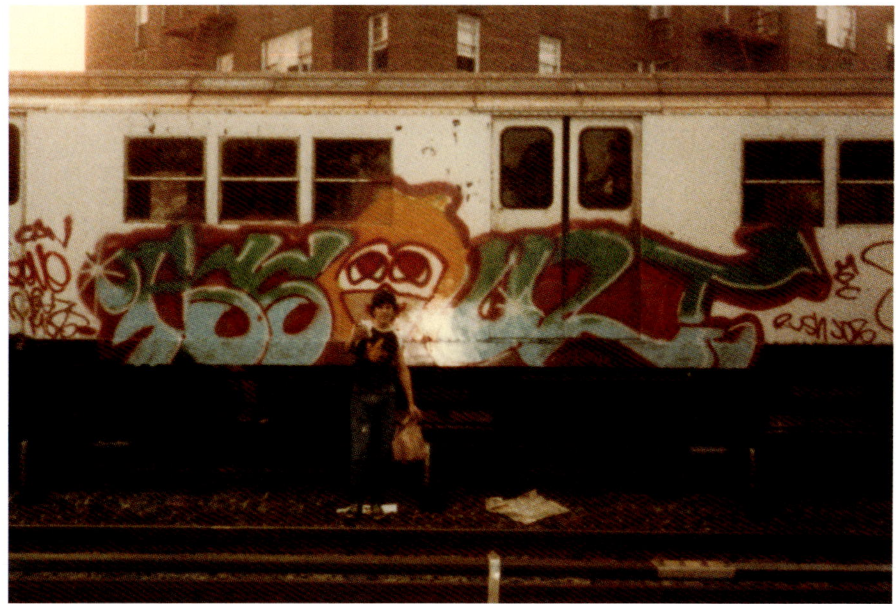

"Assault," by Pove

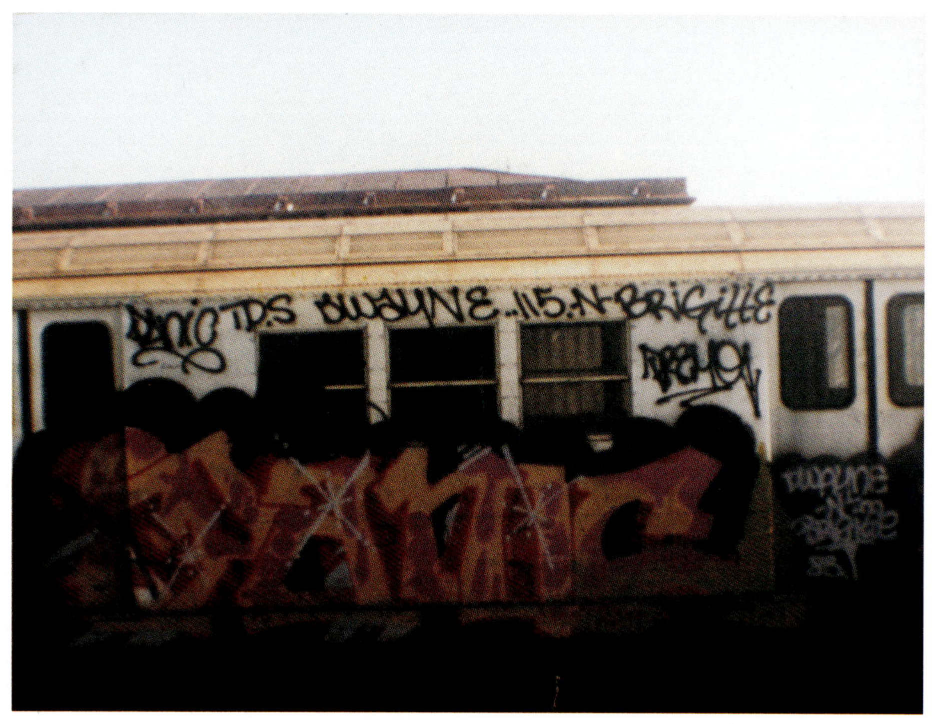

"Panic," 1983

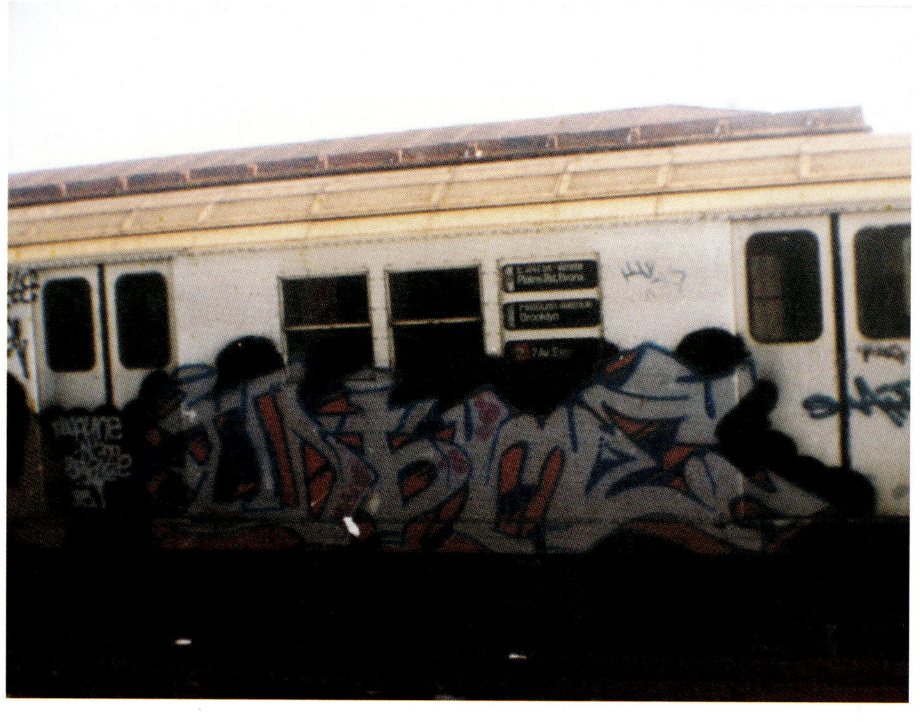

"Dime," 1983

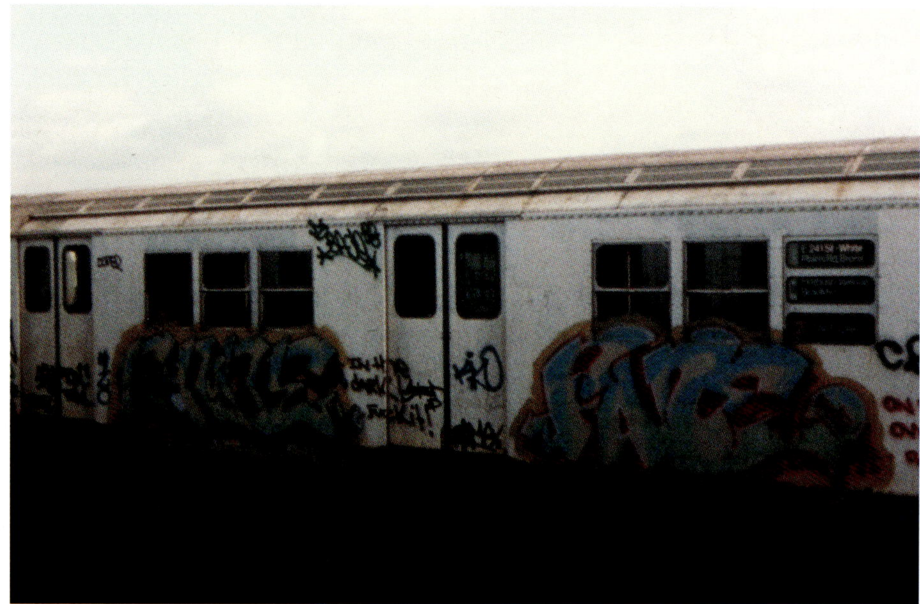

"Sade" & "Fane," 1983

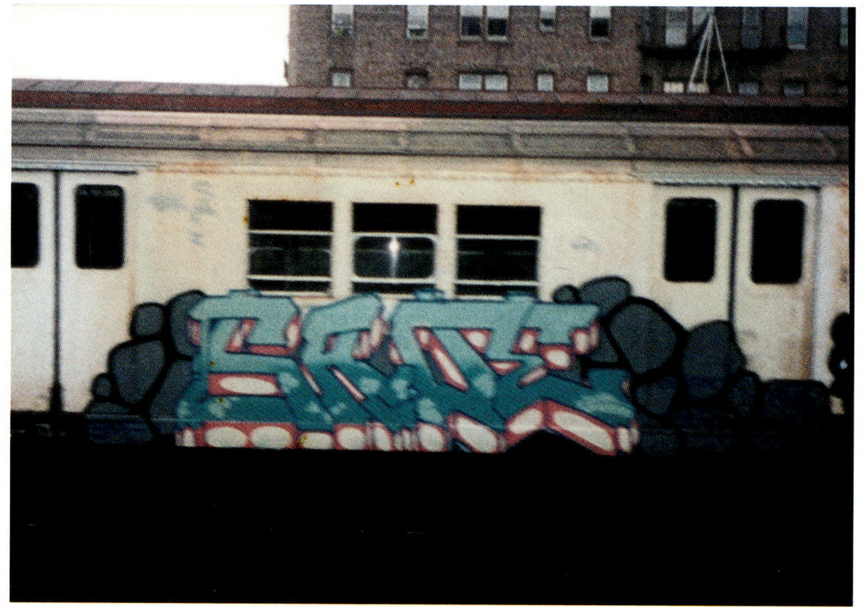

"Sade," 1983

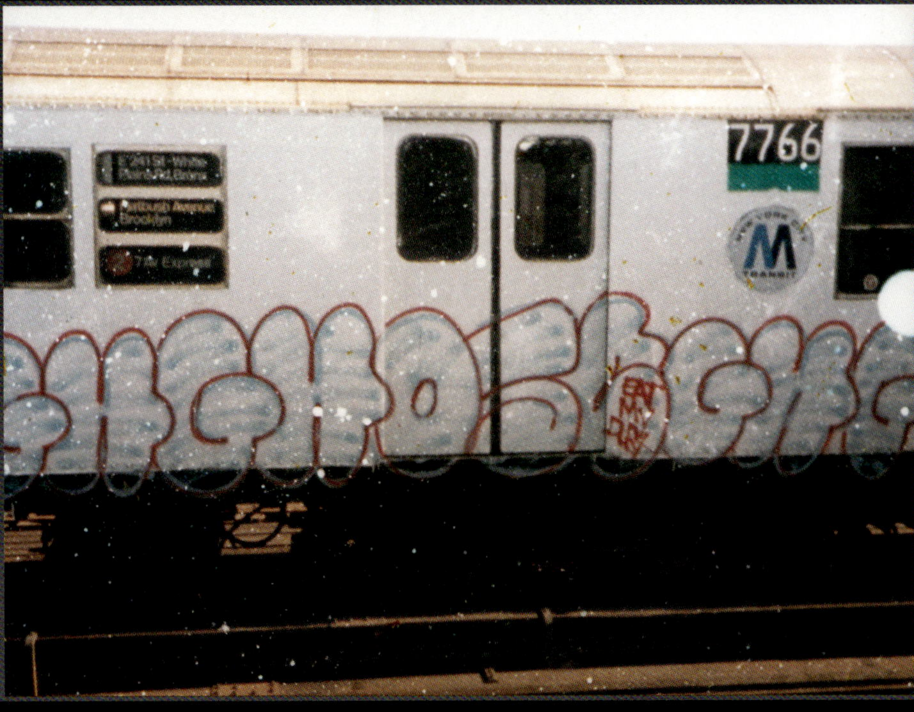

"GH," by Ghost, "Mr Big"

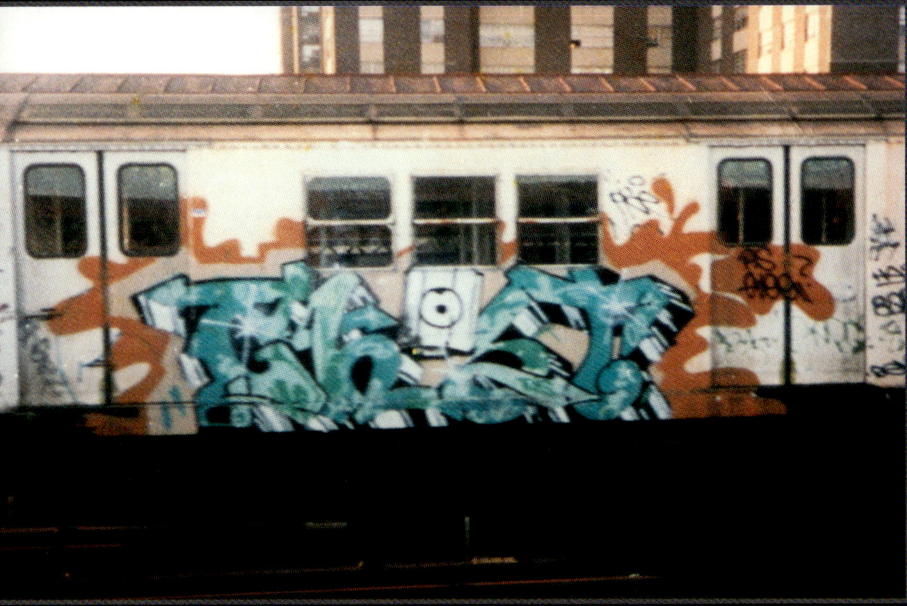

"Ghost," 1984

I remember going to the 2 yard on a Sunday afternoon. I caught all the freshly painted white trains, straight out of the barn!

I was just killing them with throwies. I love doing throw ups more than anything. Doing pieces is cool, but it really does not bring any pleasure or satisfaction like going down a set of trains just crushing shit!

–Ghost

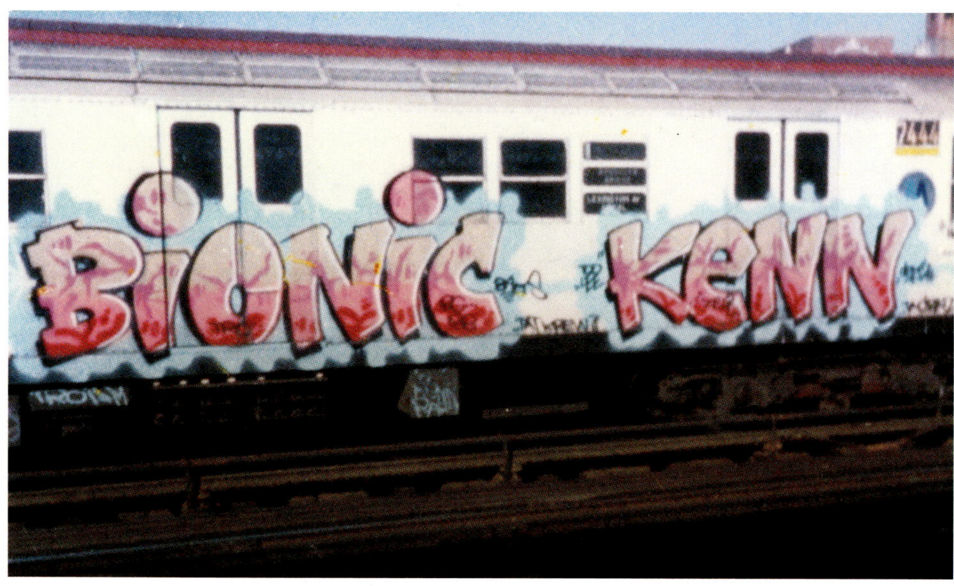

"Bionic" & "Kenn," 1983

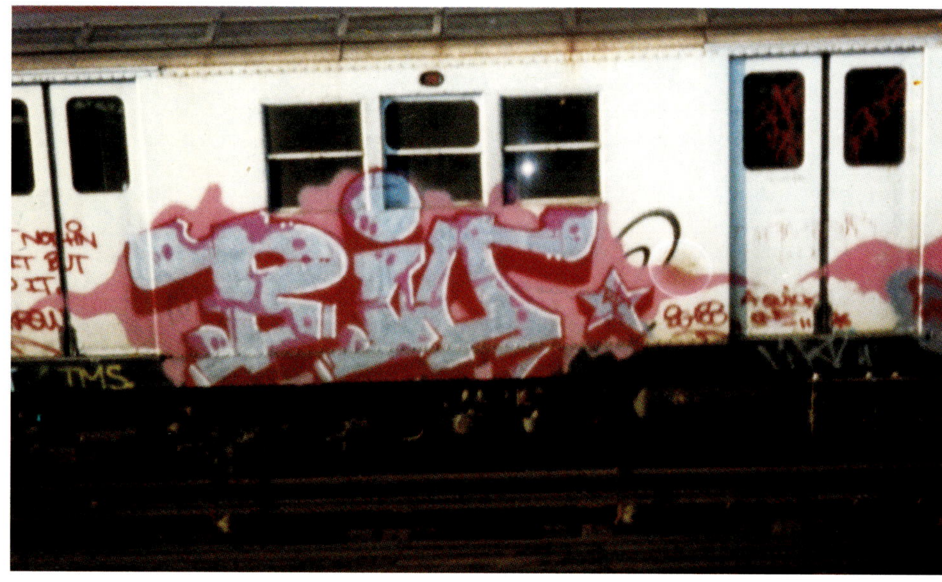

"Bio," 1983

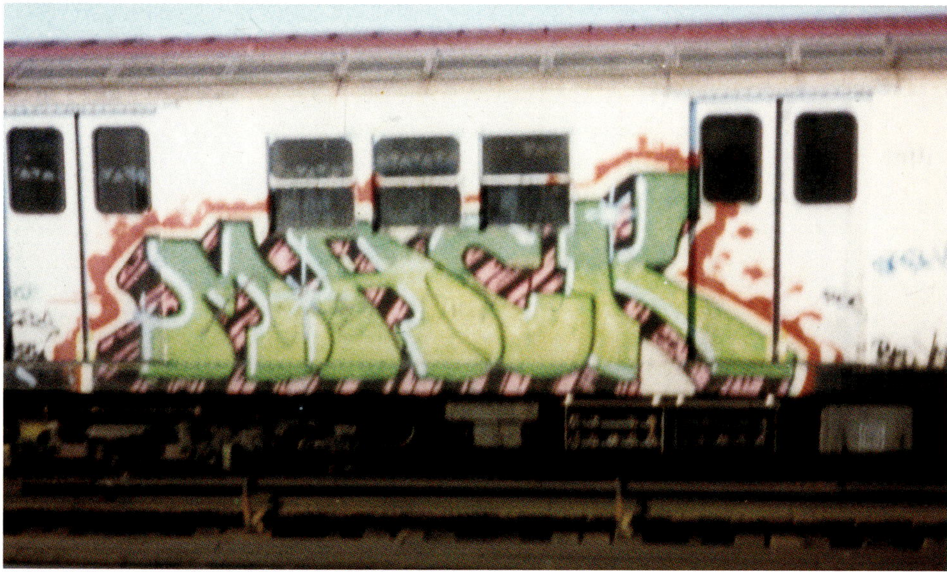

"Mack," 1983

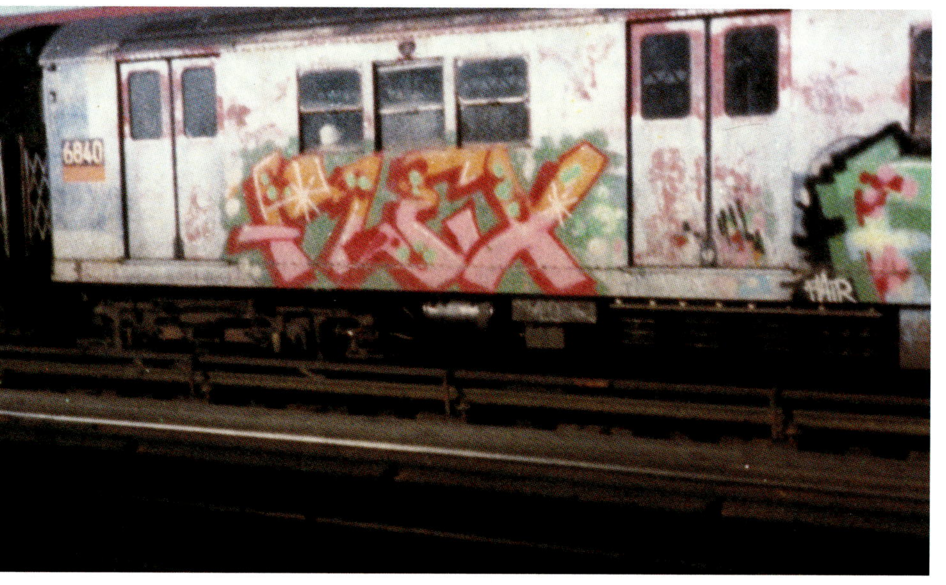

"Flex," 1983

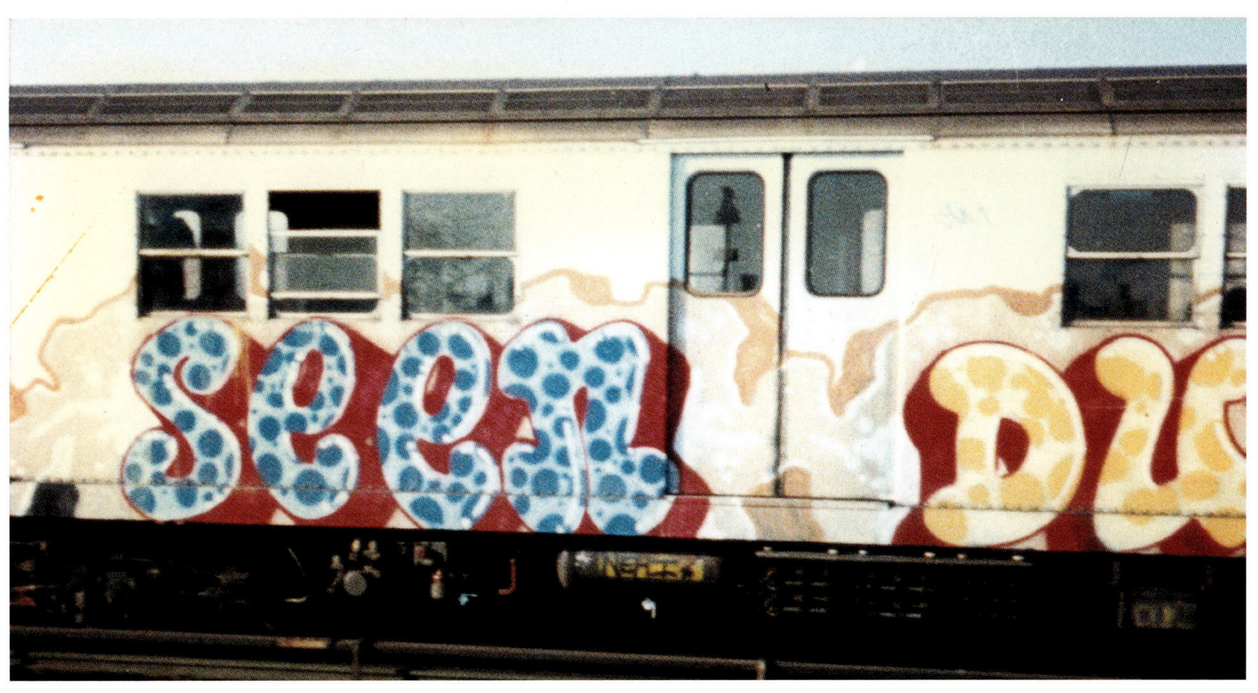

"Seen," 1983

"Seen," 1983

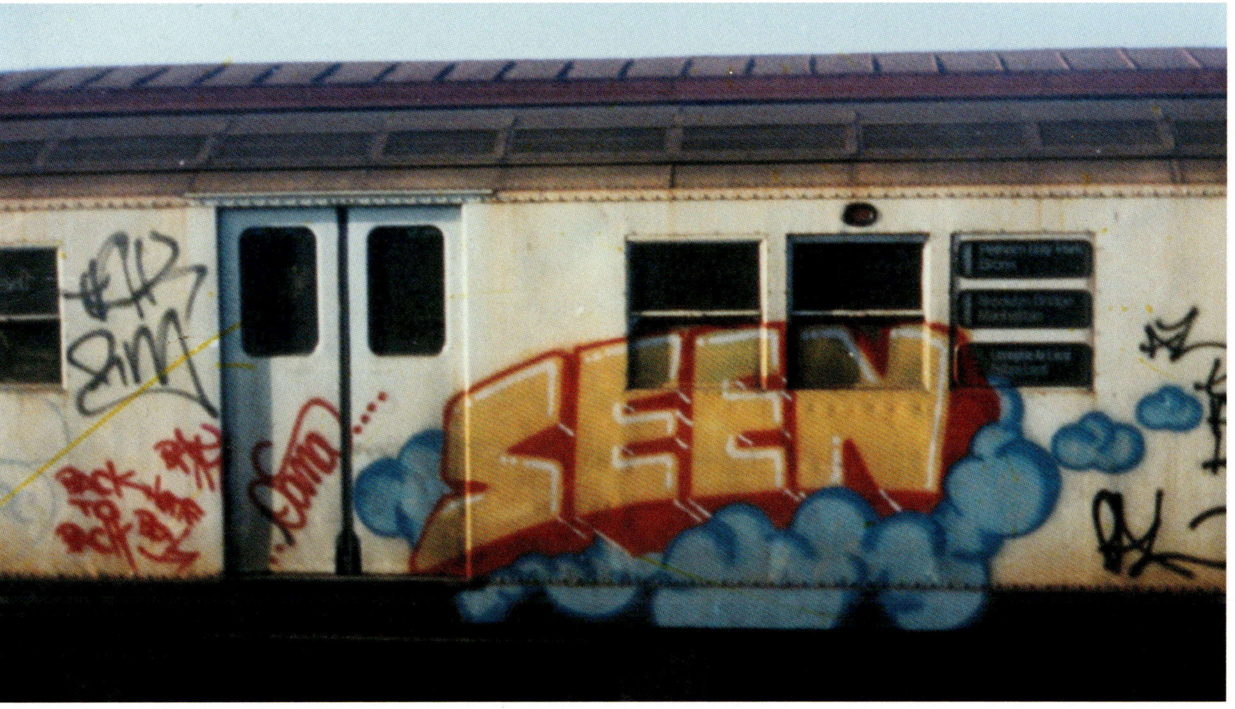

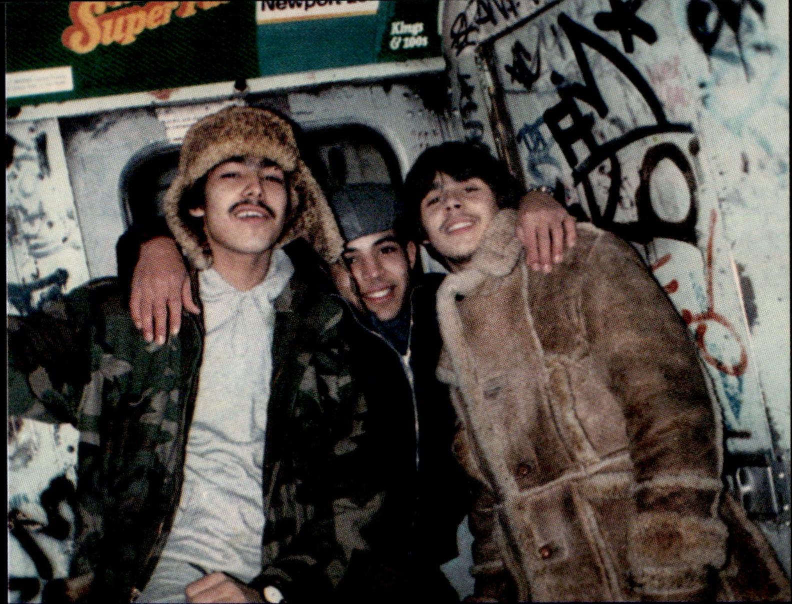

Gin, Blist & MiOne, 1984

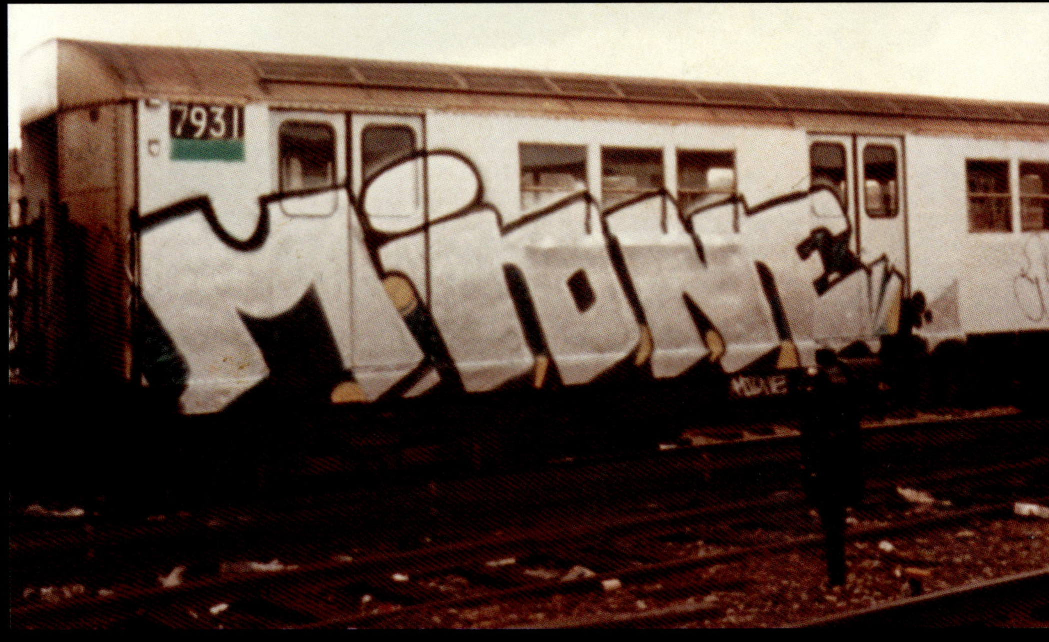

"MiOne"

It was a cold winter night in the mid 1980s. I had an idea to do a top to bottom with some red devil paint. But I had no one to go with. I was not going to climb that big fence at 241 st yard alone. As I was leaving the corner store, I bumped into Sento. He asked, "How much paint you got?" I replied enough for a top to bottom. But only enough for a MiOne. We ended up going to the yard. It turns out there was a freshly painted white car waiting for me. It was so clean, not even a tag or throw up on it. I could not resist it and the rest is history. It was not a top to bottom because it was on the first row of tracks. I could not get all the way up and had no ladder. But as everyone knows a freshly painted car had to get bombed!

–MiOne

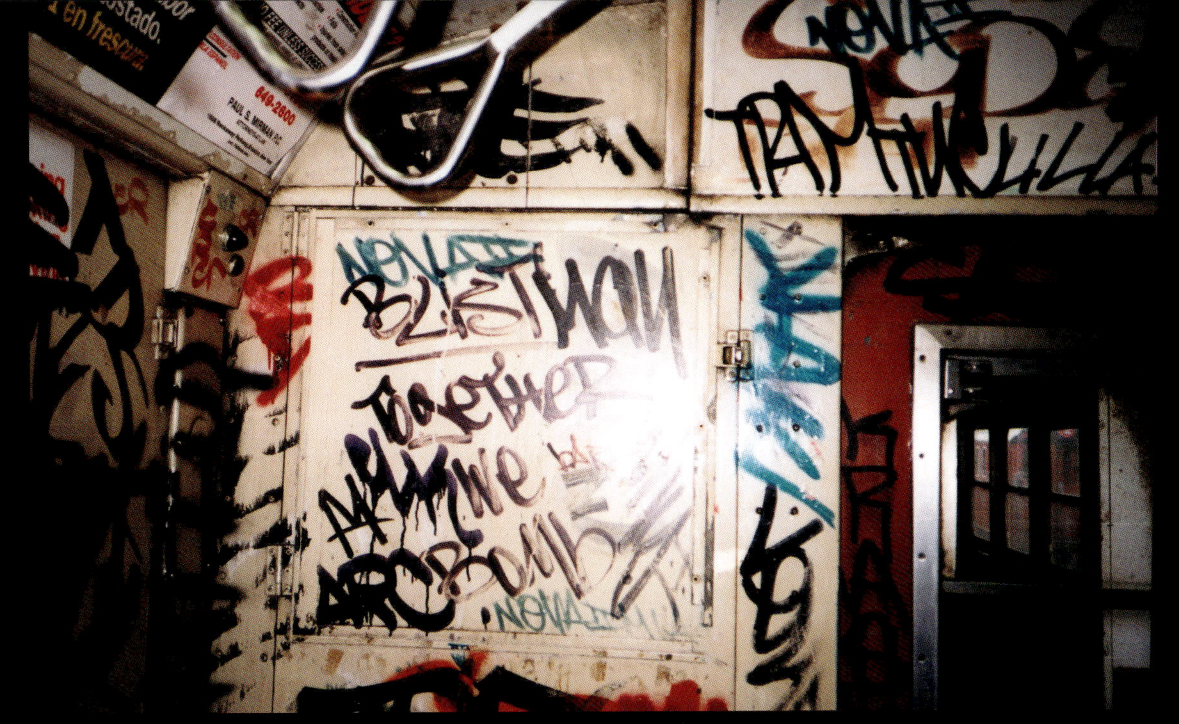

What a rush it was to go bombing, and see your throw ups go by on a train. And walking into a subway and seeing your tag there. I only did it for about 3 years. I will always love and respect the art of graffiti. Almost 30 years later I still get a chill when I see some graffiti. I never had the skills of some of the great writers of the game. But I'm proud to have been there and know and grow up with my brother from another mother, Cavster, who took the art of graffiti to another level.

–Blist

Graffiti can be painted over and washed away. But the photos that Cavster took will always bring a lifetime of memories!

–Gin one

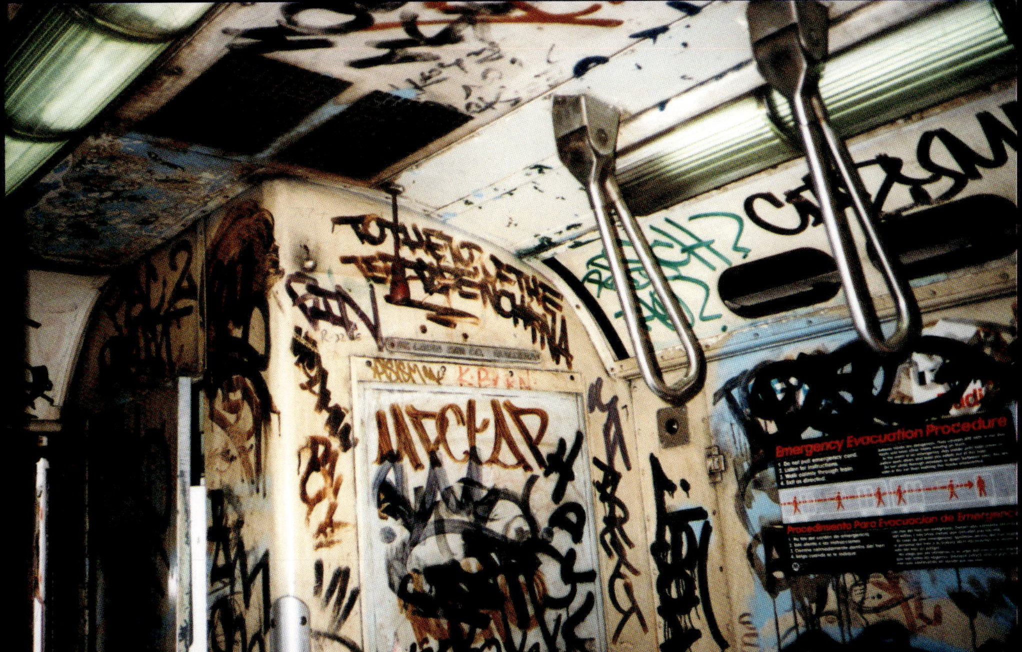

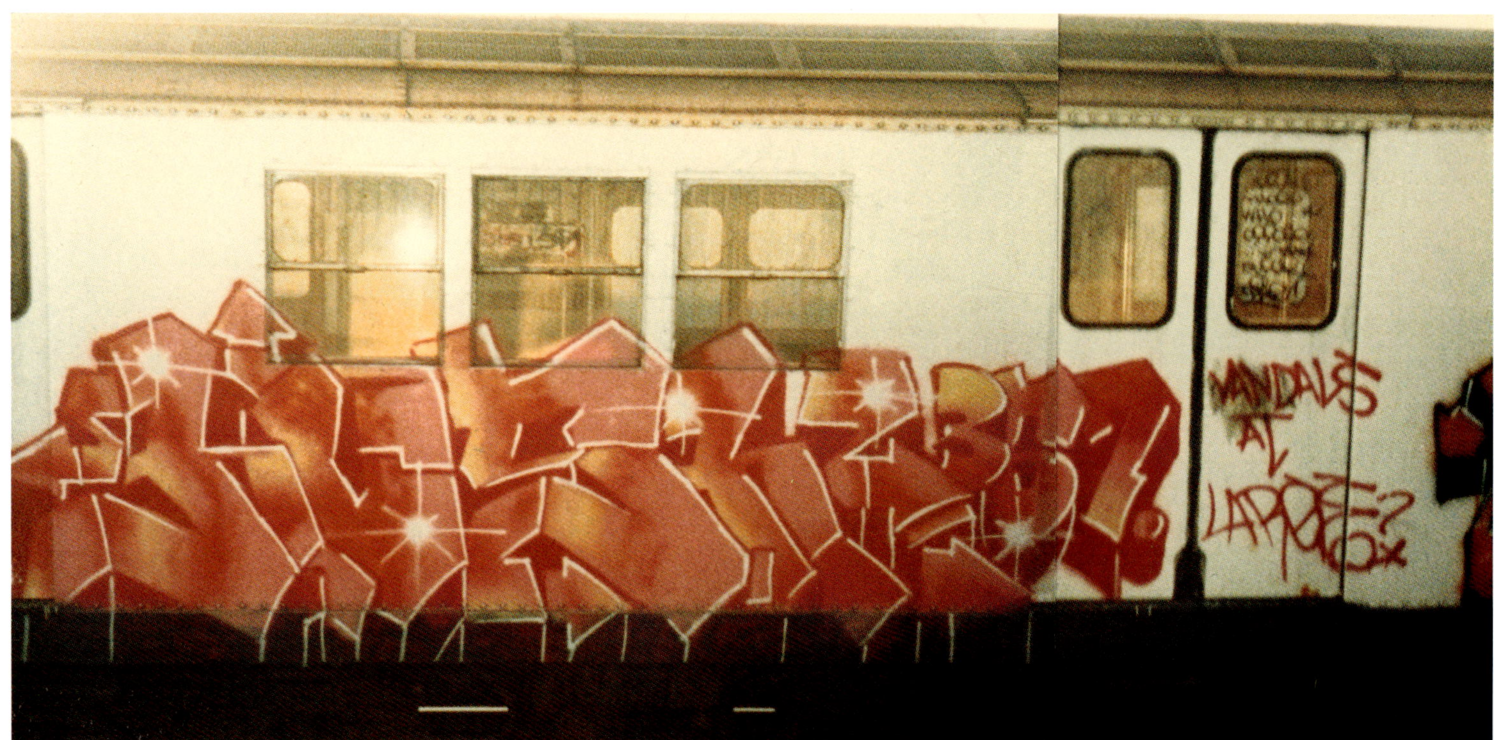

"Hush 357," 1983

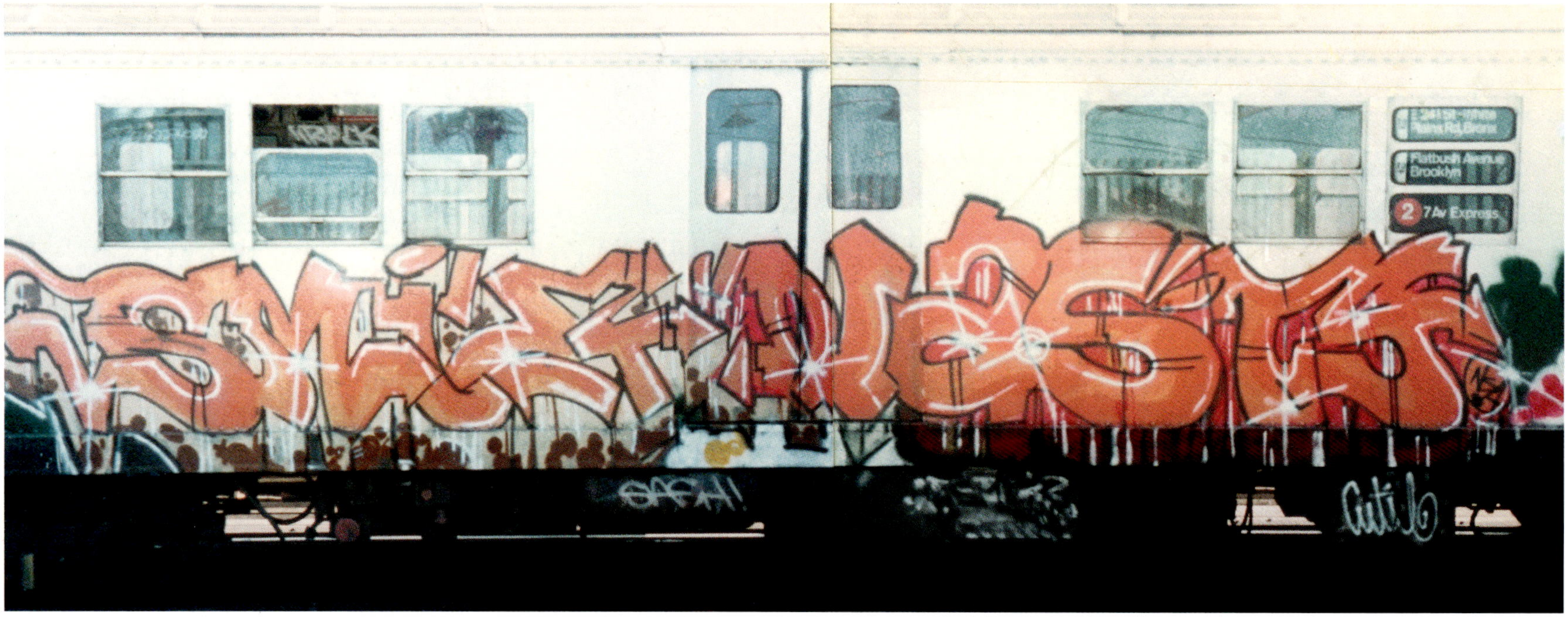

"Smiz" & "Nasty," 1983

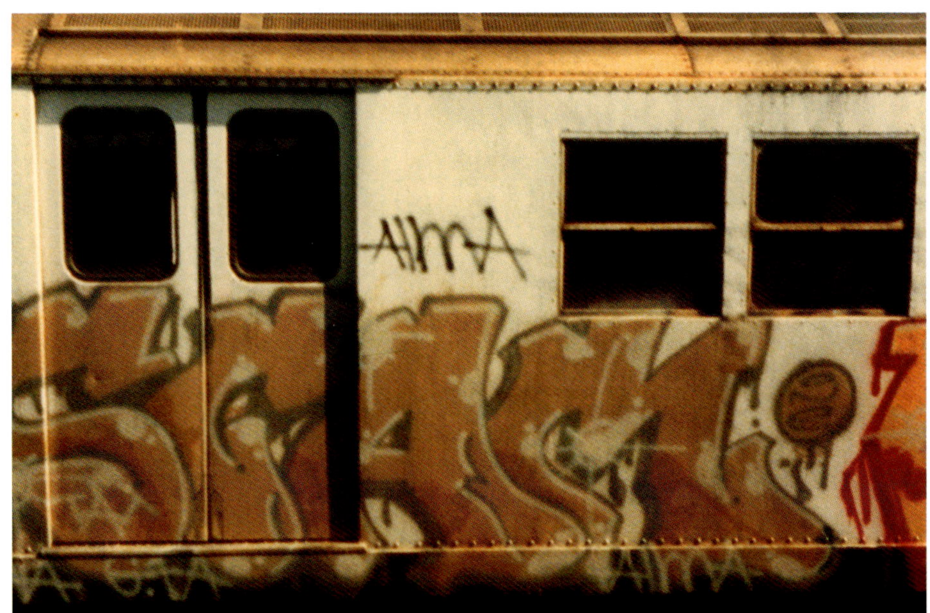

"Scam," 1983

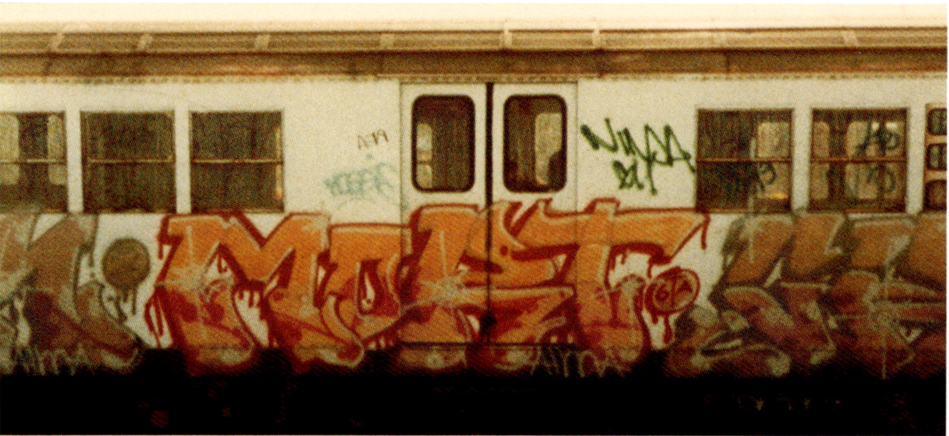

"Mort," 1983

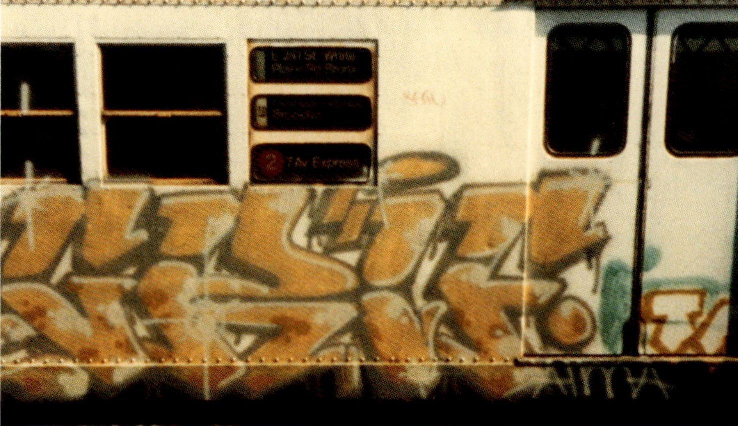

"Grif," 1983

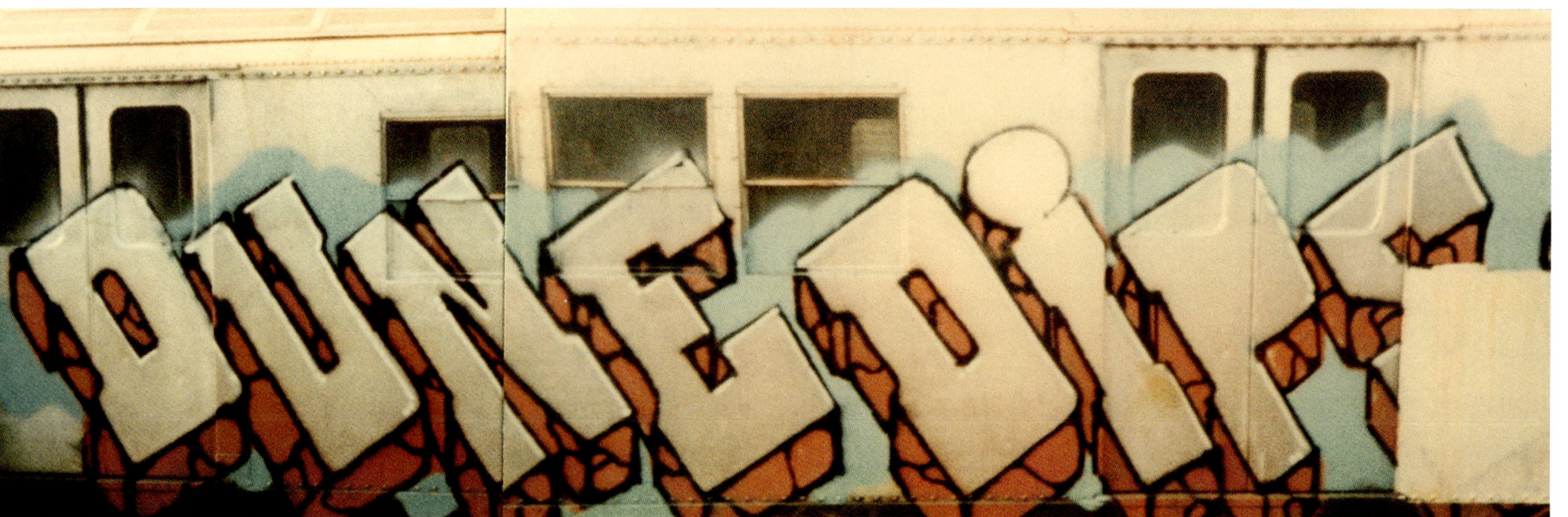

"Dune" & "Dips," 1983

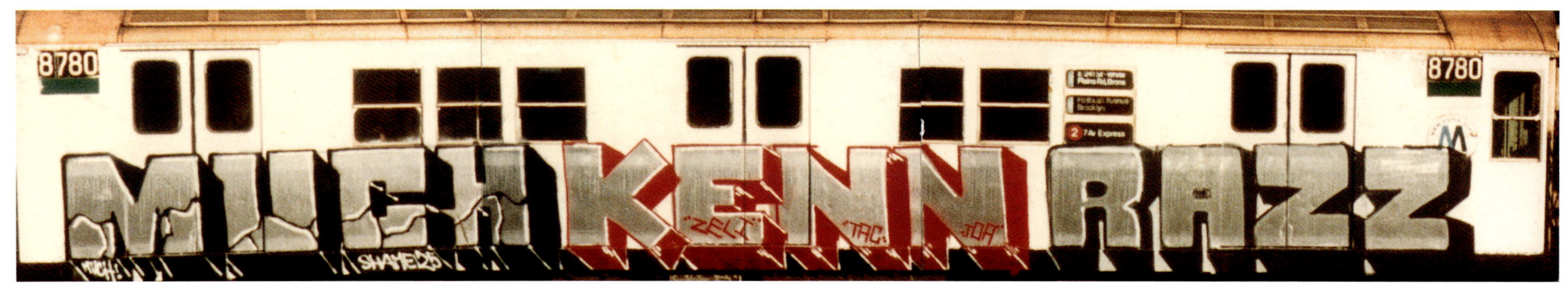

"Much," "Kenn" & "Razz," 1984

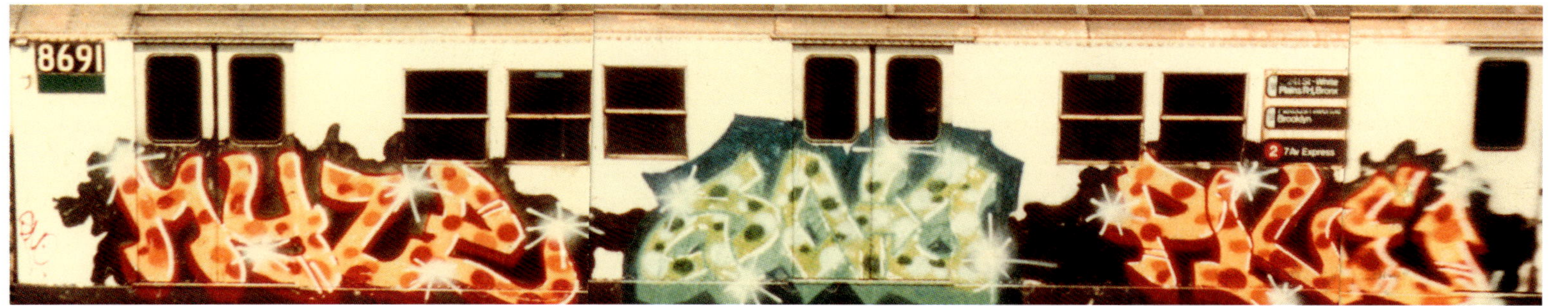

"Myze," "Sno" & "Pile," 1983

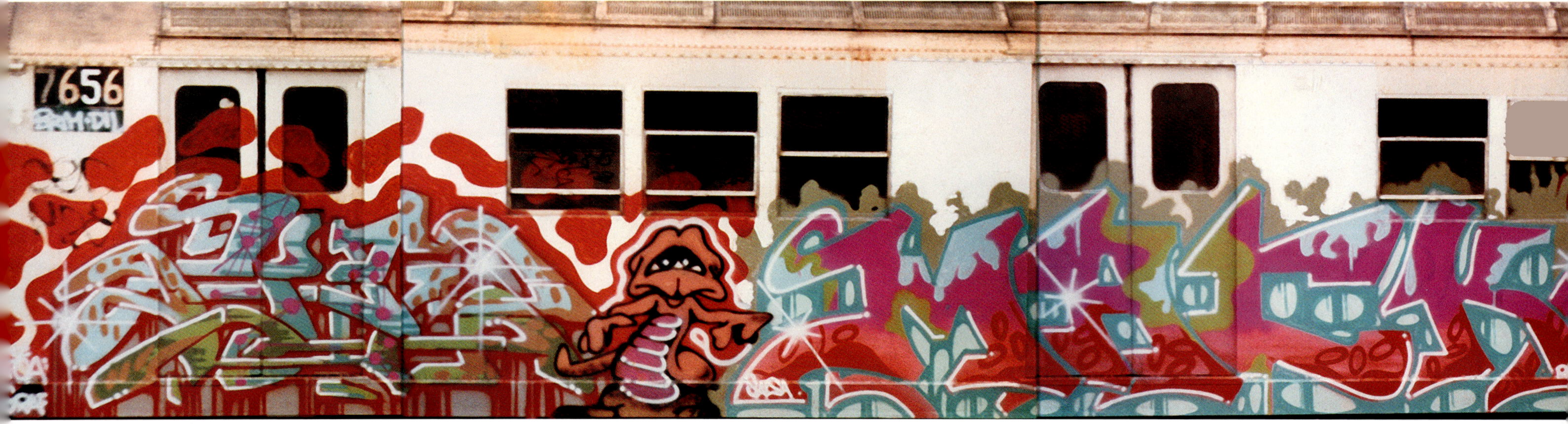

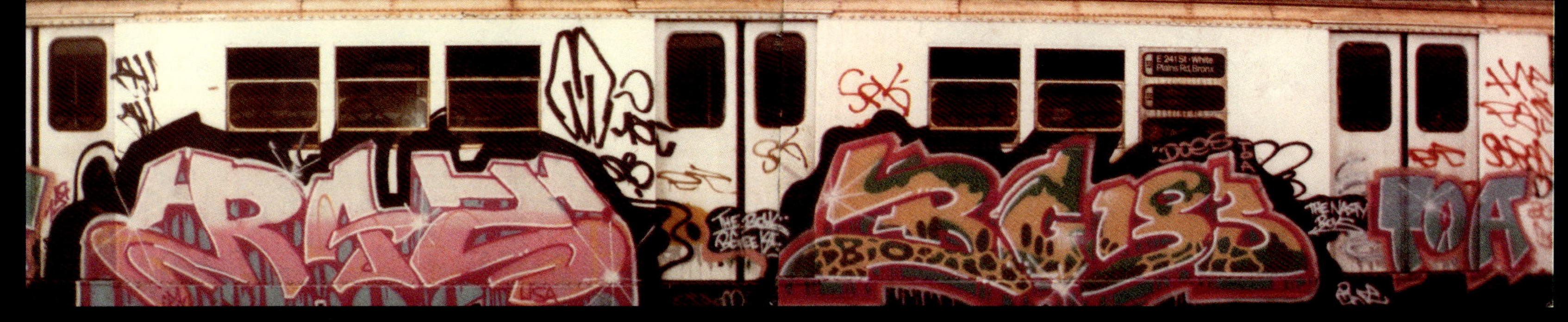

"Raz" & "BG183",1984

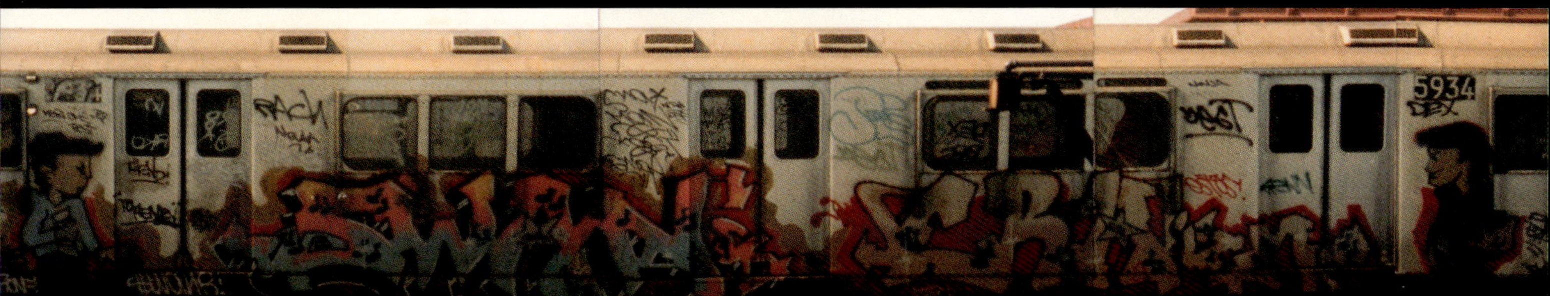

"Swan" & "Era," 1983

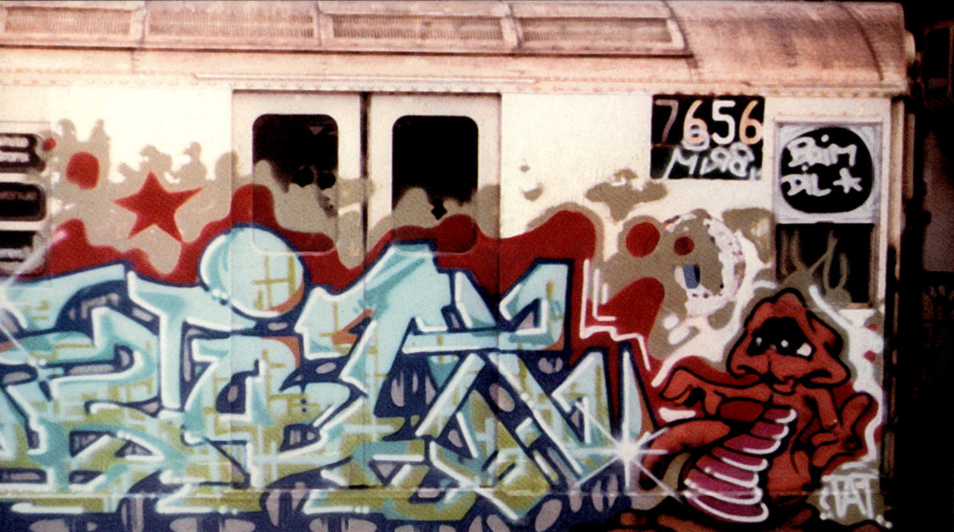

"BG," "Mack" & "Bio," 1984

Benching back in the early '80s was very exciting! Back in those days there were many different styles. But two cars stand out the most. The BG 183, Bio & Mack car with the worm characters. The other car was the Shame 125, & Cem battle car.

–Vism

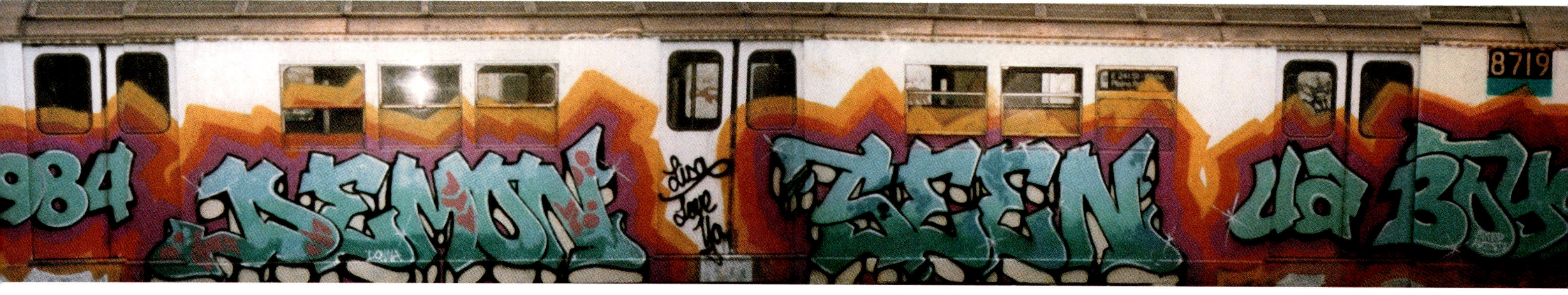

"Demon" & "Seen," 1984

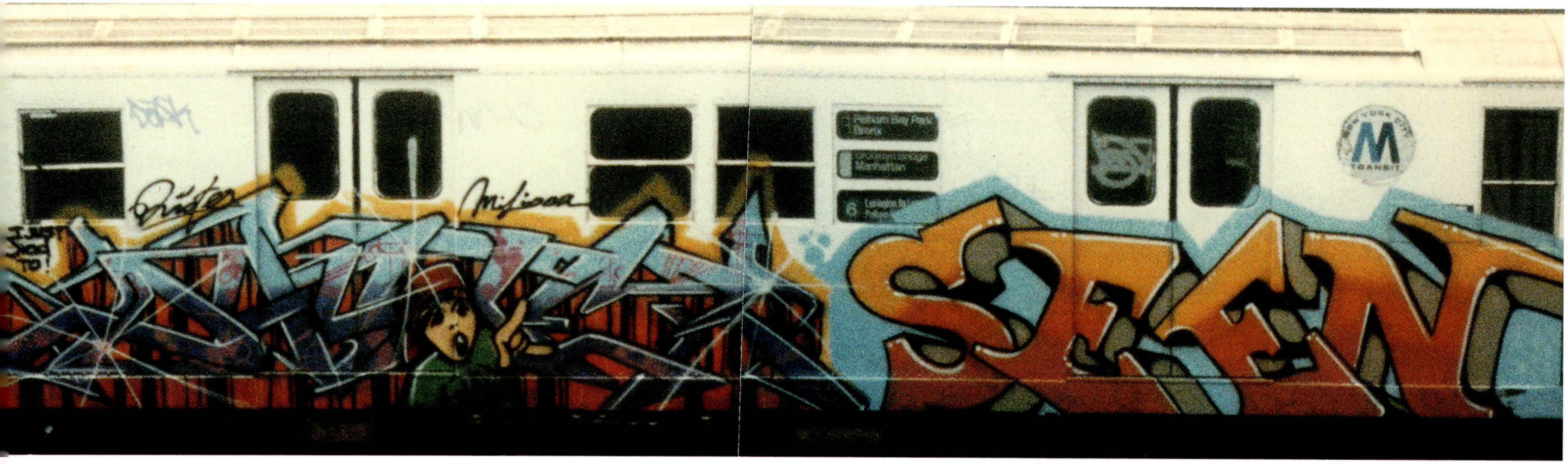

"Duster" & "Seen"

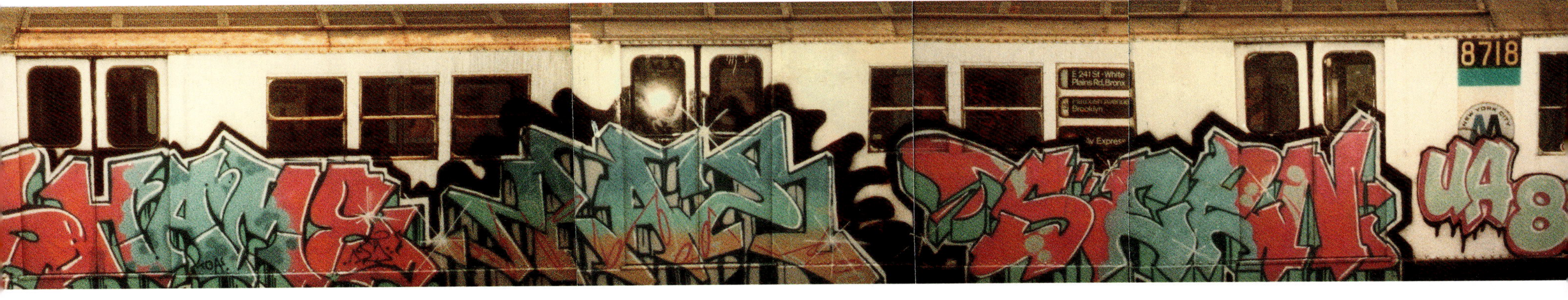

"Shame," "Raz" & "Seen," 1984

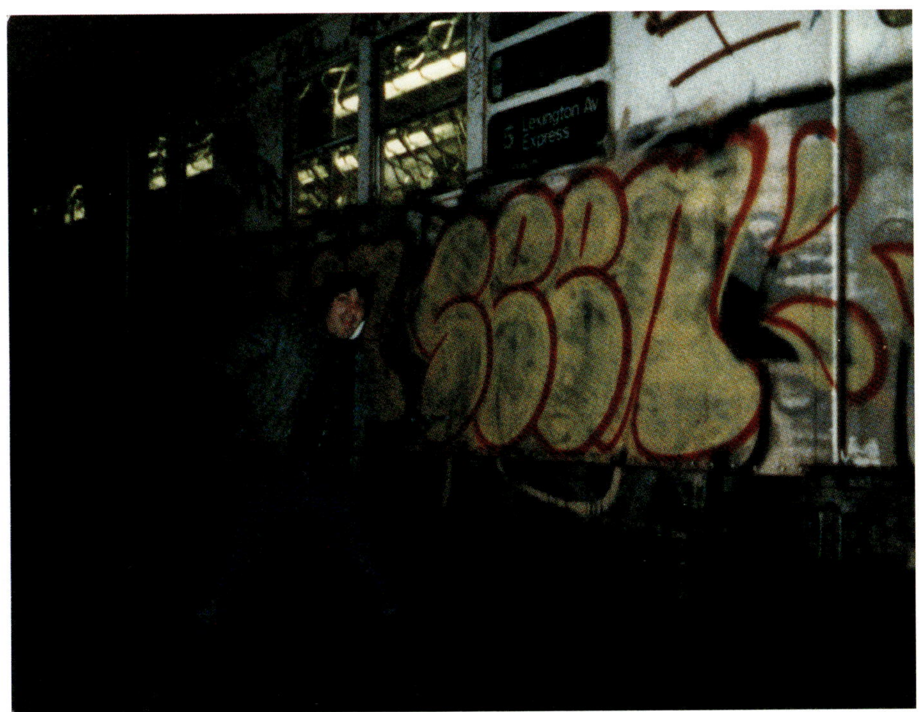

Seen in Baychester lay up, 1985.

Seen, 1985

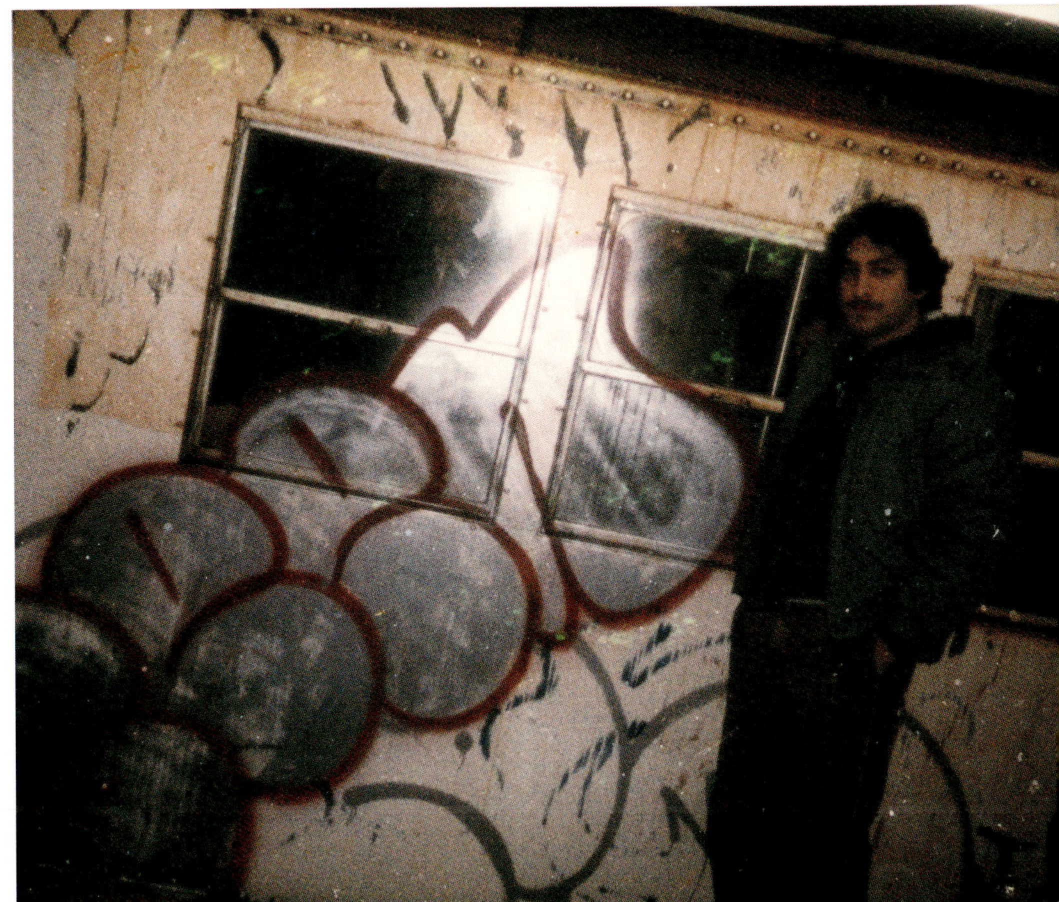

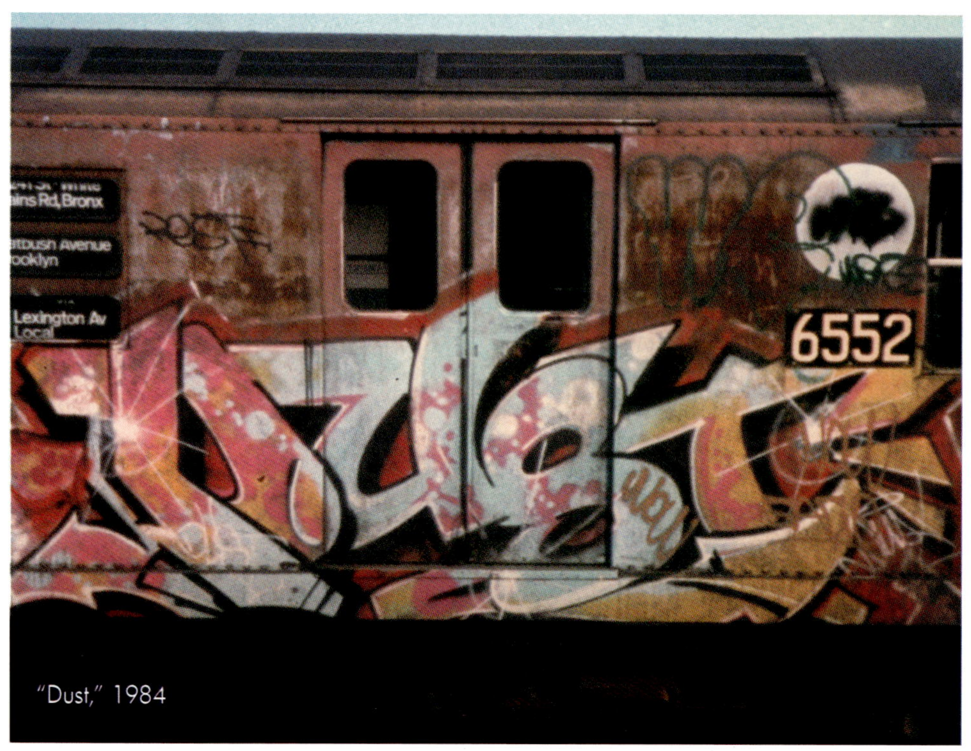

"Dust," 1984

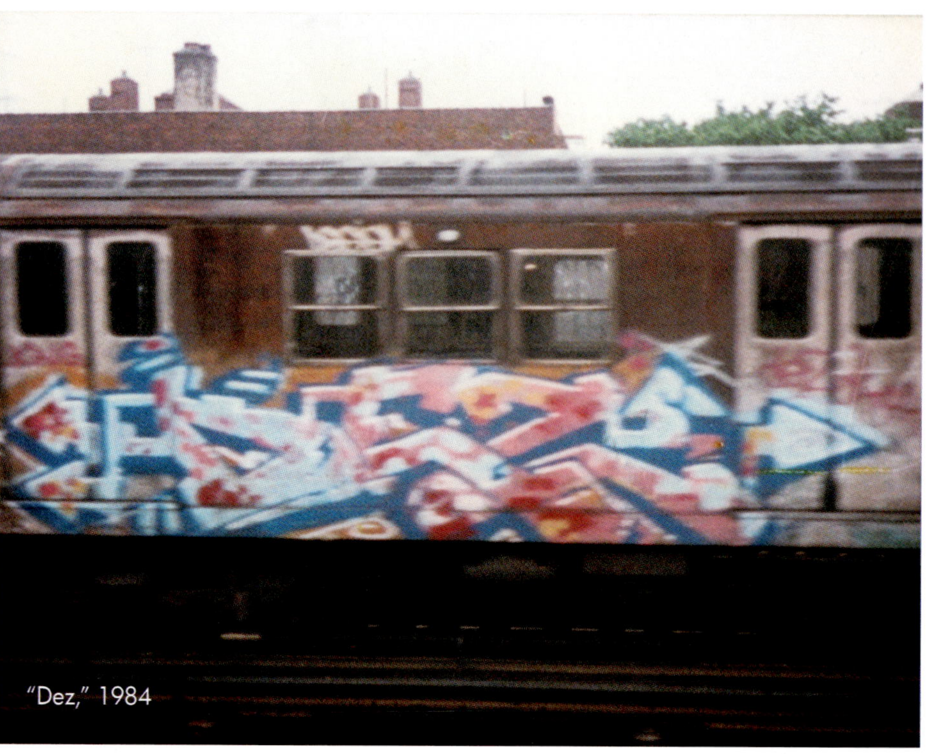
"Dez," 1984

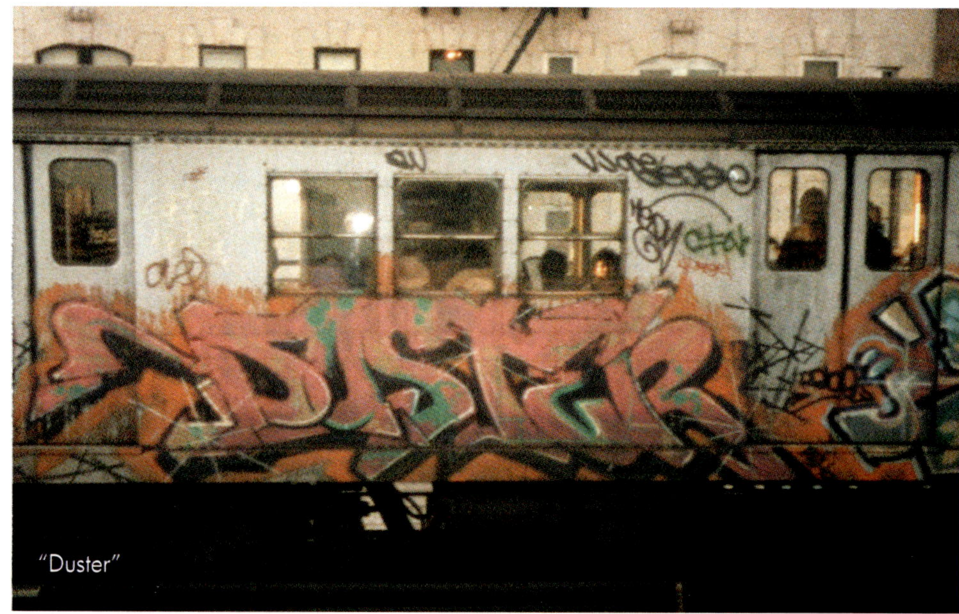
"Duster"

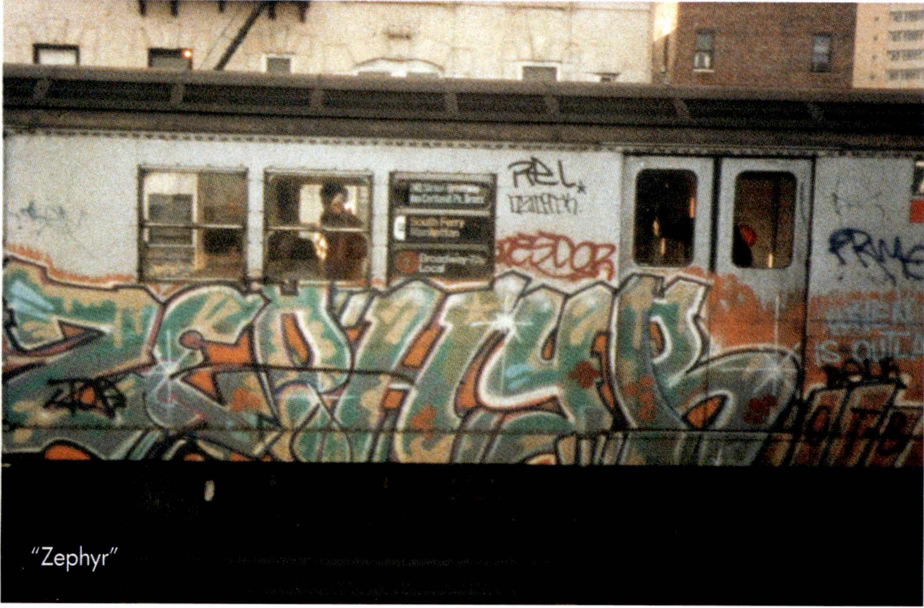
"Zephyr"

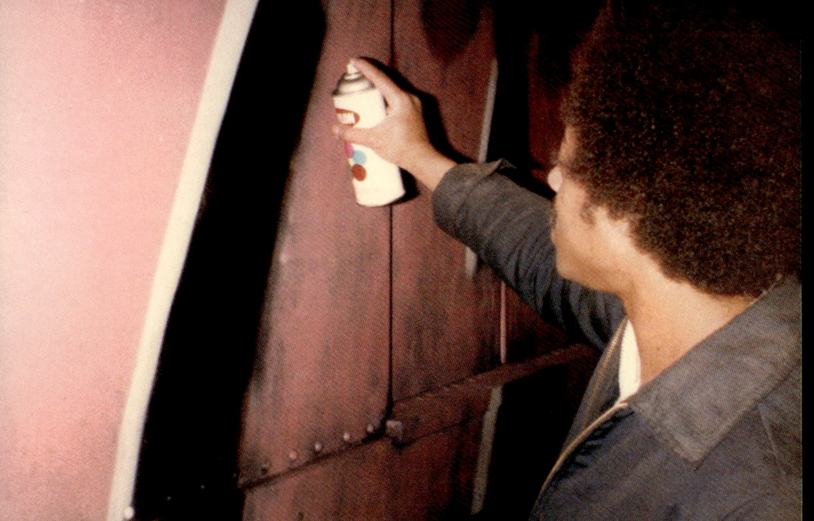

Blade in action

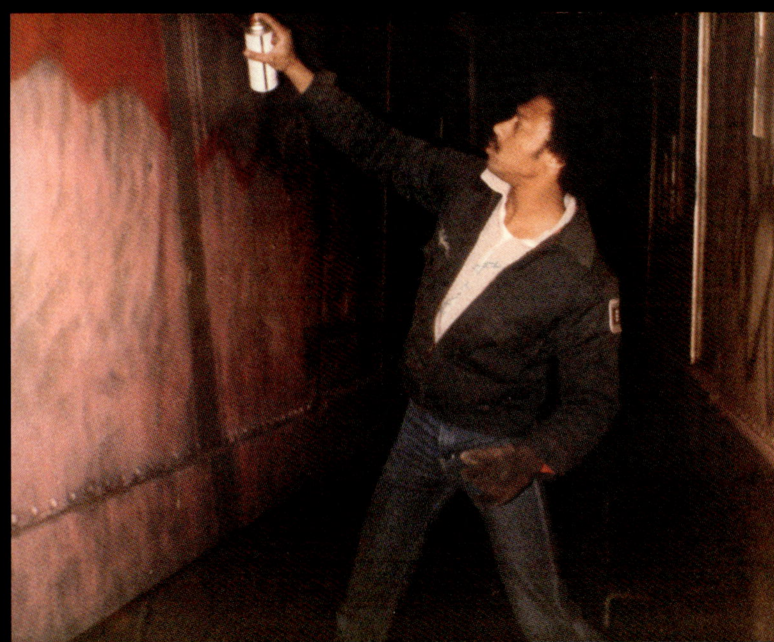

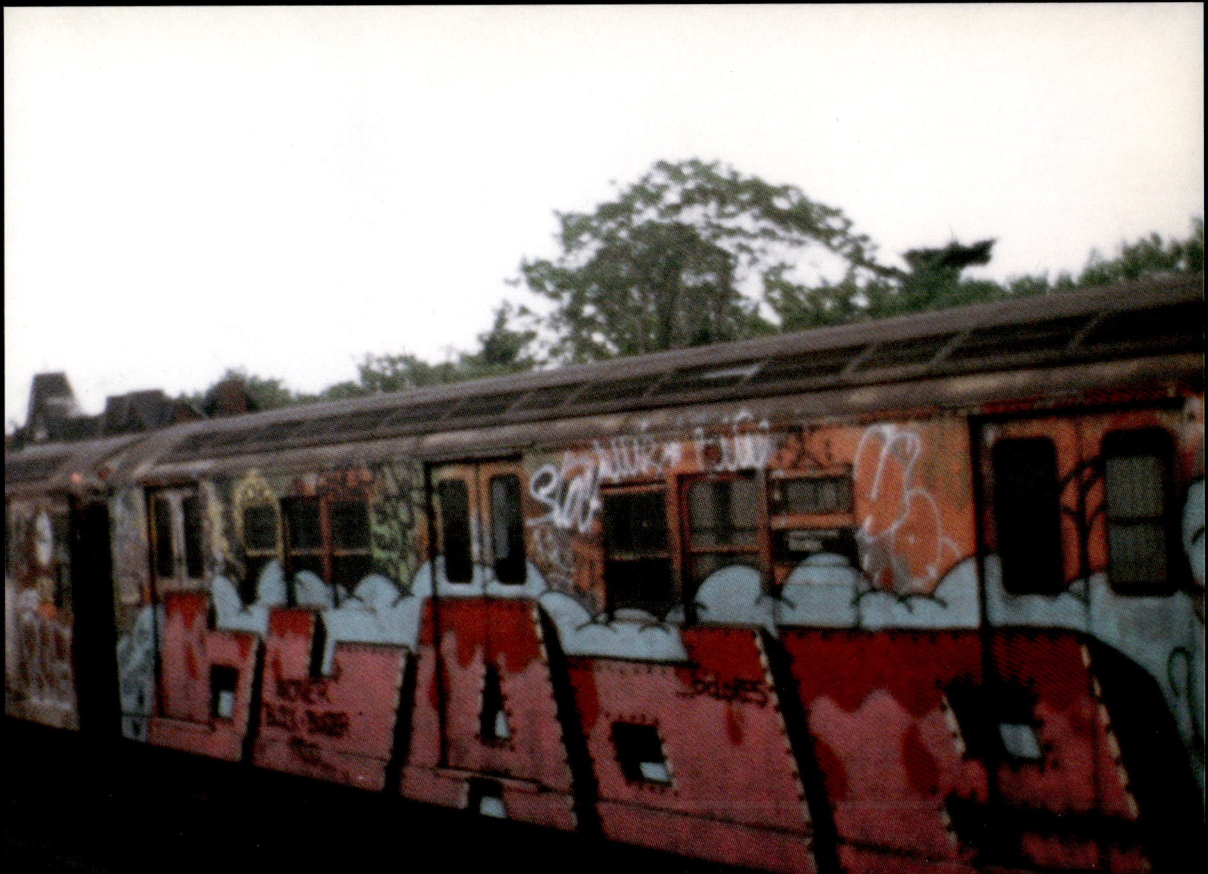

In 1984 I did a hot pink blockbuster in the ghost yard. Right by Fordam Rd. and Broadway. This was my last piece on a NYC subway car.

I had to quit because I was almost 30 years old. I directed all my energy to canvas from then until present day. Thanks to Amsterdam gallery owner Yaki Kornblit, I get to still be me at 53!

–Blade

No matter what "writing" has escalated to, trains will always be its proper place to me. From the old rolling stock writers called "coalmines," with their rusted doors & meshed seats & noisy fans that hardly worked in the summer, but with great heat in the winter months to the "flats" with those freshly buffed blue lines which were a first choice pick to piece on to the stainless steel ridges of the "fat-faces," "iron horses," "slants," and the state of the art "ding-dongs" iz where my passion and lust for writing will always be. I'll do my walls, rag tag mags, books, and even a film every so often, but nothing will ever take the place of those formative years of bombing the New York City transit system. Learning about fat caps, homemade markers out of gutted Zippos with the blackboard erasers, touch up cans or chap sticks, almost anything our young inventive minds could get our hands on and convert to meet our purpose! There are those of us who lived it. And we are still hanging around. We would wake up in the morning with one thing in mind...to "acquire" supplies to assist us in our bombing needs! If the choice was a can of "supreme quality" red devil, or rustoleum "cascade green" (#868), or something to eat, I went hungry. Some of us made many sacrifices, some with their lives. We would freeze for hours until our fingers froze to the shape of a spray can, our spray finger would literally get stuck to the spray nozzle. It would have to be pried off usually leaving a callus and then stand for hours ducking feds just to get a glimpse of yours and your boy's pieces running. We didn't take pictures then. That came later. We were in it for the fun. The competition and the camaraderie and most of all, the freedom. Well, these days it's difficult to attain that free feeling doing a wall or canvas or any "legal" substitution. But if I'm left alone long enough and if you can see my mind's eye you would see I would be in a lay up or yard facing the elements, bombing, having fun! I'm not only a participant, but am a fan as well, always will be, I'm afraid. So no matter where writing (no other true name for it) takes me, admix the global notoriety and fame (unfortunately not the fortune), I'd rather simply be on the outside of the train.

–IZ THE WIZ (RIP)

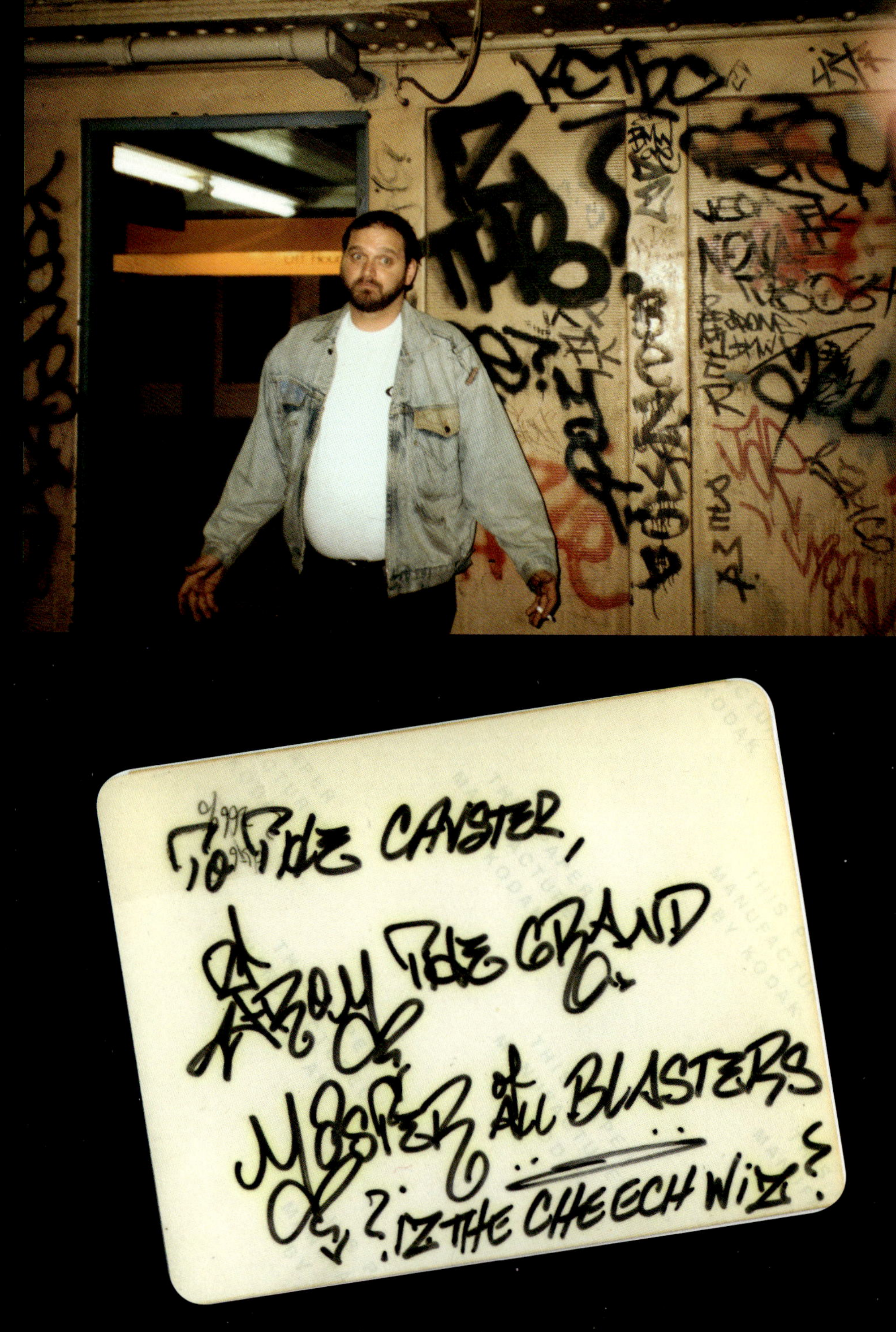

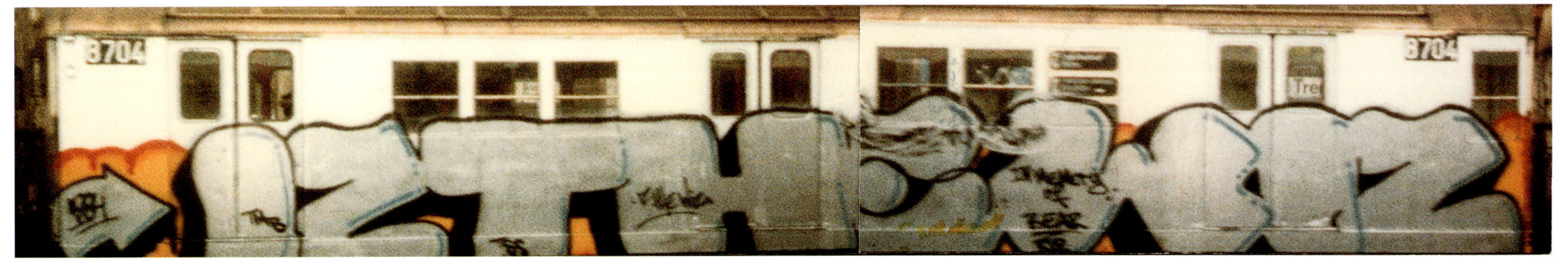

"IZ THE WIZ," 1984

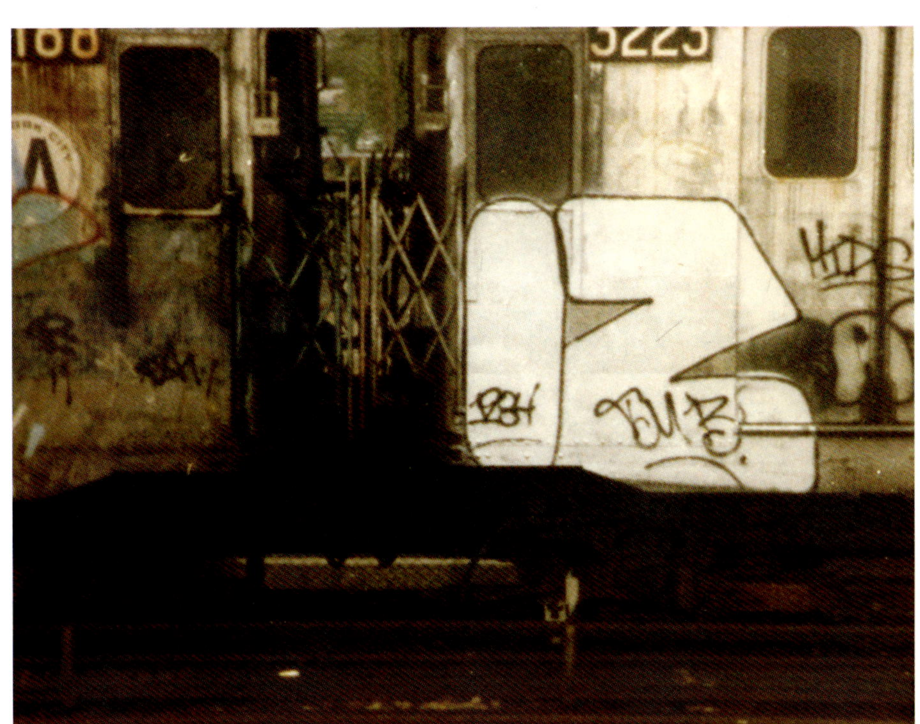

"IZ," 1984

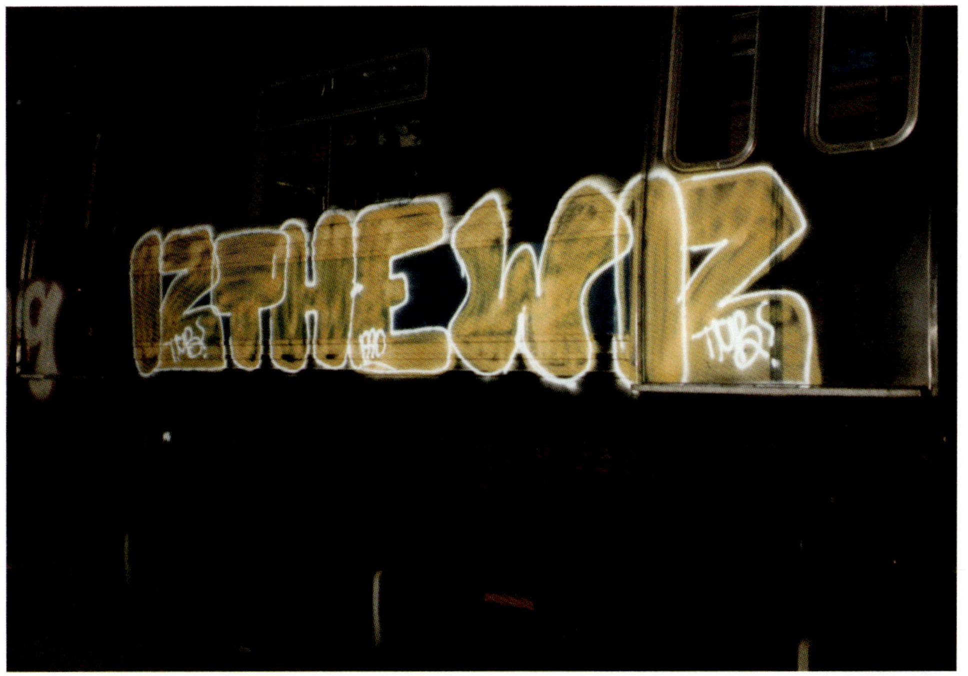

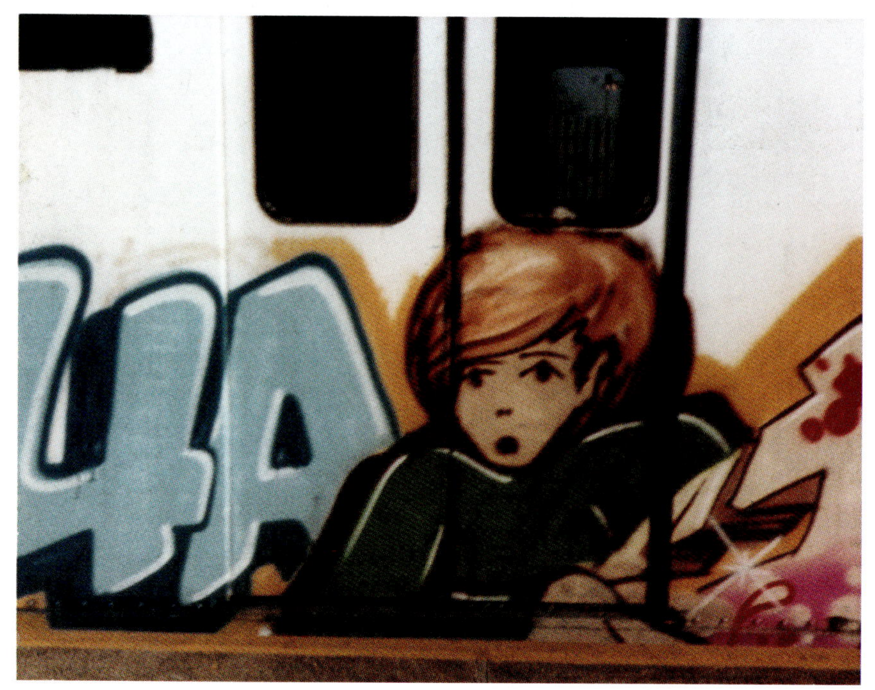

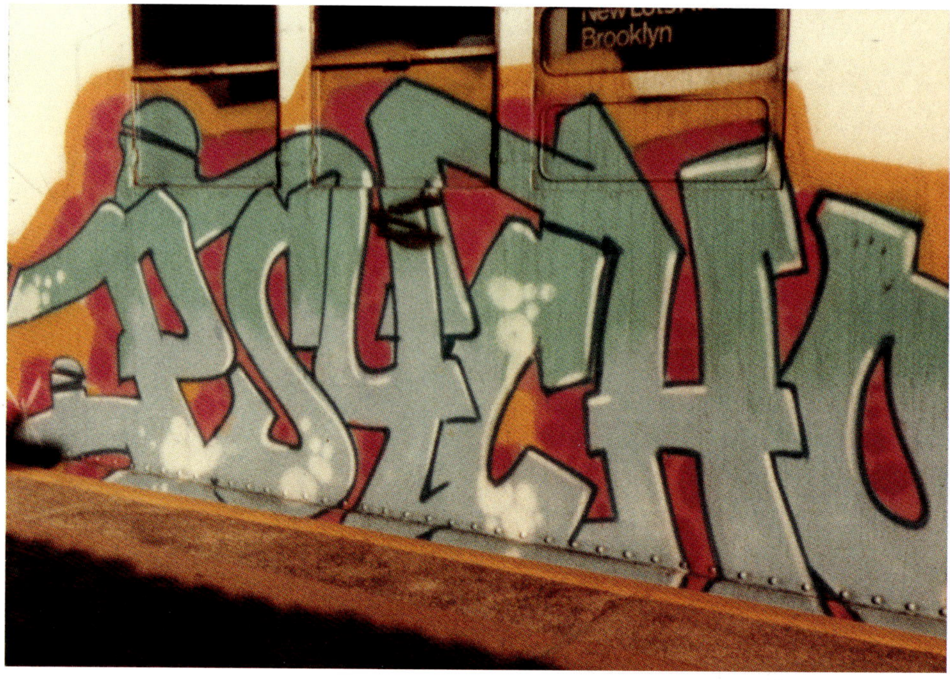

"Psycho," by Seen

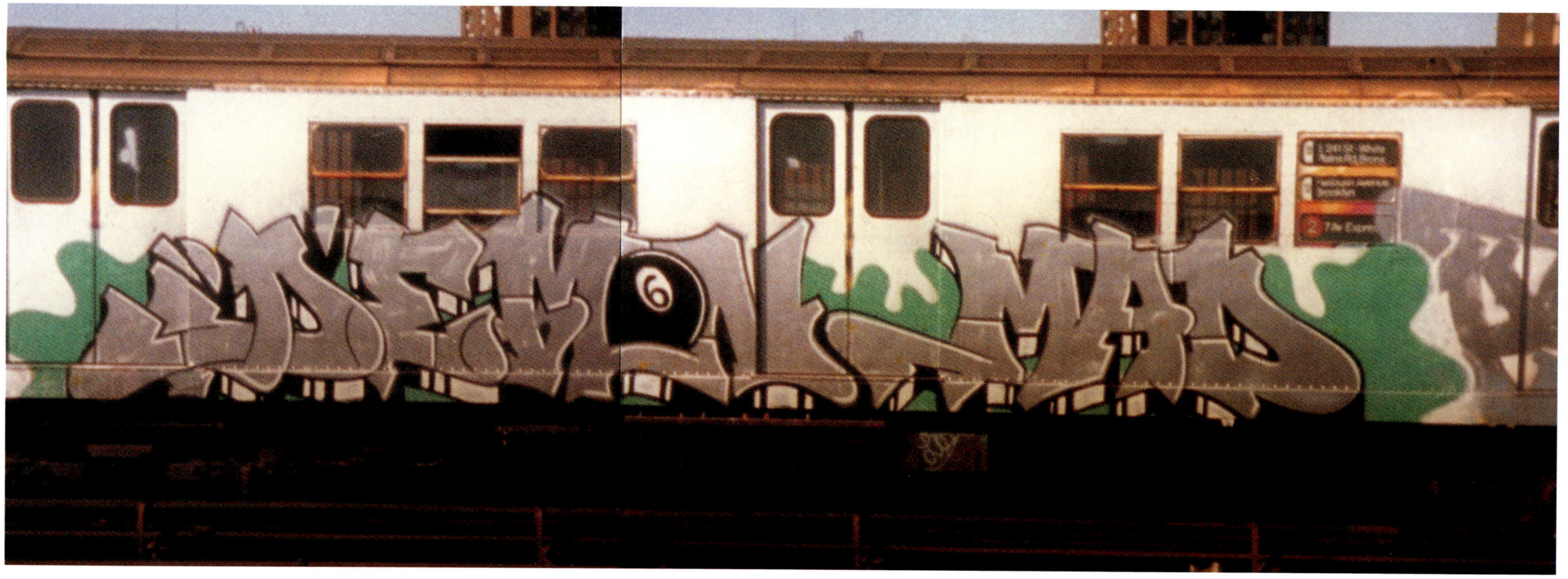

"Demon" & "Mad"

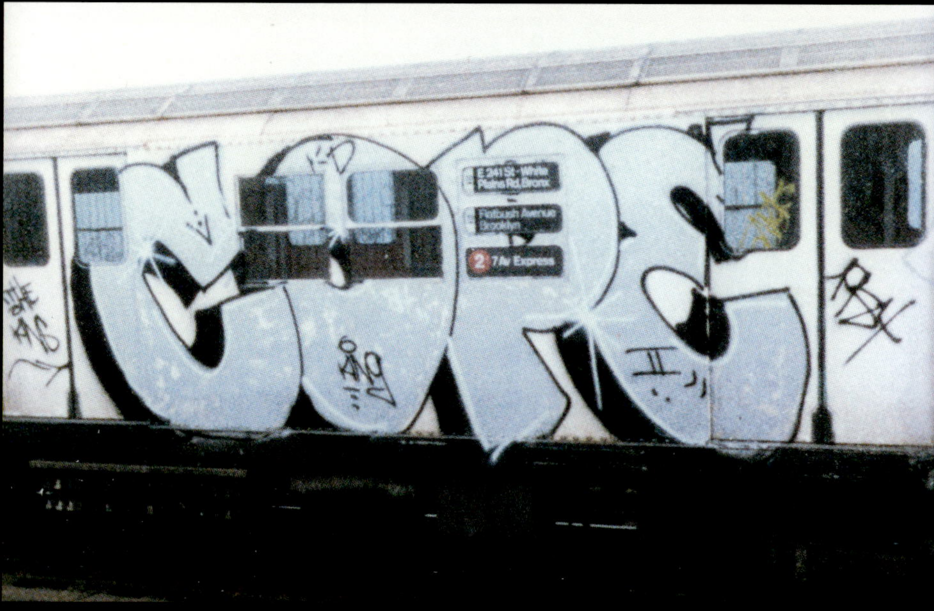

"Cope," 1984

I did this top to bottom, silver and black in the Harlem tunnel lay ups. It was in the winter of 1984. I took the 4 train down to see if they were in. They were, so I got off at 86th st. There was a martin paint on 85th st and 3rd ave. I used to smash it for years. So I went in real quick and racked up two tall metallic silvers and one gloss black. That's when Rustoleum came out with the tall cans. I took two or three orange fatcaps off the kitchen magics. I could have racked more but they knew my face in there. I got thrown out so many times. I jumped on the IRT #6 local to 116th st. As soon as the train left, I waited for the platform to be empty. It was on! I jumped onto the tracks right down to the lay up. It was early on a Saturday and I was just so open! I had to crack a quick silver and black top to bottom.

–Cope2

The Joey and Cope2 we did in the Harlem tunnel lay ups. In the winter of 1983. It was Delta2 who did the outlines for us on that car. That weekend we did a couple of cars. Cone, Delta2, Joey, Radio, and myself we killed it! I also smashed the place with throw ups. Cone and me back in the glory days!

–Cope2

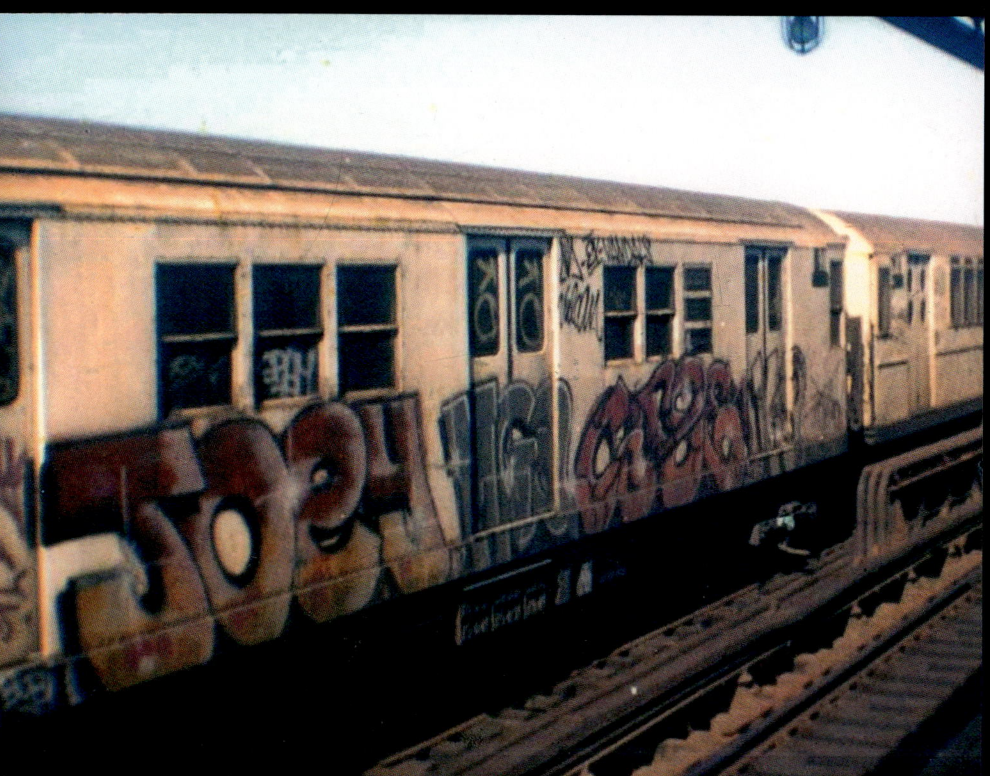

"Joey" & "Cope2"

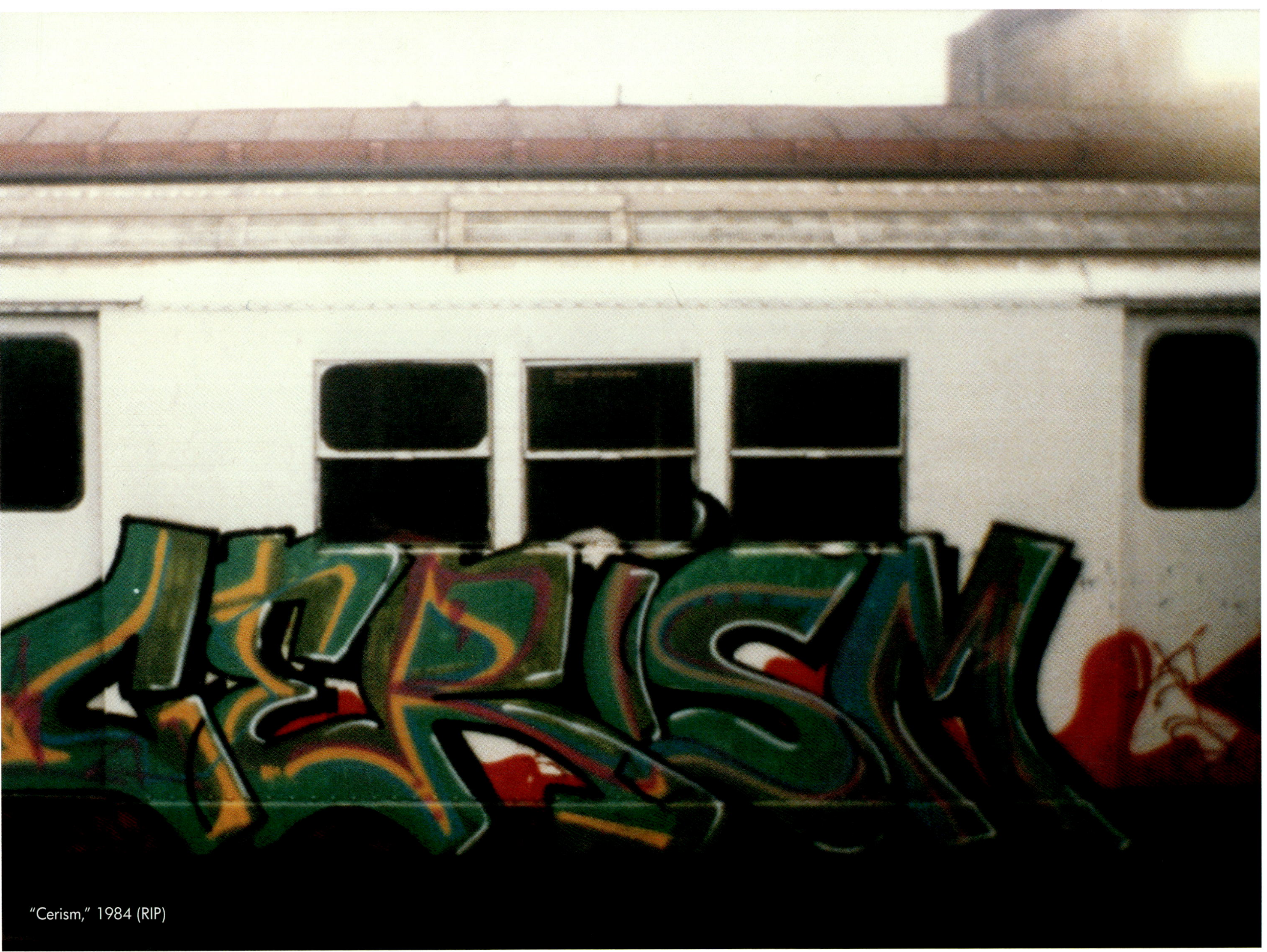

"Cerism," 1984 (RIP)

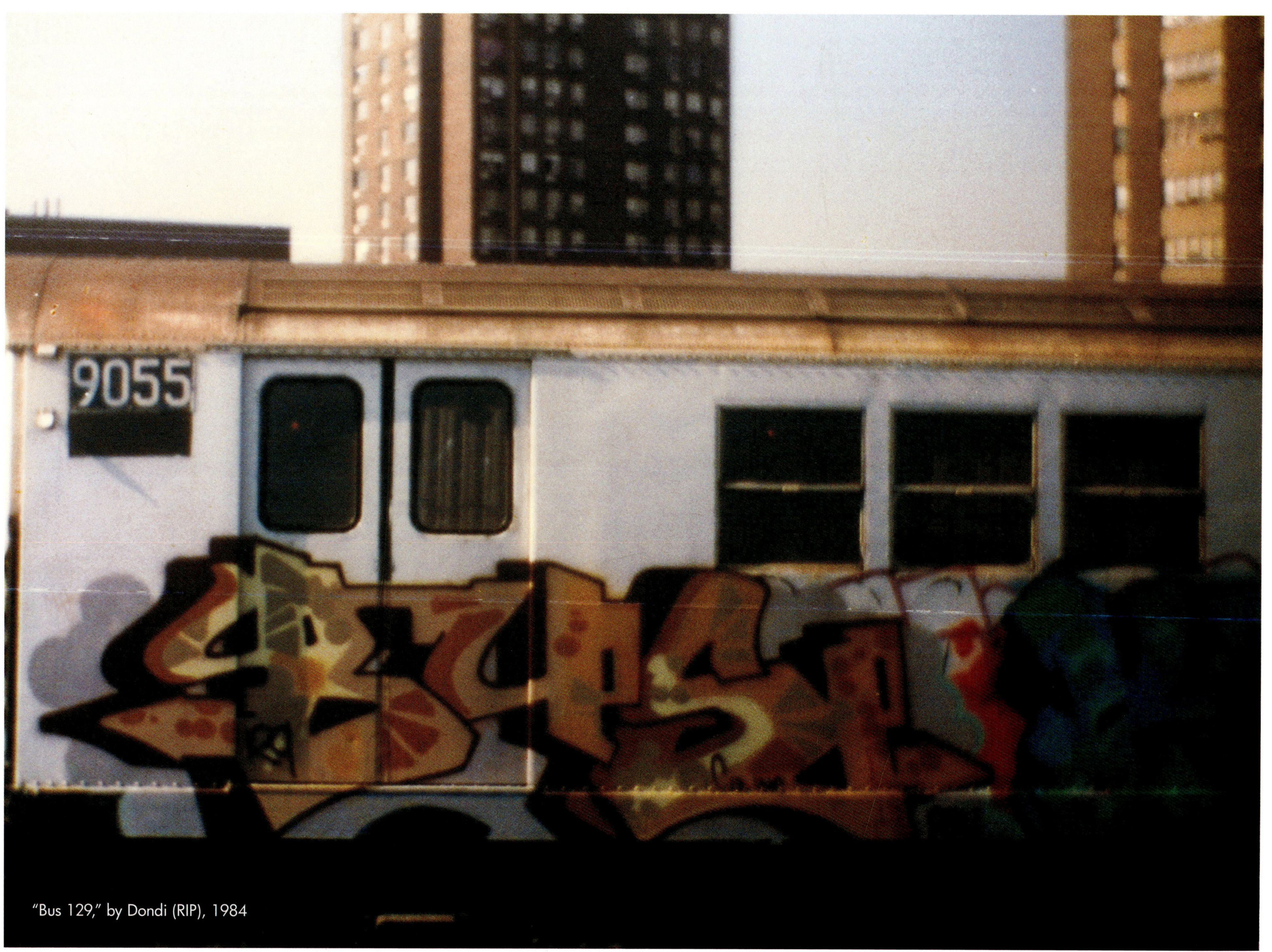

"Bus 129," by Dondi (RIP), 1984

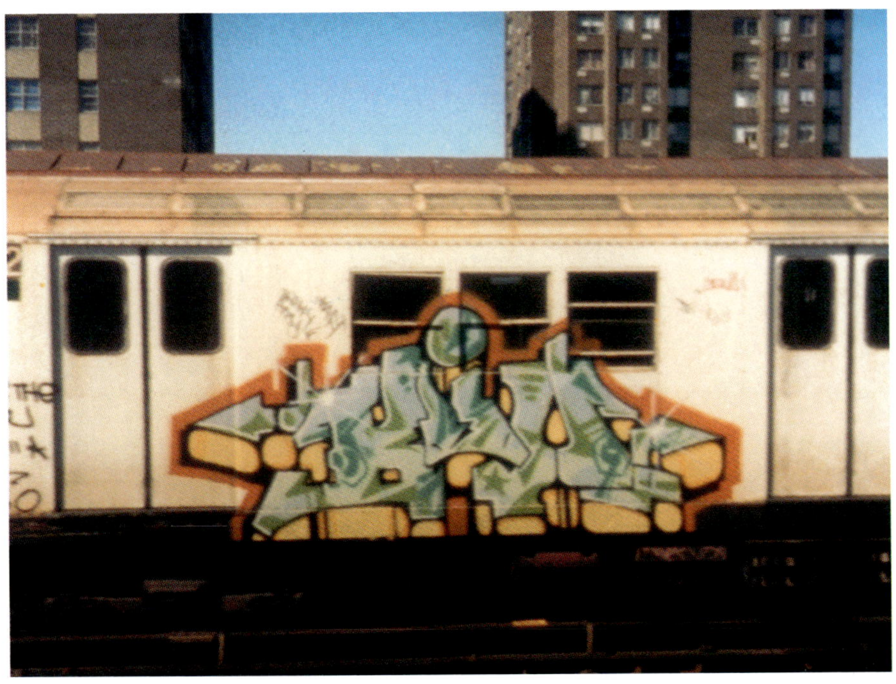

"Bio," 1984

"Mack," 1984

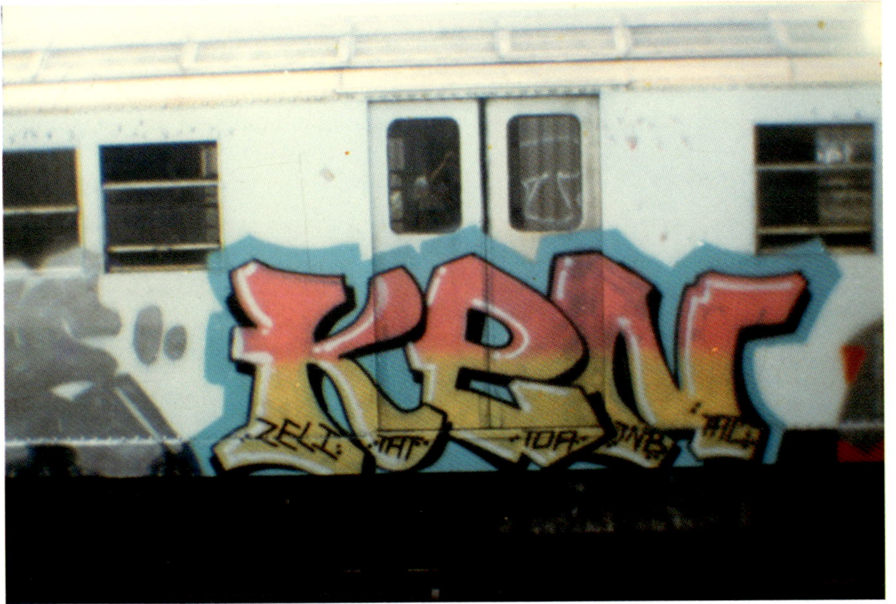

"Ken"

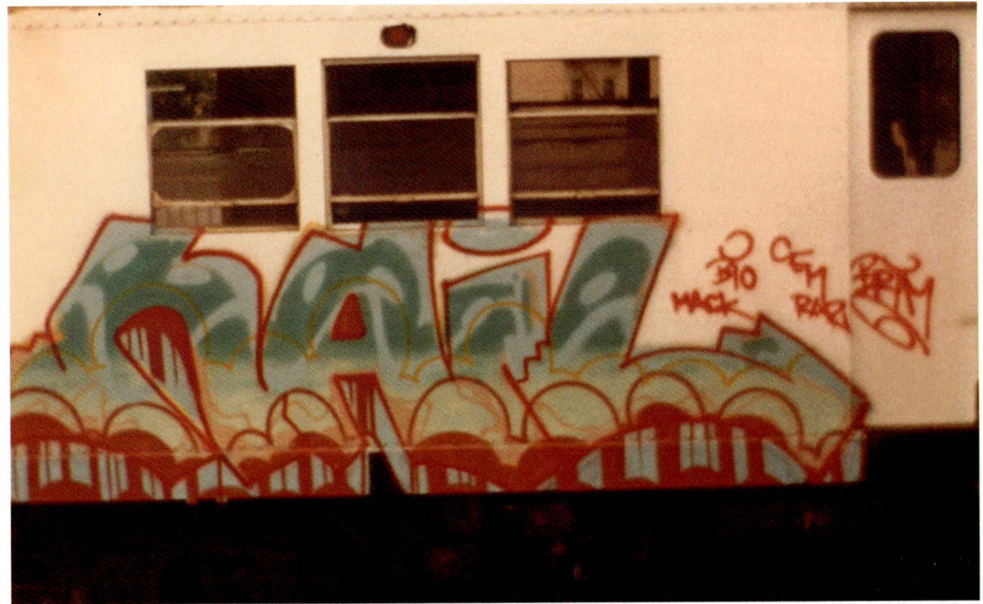

"Nail," by Brim

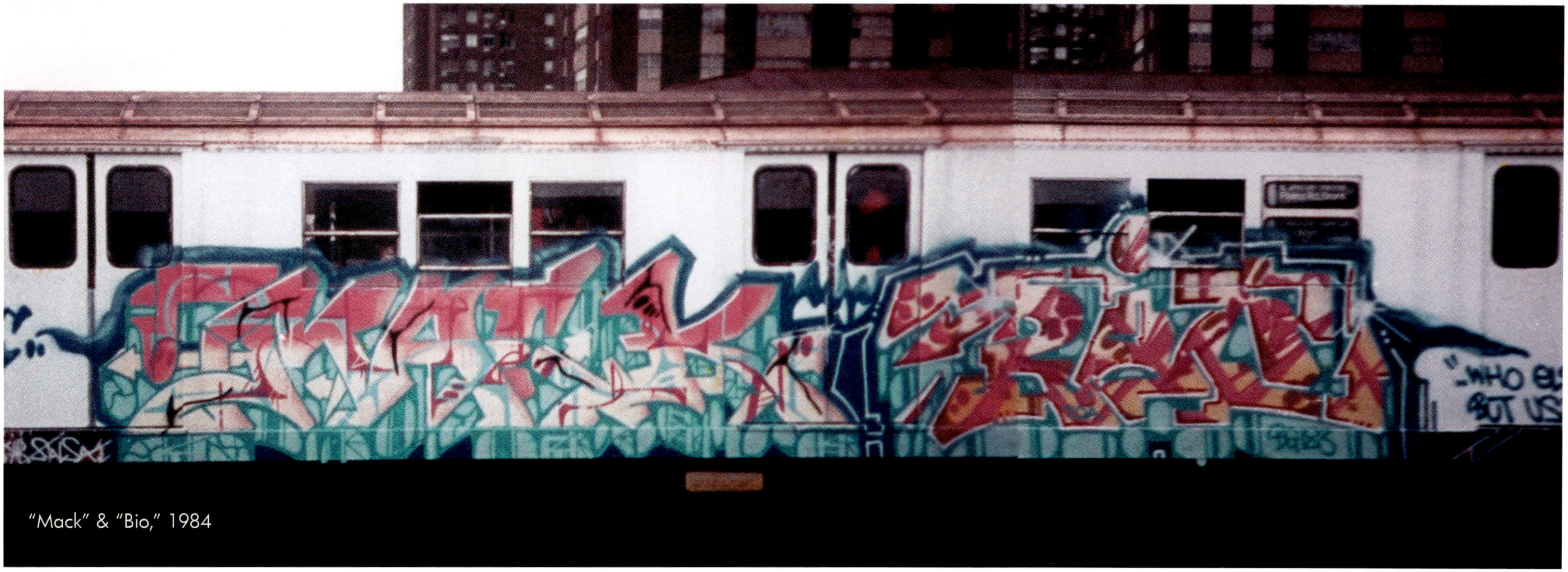

"Mack" & "Bio," 1984

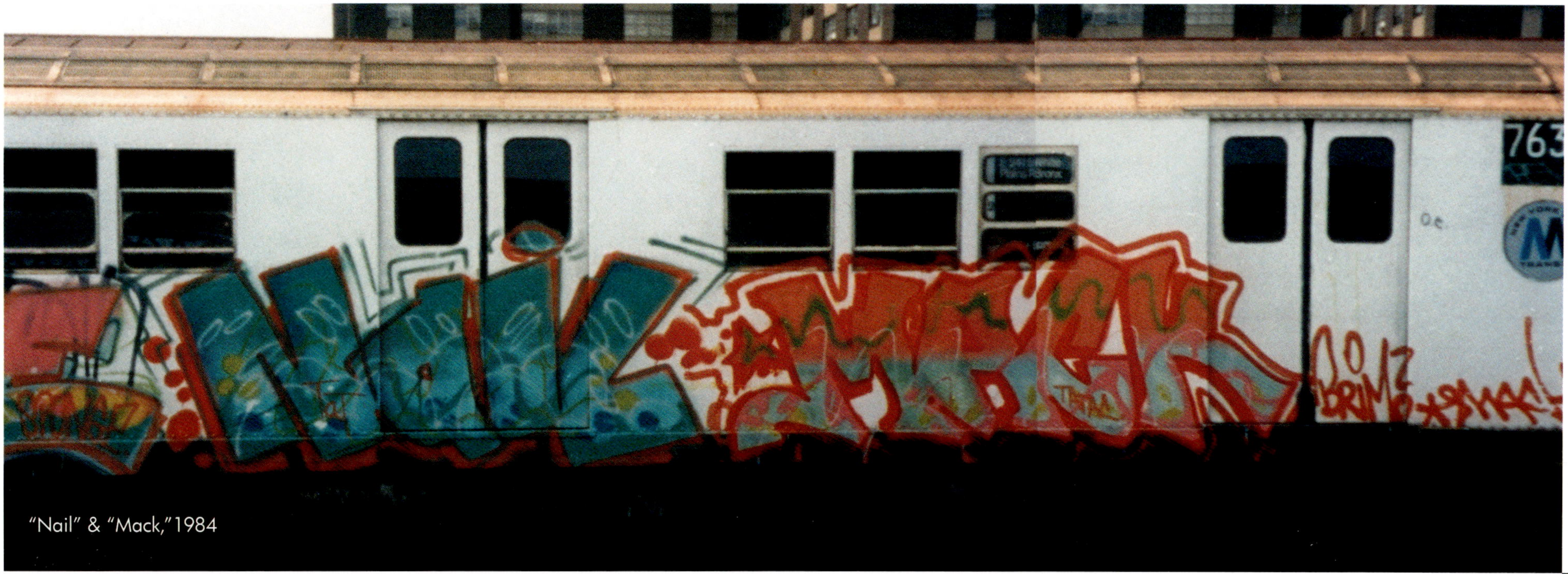

"Nail" & "Mack,"1984

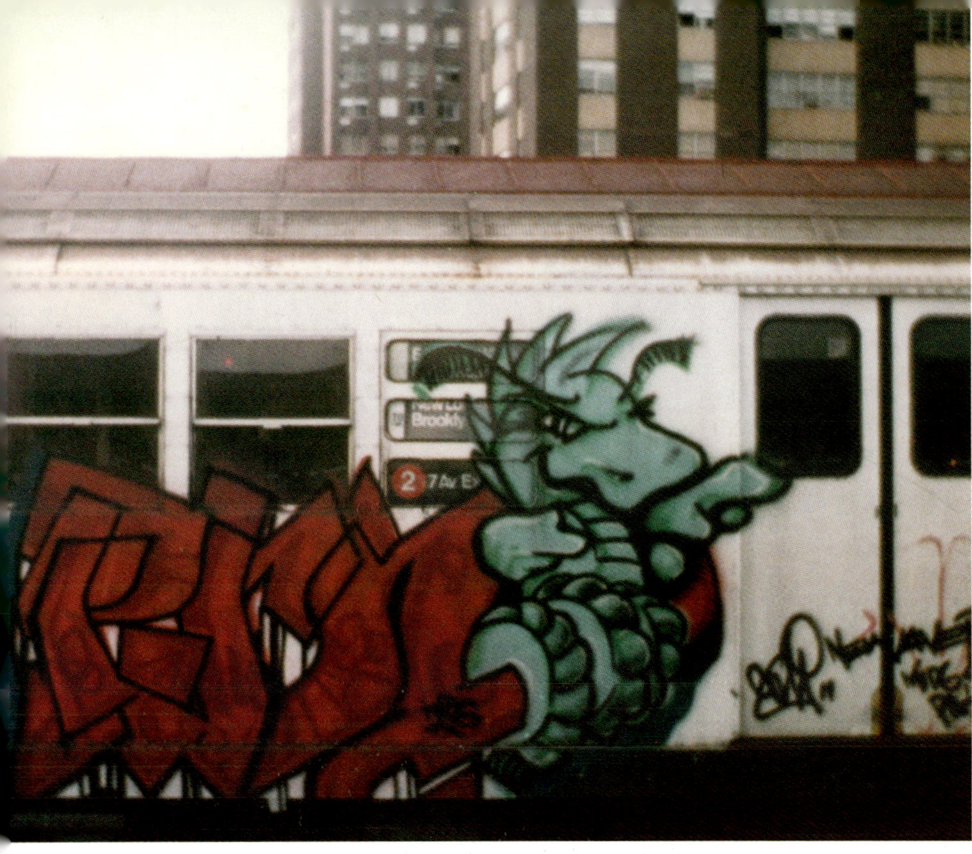

"Erni," 1984

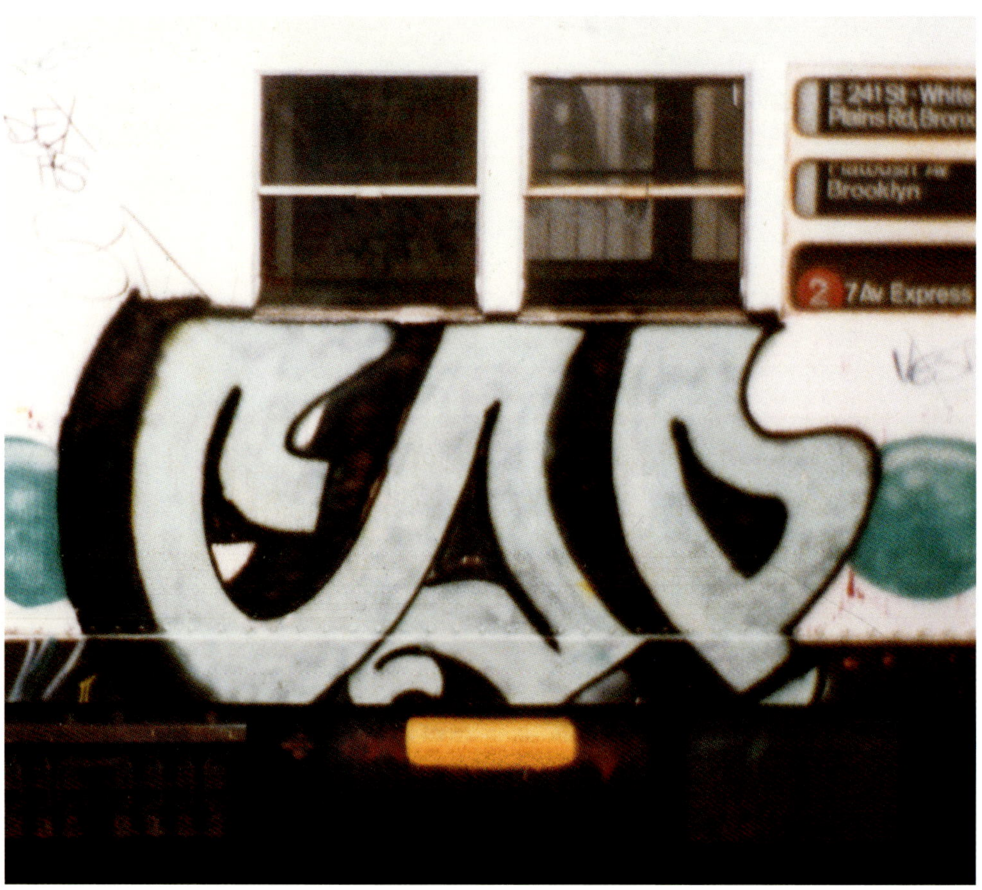

"Cap," 1984

"Ken," "Jop," "Shaz" & "Much," 1984

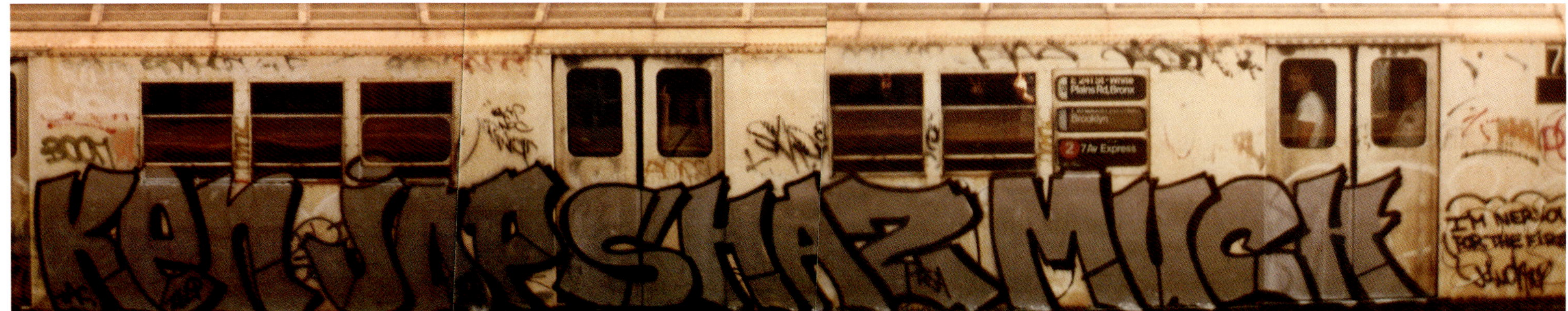

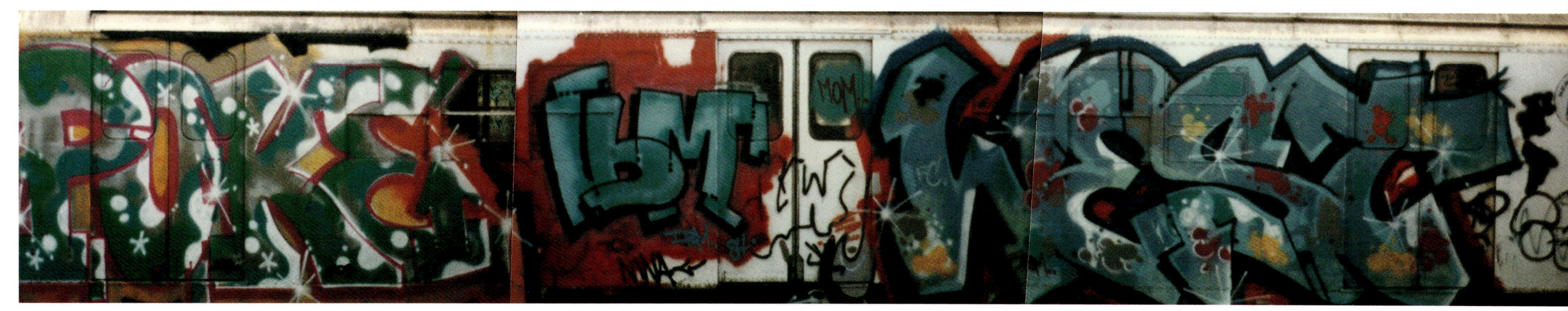

"Poke" & "West," 1984

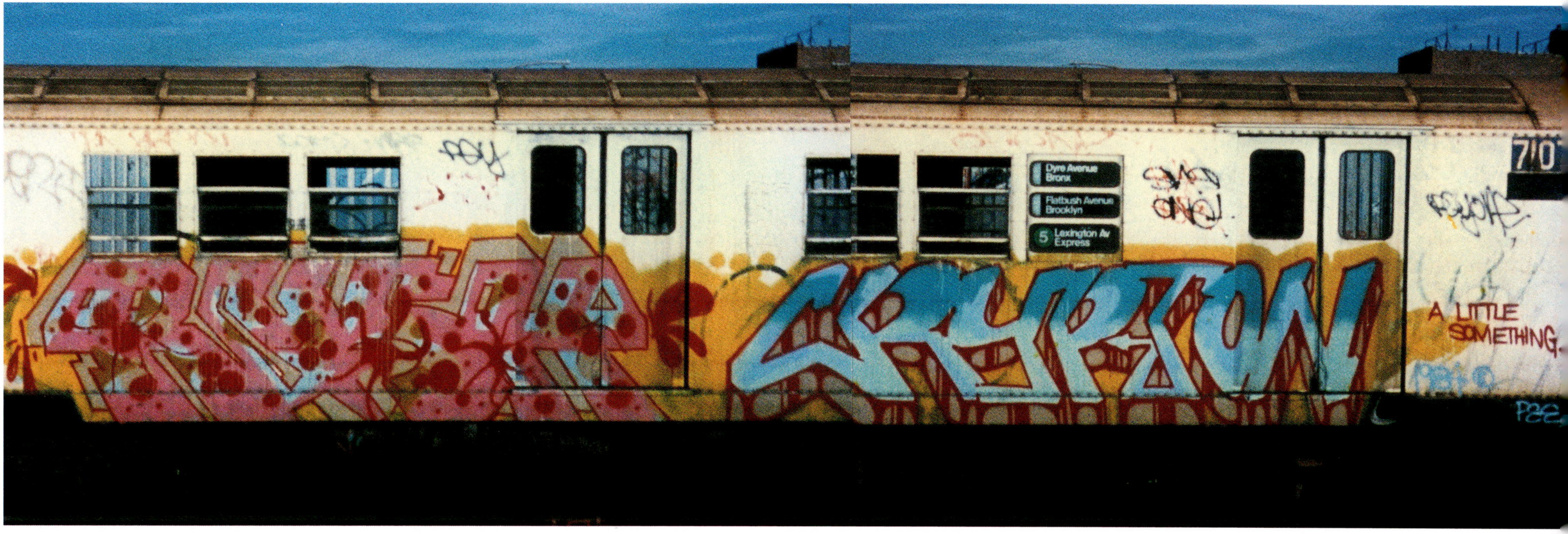

"Rush" & "Crypton," 1984

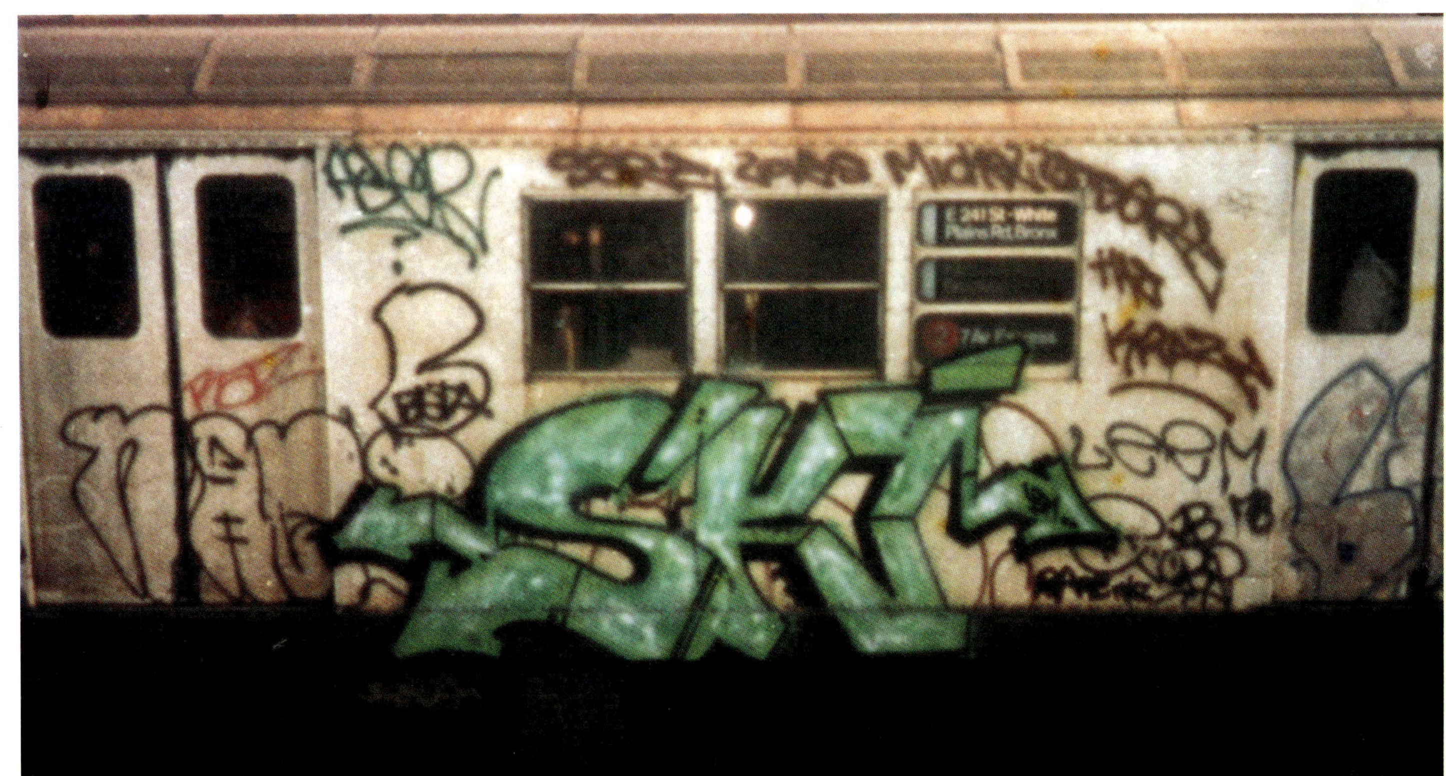

"Ski," 1984

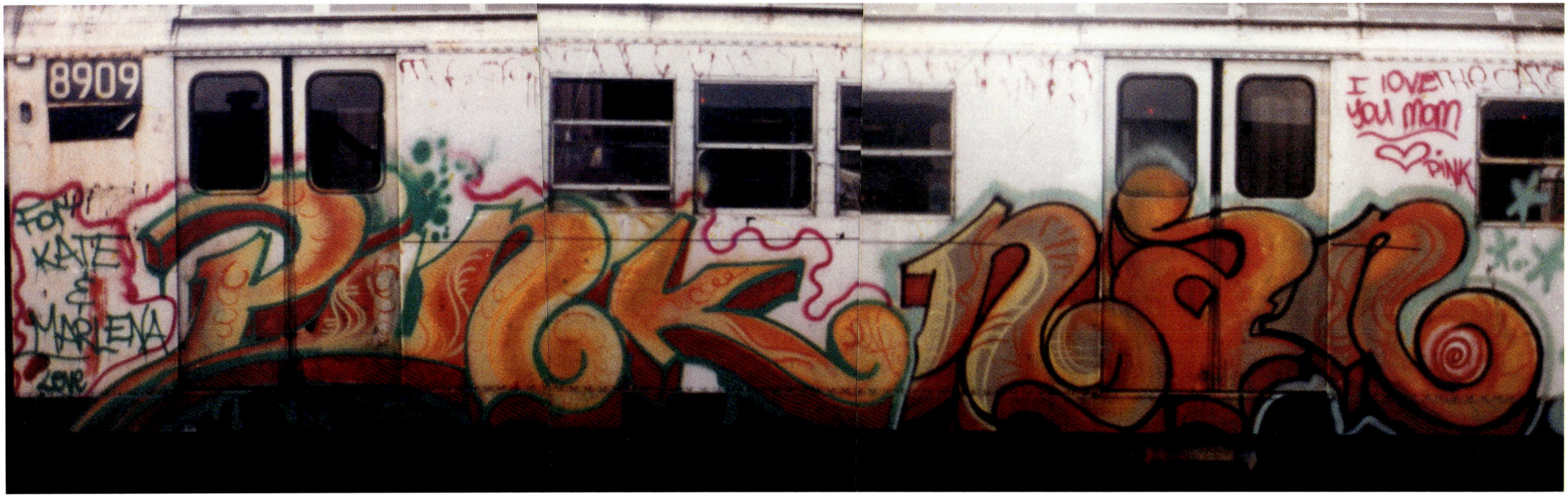

"Pink" & "Nan," 1984

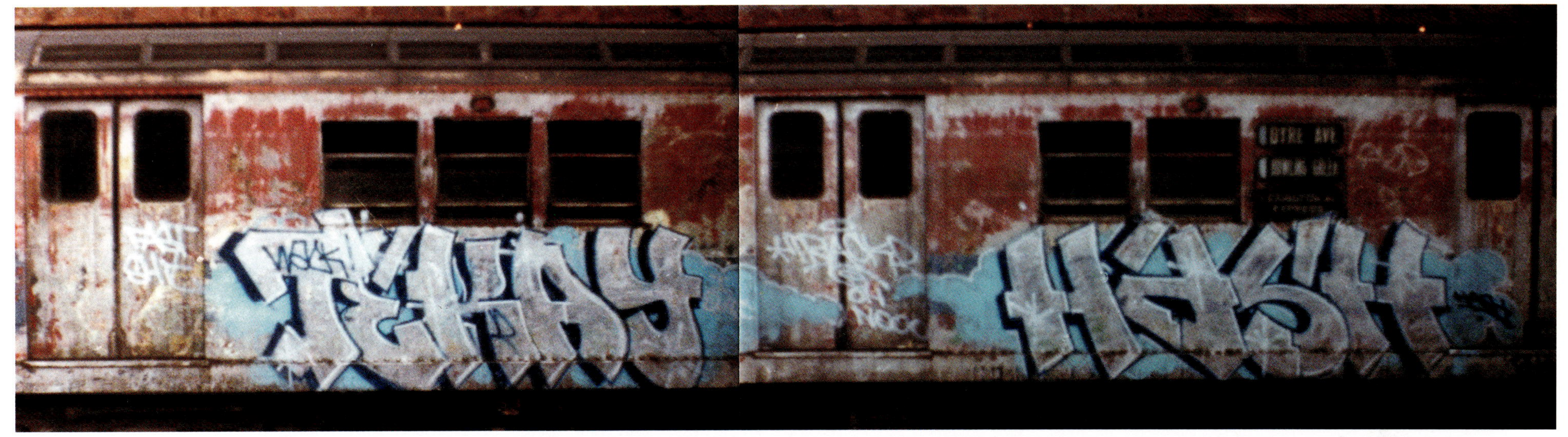

"Tekay" & "Hash," 1984

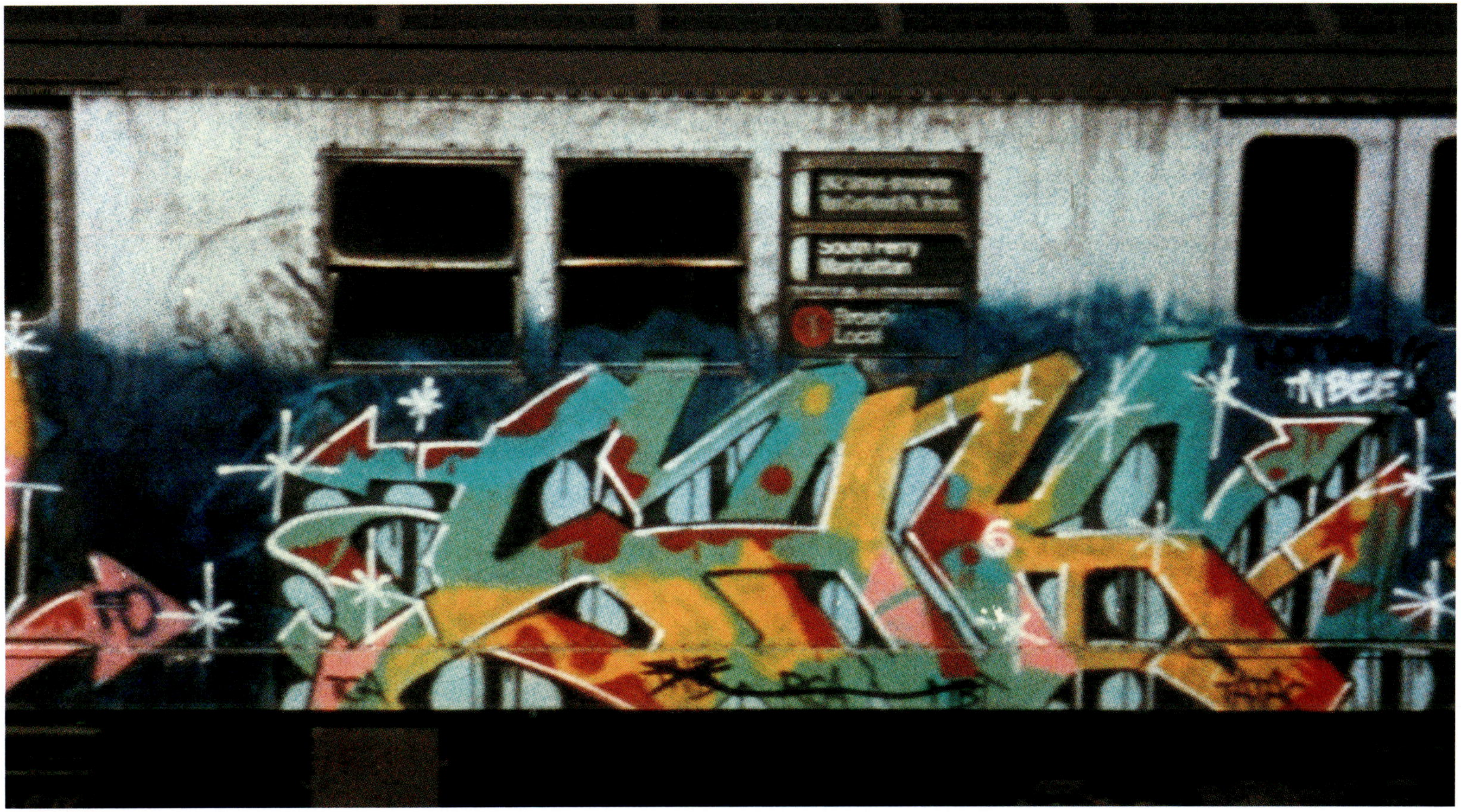

"Sak," 1984

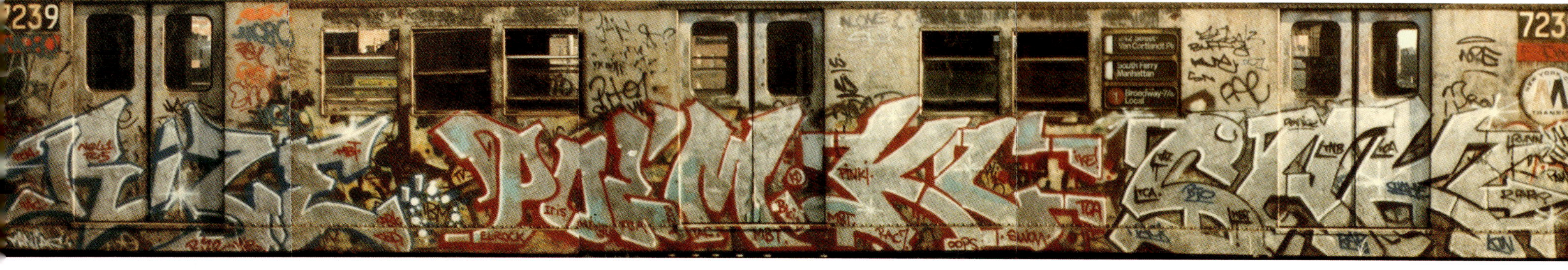

"Rize," "Poem," "KC" & "SAK," 1984

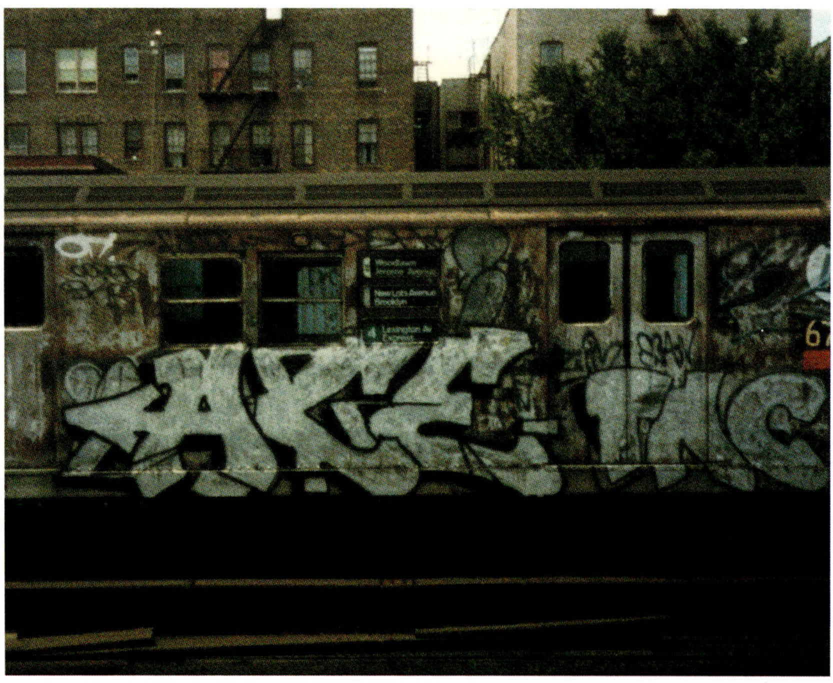

"Ace" (RIP), 1984

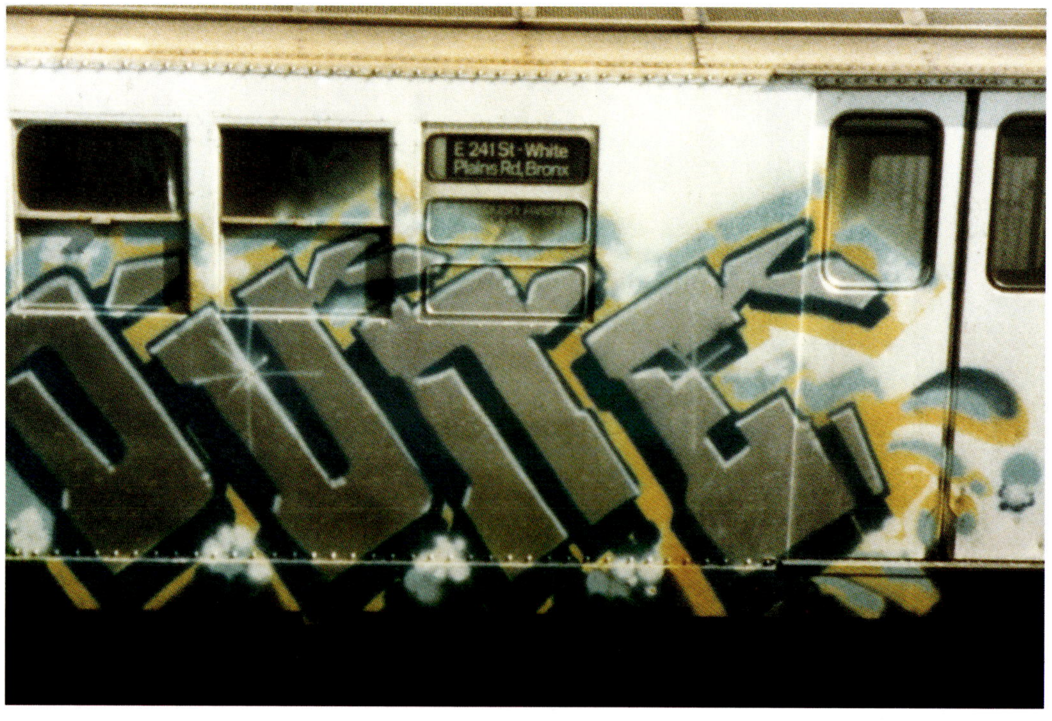

"Dune," 1984

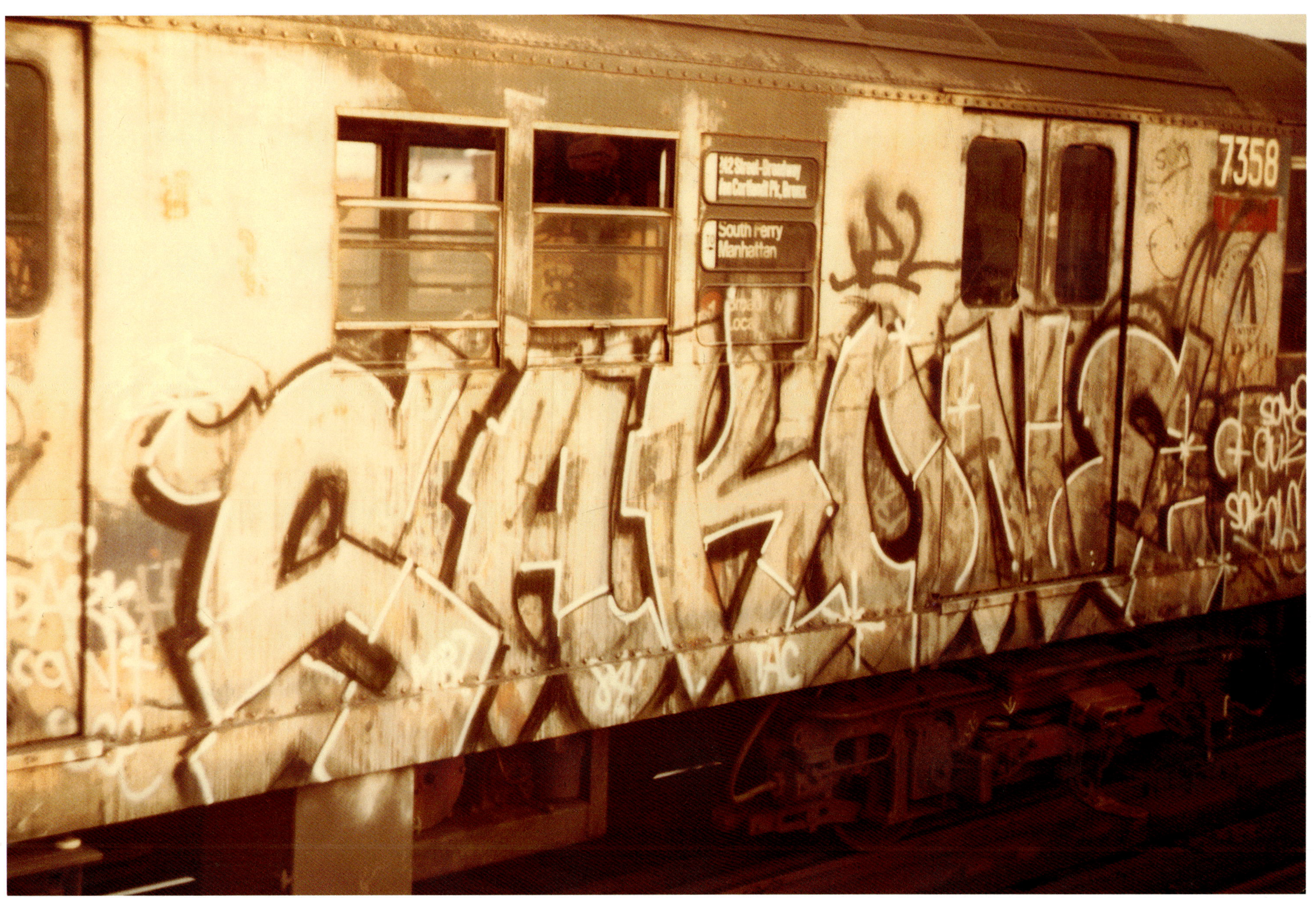

"Sak," 1984

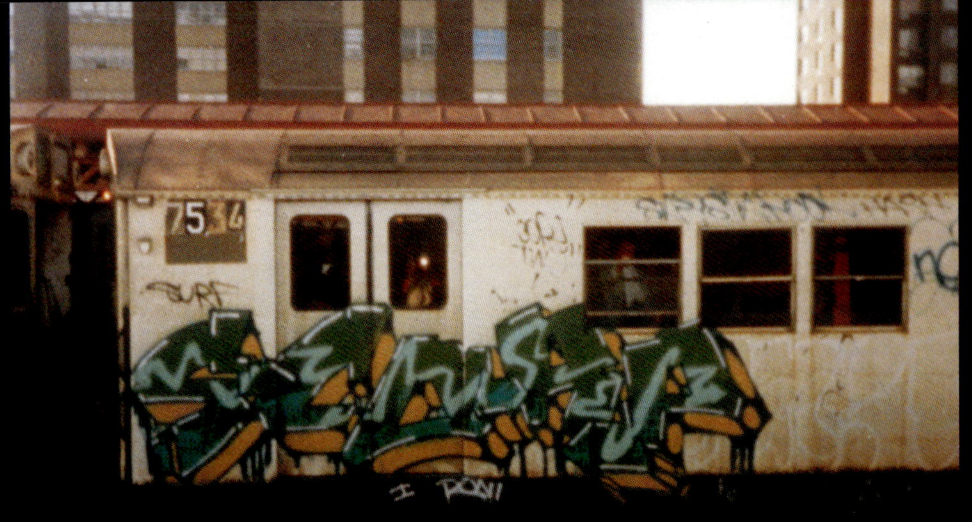

"Scorp," 1984

"Seck," 1984

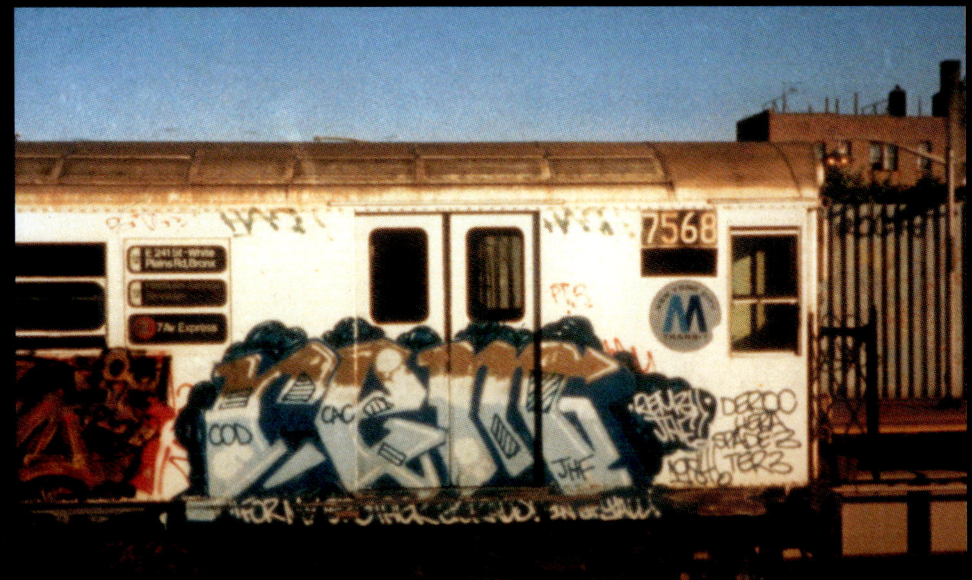

"Rem 311" (RIP)

This night is memorable because it was not only my first piece on a subway train, but ironically was my last "Seck" piece as well. Soon after I started up with the name "Vet," and moved to a whole different level. I haven't looked back since.

–Vet

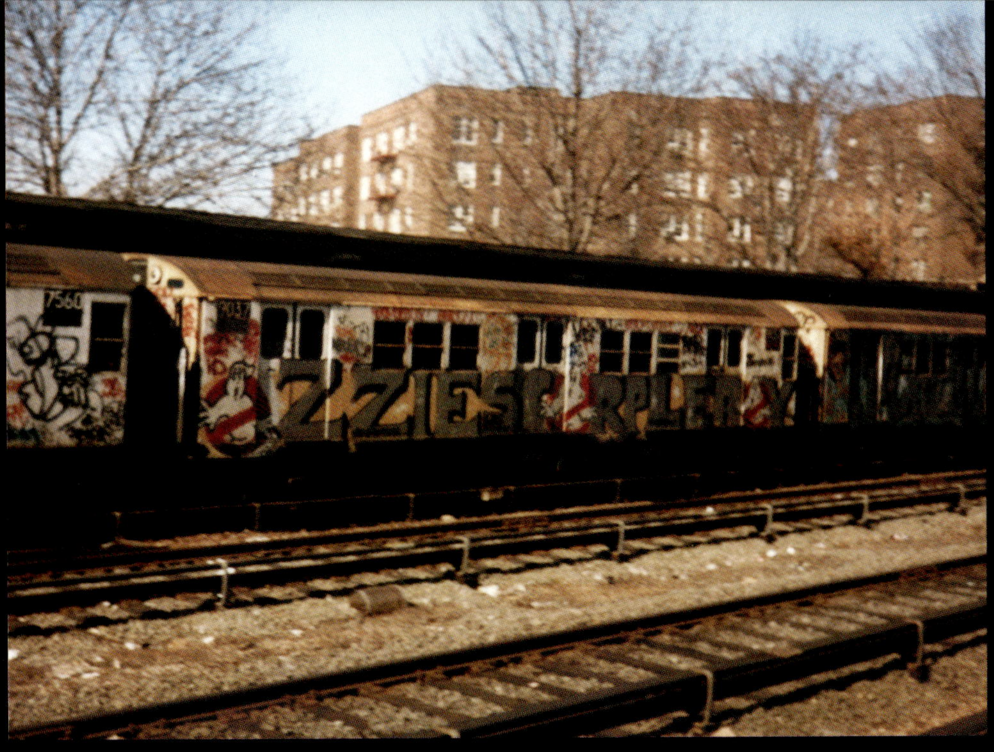

"Ozzie," "Scorp" & "Leroy"

A magical night in 1984 that brought two crew leaders together, to create something special. Michelob was a great painter with exceptional can control, opposite my colorful party-guy style. The contrast worked well!

-LM4

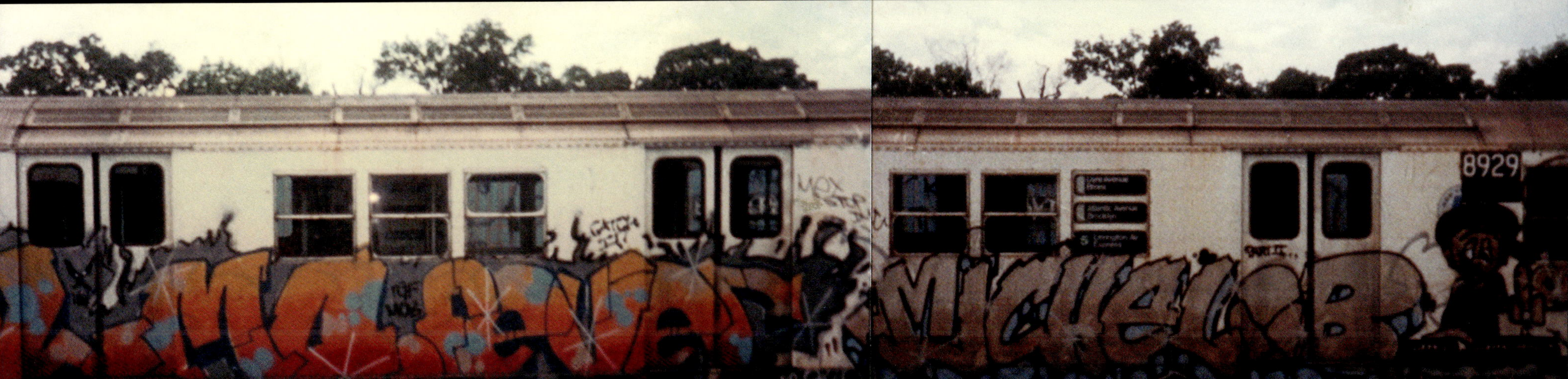

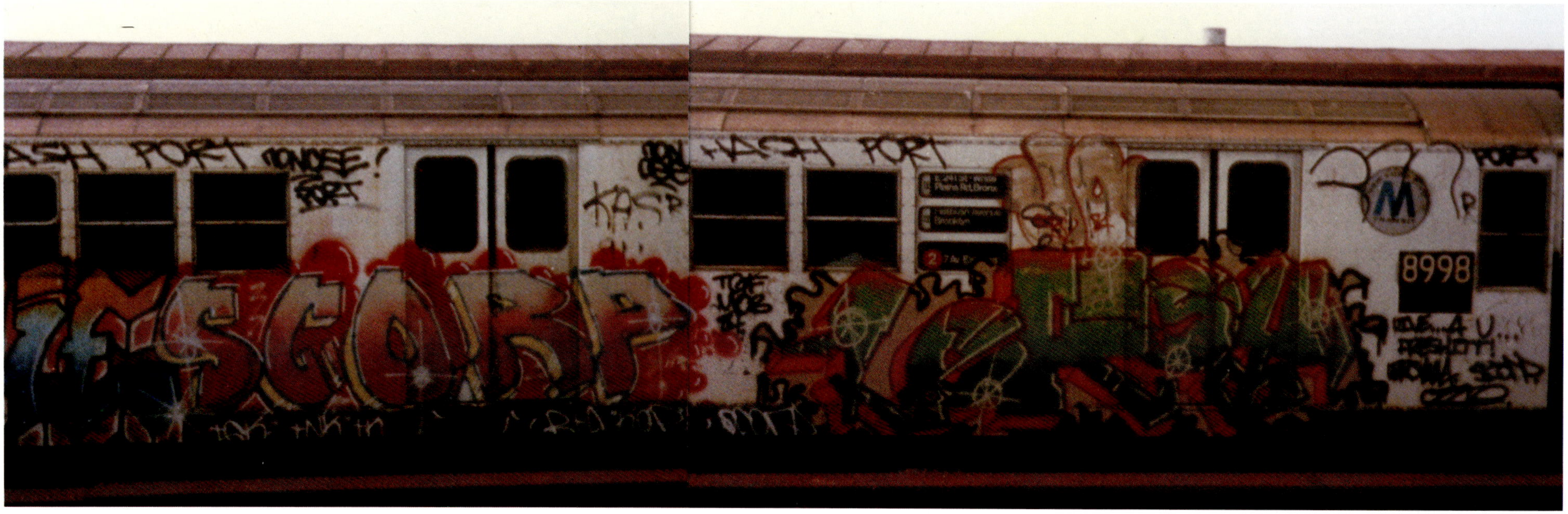

"Scorp" & "Leroy"

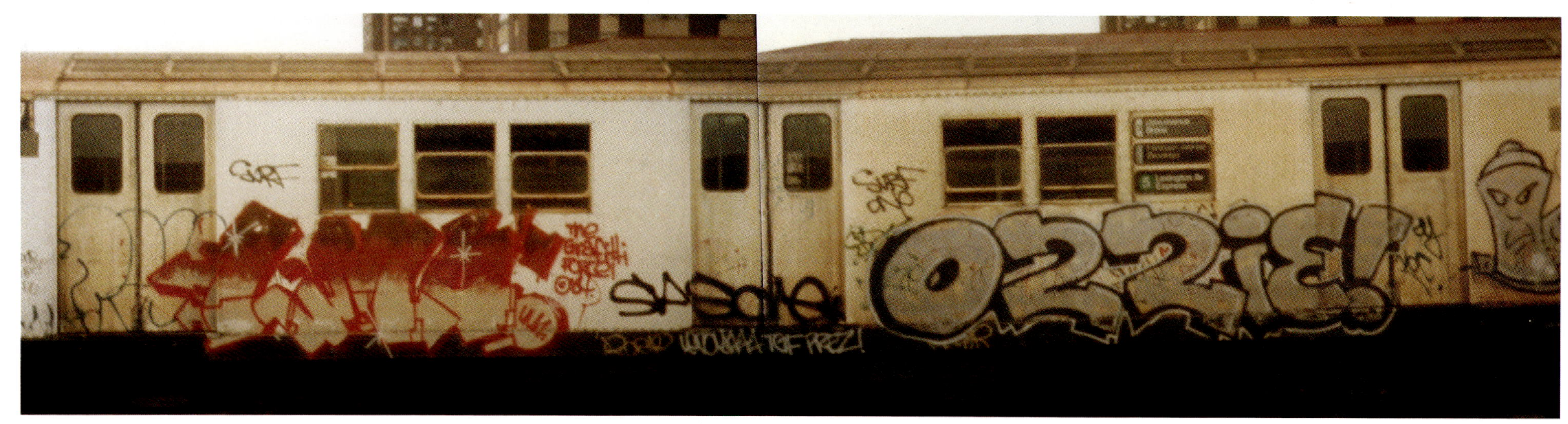

"LM4" & "Ozzie"

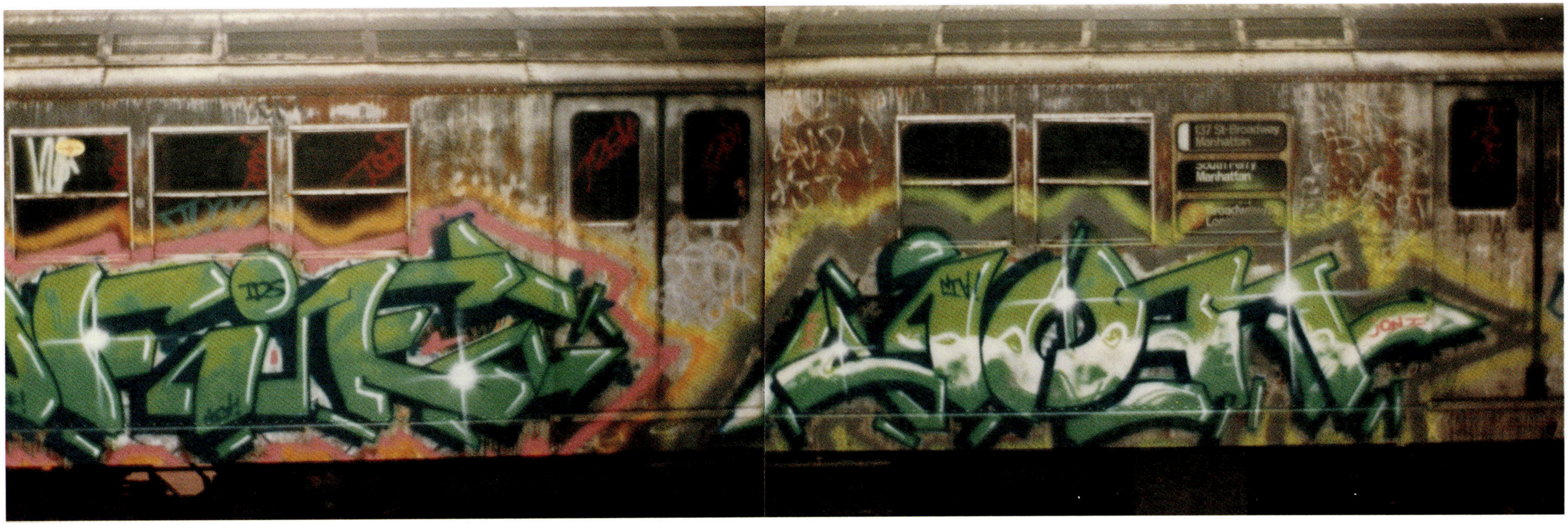

"Flite" & "Jon," 1984

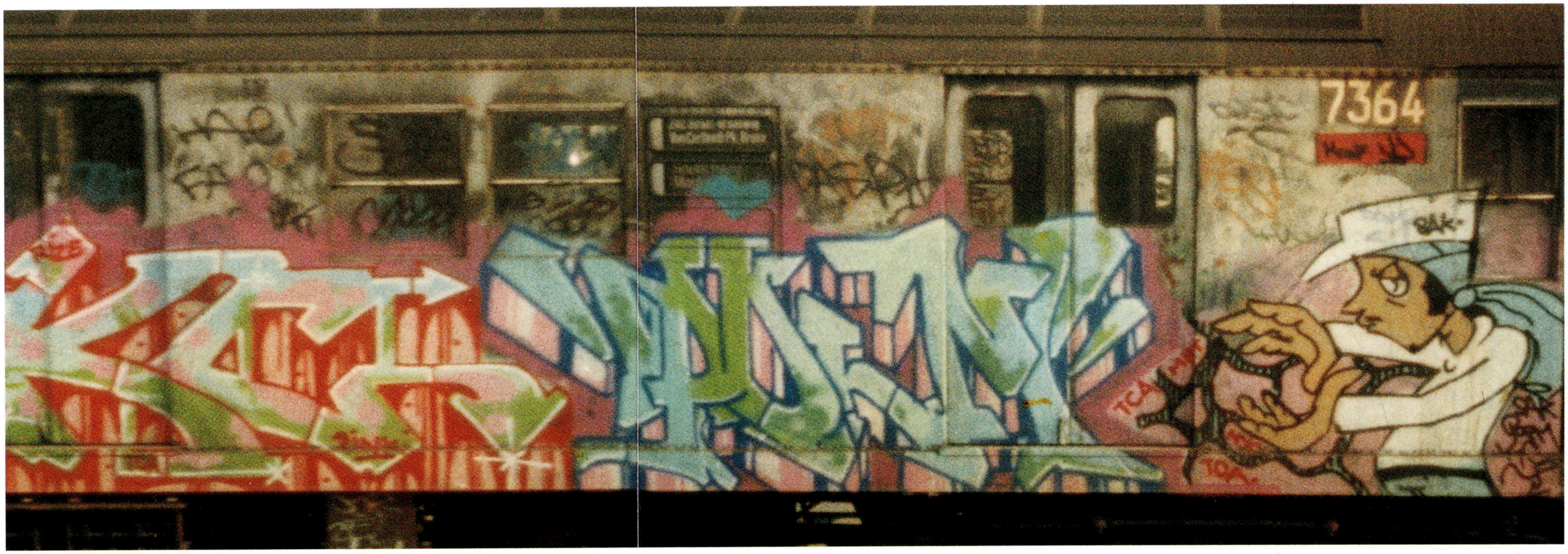

"KC" & "Poem," 1984

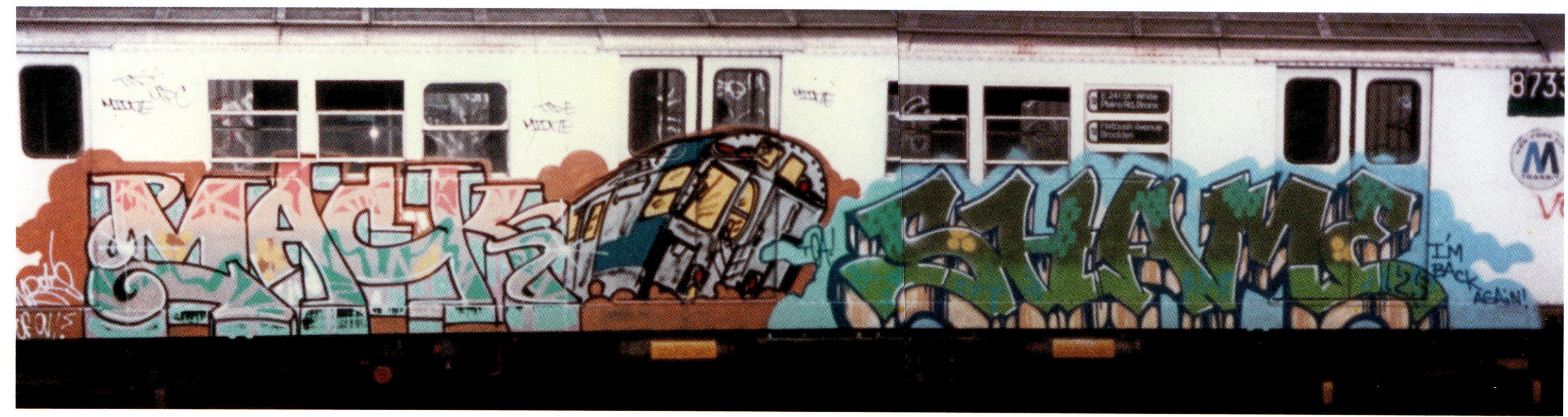

"Mack" & "Shame," 1984

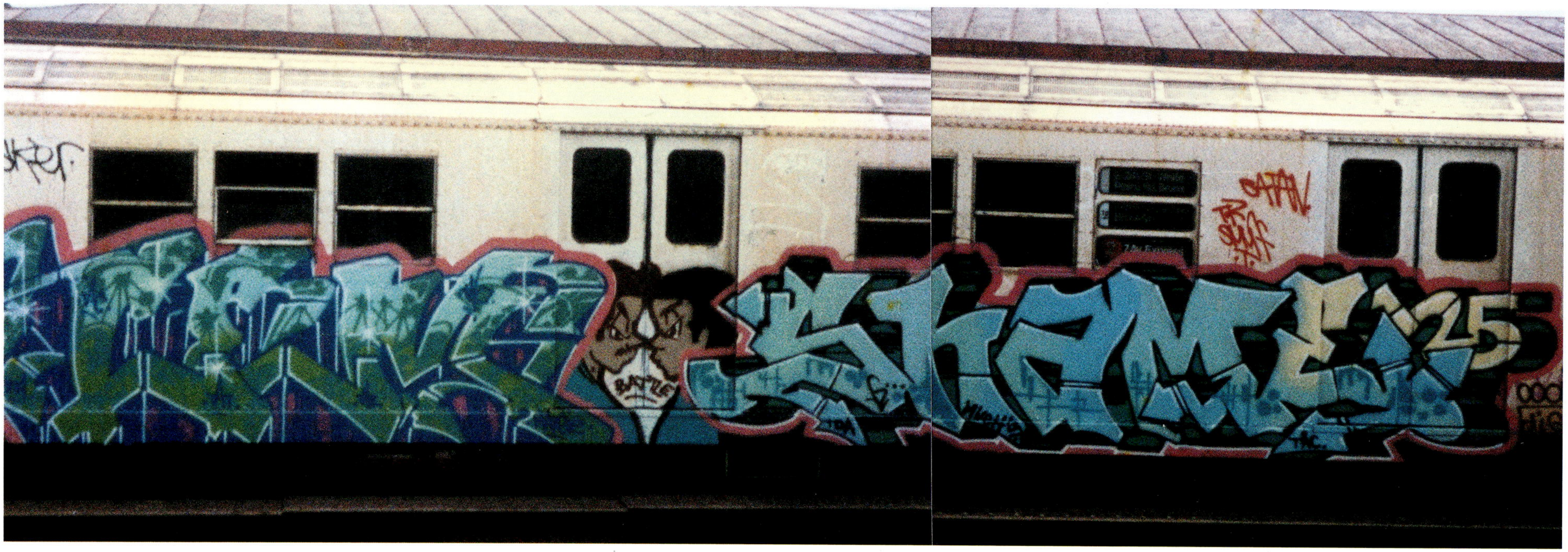

"Cem" & "Shame" Battle Car, 1984

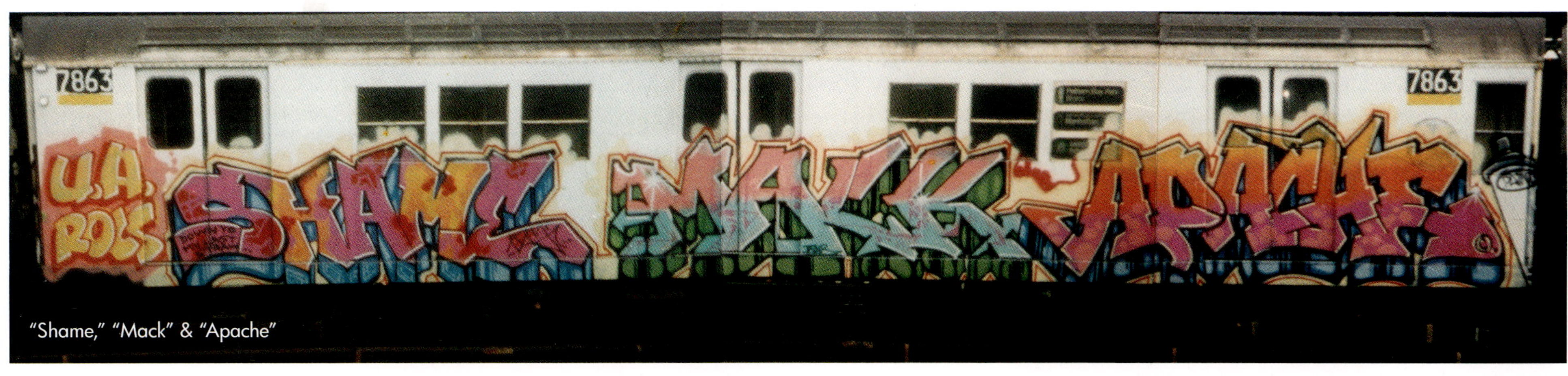

"Shame," "Mack" & "Apache"

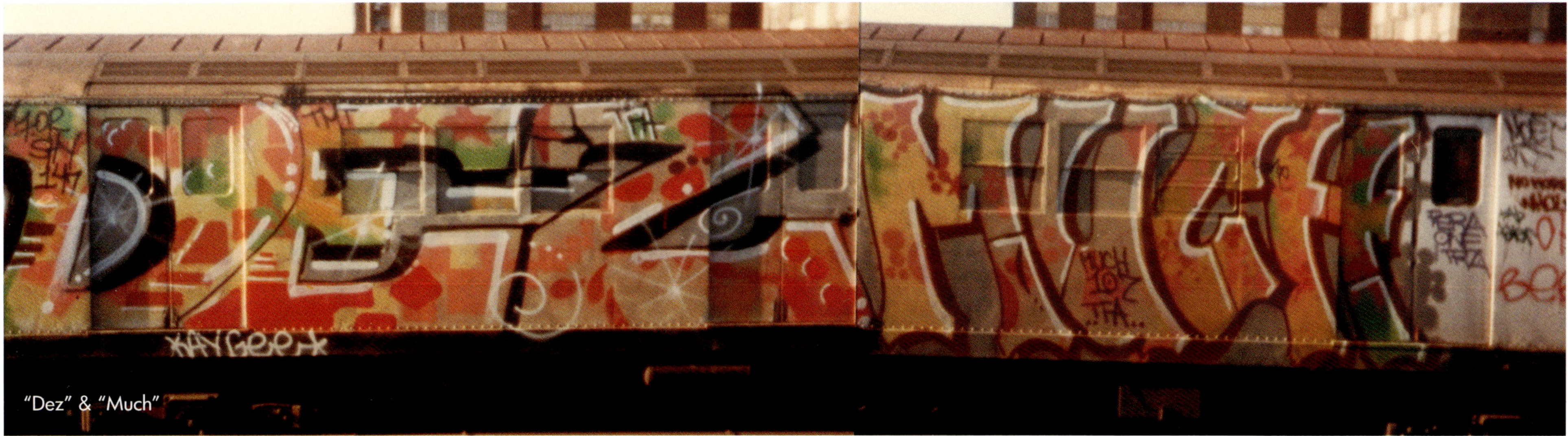
"Dez" & "Much"

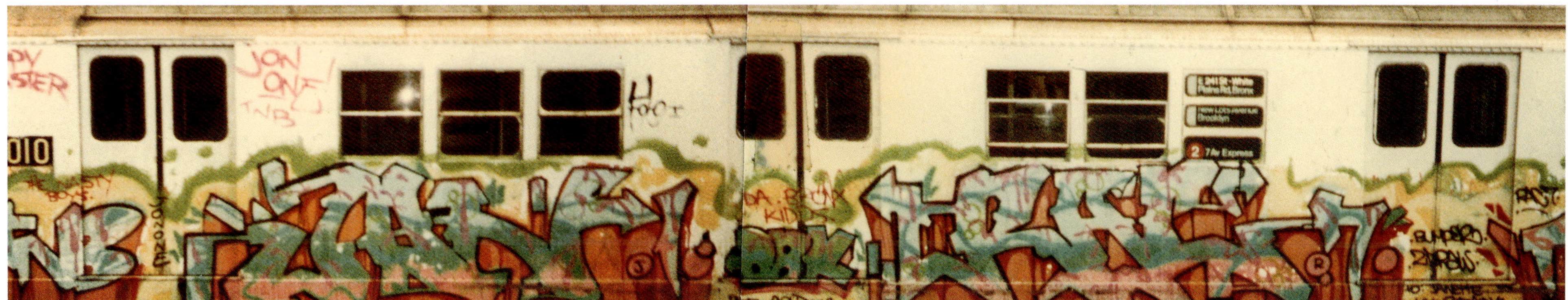

"Jon-one" & "Rac7," 1984

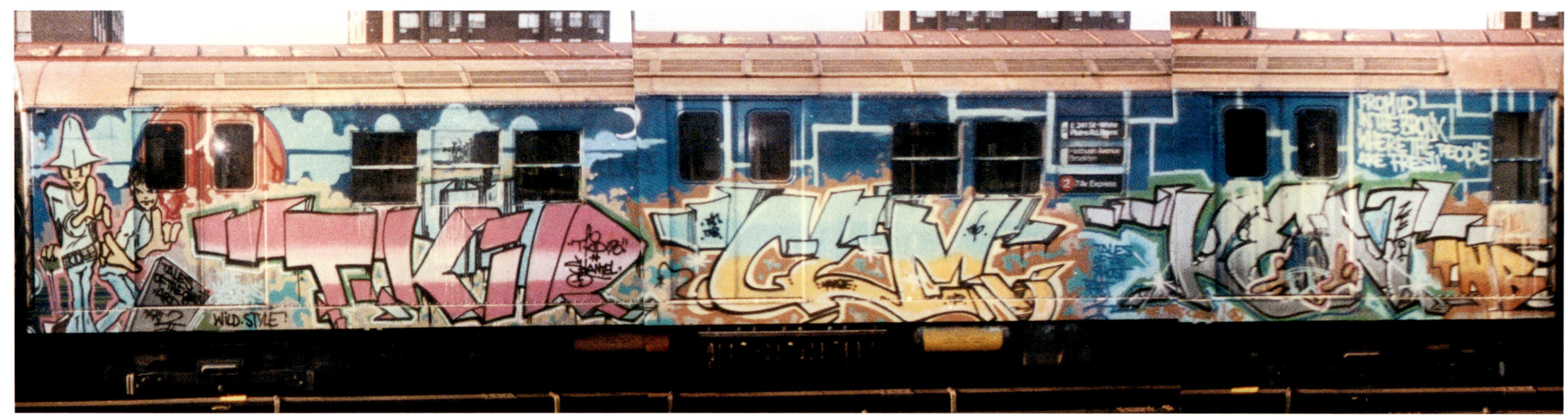

"Tkid," "Cem" & "Ken" in *Tails of the Ghost Yard, Part II*

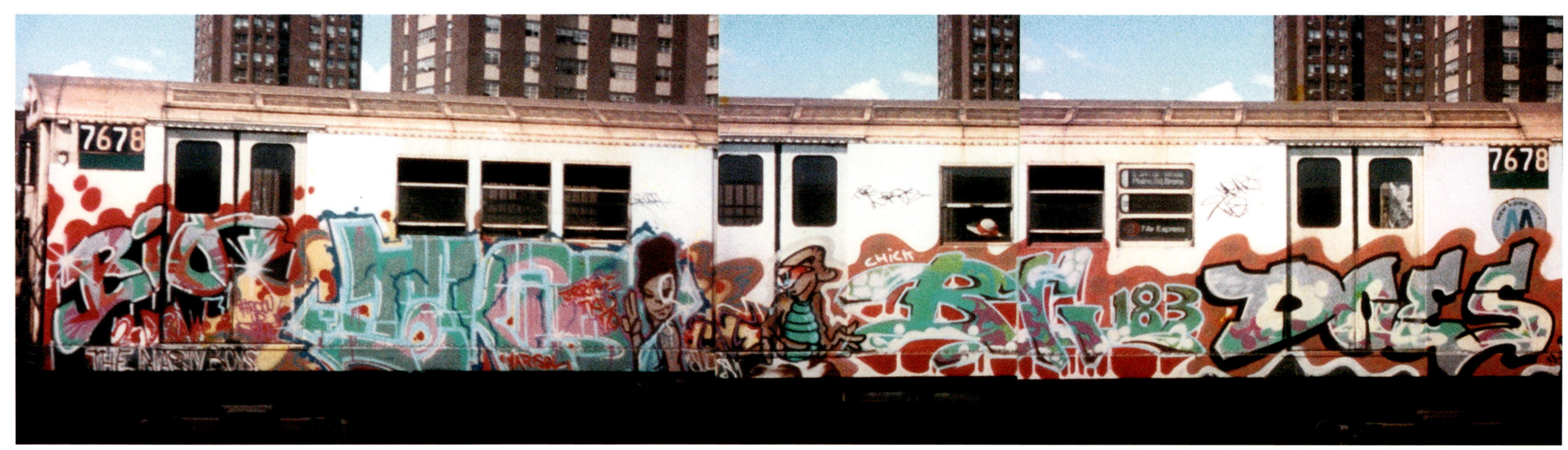

"Bio," "Tkid," "BG183" & "Does," 1984

The Ghost became my yard. I rocked whole cars, end to ends, and window downs. You name it, I rocked it in there! You stayed out the Ghost because you knew I was there. If you got caught in there, you and your shit were ghost!

–Tkid

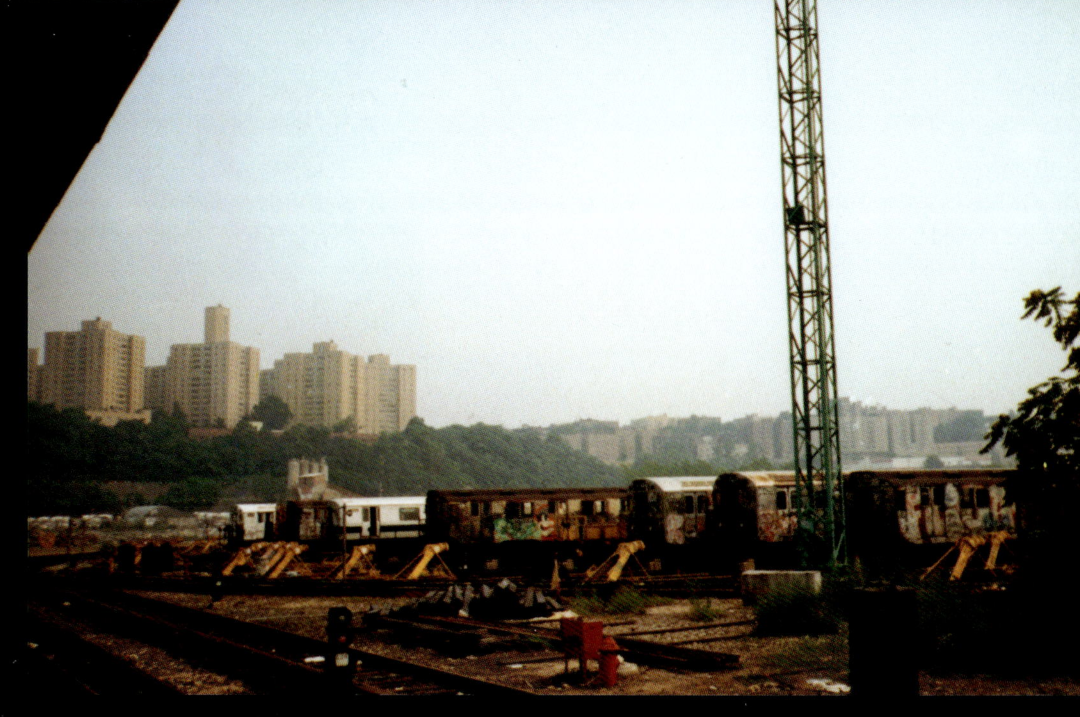

Ghost Yard

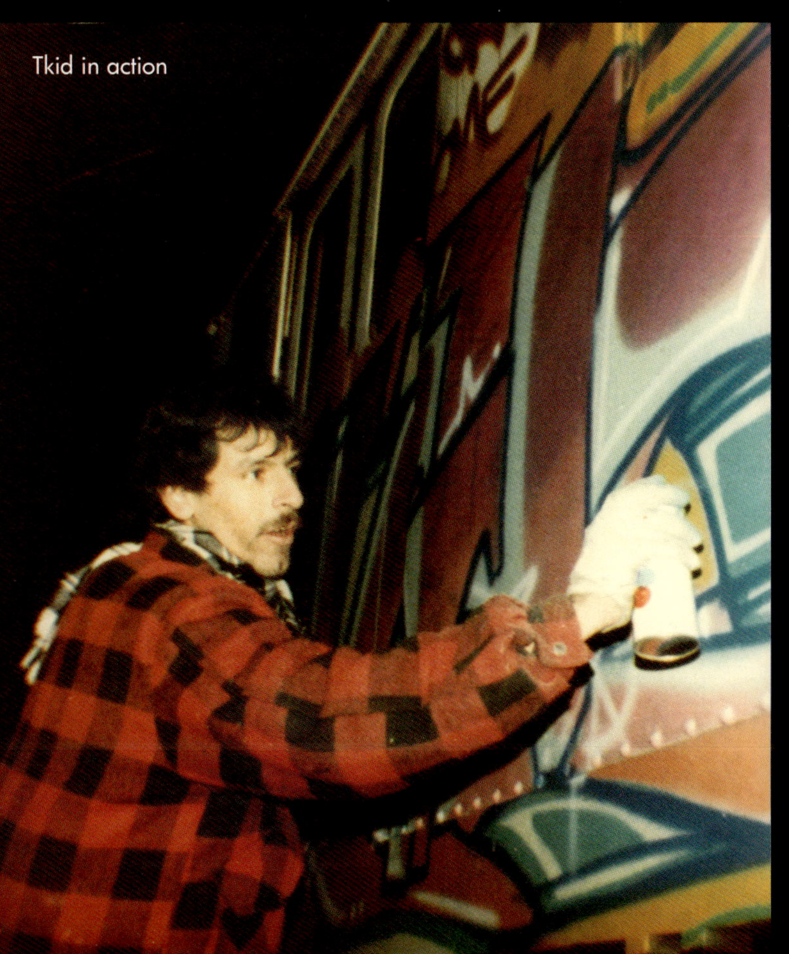

Tkid in action

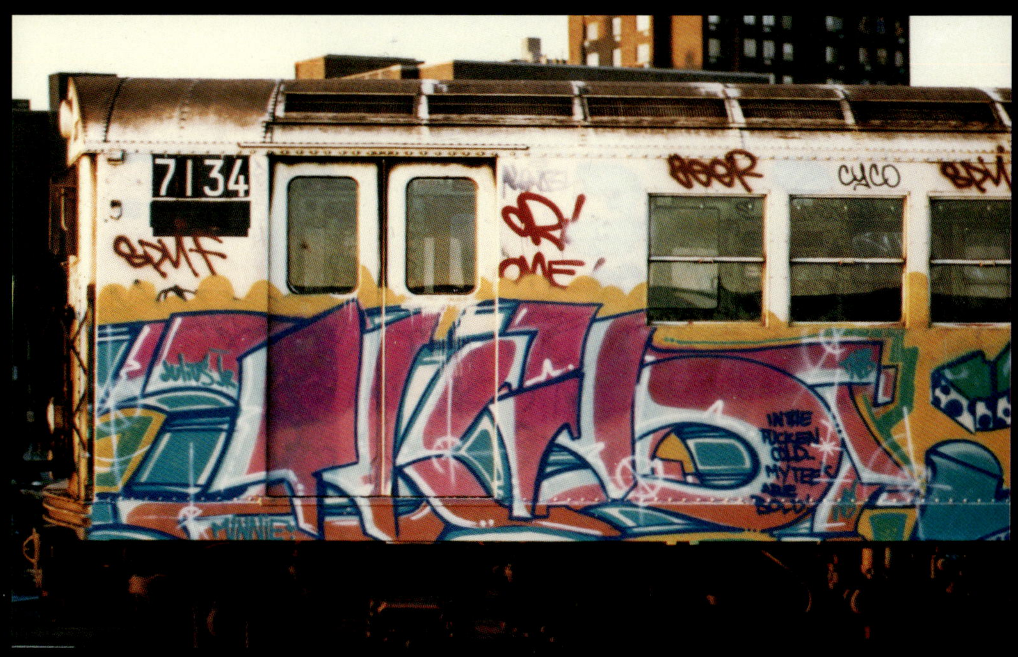

"Tkid"

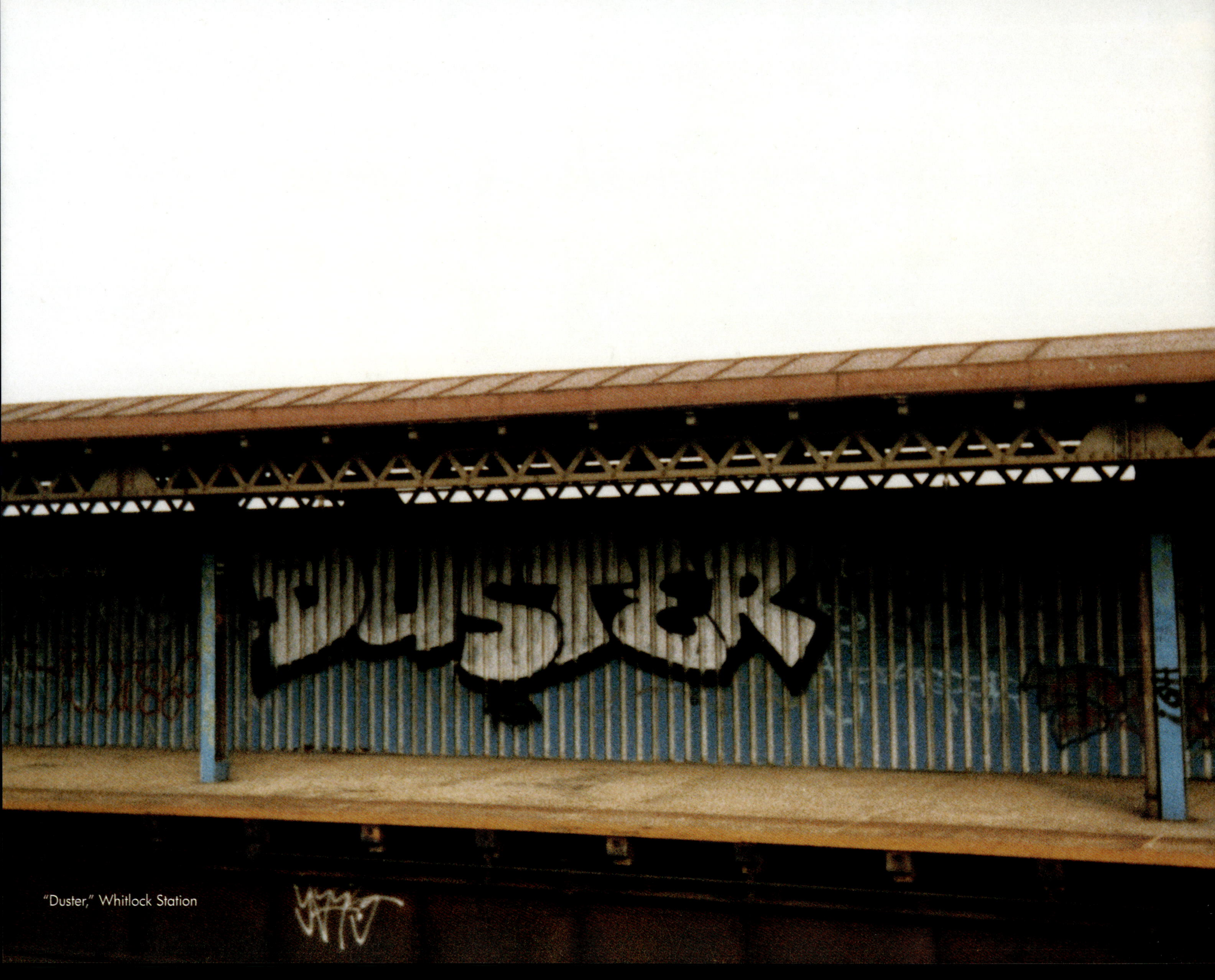

"Duster," Whitlock Station

Cavs and I first met in autumn of 1984 at East Tremont Station on the 2&5 line. From the very first meeting with Cavs we would forge a tight friendship based around capturing graffiti art on trains. Over the course of the next several years I would continually make the two hour trek from Brooklyn to the Bronx to bench at East Tremont. The train stations of the Bronx became a second home to me. Even without a planned meeting Cavs and I would always run into each other like clockwork at East Tremont while benching. We spent countless hours from morning to dusk waiting for the catches of the day. Cavs was a great benching partner who was always down to bench regardless of the weather conditions. We would spend countless hours at Tremont benching in sub frigid weather. Often times it was so cold we would wait around the heaters in the mezzanine area waiting for the bell to signal the arrival of the next incoming train. All in anticipation to catch the many whole cars painted by various writers in the Harlem Tunnels the nights before during the MTA's cold weather storage program. Cavs and I always had a backup plan to photograph a train we were trying to catch in the event that a train riding in the opposite direction blocked our camera view finder. Situations like this would often cause us to wind up on many other stations in the Bronx such as Baychester and Intervale when this occurred. In many instances one of us would jump in the train we wanted to photograph and pull the emergency cord. This would give us a good 10 minutes to capture a whole car perfectly on film. We would repeat what became to be benching habits all over the city subway lines for the next several years.

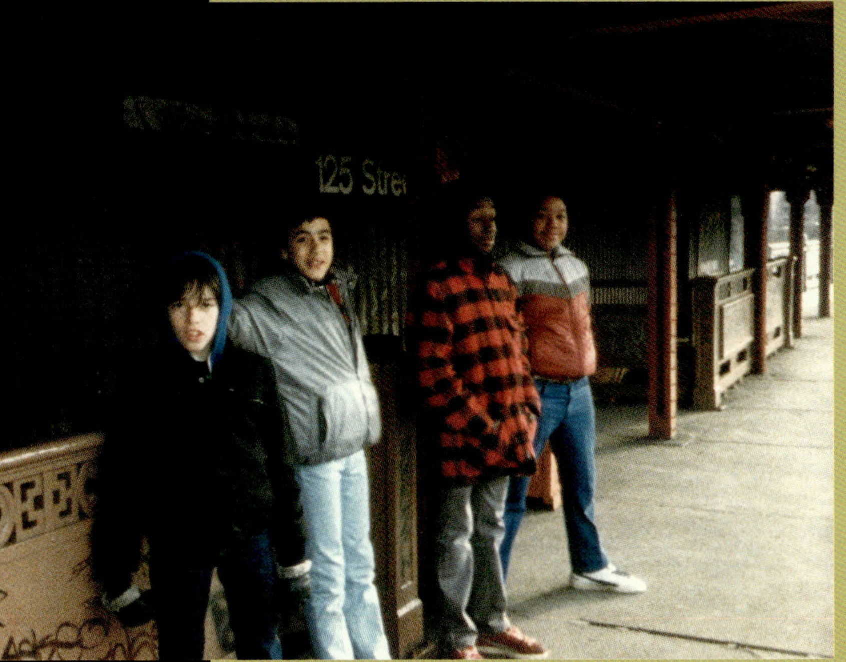

Ven, unknown, Wane, Vism, 1984

Another reason Cavs made a great benching partner is that we always backed up one another with photos if for some reason our own shots were blurred or if one of us ran out of film. I vividly recall trying to capture Raz Apache (Seen) end to end with a dog character holding a paintbrush while with Cavs at 238st station. Cavs and I had been alerted about this car by Seen. Several days later while benching in snowy weather at East Tremont this train would barrel through the uptown side of the station with horn honking to alert passengers on the station that it was out of service. Cavs and I quickly decided to chase down the train in hopes of catching it before it pulled into the 2 yard at 238st Station. We knew it was very common during this time period for burners to be painted by the MTA over in white at the 2 yard. With Cavs and I in hot pursuit of this car we enter 238st station on the next in-service train. Upon entering the 238st station we see a 10 car set in laid up in the middle track ready to pull into the 241st yard. Glaring through the train's windows of the laid up train we can tell this is the Raz Apache car by seeing the windows painted over through the interior of the car. Quickly we exit off the train and cross underneath the station to the downtown platform on the other side. As we come up on the platform we realize that time is very limited for the catch when we hear the train's air compressors being charged for departure. With time running out quickly we stand on the yellow platform line to catch sequenced join up shots. As I hear my camera click capturing the first image I soon realize that this will be the final click of the day. My film had simply run out. Cavs saves the mission and catches the entire car in a series of sequenced shots. Within seconds of the catch the train heads into the 2 yard. The following day Cavs goes for a walk by the 2 yard and sees the car sitting there. He enters in and even catches better shots. This would be the last time anyone would see it other than the workers who painted over it. A few days later Cavs and I meet at the legendary one hour photo lab on Canal Street where we exchange photographs of the week's catches. In that exchange are prints of Raz, Apache for me. This is the sign of a true benching partner!

-Ven

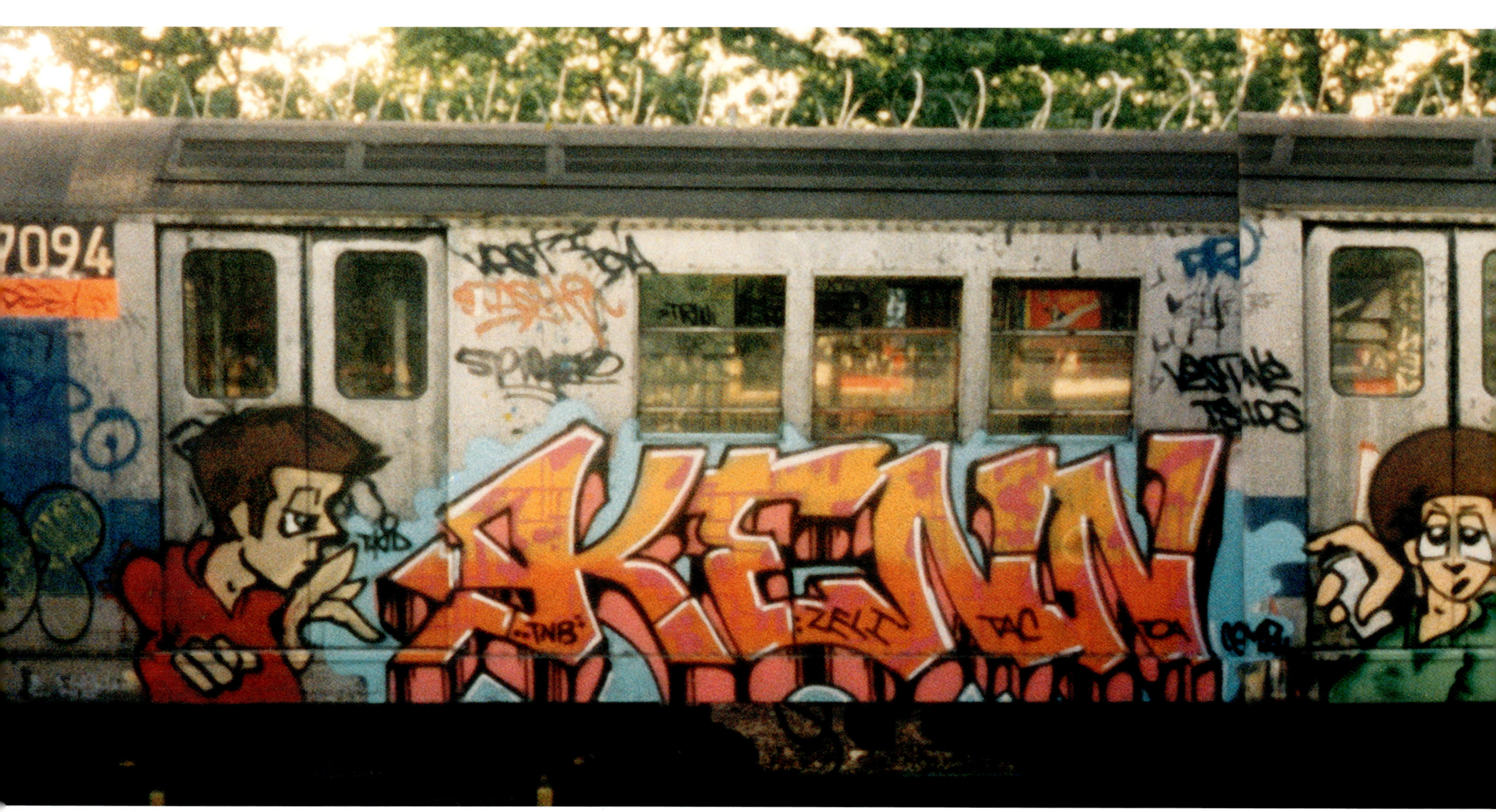

"Kenn" & "Shame," Esplanade lay up, 1984.

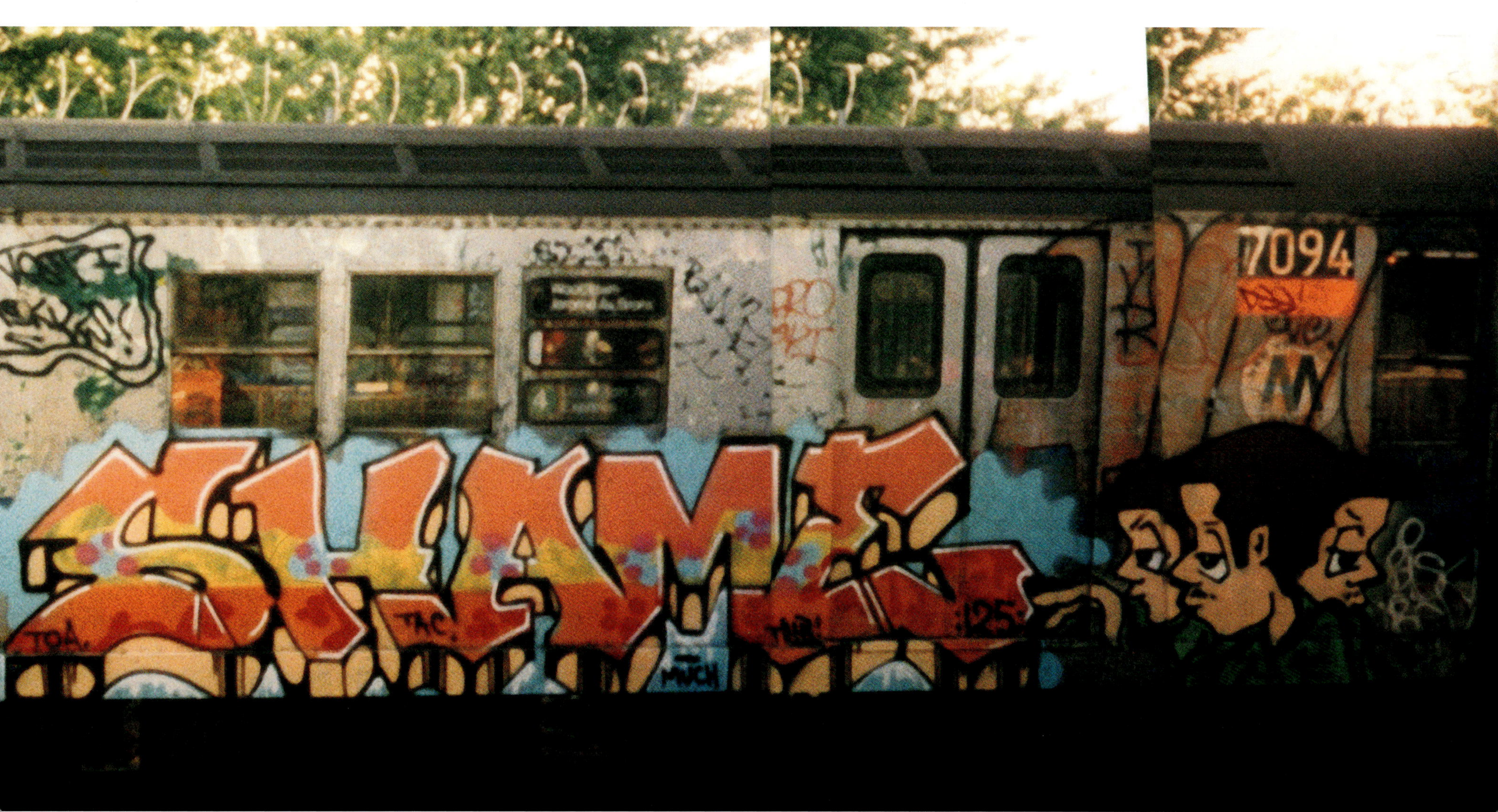
7094

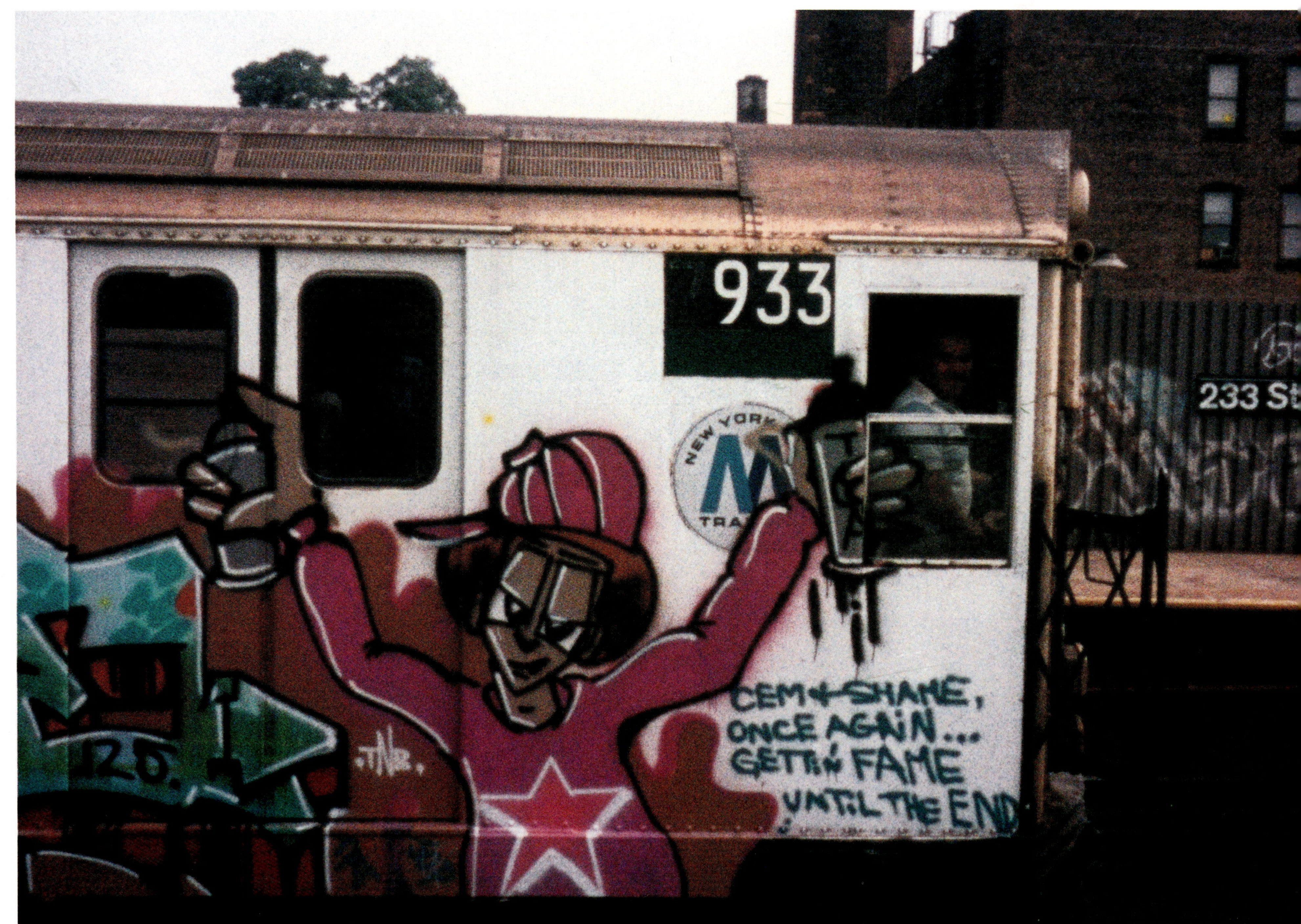

Character by Shame125

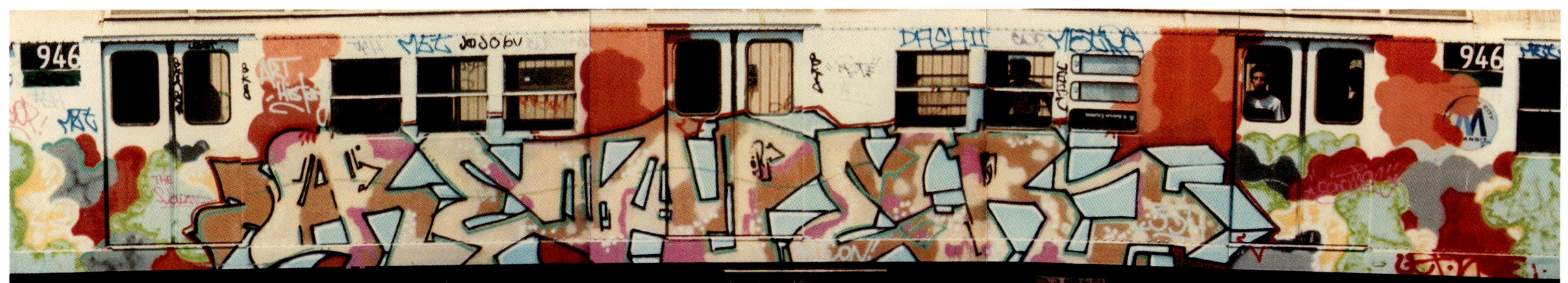

"Reaper," 1985

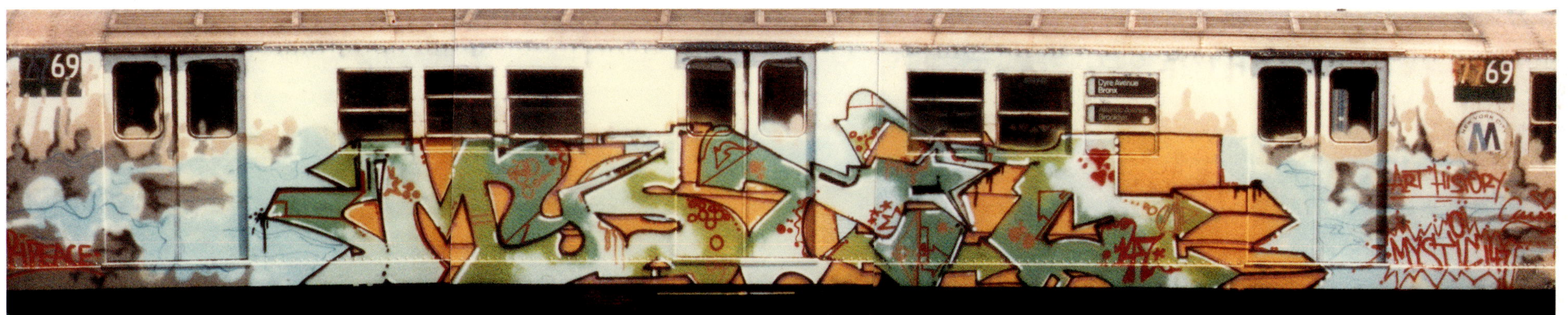

"Mystic,"1985

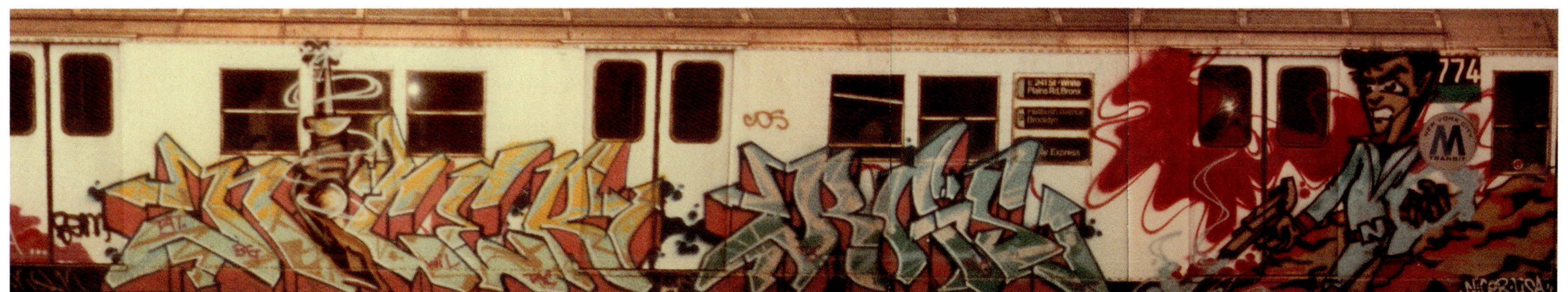

"Nicer" & "Ras,"1985

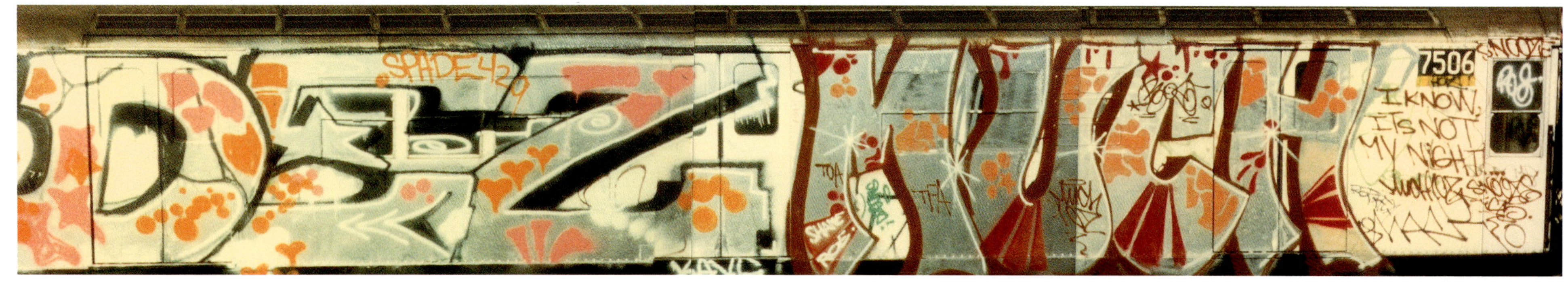

"Dez" & "Much," 1985

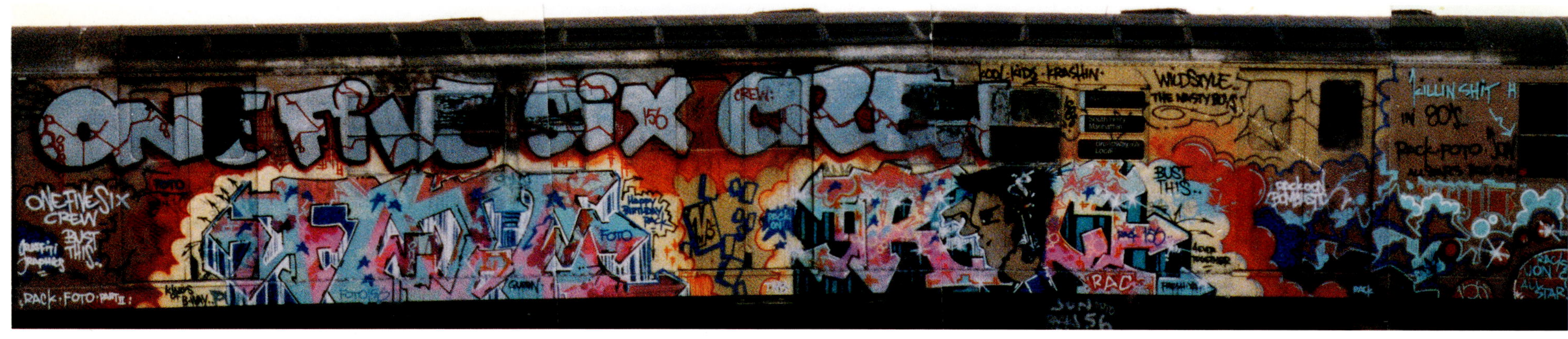

"Foto" & "Rac7," 1985

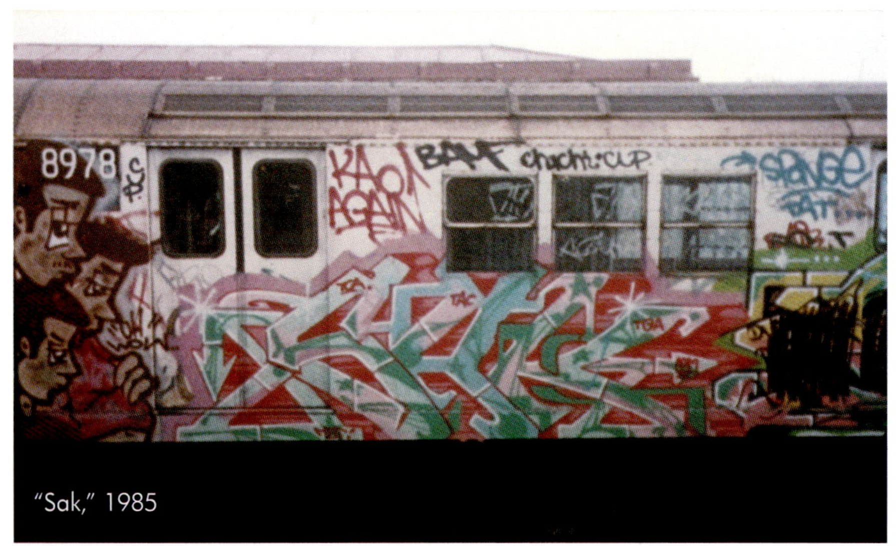

"Sak," 1985

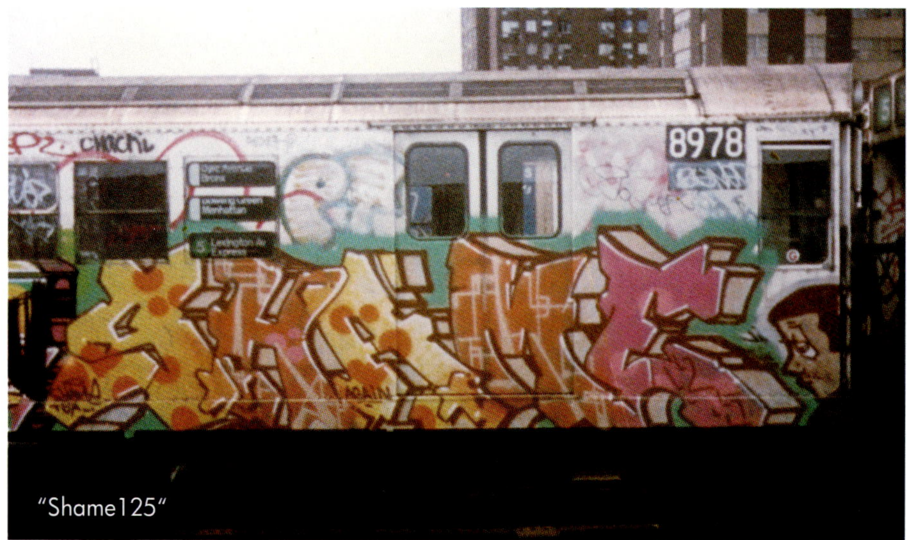

"Shame125"

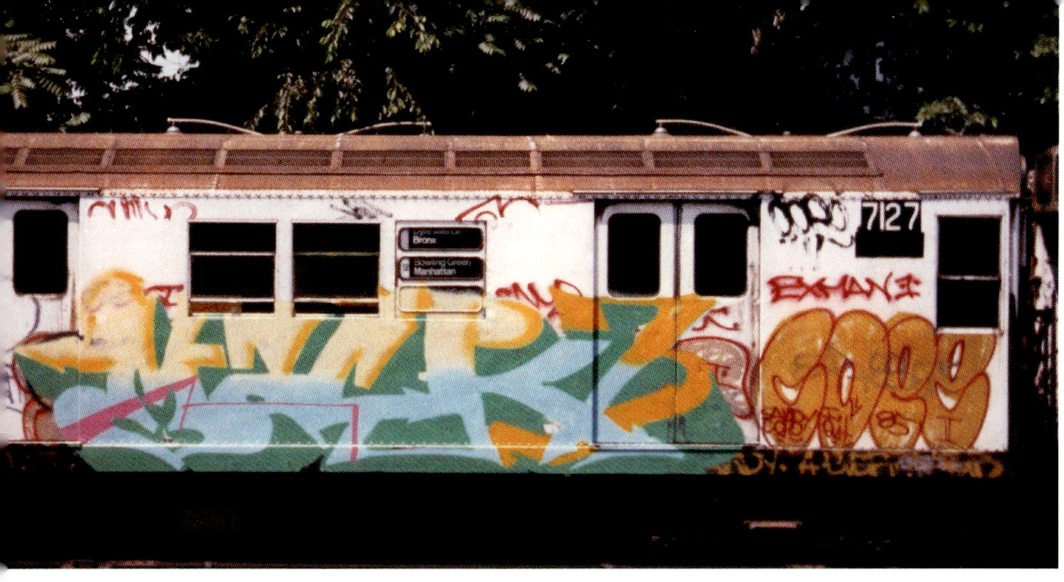

"Mack," 1985

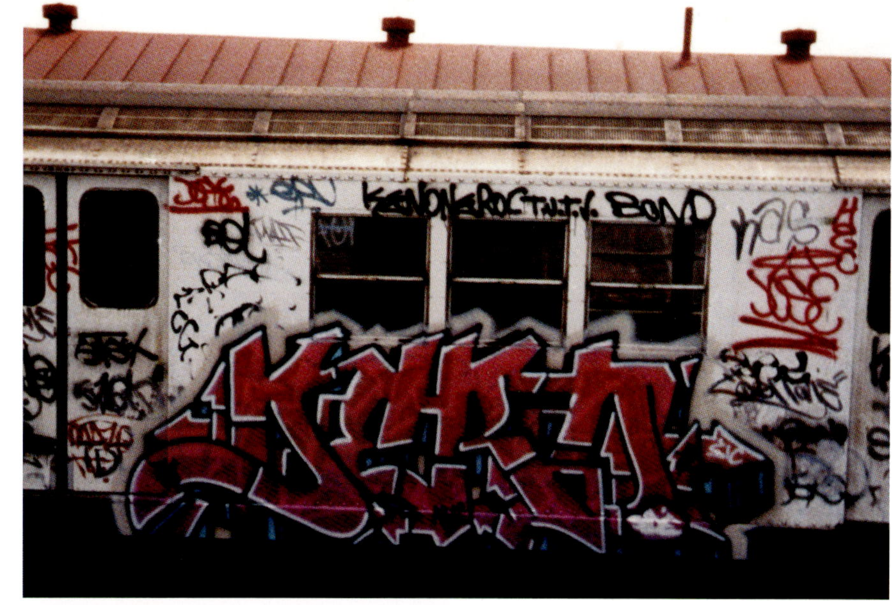

"Dero"

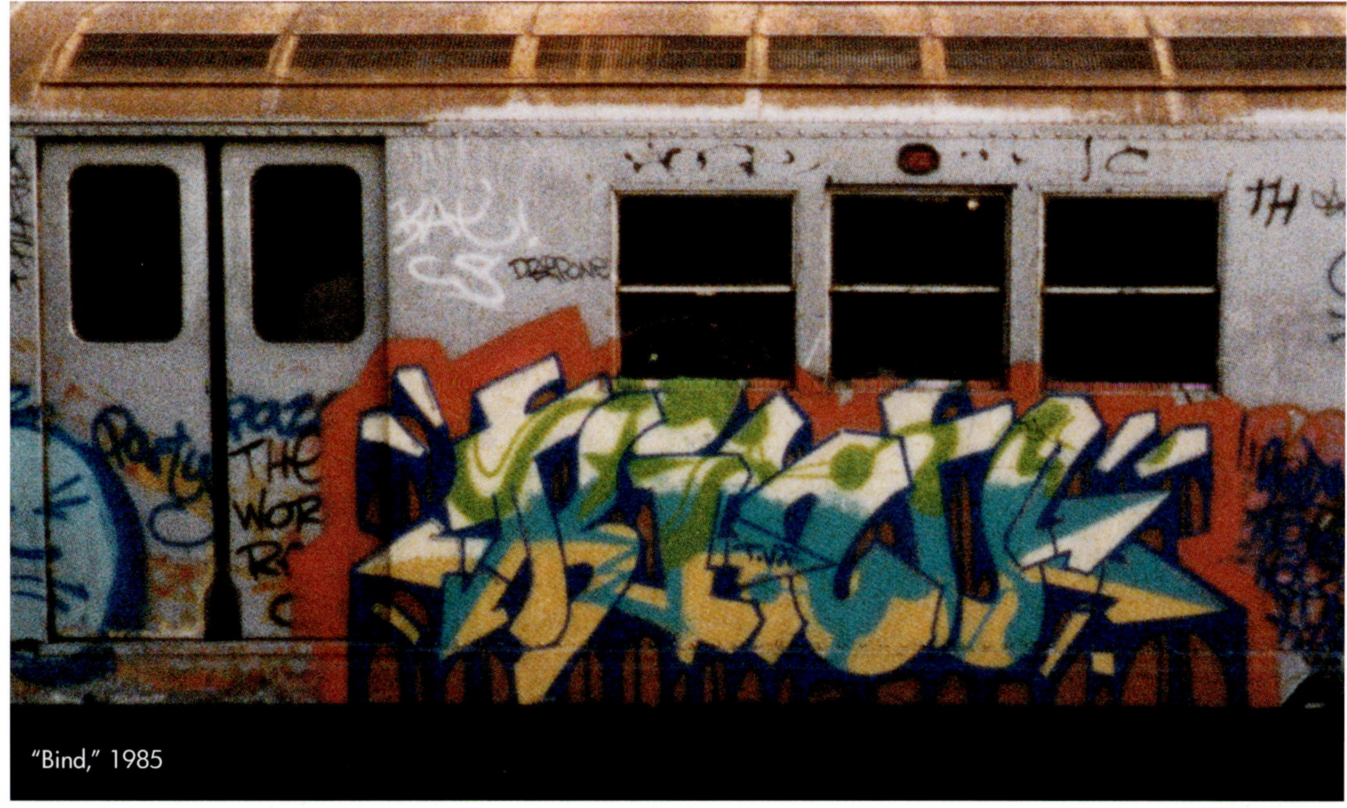

"Bind," 1985

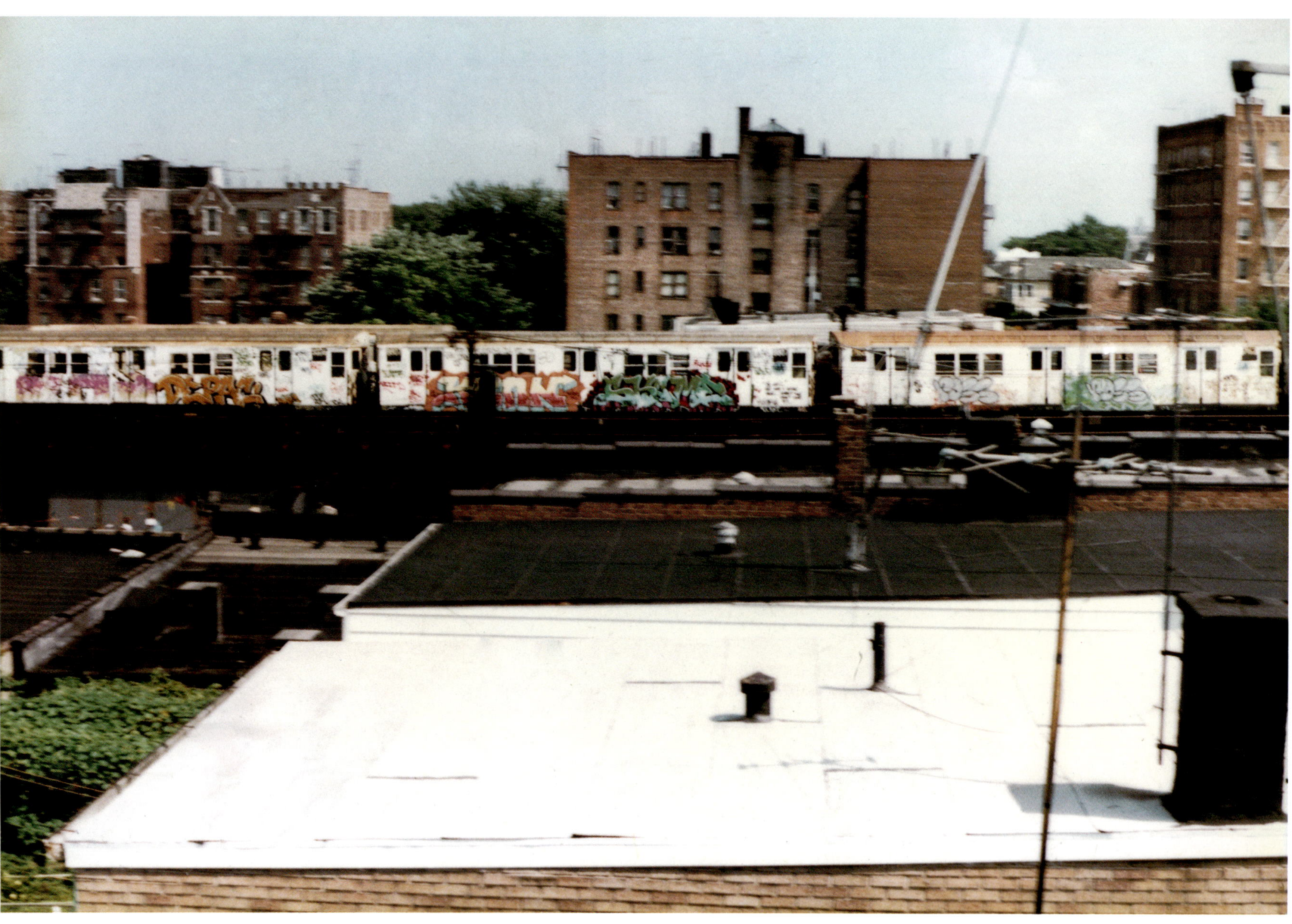

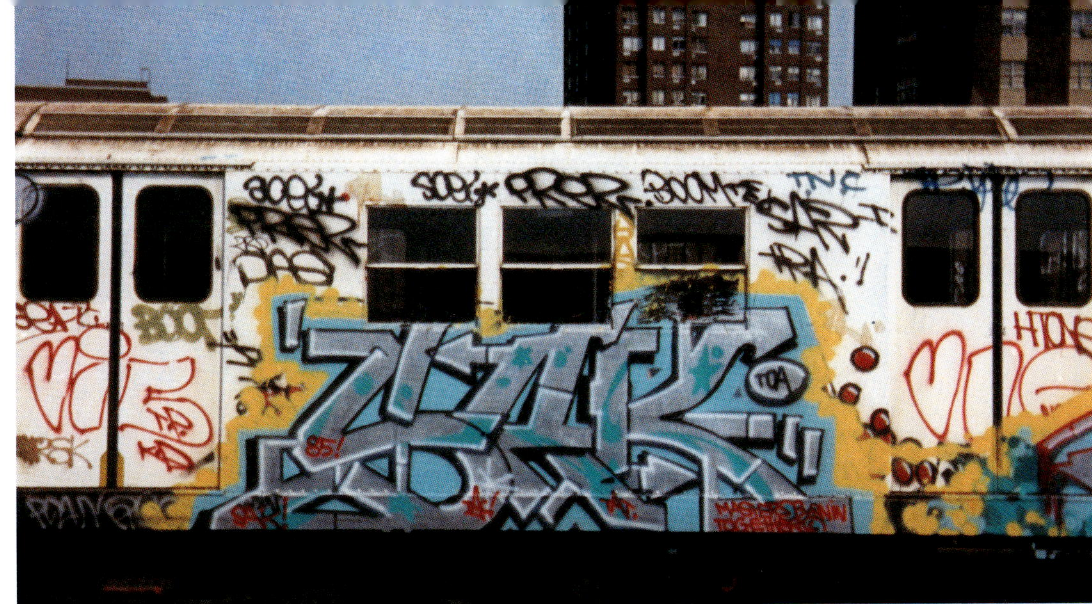

"Sak," 1985

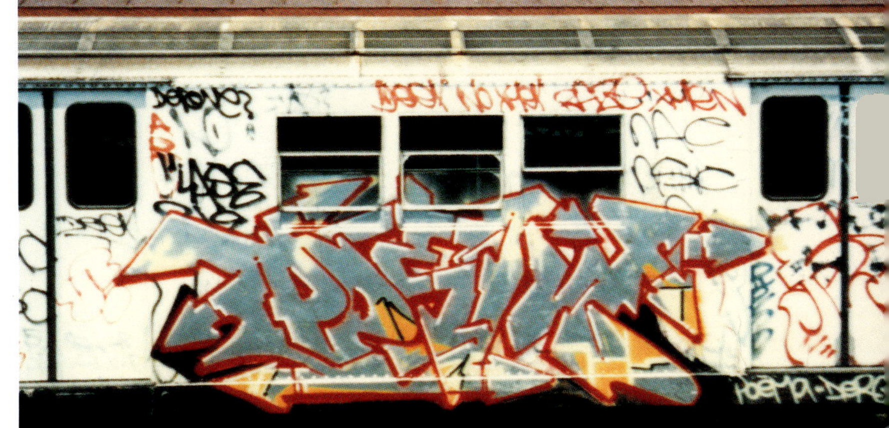

"Poem," 1985

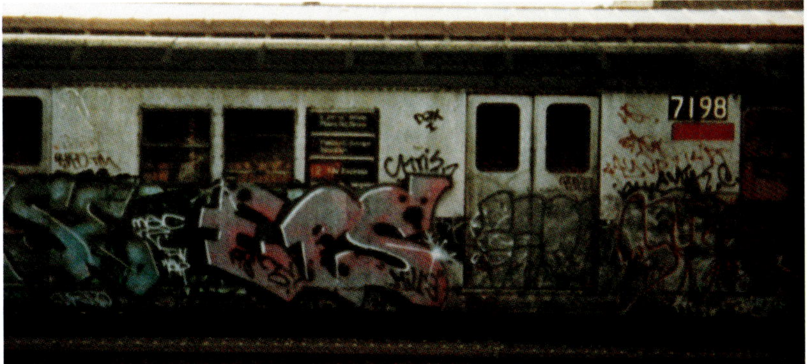

"Eps," 1985

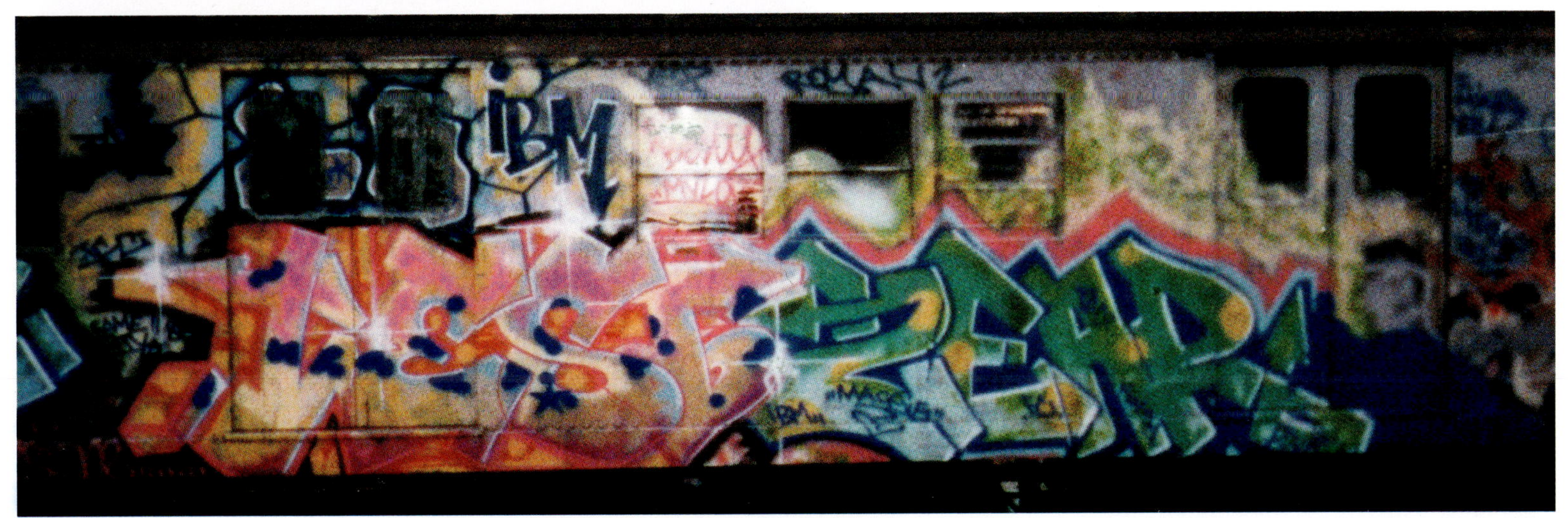

"West" & "Zear," 1985

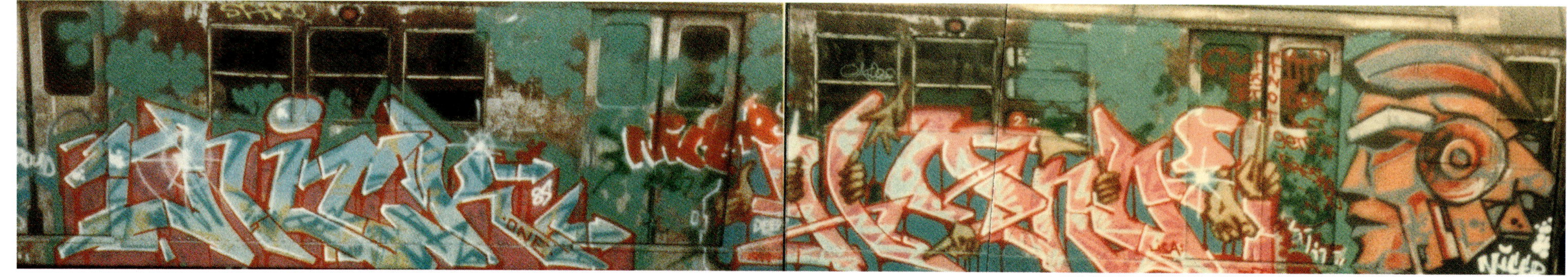

"Nick & Hand," by Nicer, 1985

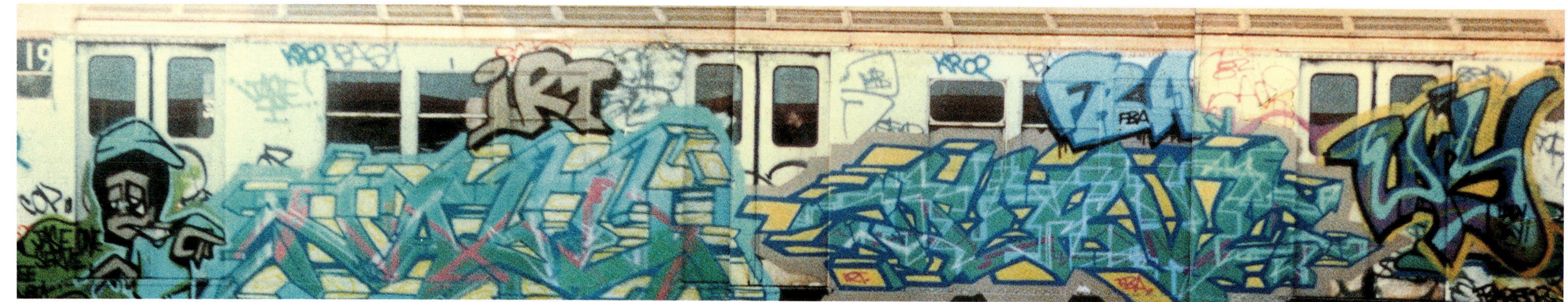

"Jase" & "Serve," 1985

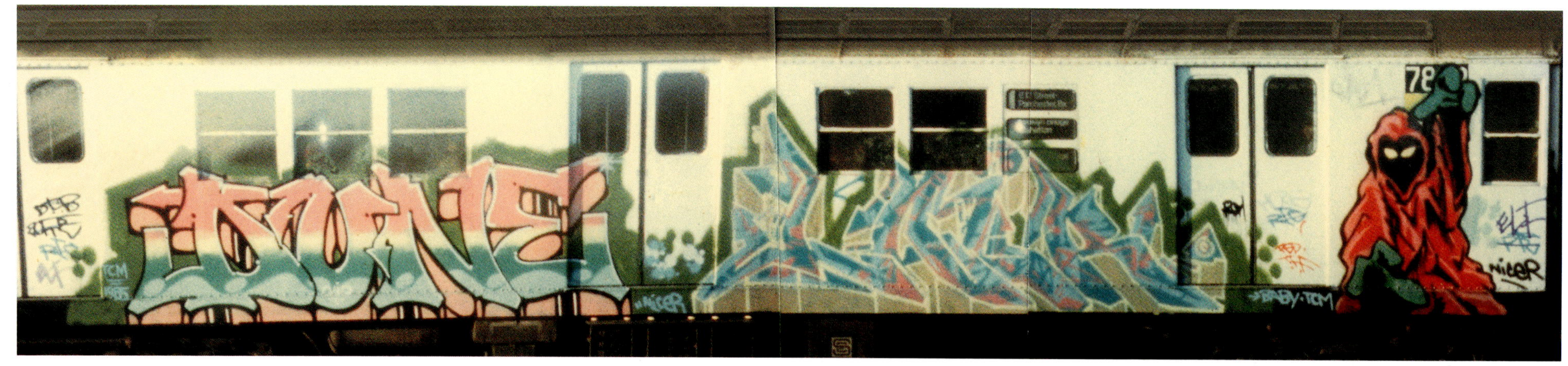

"Dune" & "Lair," 1985

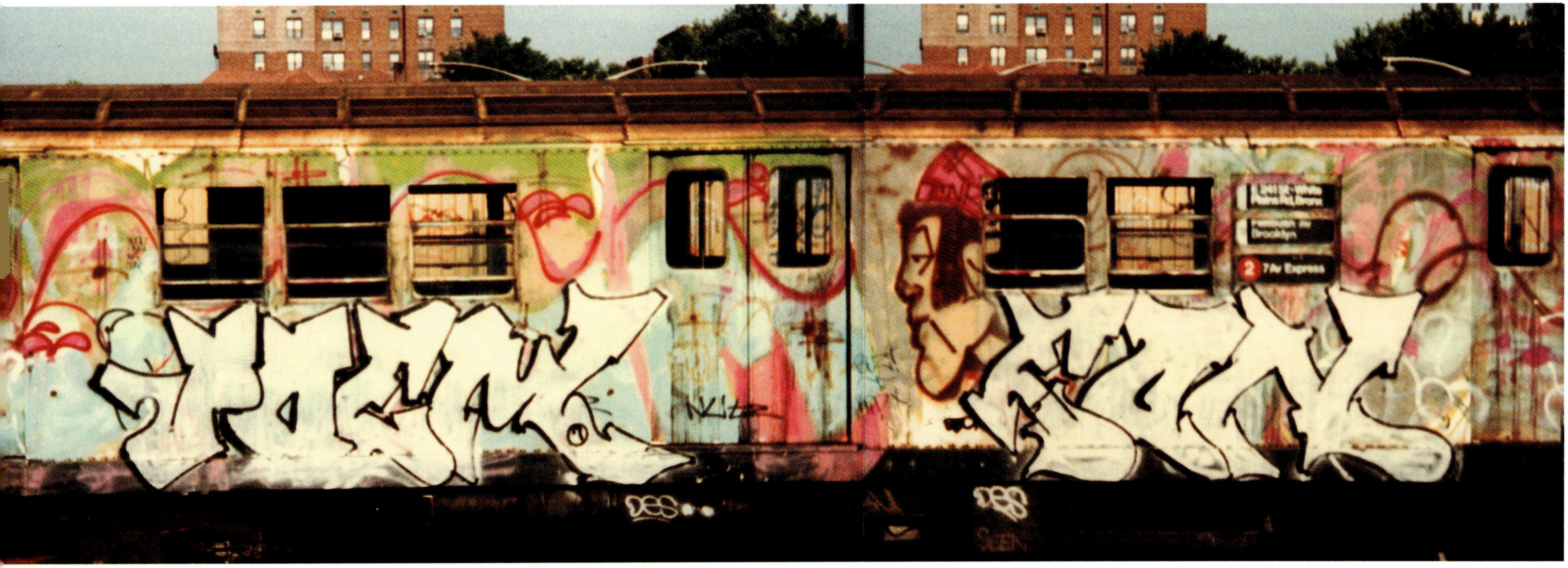

"Poem" & "Eon"

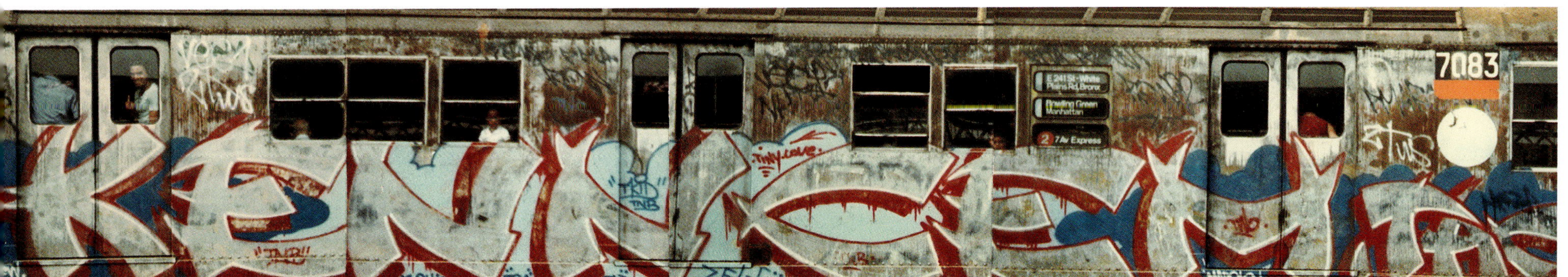

"Kenn" & "Cem"

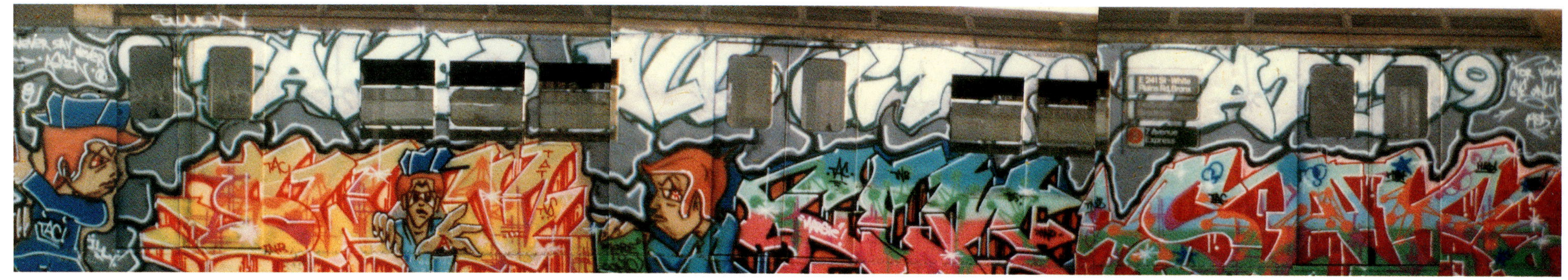

"Swan," "Cem" & "Sak," 1985

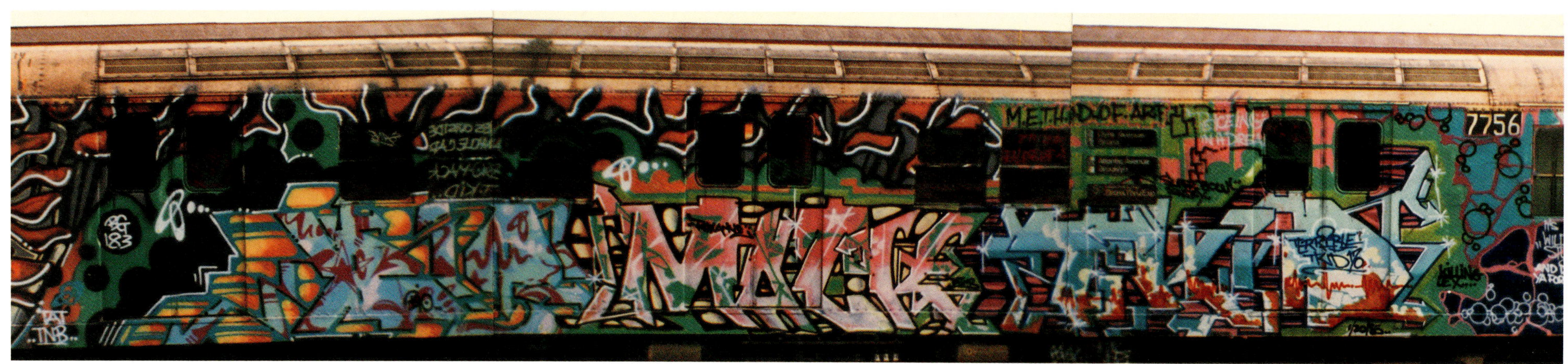

"Bio," "Mack" & "T-kid" in *Method of Art,* 1985

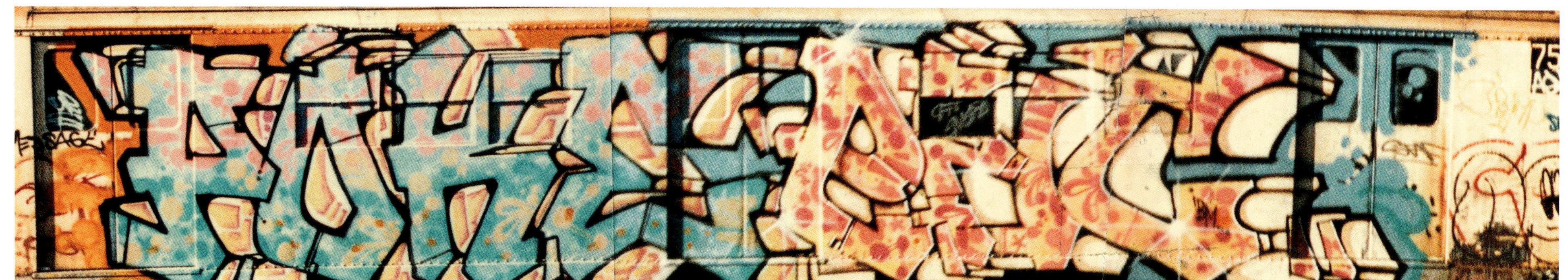

"Poke" & "Epic"

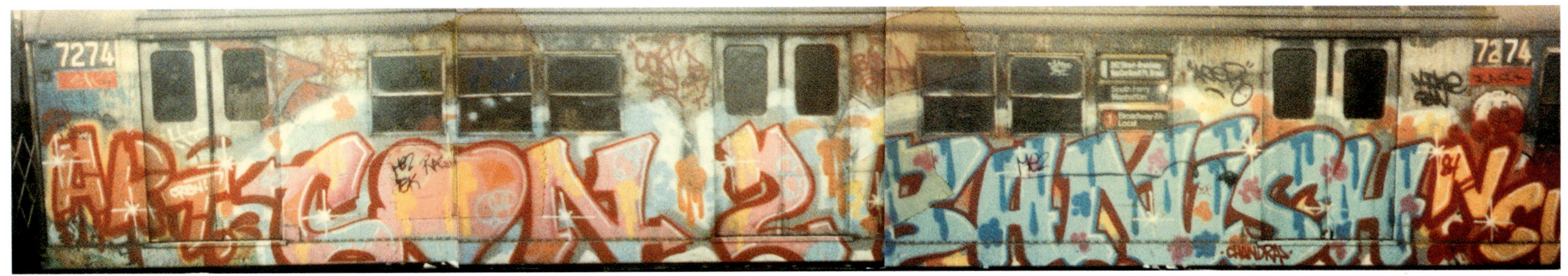

"Con2" & "Banish"

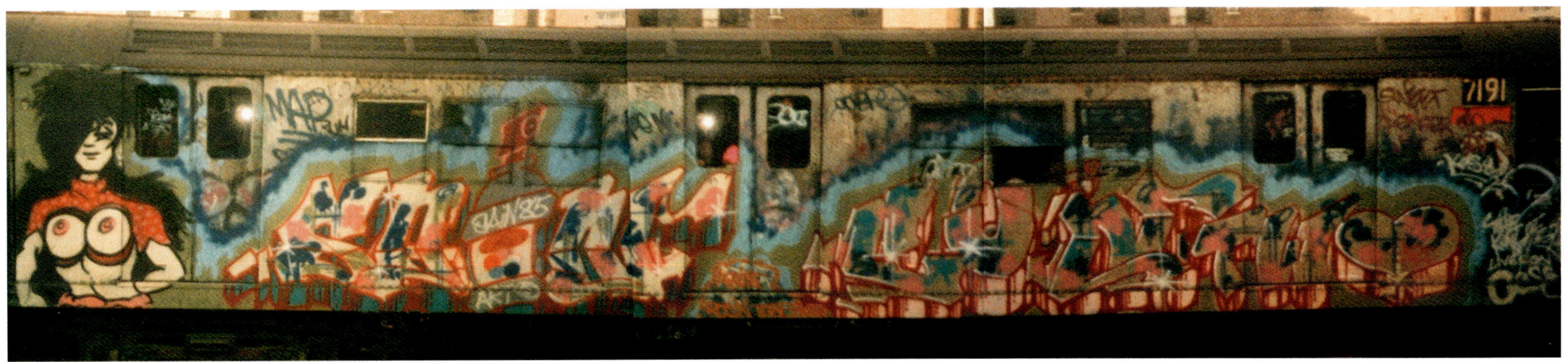

"Sain" & "Con2," 1985

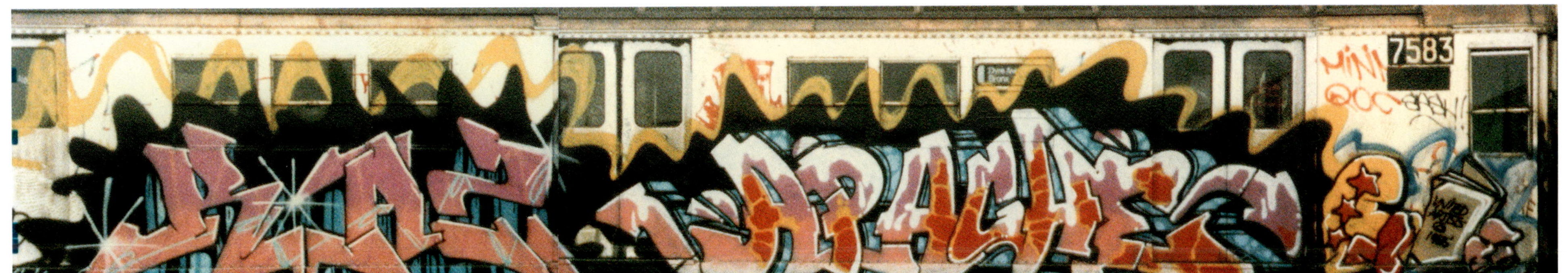

"Raz" & "Apache"

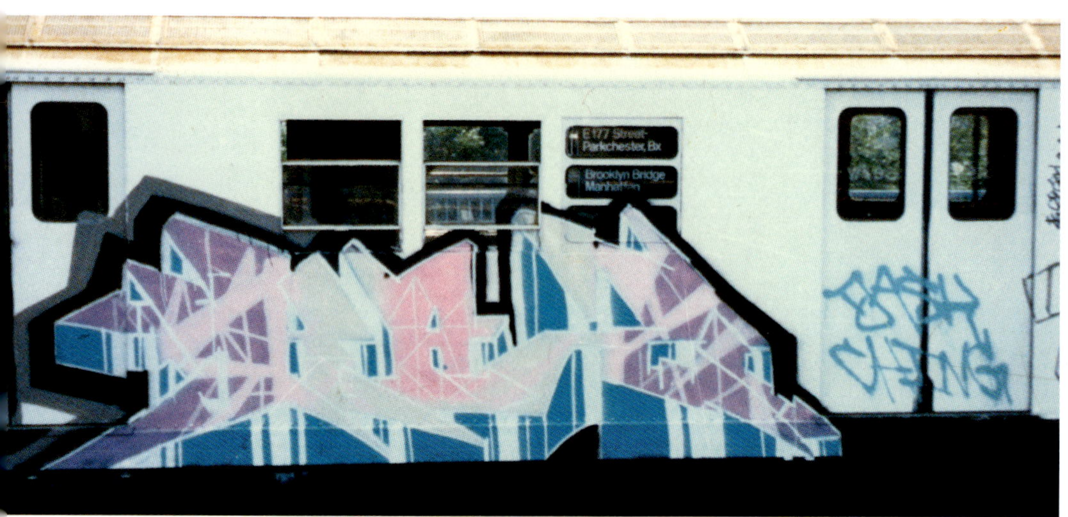

"Raz"

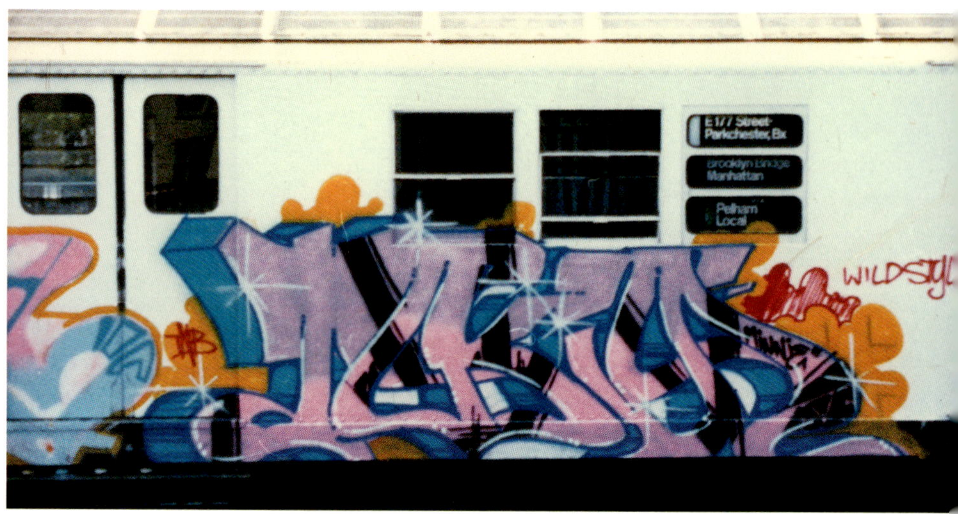

"Tkid"

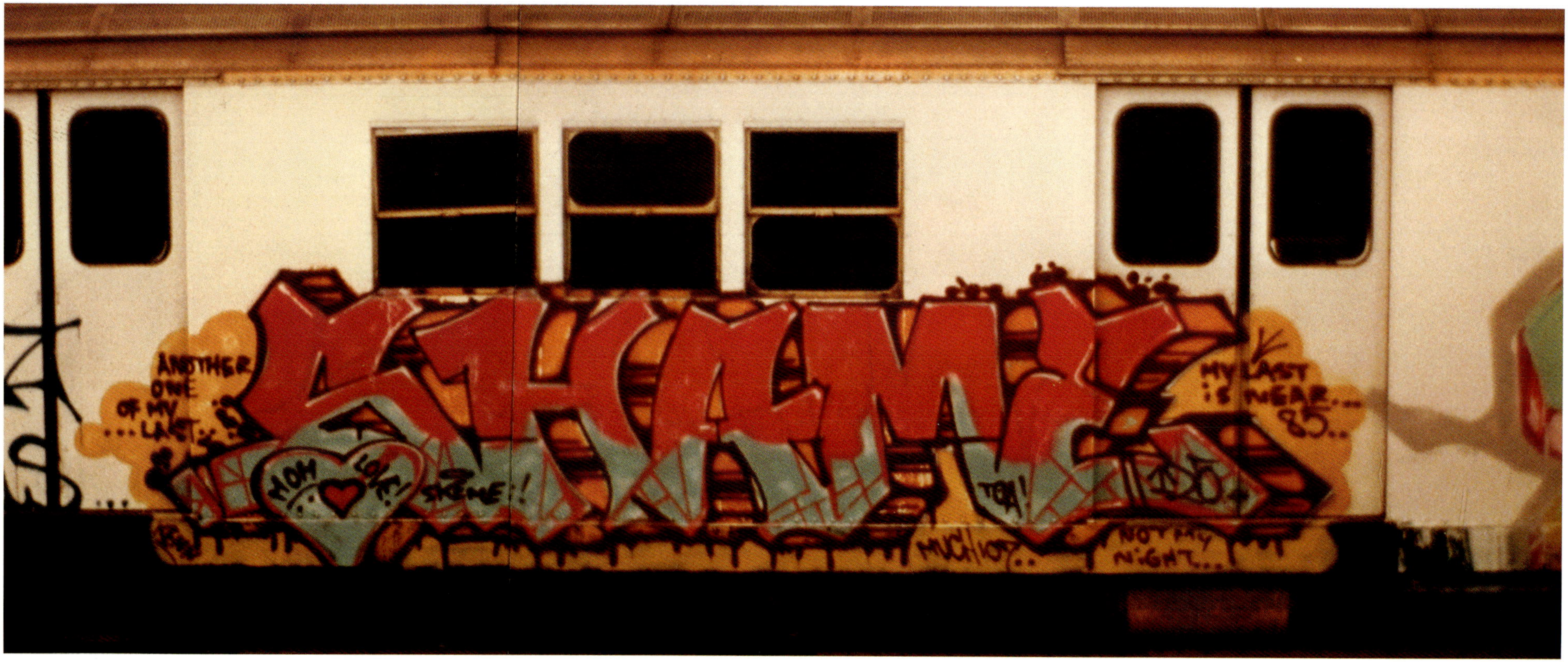

"Shame125"

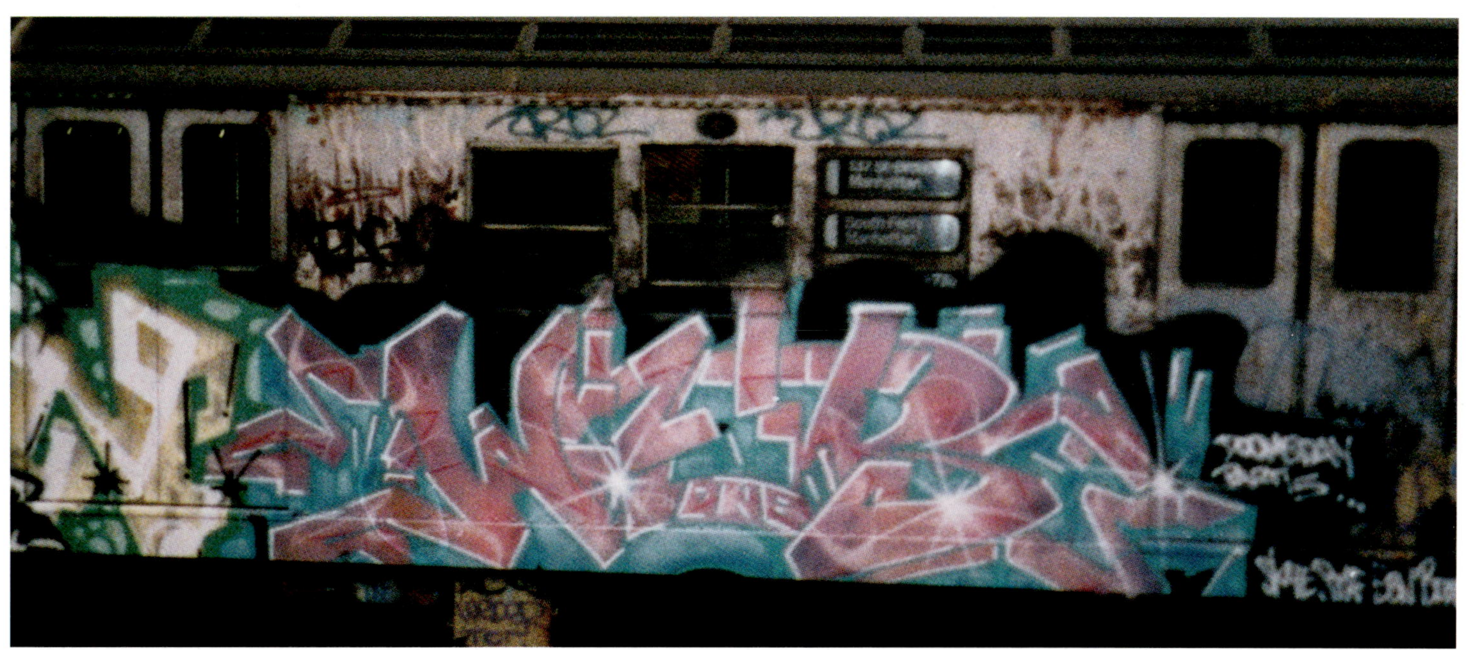

"Web"

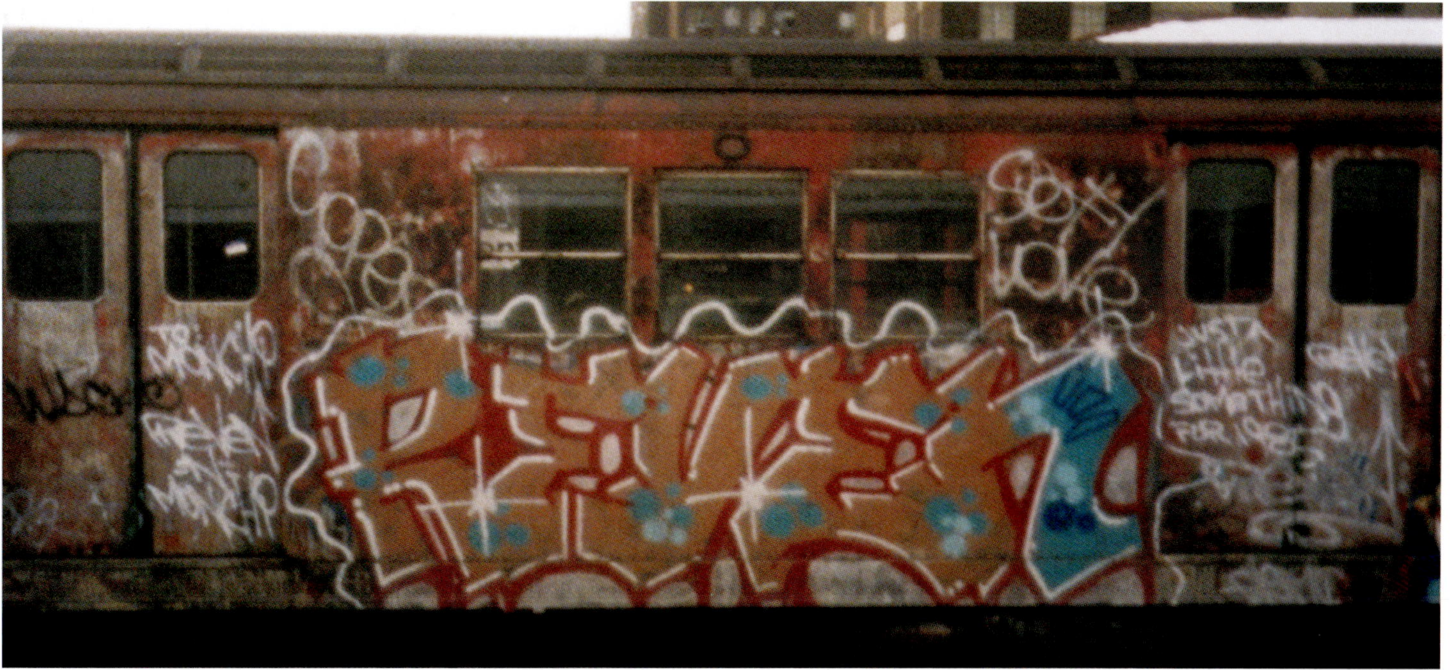

"Reven"

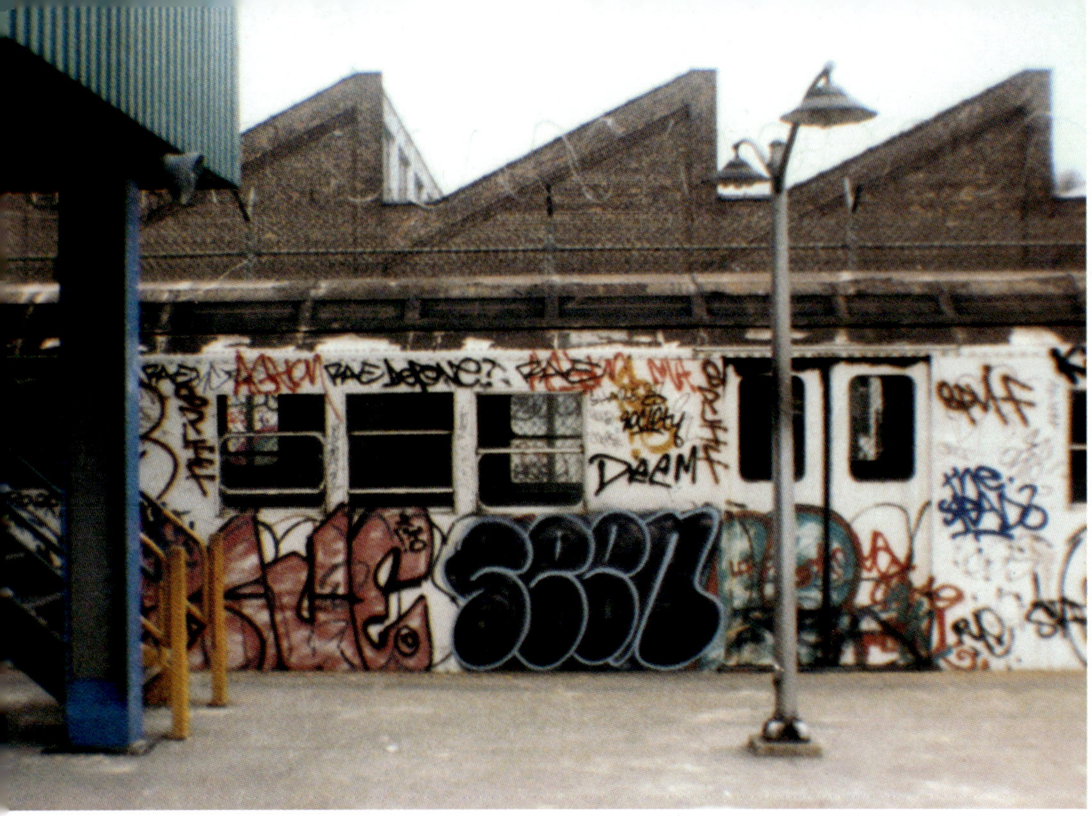

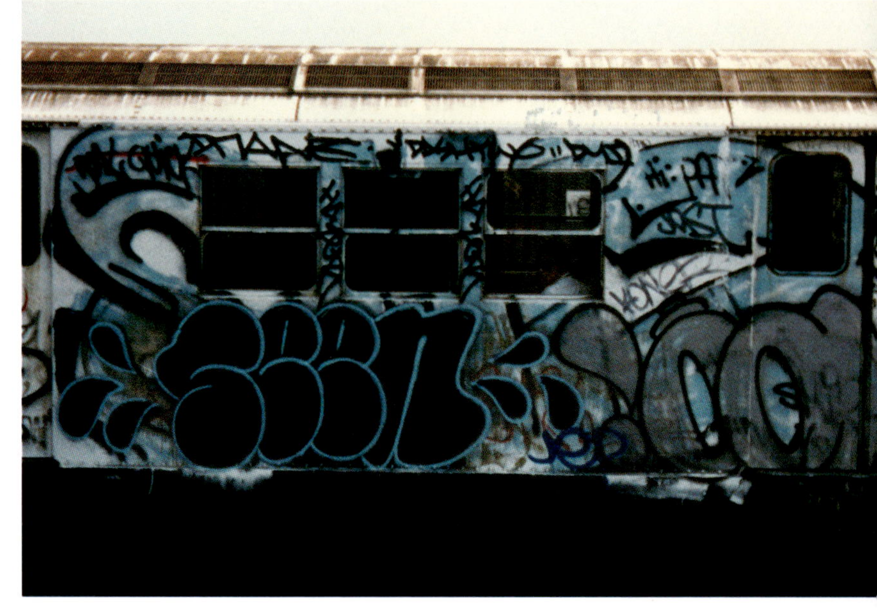

"Seen"

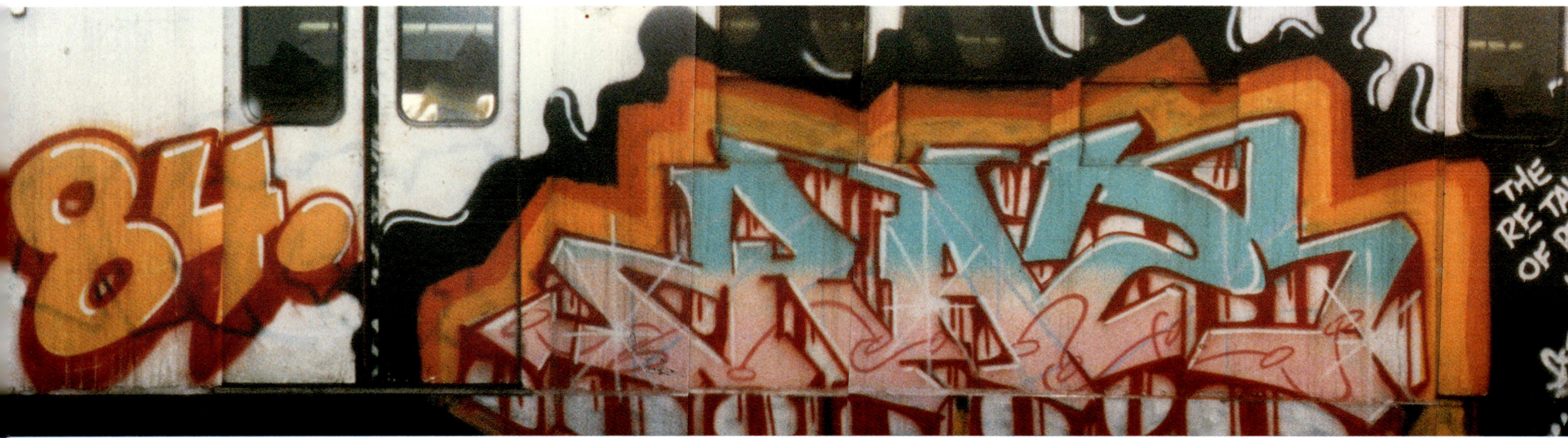

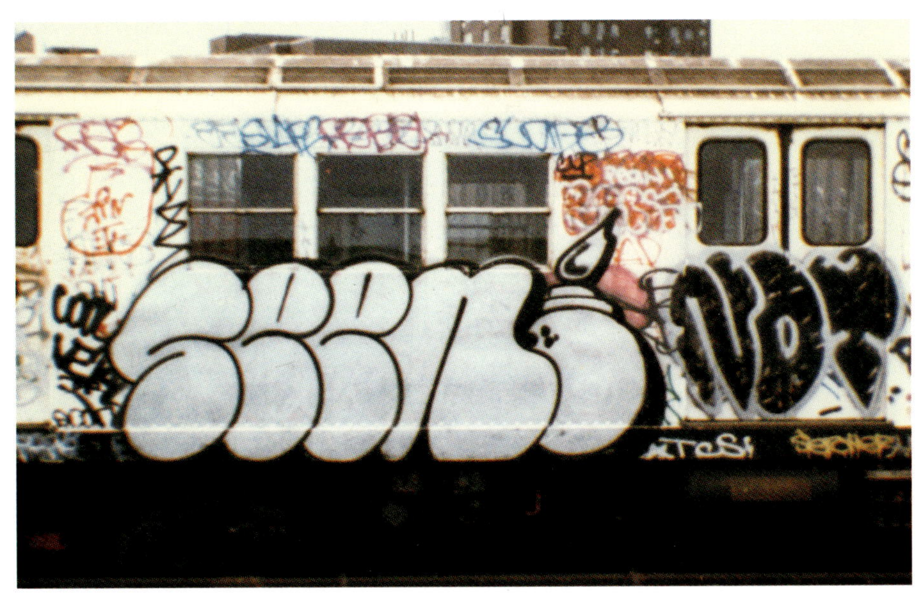

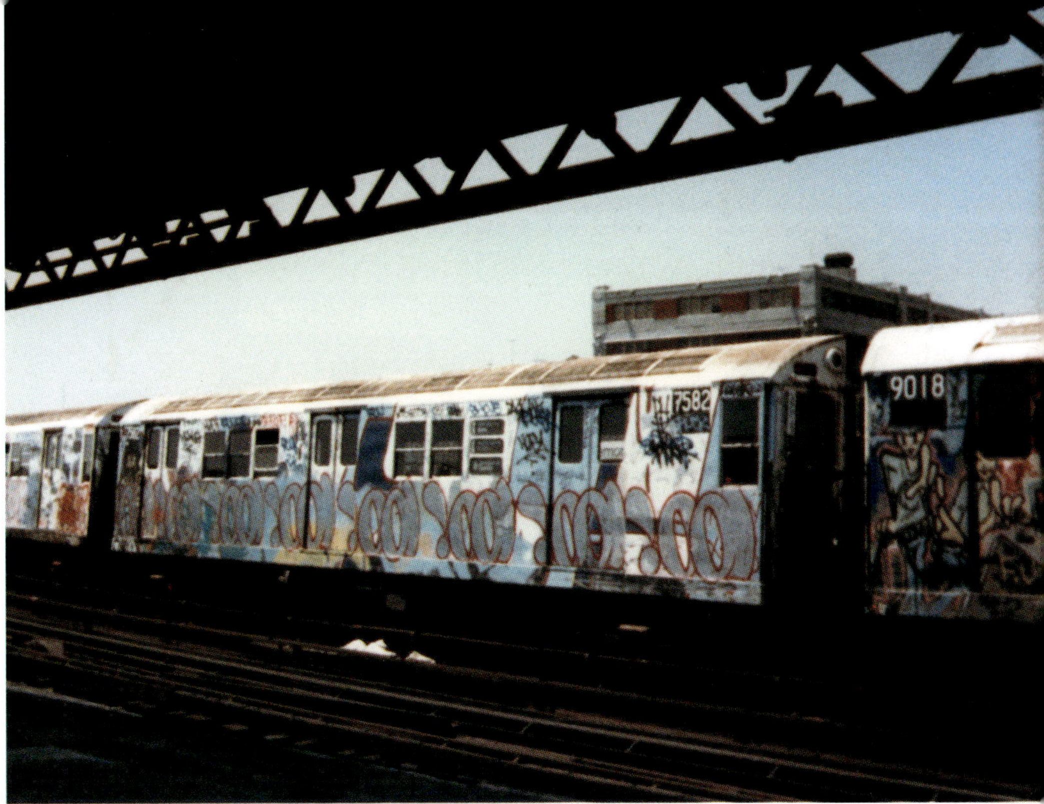

"OD3"

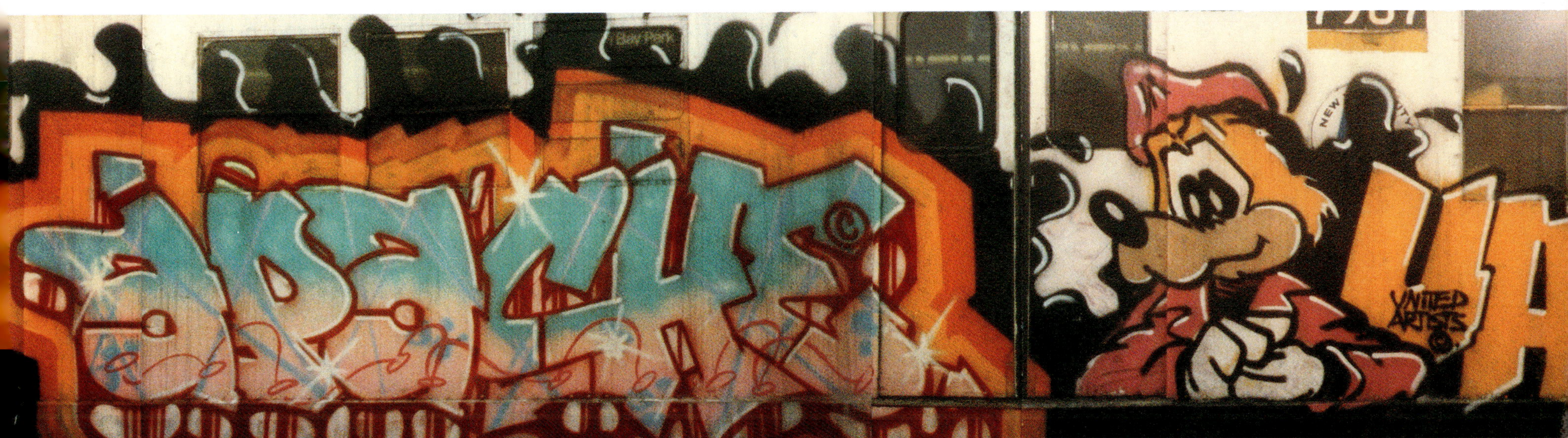

"Raz" & "Apache"

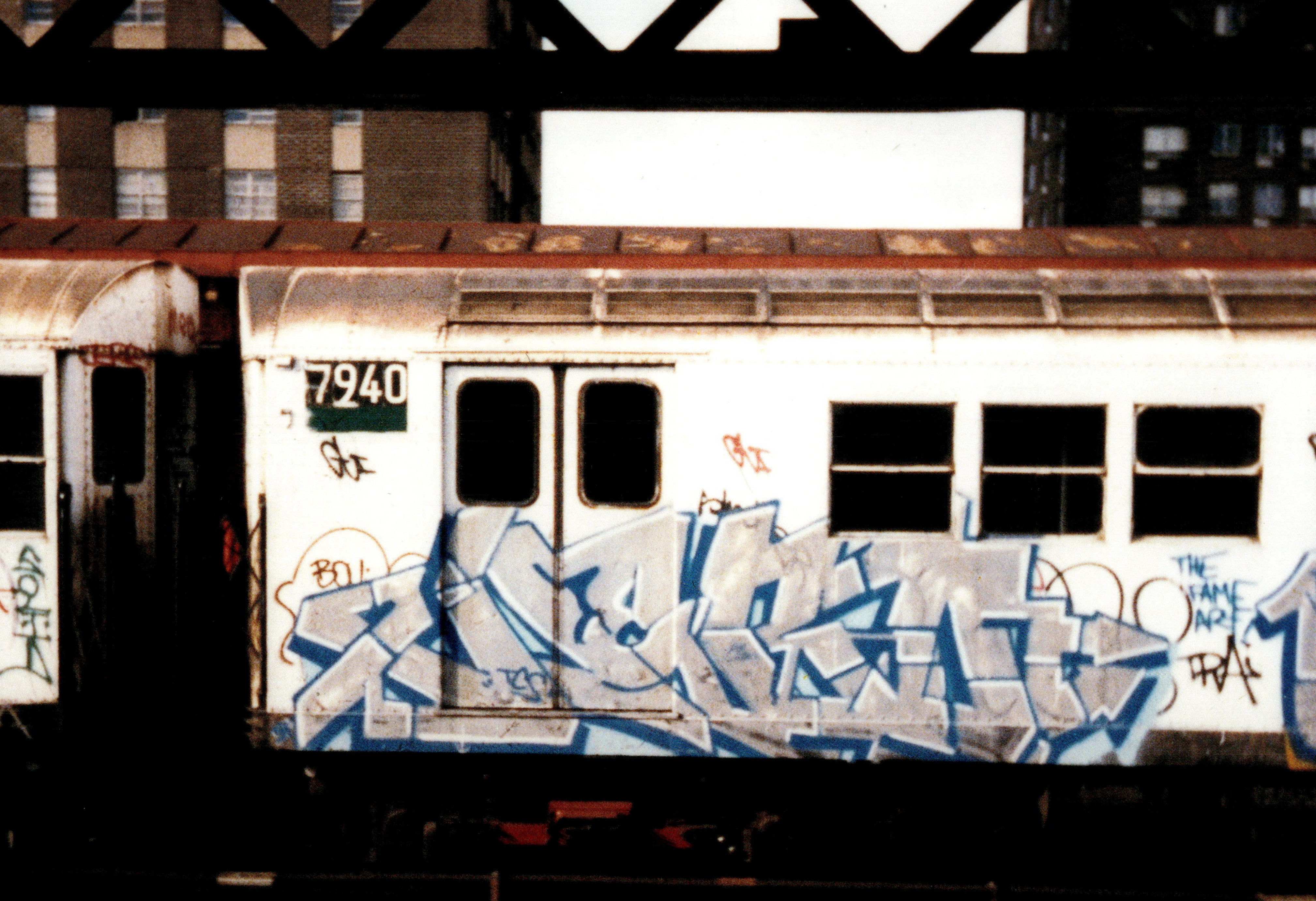

"Dero"

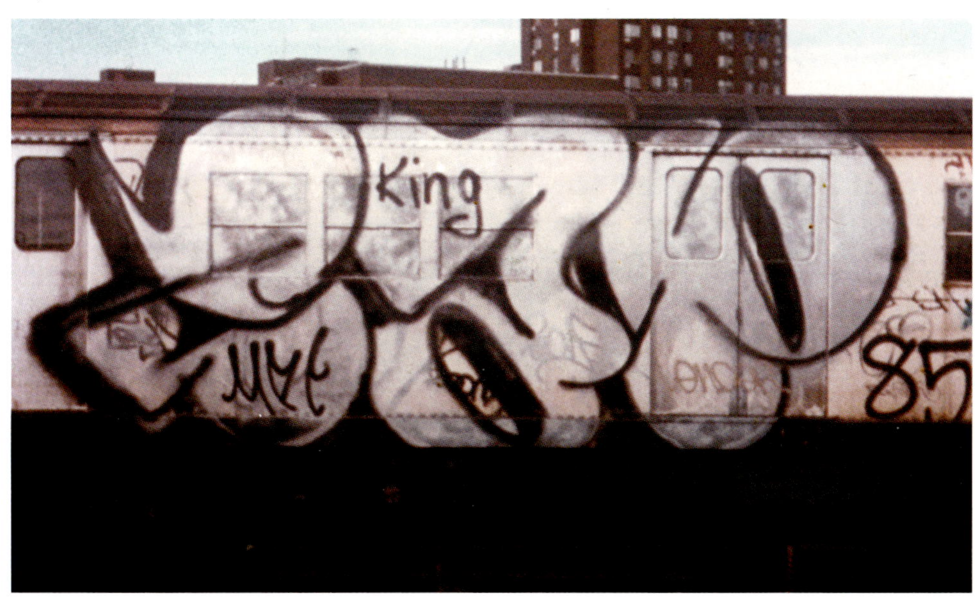

"Cap"

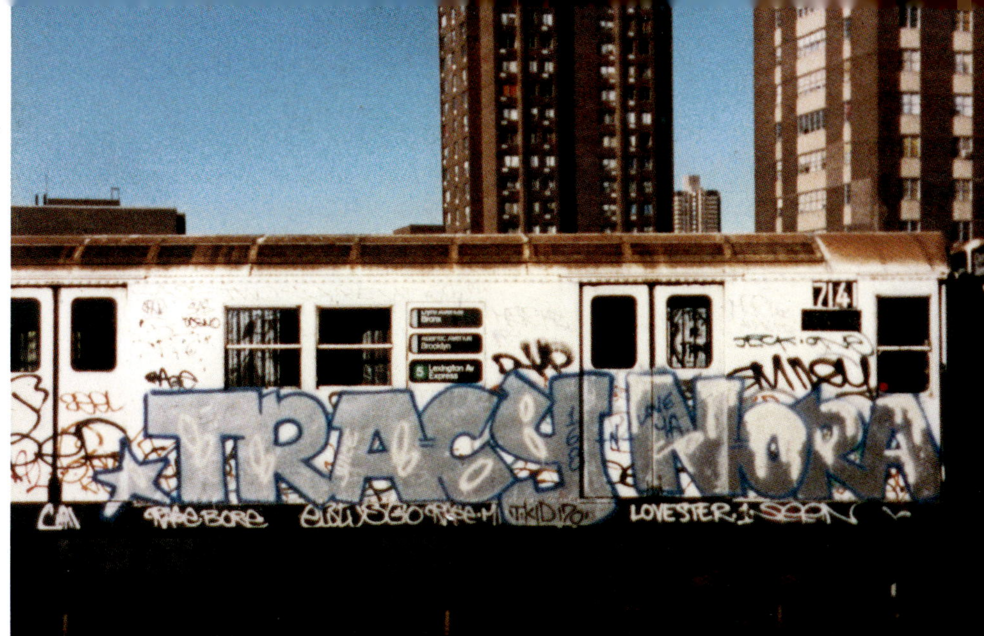

"Tracy"

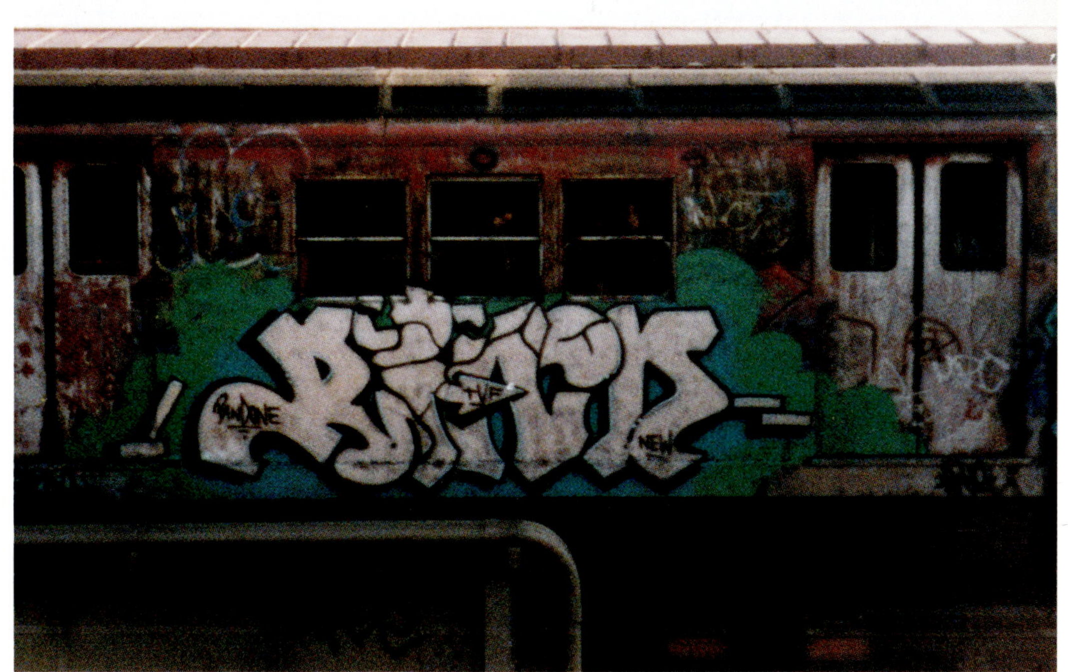

"Bind"

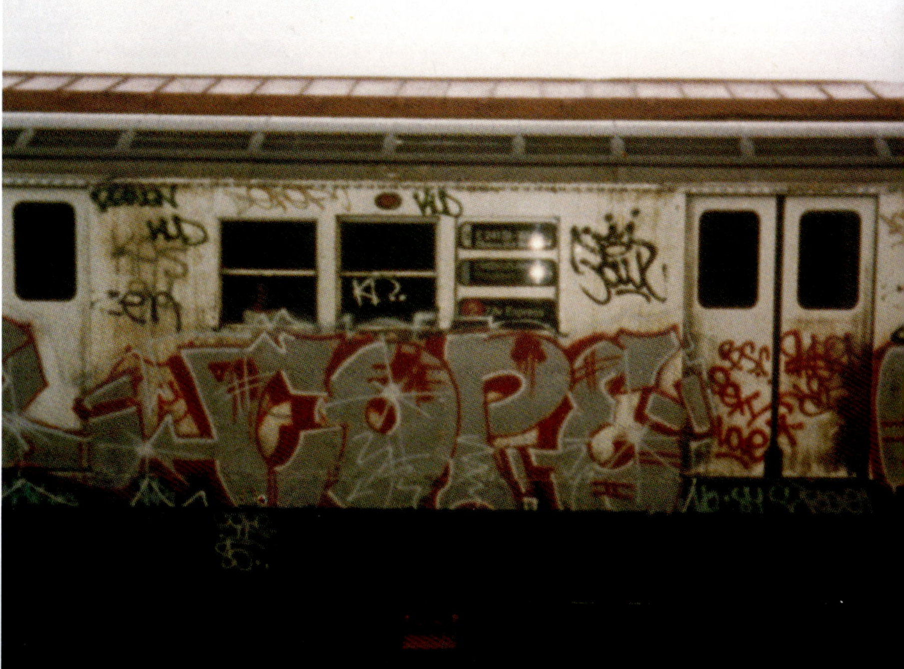

"Cope2"

"Sade" & "Dune," 1985

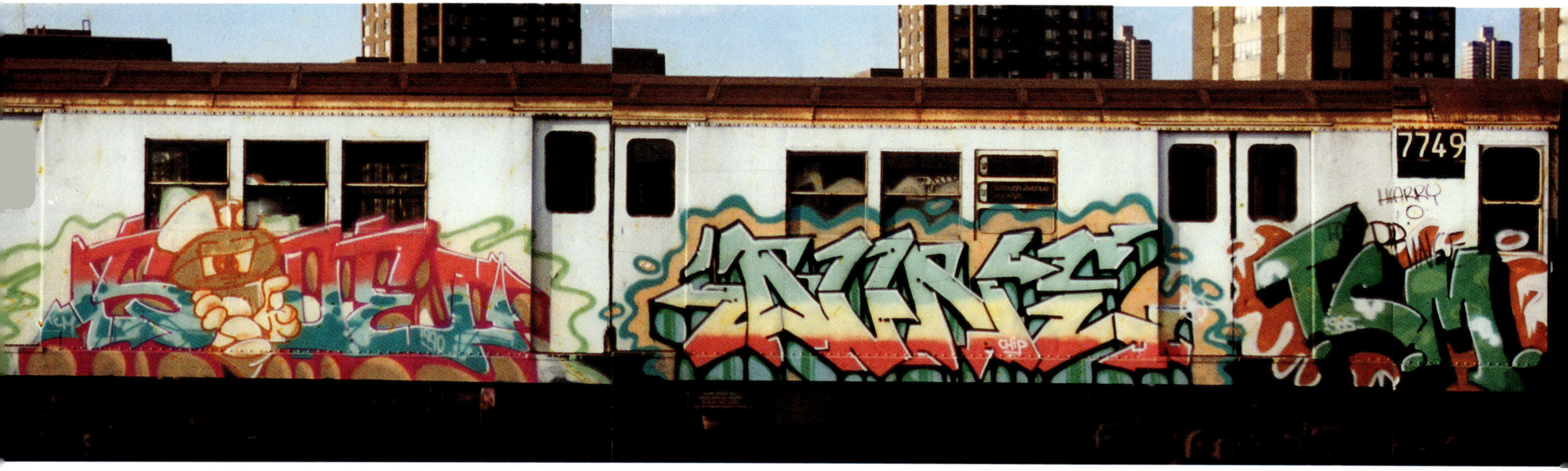

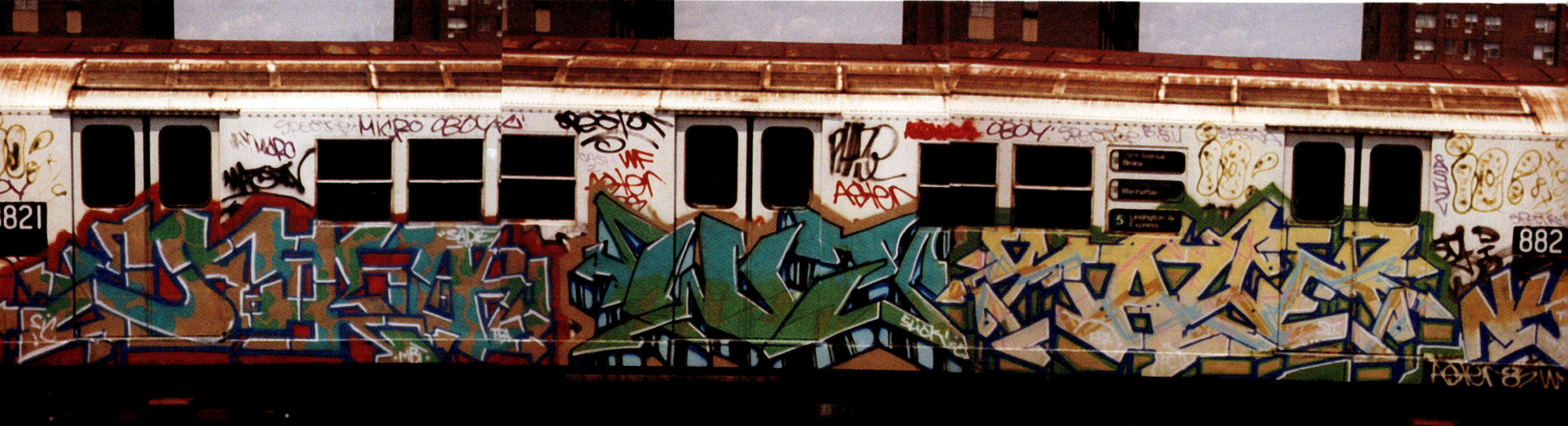

"Dero," "Wuz" & "Jase"

Dyre Avenue
Bronx
Atlantic Avenue
Brooklyn
5 Lexington Av
Express

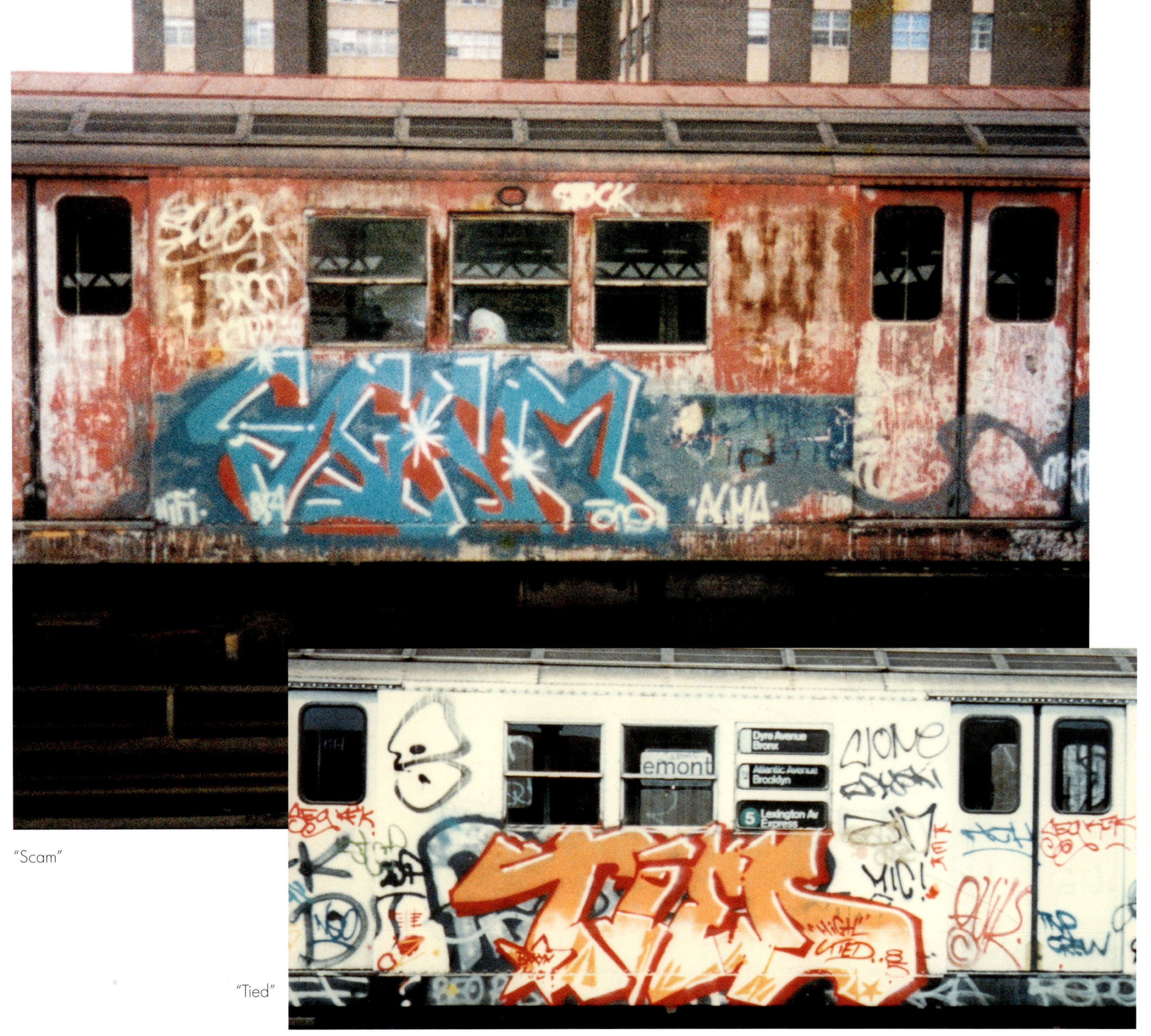

"Scam"

"Tied"

Graffiti to me was a hobby until I did my first lay ups at Esplanade, then it became an addiction. The smell of the tracks and mist of paint, sometimes in scorching hot weather or freezing snow, it was always an adventure. When I started to bomb regularly, it almost became the only thing I thought of doing, no matter where or when. We always had to scope out the tracks for work bums, other rival writers, and of course, the transit cops. Nowadays the writers are missing the most exciting thrill, walking up to a steel canvas and emblazoning it with their name and watching it run from the Bronx to Brooklyn!

–Des KTC

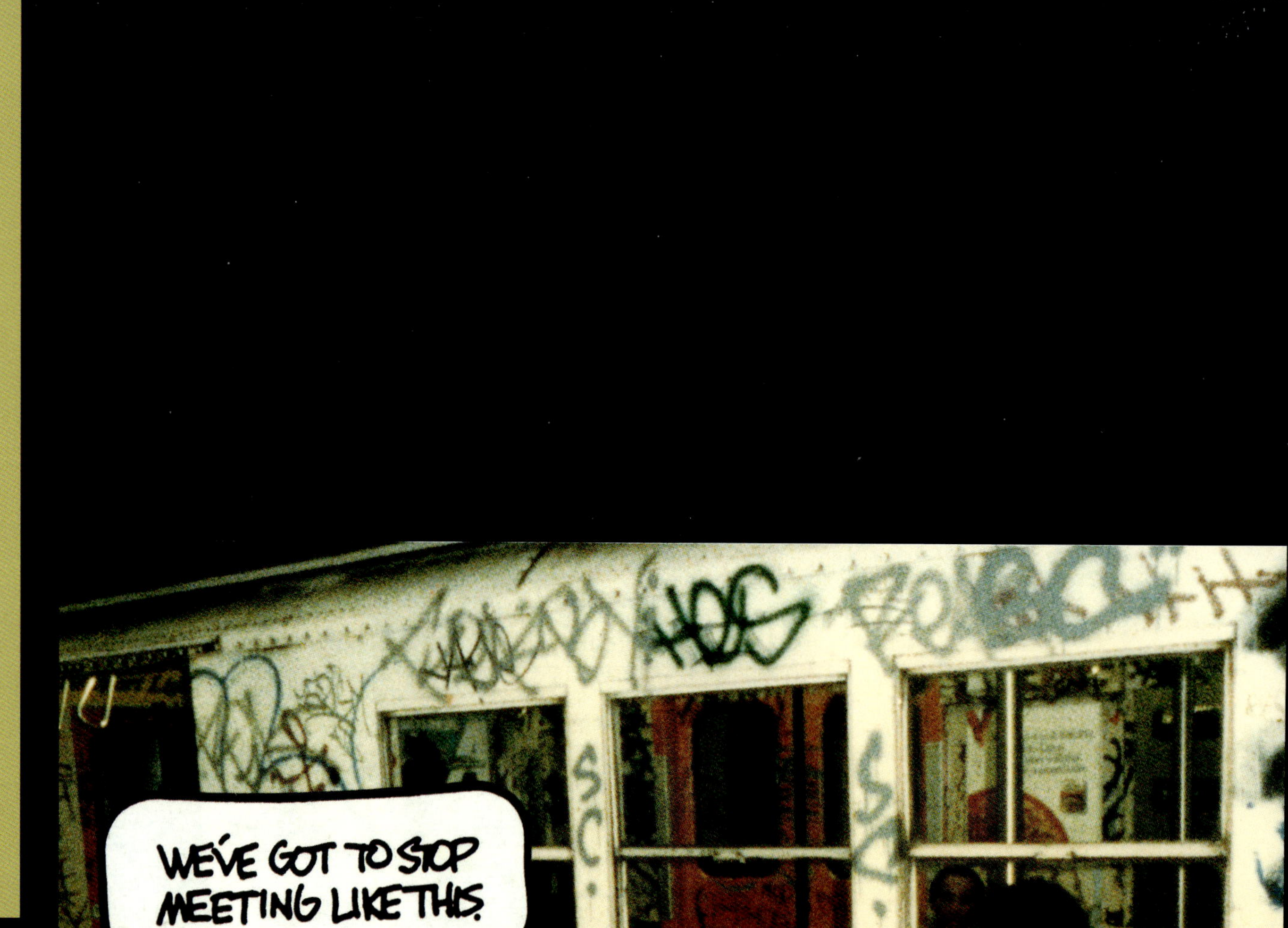

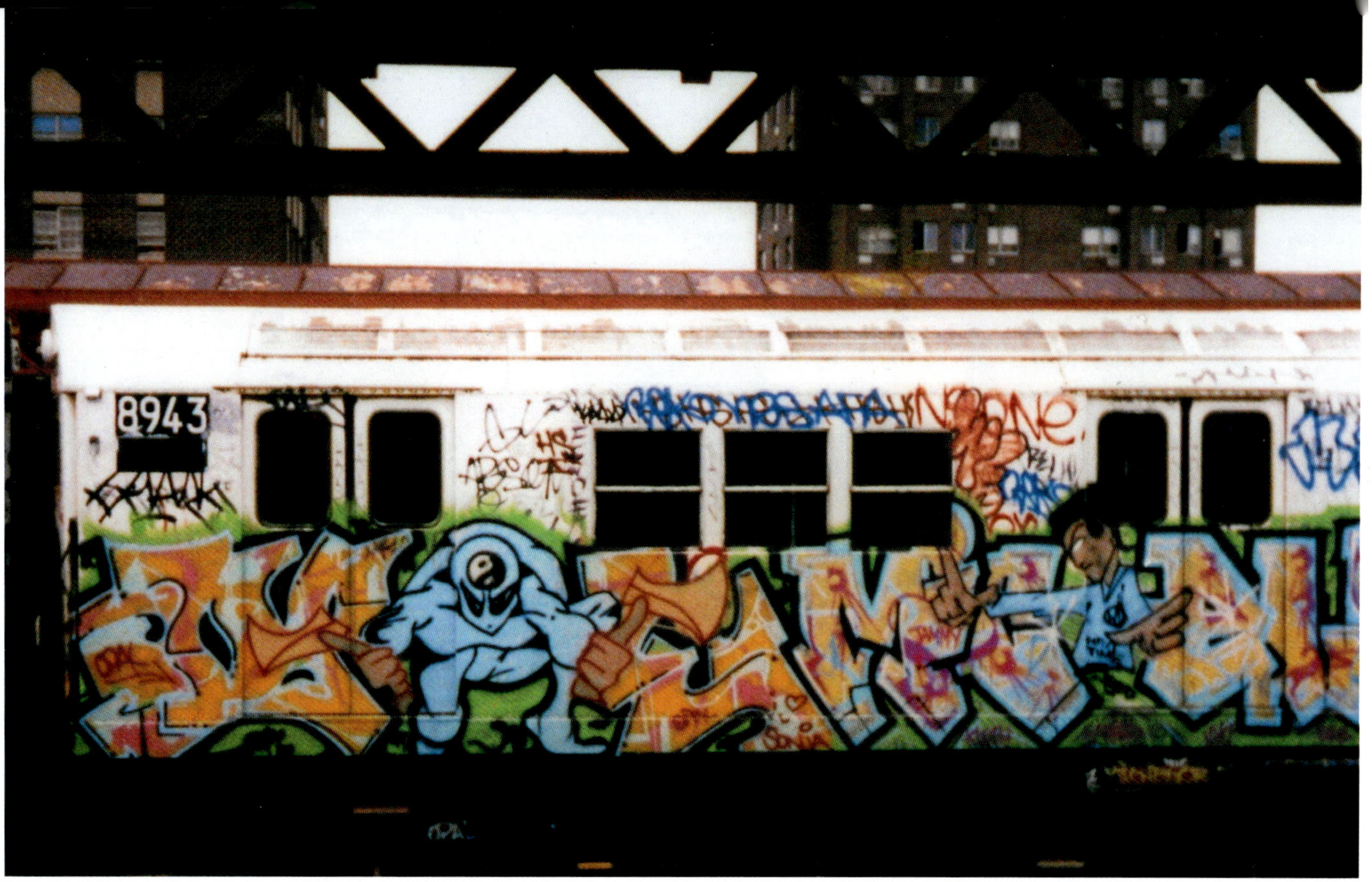

Opal

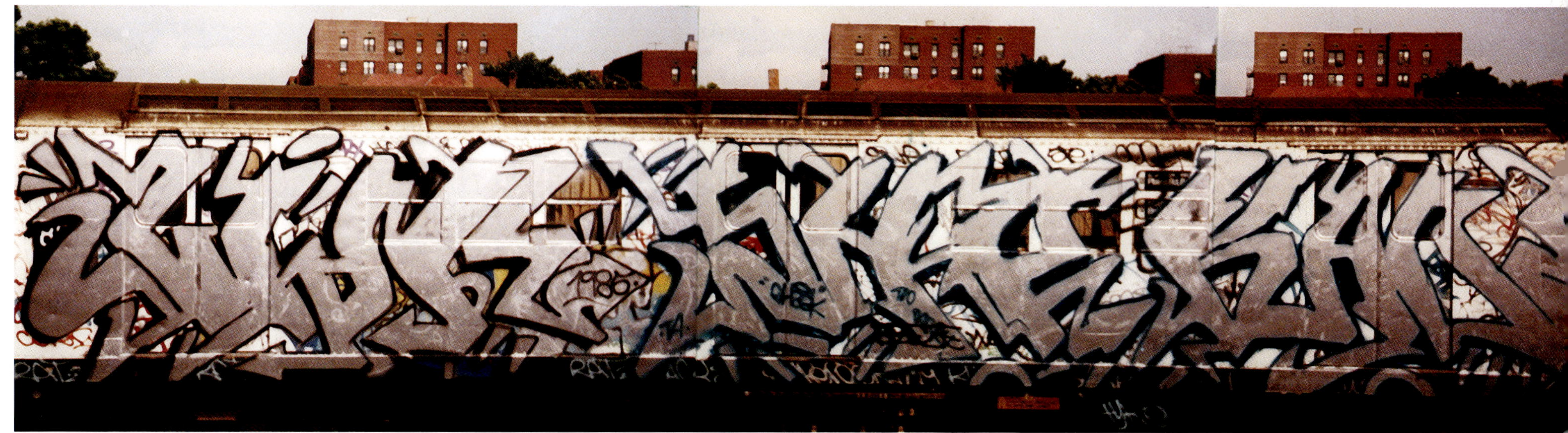

"Lin," "Sheek" & "Kade"

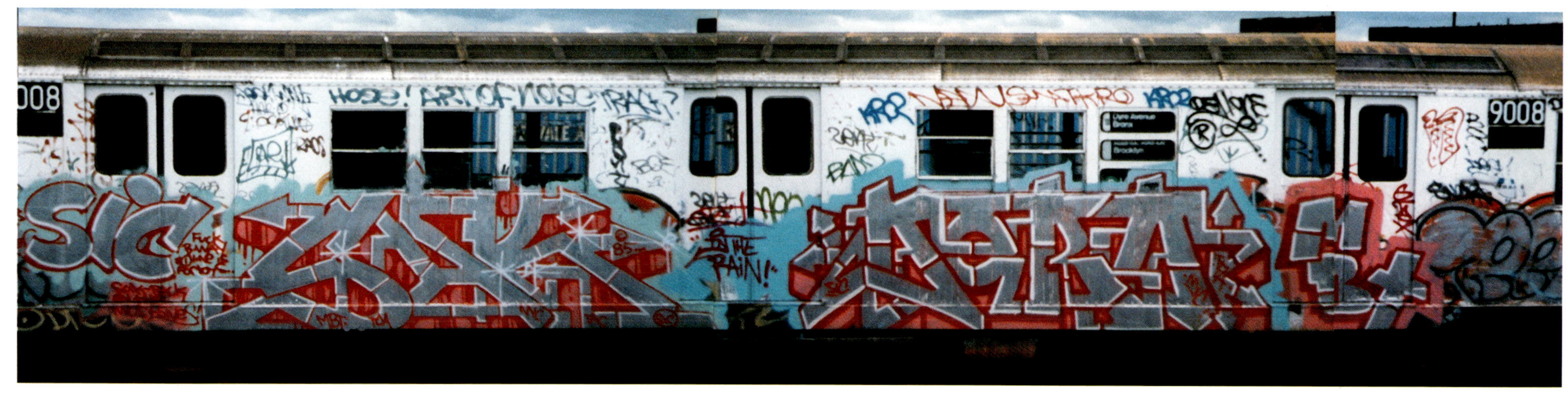

"Sak" & "Dero"

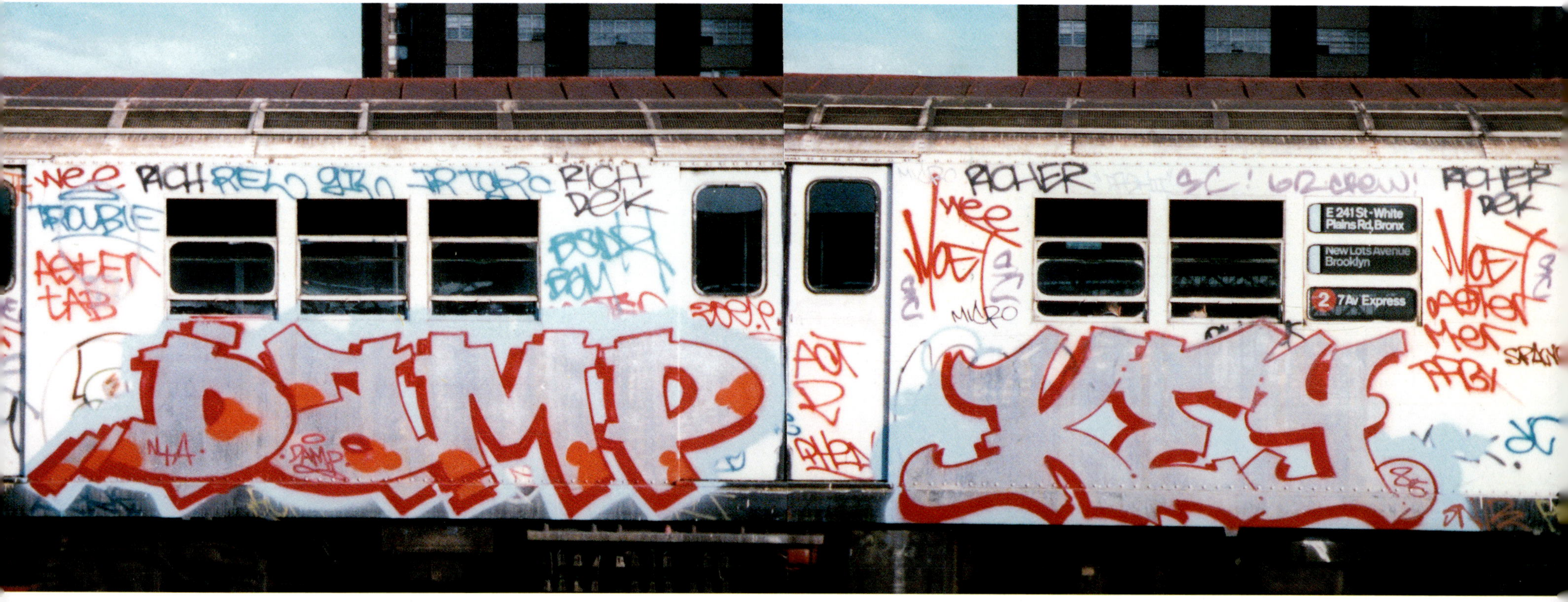

"Damp" & "Key"

I started taking pictures between the years of 83-84. The trains were very rusty back then, and the MTA had just started to paint them white. I would take pictures by myself on my home station which was 238th street on the 2 line (although I did venture to 233rd street once in awhile also). I would get out of school, and then hop the train with my 110 camera. I took pictures of all types of graffiti on the trains. Pieces, throw ups, window downs, e to e's, etc. After a while I started venturing out to other lines. Sometimes I would be alone, and other times I would be with other writers. My favorite spot to go to was East Tremont Ave. because you could go to either side of the station without having to pay an additional fare. After 180th you could only do that at the Tremont and Intervale Avenue stops. I would go to Intervale from time to time, but I felt most comfortable benching at Tremont. Some of the people that I met would only bench, but I was meeting the writers that were painting them as well. It was pretty cool when I met up with writers and became friends with them. They would call us and tell us when they had done a car so that we could get a head start on getting the photos. Some writers depended on us to get the pictures because they didn't have the patience to be out there and get them. We were out there in the rain, sleet, or shine, sometimes freezing our asses off to catch the photos before they were either buffed, or dissed. We benched so much that we knew how long it would take for a train to go downtown and come back uptown. We had the schedule down pack. Sometimes we would ride inside the train, make sure all the windows in the cars were up, and then pull the emergency brake. This would insure that we could photograph anything we wanted from all 10 cars. It was cool being out there in lay ups or yards exchanging war stories. It was a whole subculture that I am happy I was a part of. Riding the lines, taking photos, going to other lines. It was like being a reporter, and going out and getting a story. Doing your homework and finding out where all of the work was being done. At one point the workers even knew who I was. They would tease me about putting in overtime when they would see me on the weekends and holidays. What an era to be a part of. Growing up and being a student of the game. Listening, learning, and accepting criticism from the more experienced writers. Developing friendships that continue to this day. This is an era that I will always remember. The good old days.

-Key

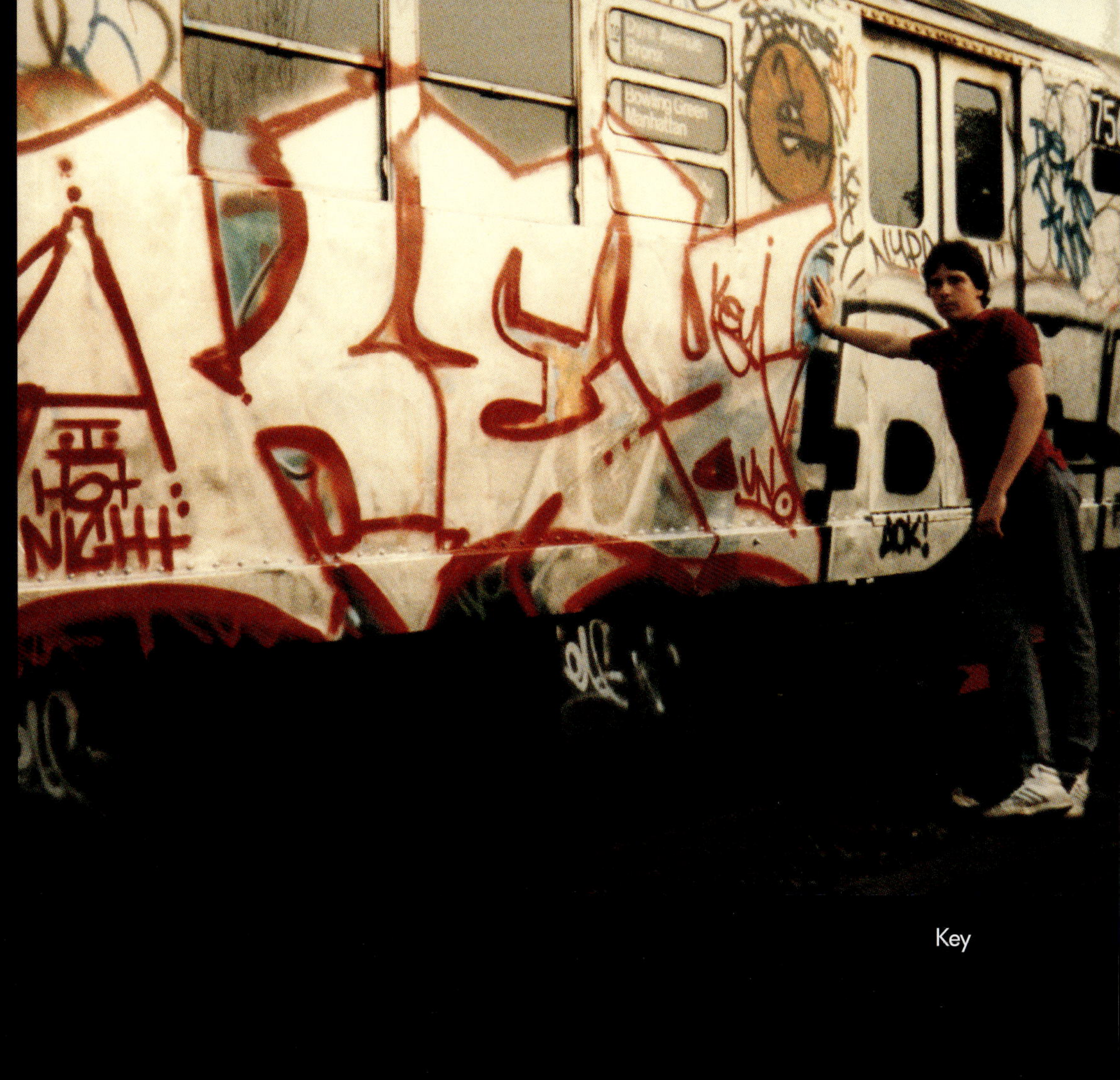

Key

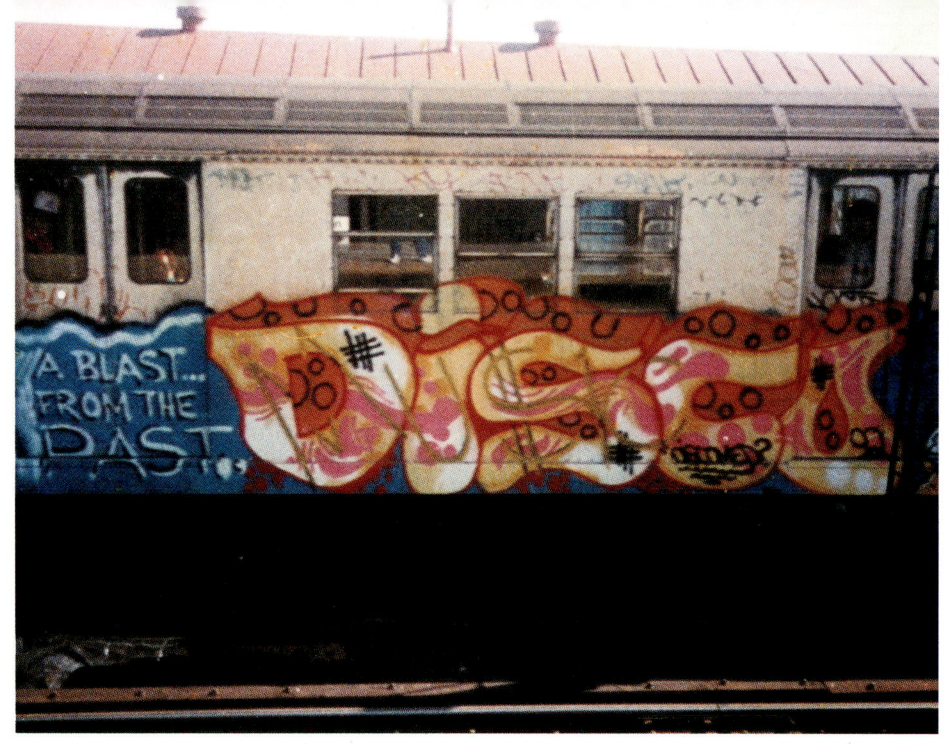

"Disco," 1985

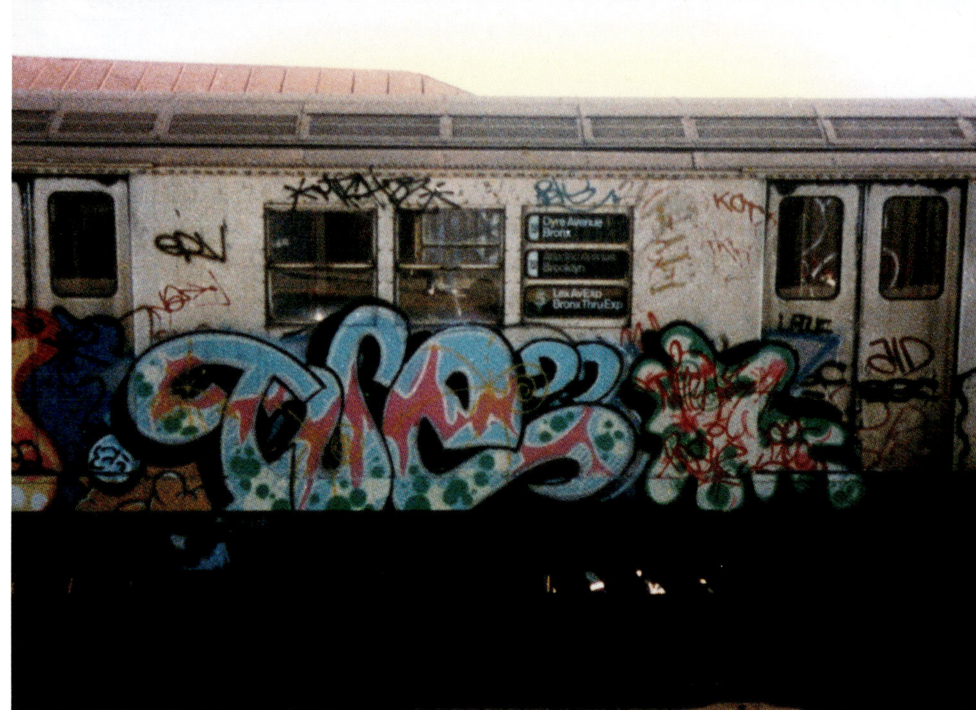

"Tue," by Mitch77, 1985

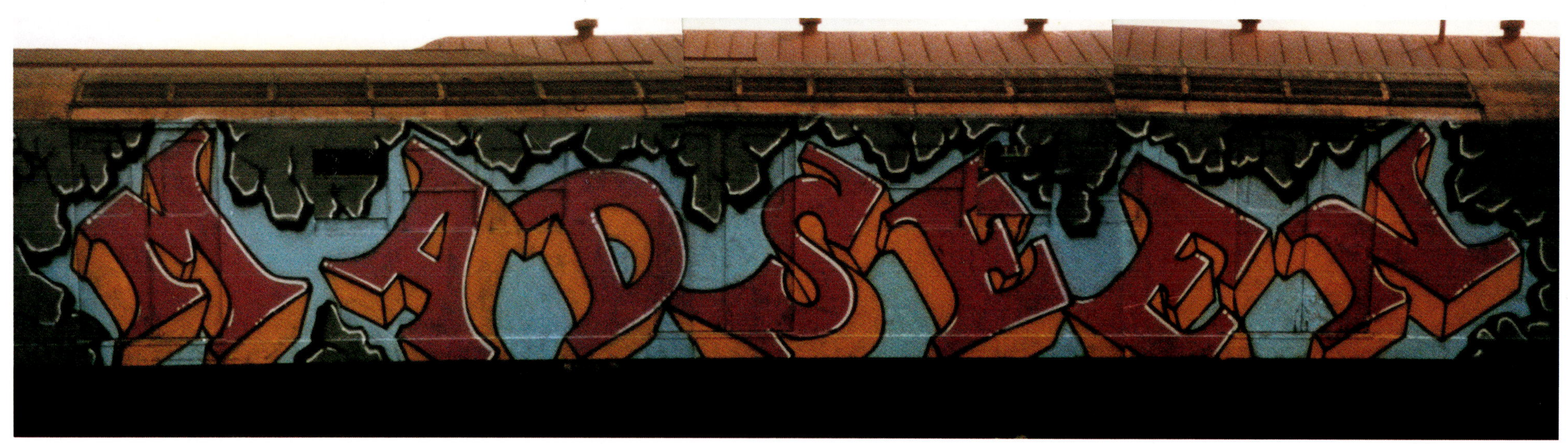

"Madseen," 1985

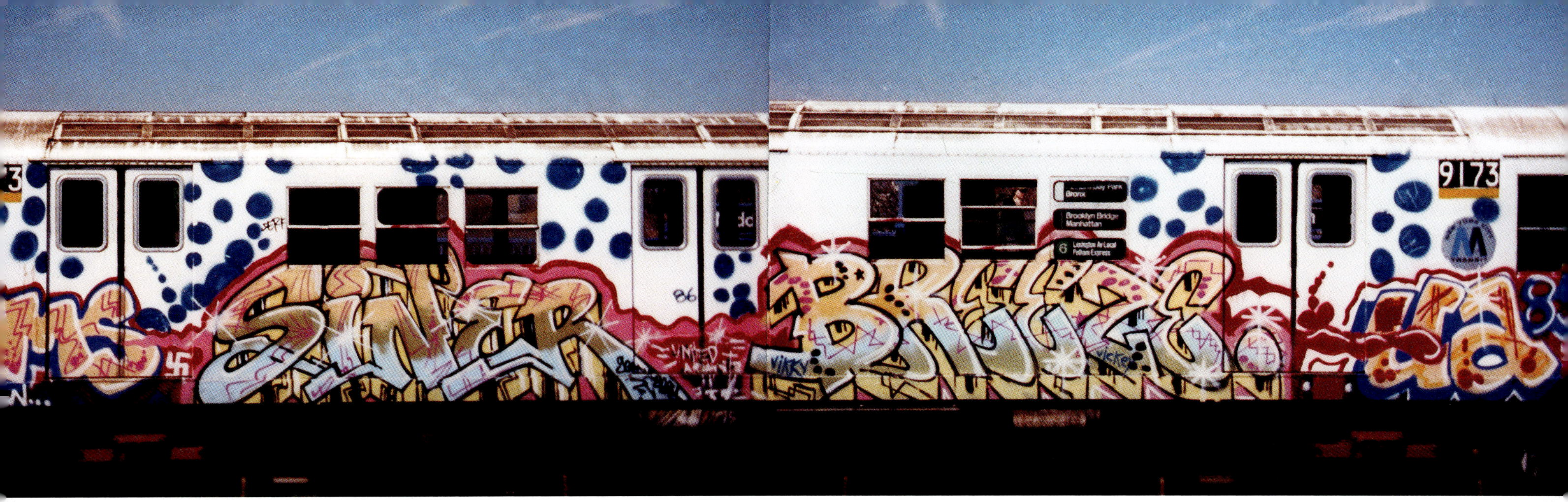

"Siner" & "Breeze"

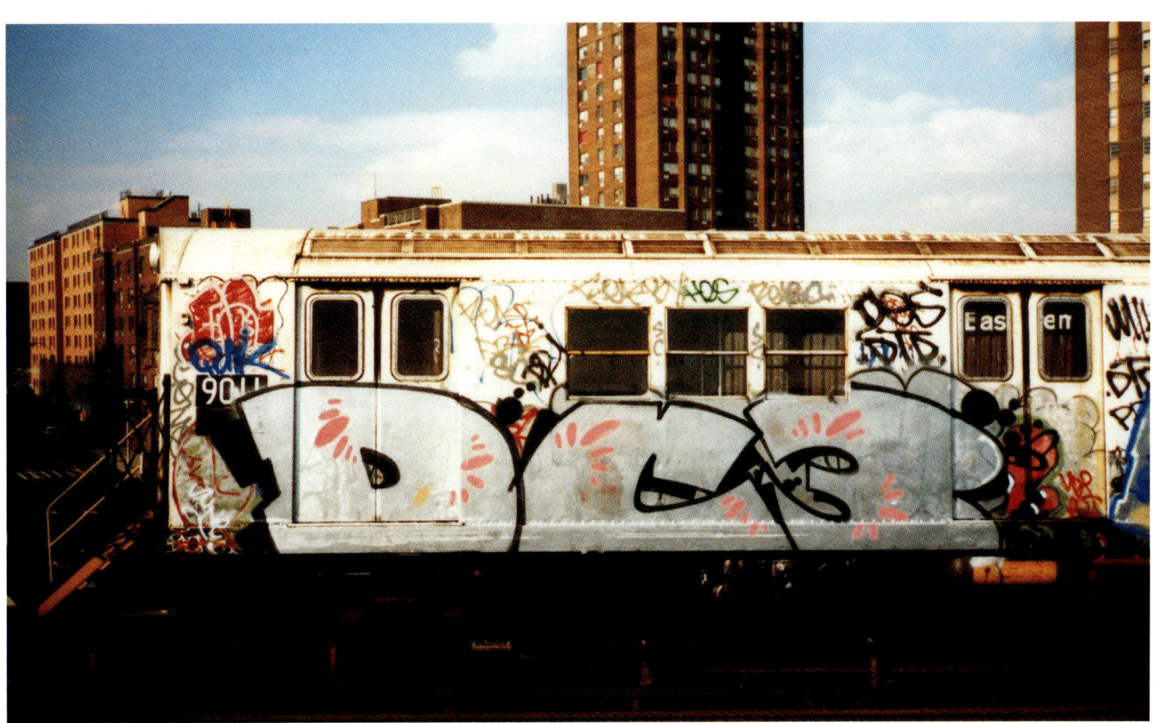

"DC3"

As a small child I was constantly creating comics for my fellow classmates, perhaps when I should have been listening to the instructor. I was quite prolific then too, yet my drawing skills were beyond weak, so they simply became personal. I guess that's where the introversion and insecurity began regarding my being and artistic abilities. Soon I began to paint the subway trains of New York with ferocity. On the trains my work commanded and demanded viewing, regardless of respect or permission from society at large. I forced my work upon the "audience." We graffiti painters became subway terrorists, taking control of the surfaces for our expression.

My experience in art universities has been frustrating also, thus more rage and anger began to compound itself inside of me. This combined with the frustration of being a Black American and the social and professional limitations within that parameter (racism) fostered yet more creative and destructive energies. The subways were an opportunity to have as much "canvas" on which to paint. I recall watching my hundreds of graffiti's go past...I had created miles of work!

The ability to paint and create professionally within the art world and throughout many aspects of the commercial visual design arenas is simply a continuation of my image making. I prefer to accept myself as an image maker. Naturally, I use paint... thus I am a painter. I don't truly like the words "artist" or "famous", which are used quite often when mentioning men of my genre from New York.

The era of painting trains was one of the most enjoyable times of my life. The physical and actual aspects of it all have been documented hundreds of times over in books and films, so I don't need to describe that in detail. Yet the smell of the paint combined with the grease, oils, and machinery were as thrilling as a hike across a mountaintop at that time in my life. The adrenaline rush, along with the action of the creativity was exhilarating! Train painting was my sport and addiction, and I never slept better than those hundreds of nights after successful bombing. I was busy with so many things in those days: school, work, relationships...yet painting trains was more satisfying than even sex.

I recall working days at IBM; going out to dinner and concerts with Jamie (my ex-wife); having sex, and then feigning fatigue; drop her off at home claiming I was going home too. Yet, all along the trunk of my car was filled with paint, and I would rush off to make my 1: am or 2: am appointments with the guys.

Once I was older and experienced in the game, we of the ROLLING THUNDER CREW (namely BILROCK, MIN, SACH, RICH, REVOLT, and DEMO) approached the action with military style finesse. We were on a mission, and were determined to be successful every time. It's also like gambling if one goes against the law or the system; sometimes you win and sometimes you lose. I lost a couple of times, yet in comparison to how many thousands of trains I painted, I was a professional.

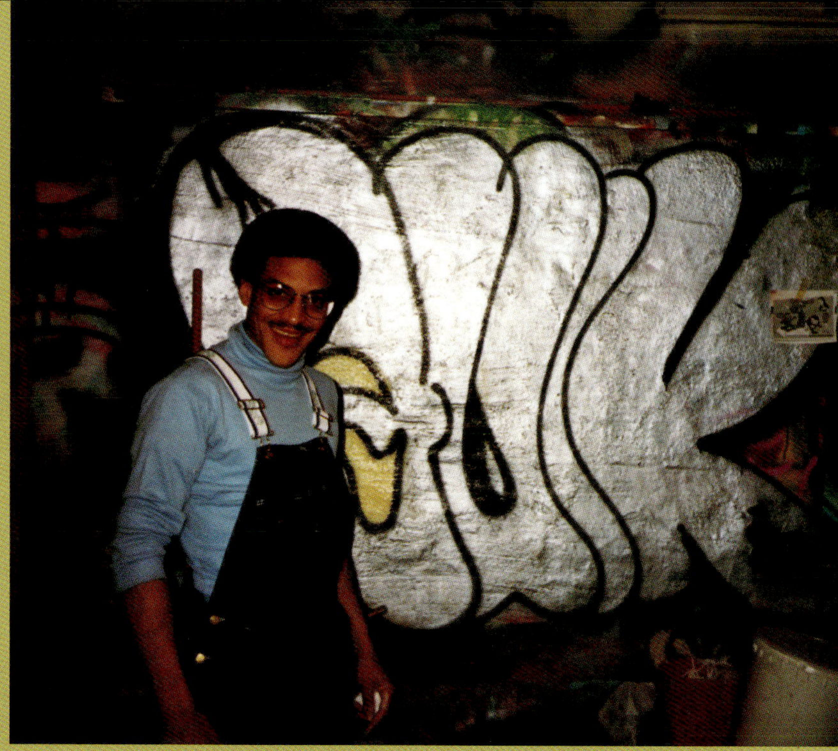

Many writers were naturally dedicated to doing beautiful creations, whereas I was bent on destruction and aimed to dominate the carriages with my ugly unique throw ups like my earlier mentors JESTER, TRUE 2, and IN. Occasionally I would attempt nice work, but bombing was my forté. Unfortunately, I realize now that all this pent up rage and frustration was not mentally healthy. Normal people do not paint trains!

Some how as a young man I believed that the days of train painting would never end. To me it was normal as going to the park to play baseball, handball, or basketball. Luckily I've been able to continue spray painting around the world as this phenomenon grew into an international culture. I am not the best, never was and never will be. I was not the first, nor shall I be the last train painter. Yet, I bombed...and I wish those days never ended.

–Quik

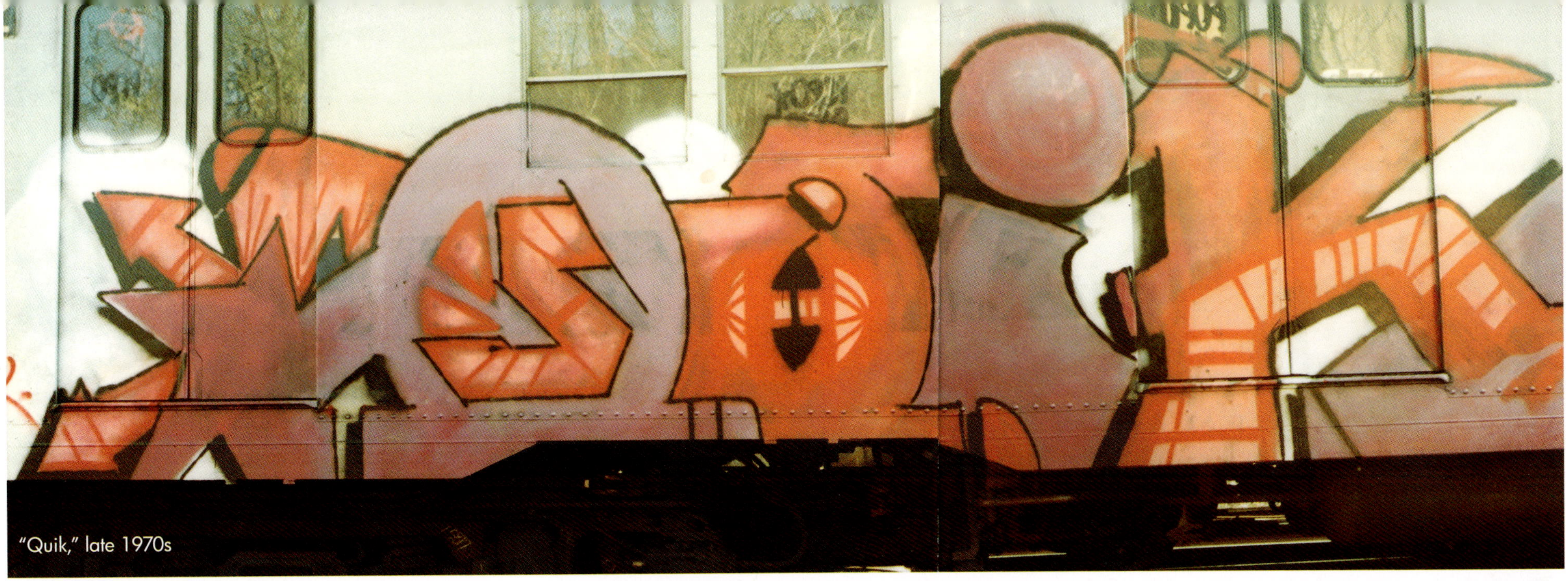

"Quik," late 1970s

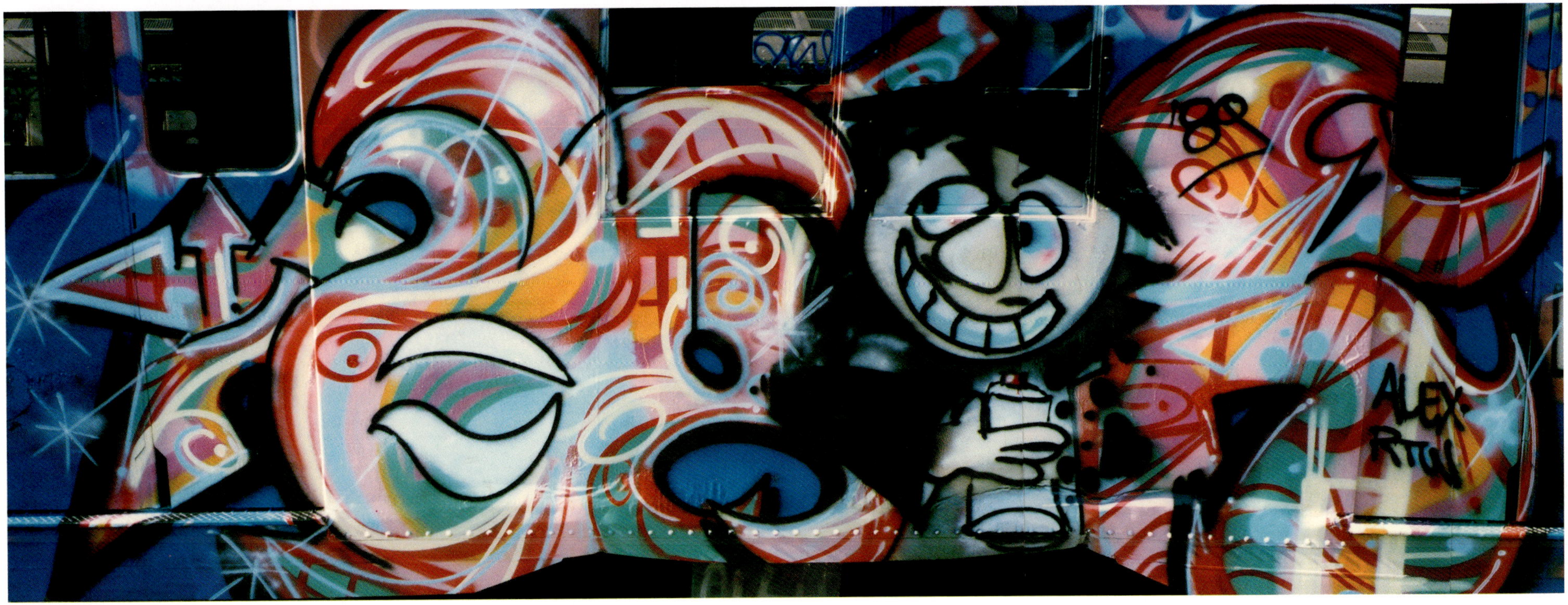

"Quik," 1989

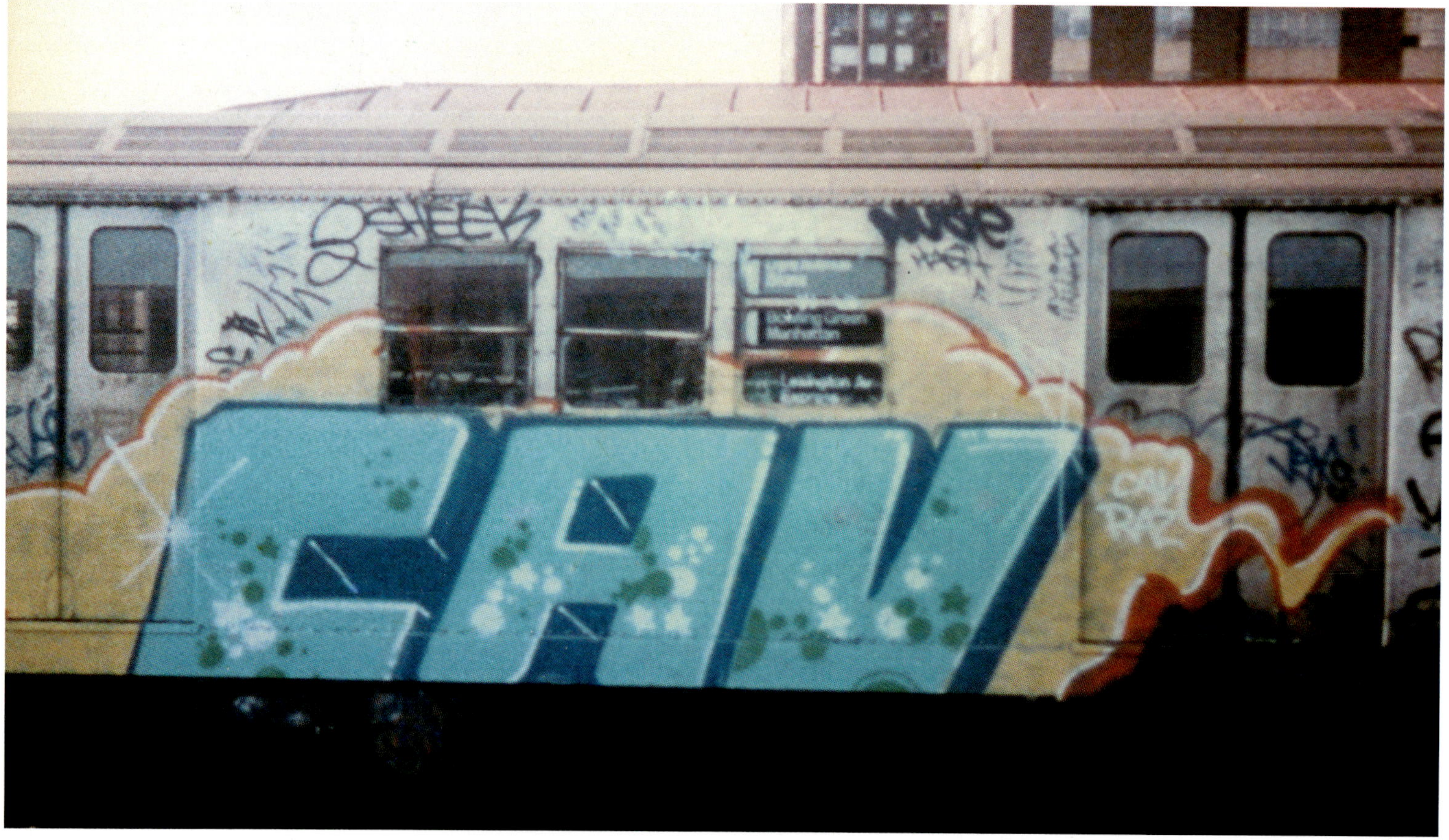

"Cav," 1985

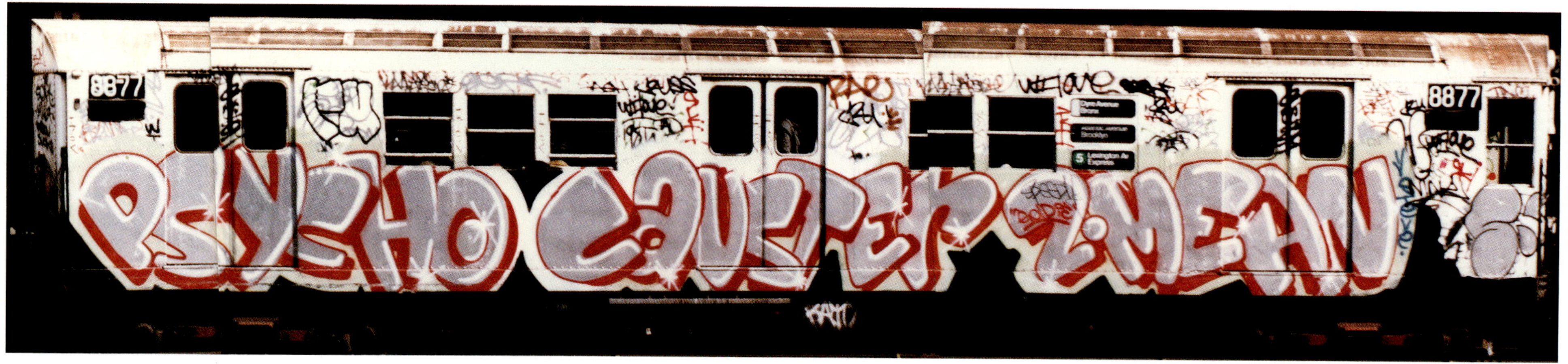

"Psycho," by Seen, "Cavster" & "2Mean," 1985

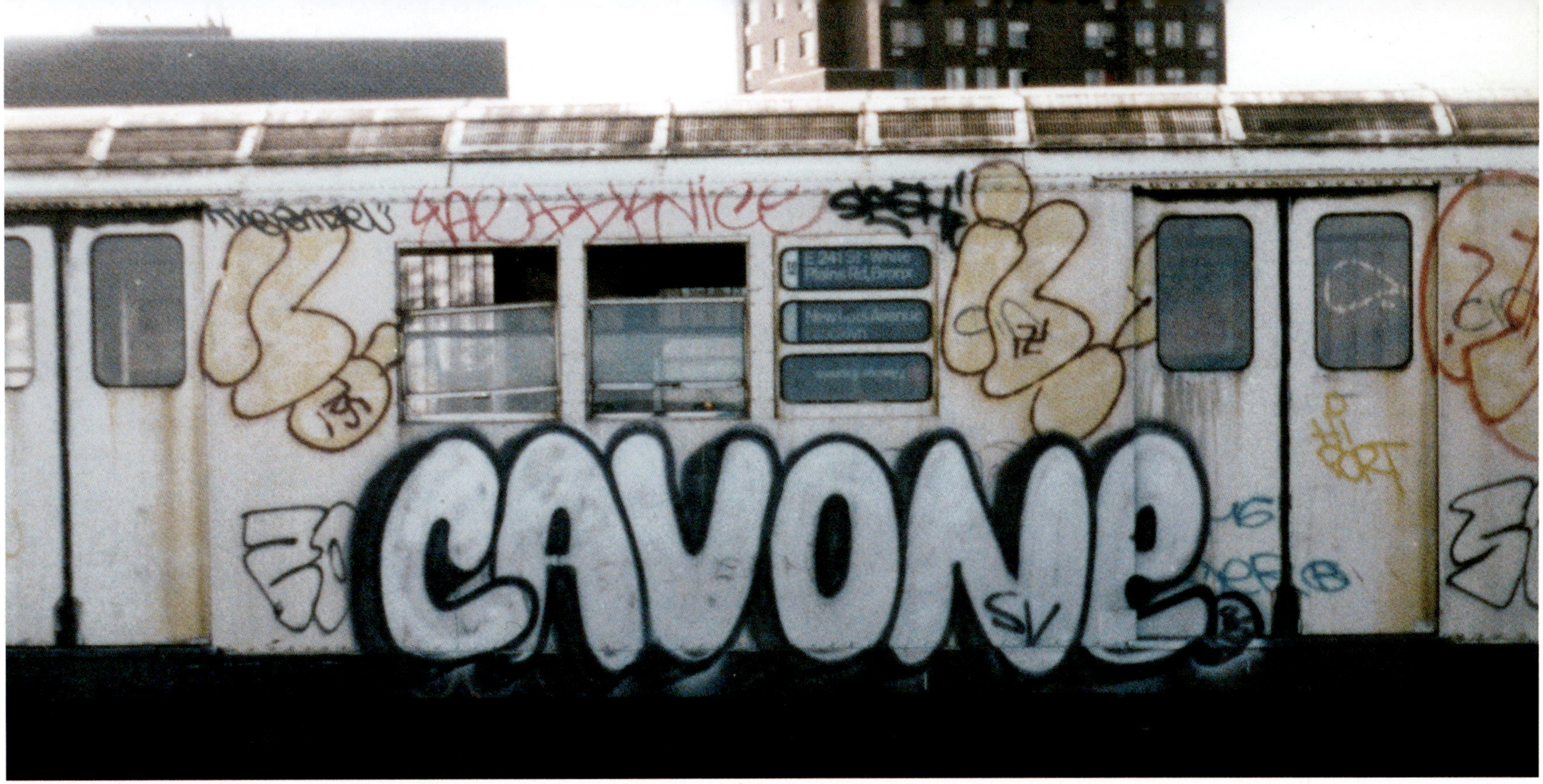

"Cav-one"

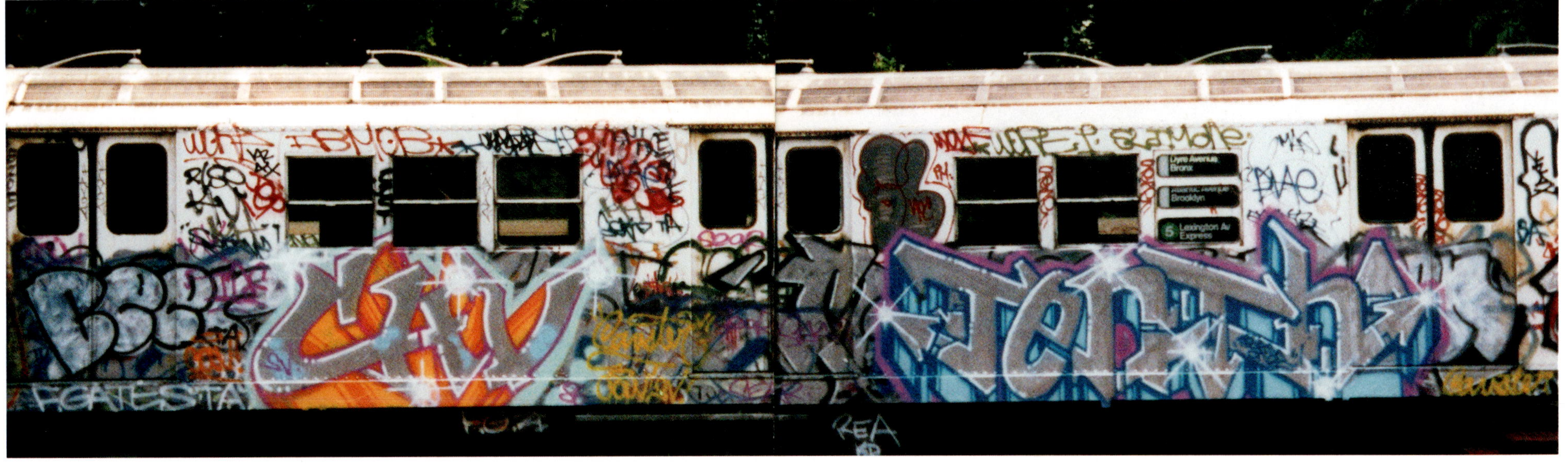

"Cav" & "Tenth"

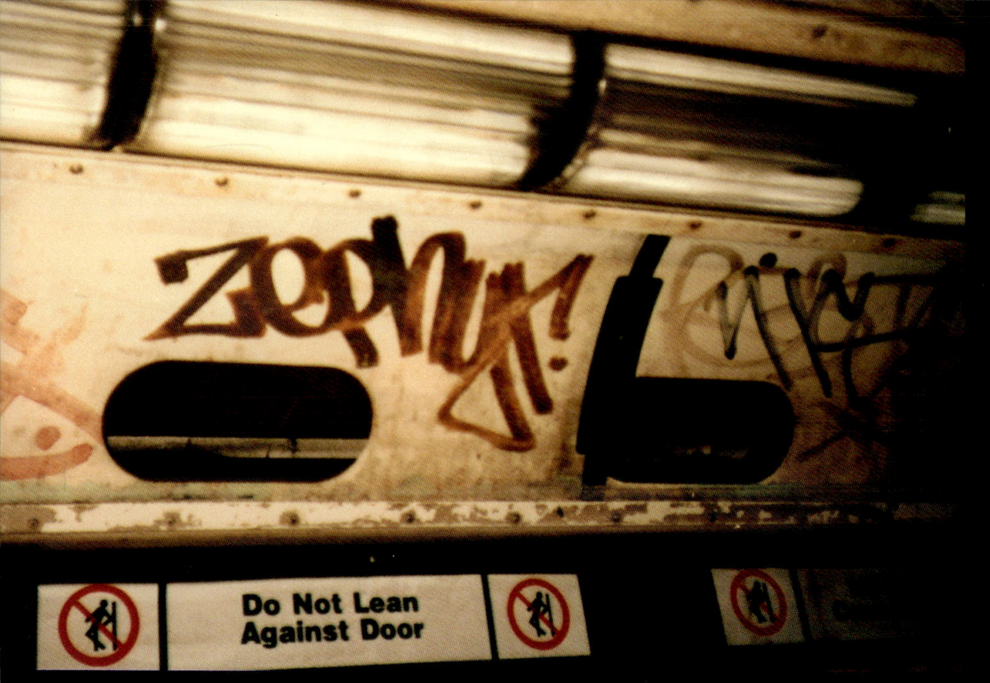

I first discovered the wonders of painting subways in 1977. What I discovered was a liberating form of self-expression that changed my life. But I also discovered the perfect medium. A subway car, each of the 2 metal panels that lie between the doors and below the windows of an R-28 IRT car measure approximately 4' x 12'. To this day, these panels remain the greatest things I've ever painted on. Nowadays I'm still painting as many pieces as I can. Freight trains, which I sometimes refer to as the "national movement" or the "final frontier," get mixed reactions from many graff purists. But you can't argue with the fact that they offer our paintings more longevity than the NYC subways do. Ill always say this. As long as I'm having fun and enjoying the process, I'm going to keep at it. And after 30 years of painting, I'm still having a blast.

–Zephyr

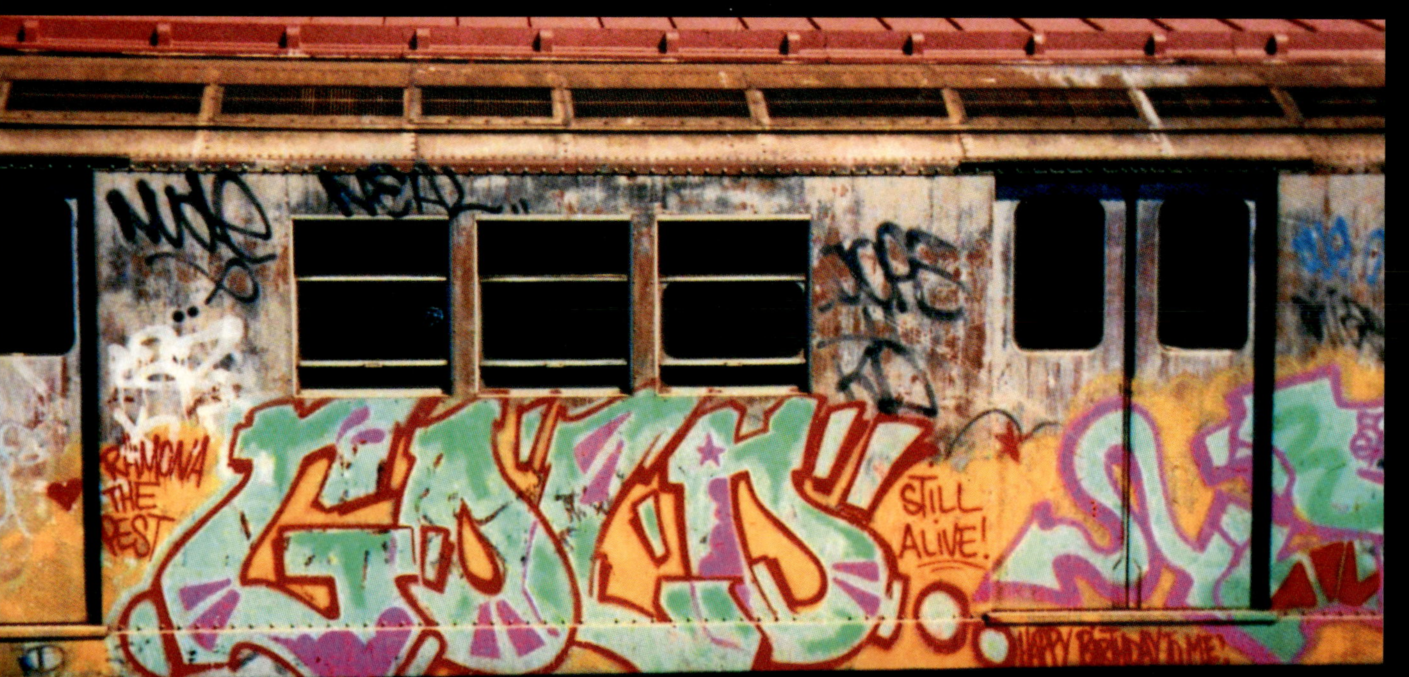

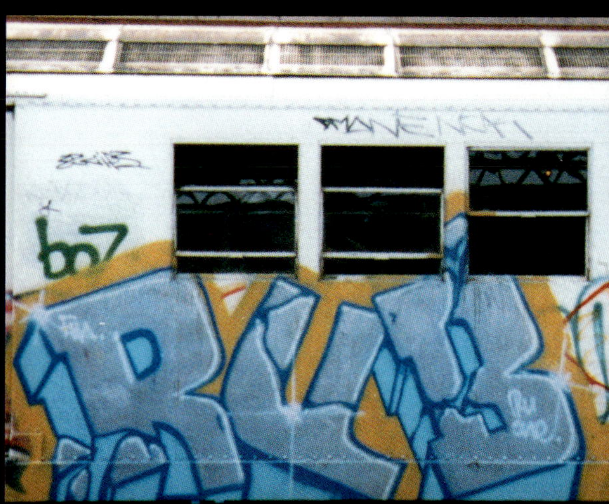

"Gold," by Zephyr, 1985

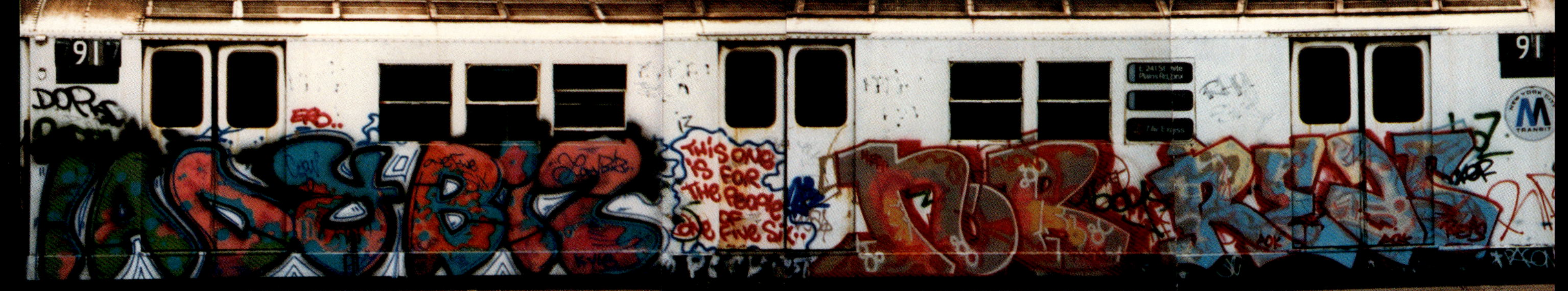

"Lady Biz," "Nob" & "Reas," 1986

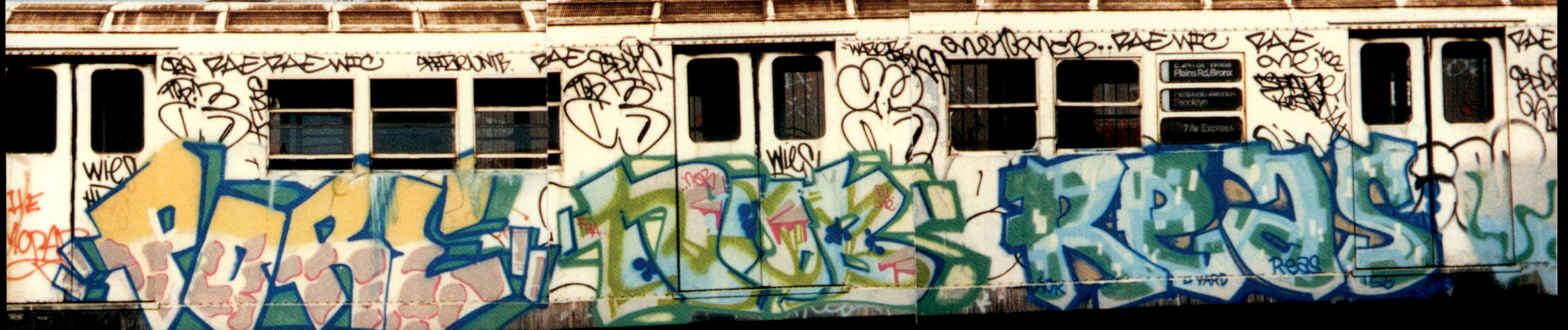

"Pore," "Nob" & "Reas"

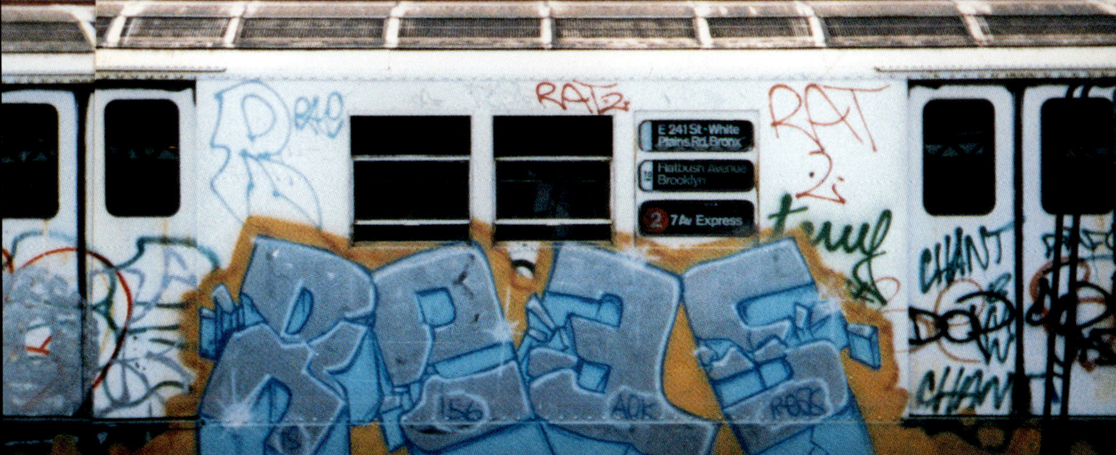

"Rub" & "Reas"

We did three or four cars that weekend. We did the Rub, Reas in the D yard. There was a new hole in the fence during a super cold snow storm. Jon 156, Omni, Chow, Raze & Seze were all doing stuff as well. It was a rare weekend; there were few distractions. The cars we did ended up literally being some of the last buffed on the 2s & 5s.

–ReasAok

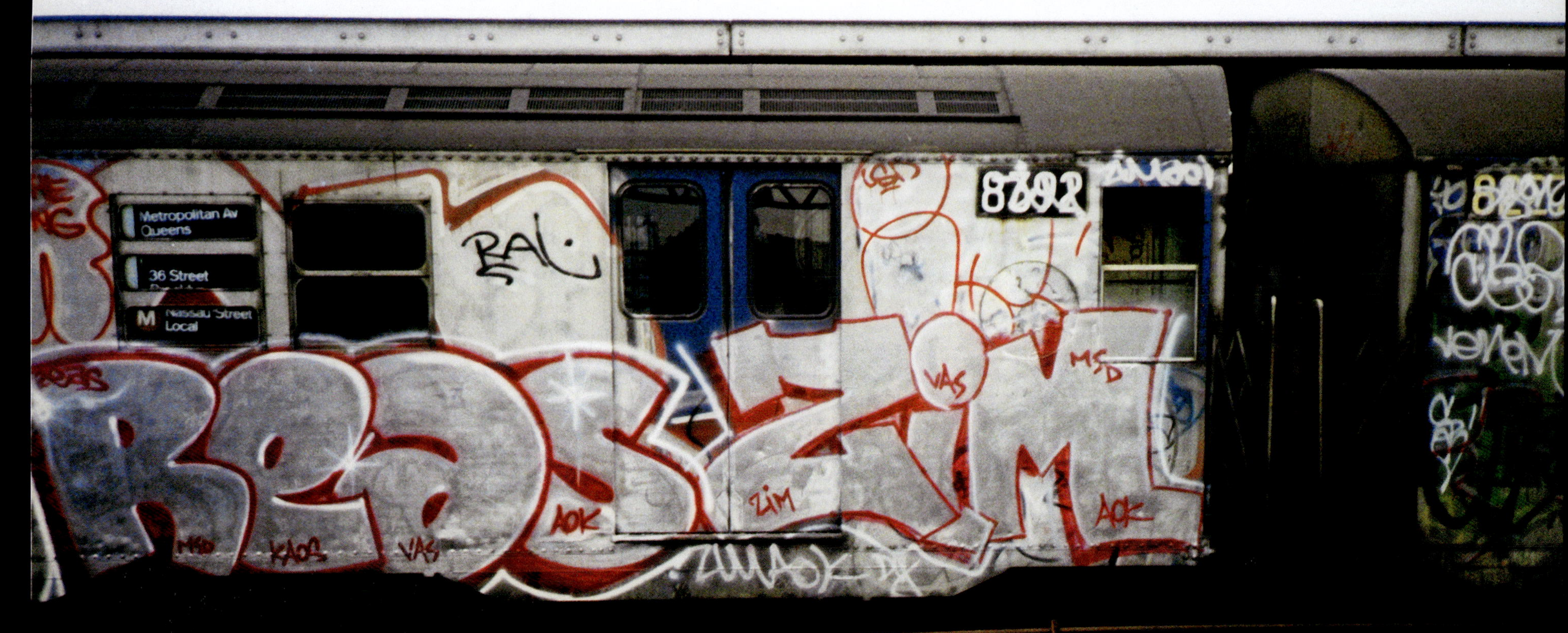

"Reas" & "Zim"

This was the first time Reas & Mesh came to the M yard. Reas met Show, DG, Poes, Noe, Dek, Mag & Sept. Show put Reas & Mesh down with MSD crew and DG put them down with VAS Crew. I was lucky to have partnered up with Reas. He showed me alot. He is one of the best writers of our time! I`m also proud to be an original AOK member.

-Zim Aok

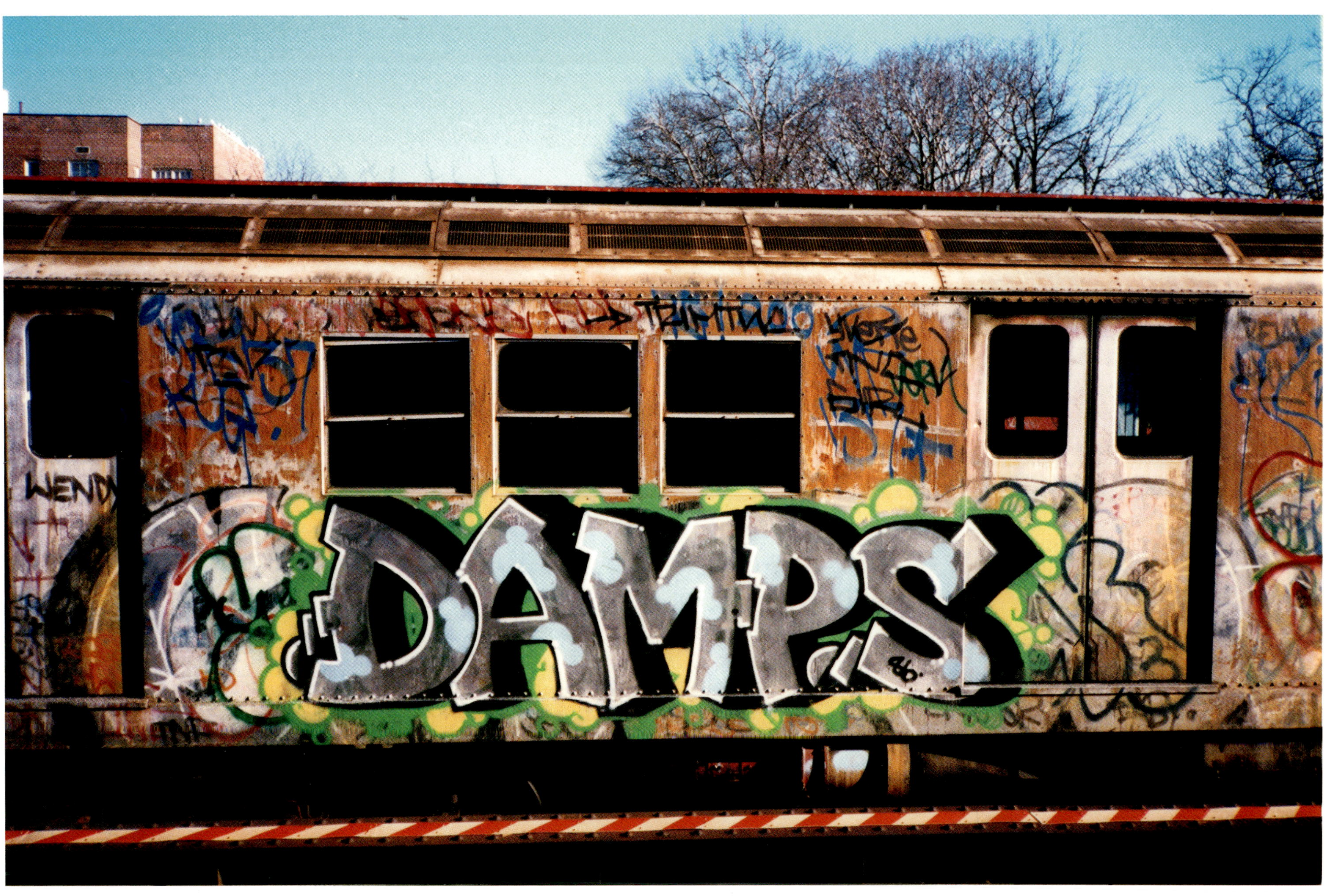

"Damps," by Sent

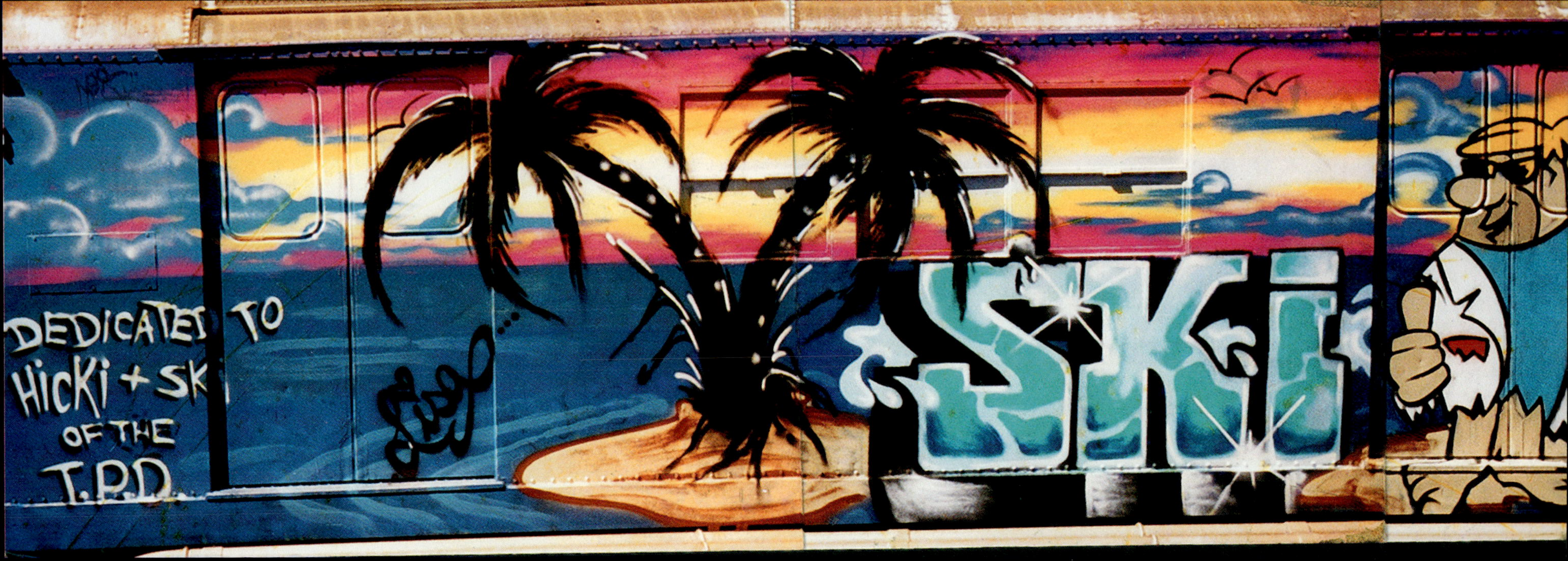

"Ski & Hicki," by Seen, 1986

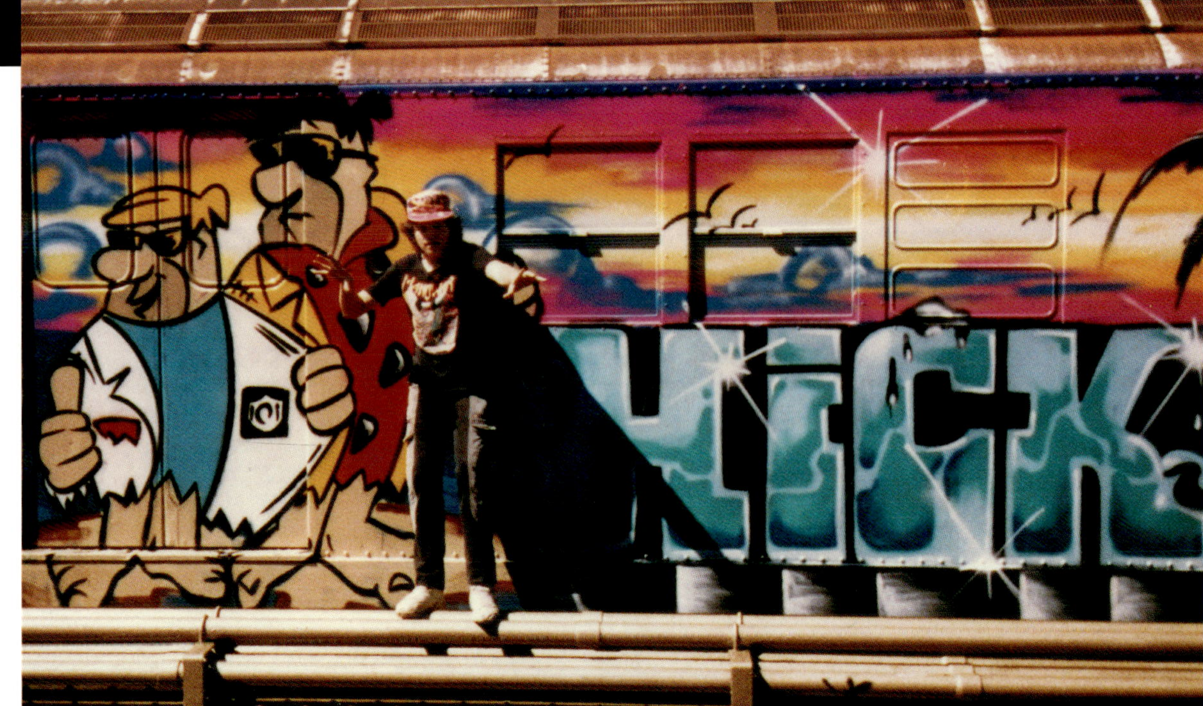

Cav at Zerega Ave Train Station

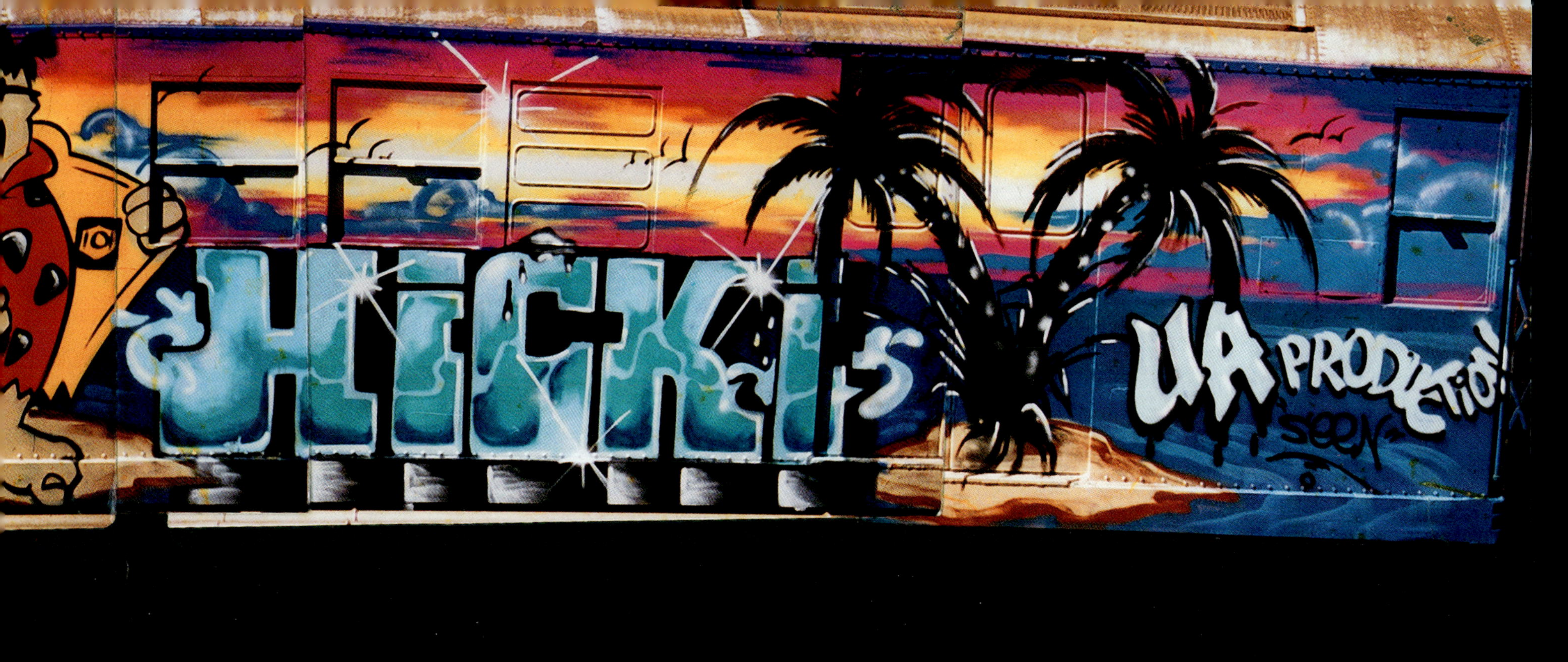
UA PRODUCTION
SEEN

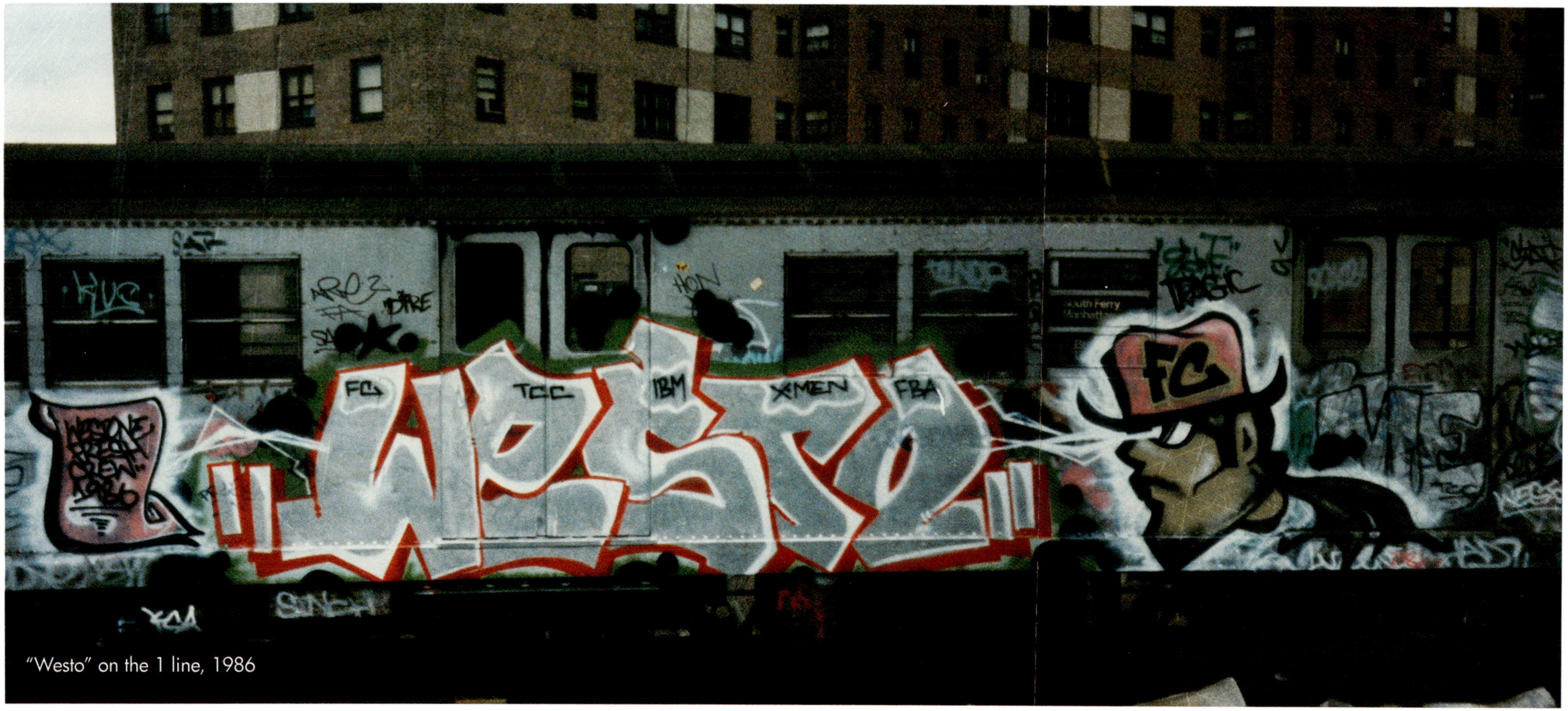

"Westo" on the 1 line, 1986

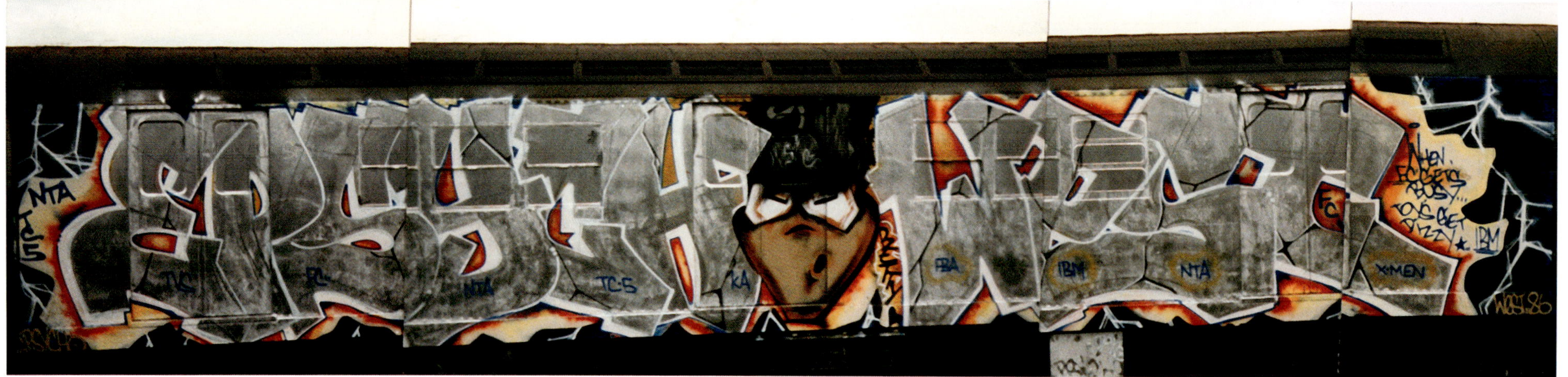

"Epsycho" & "West"

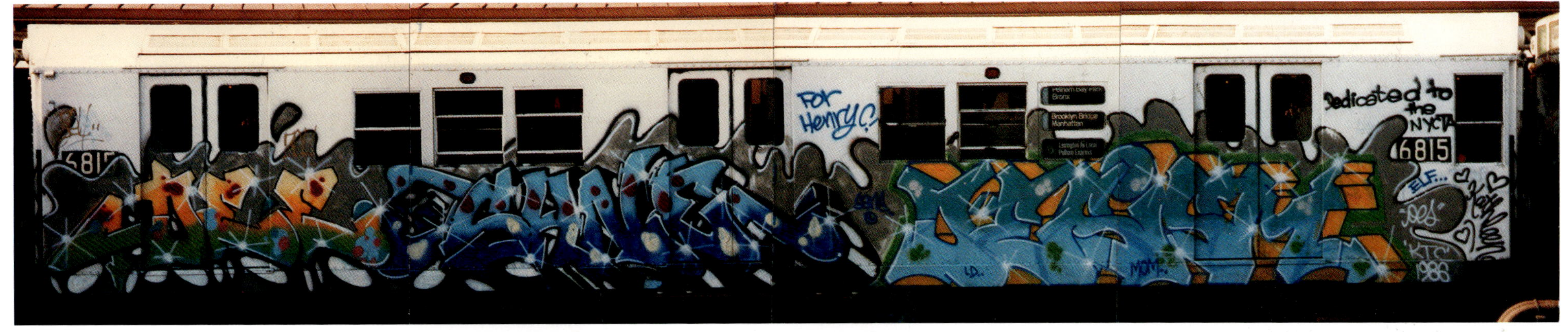

"Dee," "Sane" & "Desism"

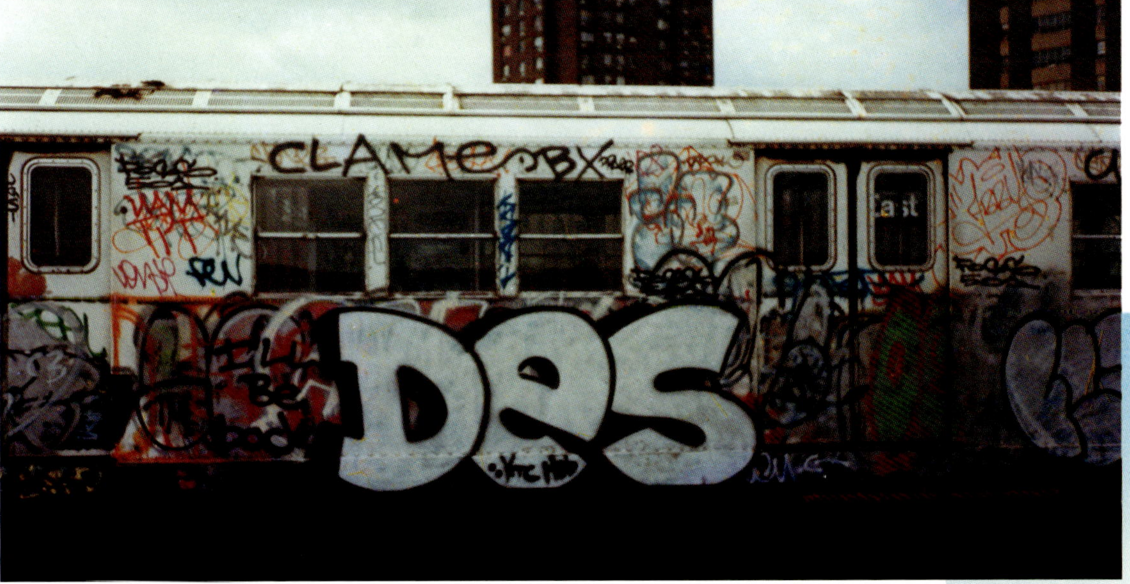

"Des"

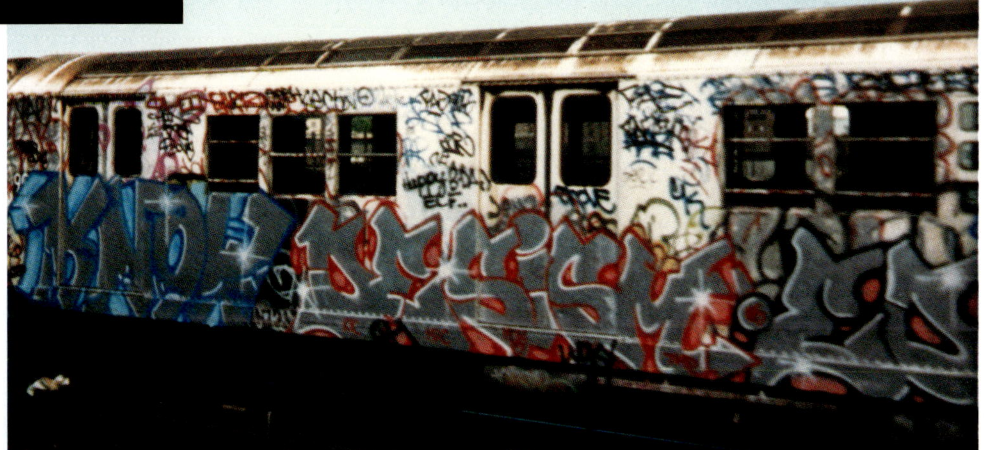

"Know," "Desism" & "Ed" (RIP)

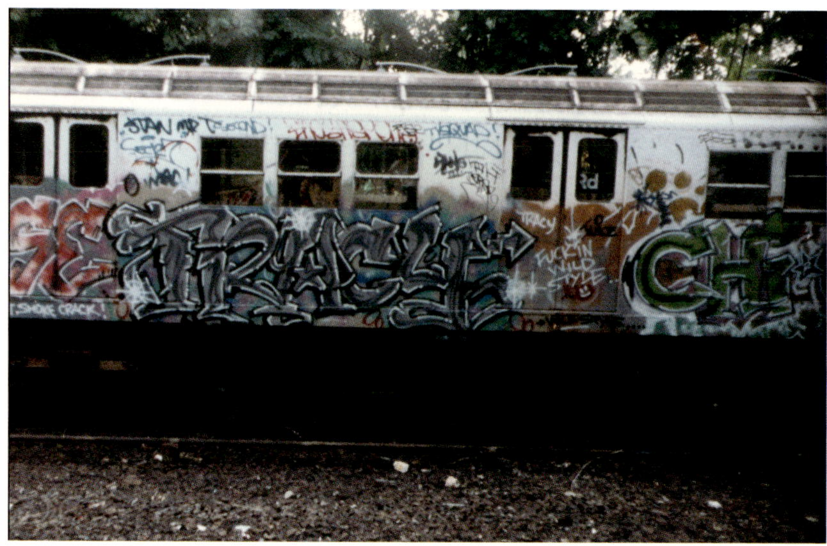

"Tracy168"

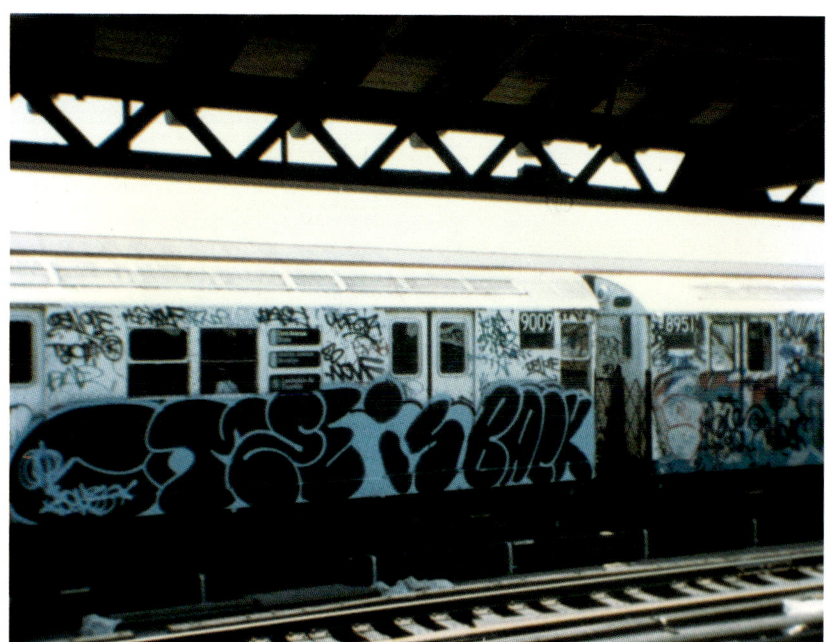

"Comet is Back"

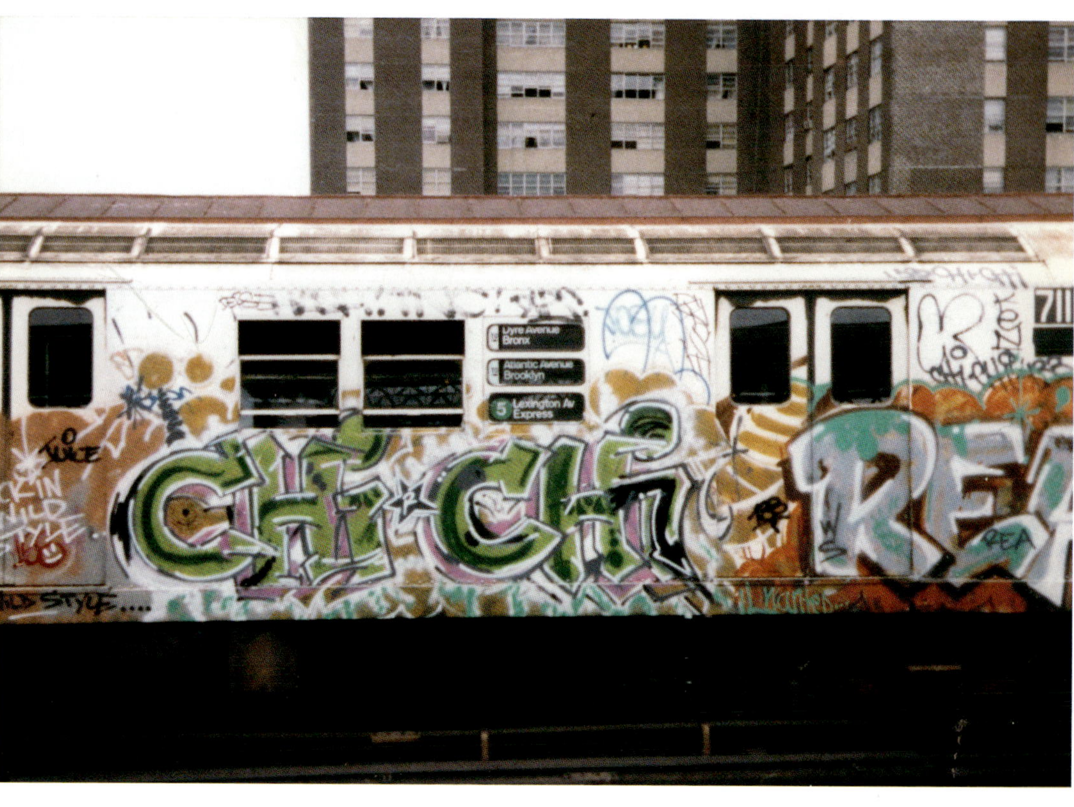

"Chi-Chi"

"Comet," 1986

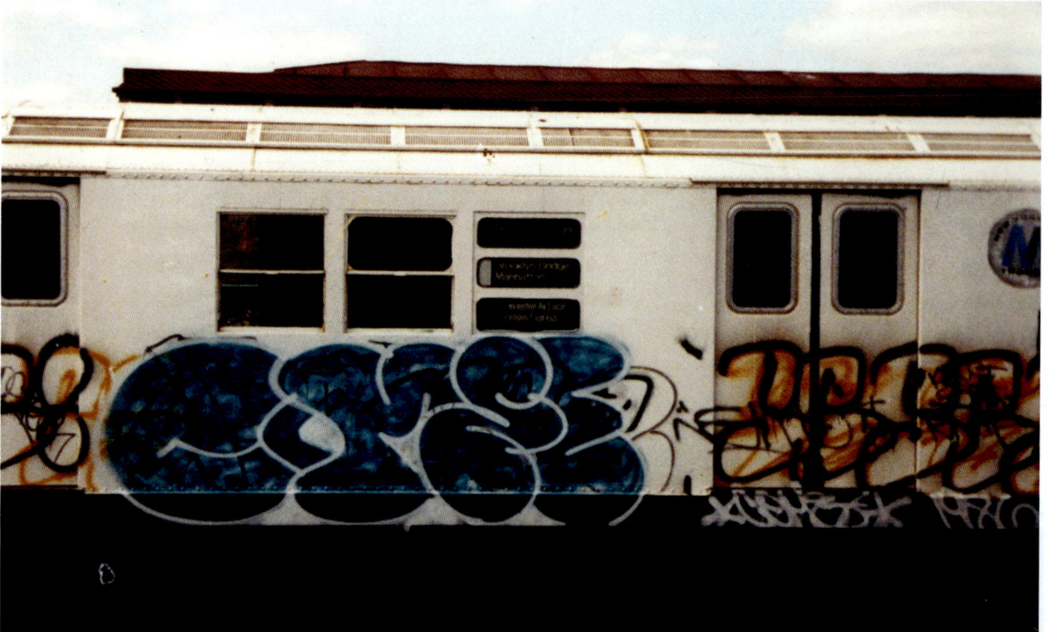

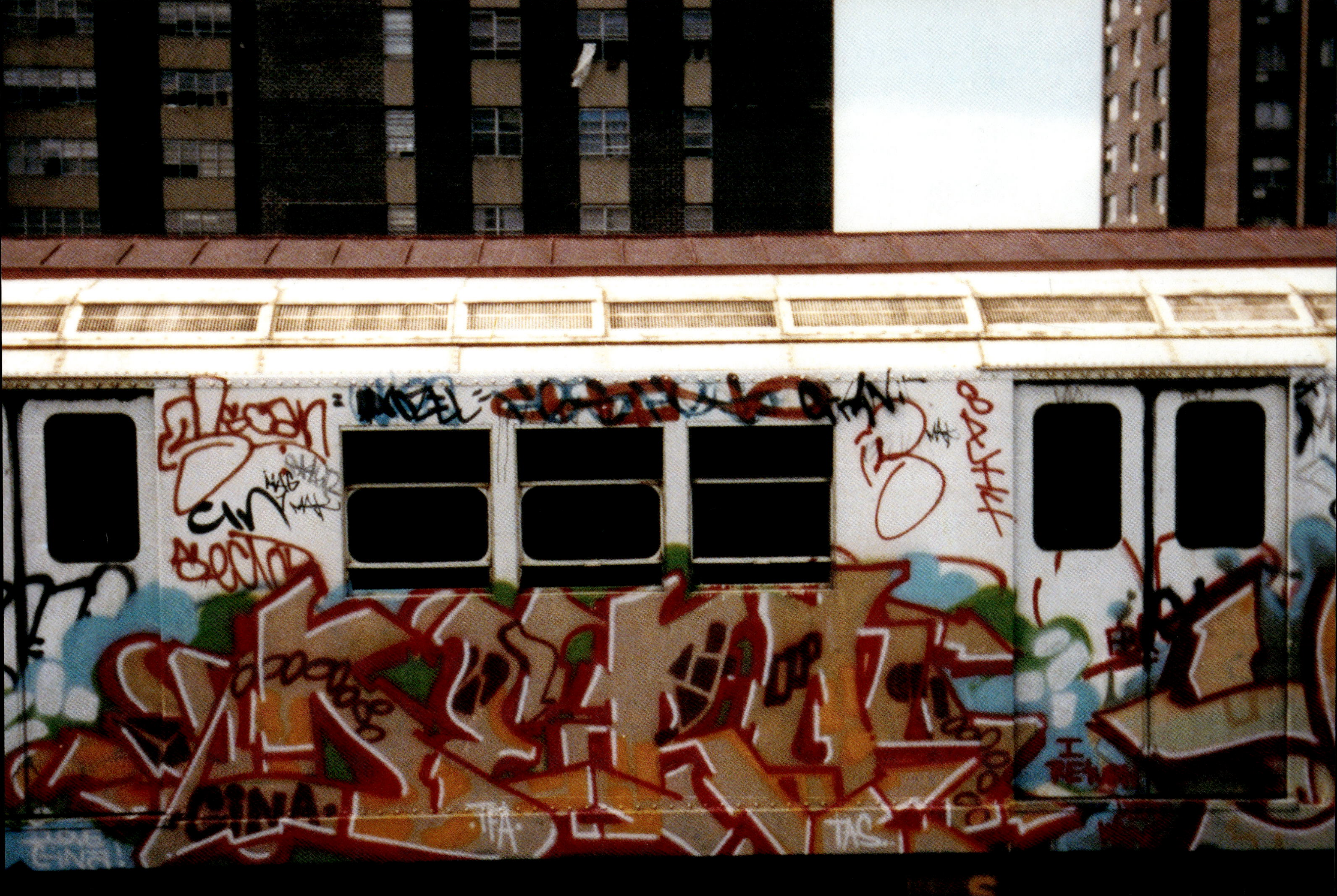
CINA.
TFA
TAS.

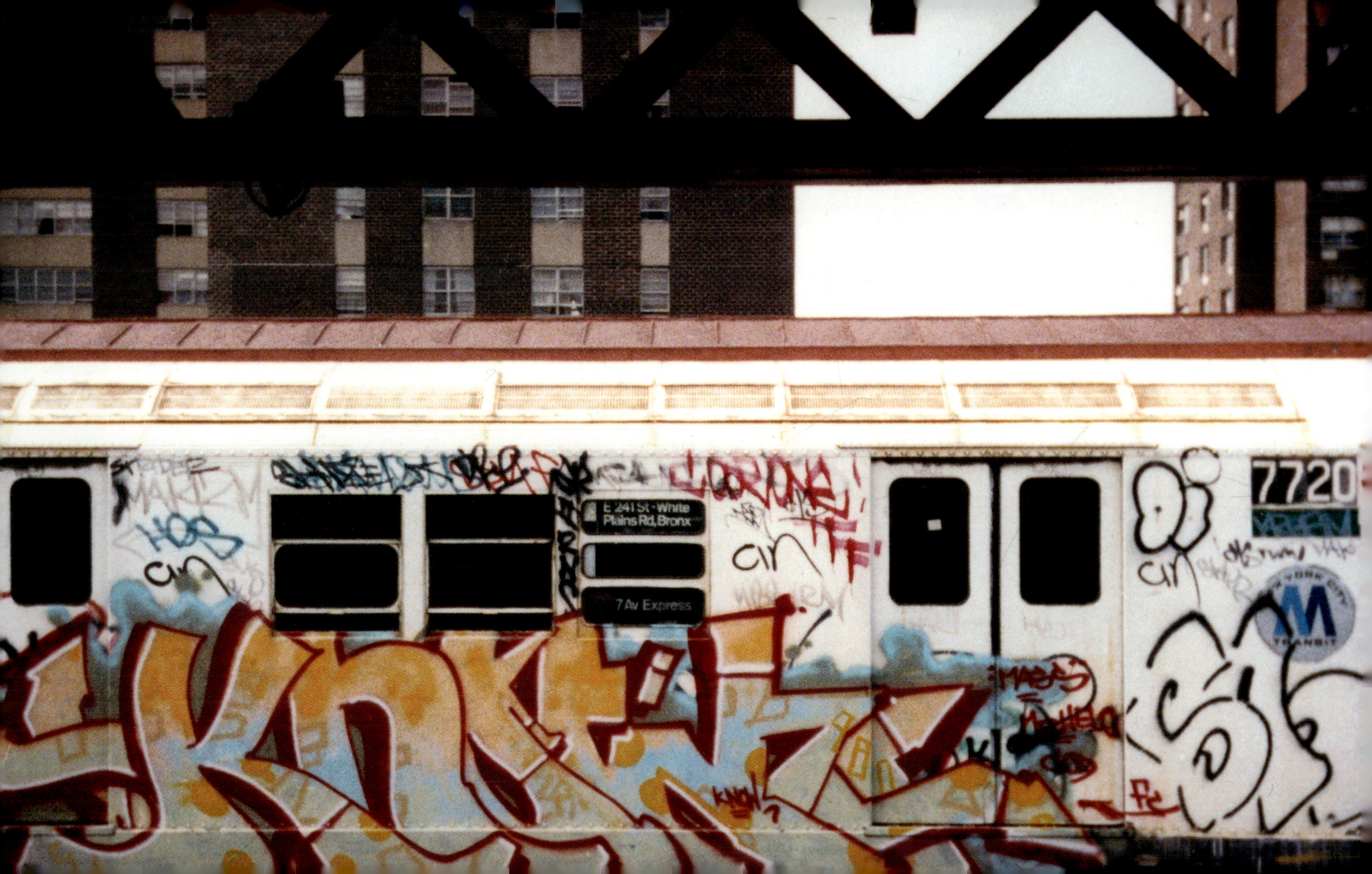
7720
E 241 St - White
Plains Rd, Bronx
7 Av Express

"Him" & "Nine"

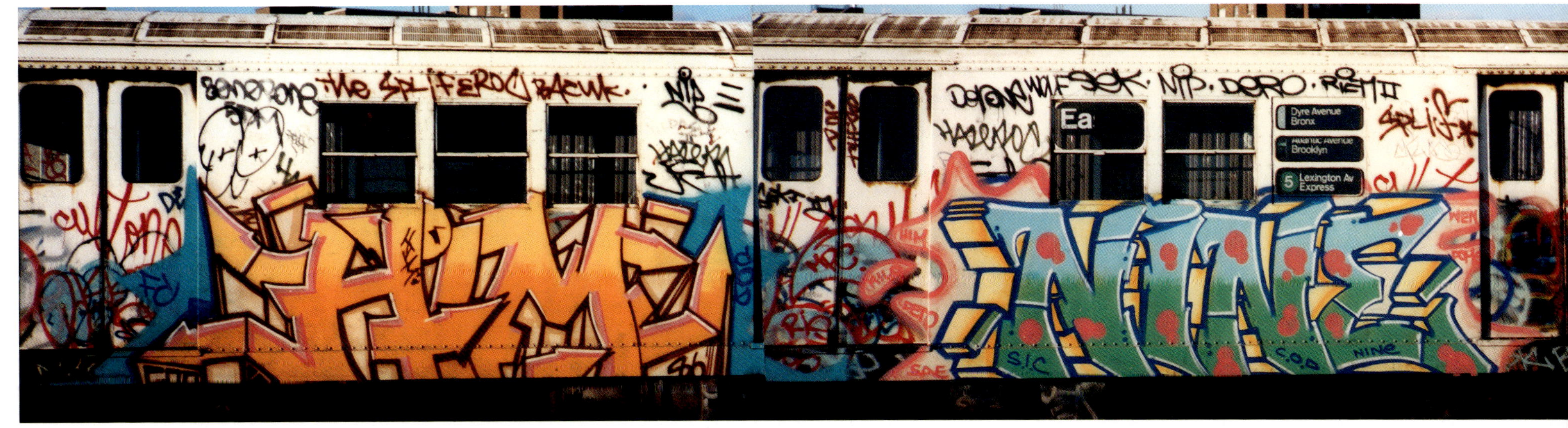

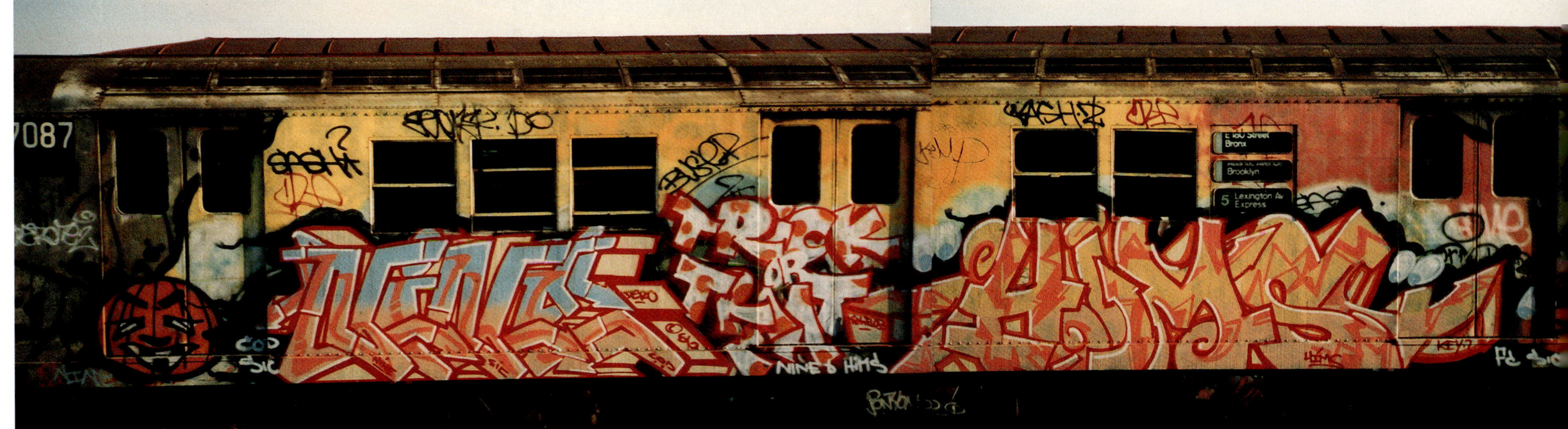

"Nine" & "Hims"

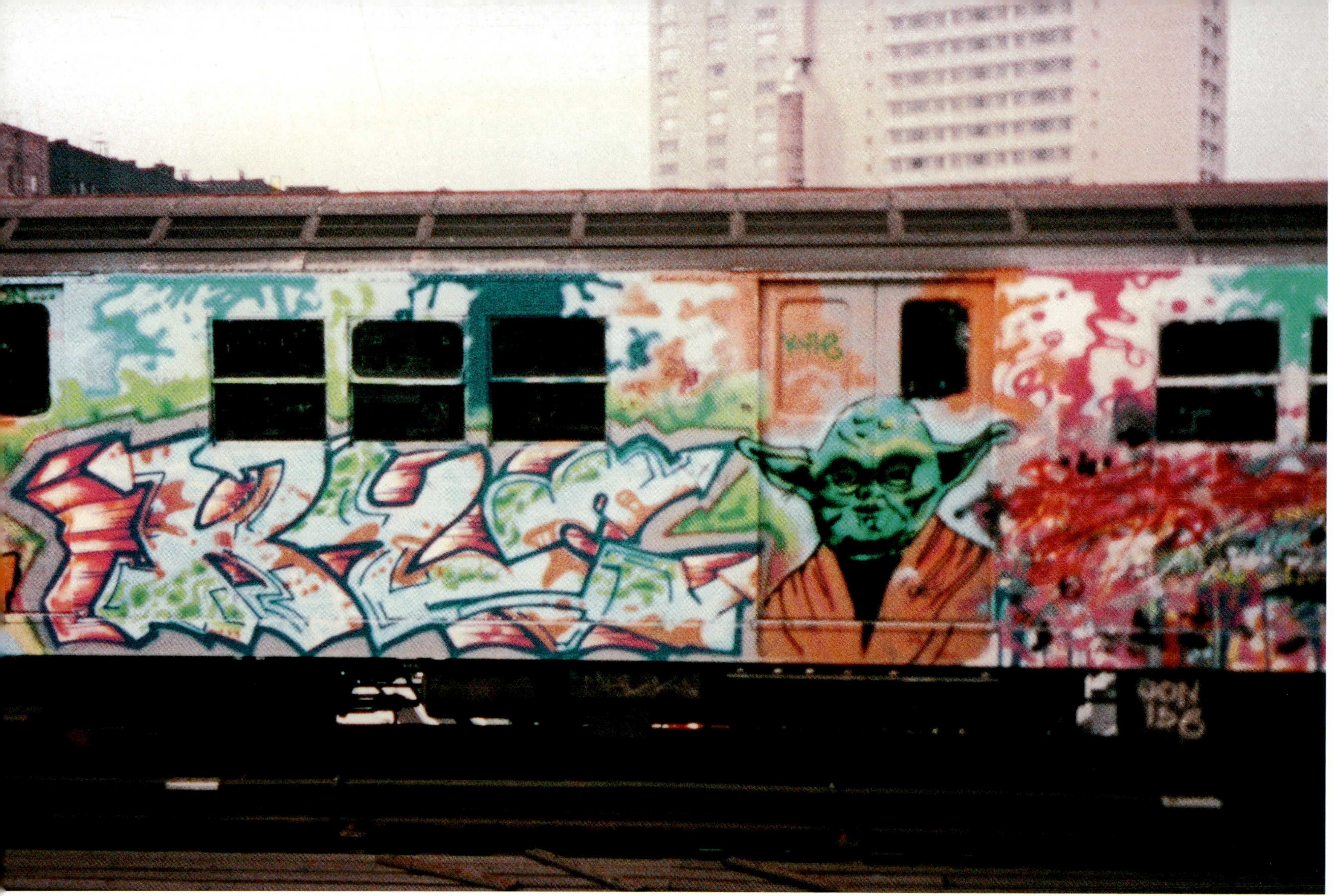

"Kyle"

148 St-Lenox
Term, Manhattan
New Lots Avenue
Brooklyn
3 7 Av Express
Jonone
Liz

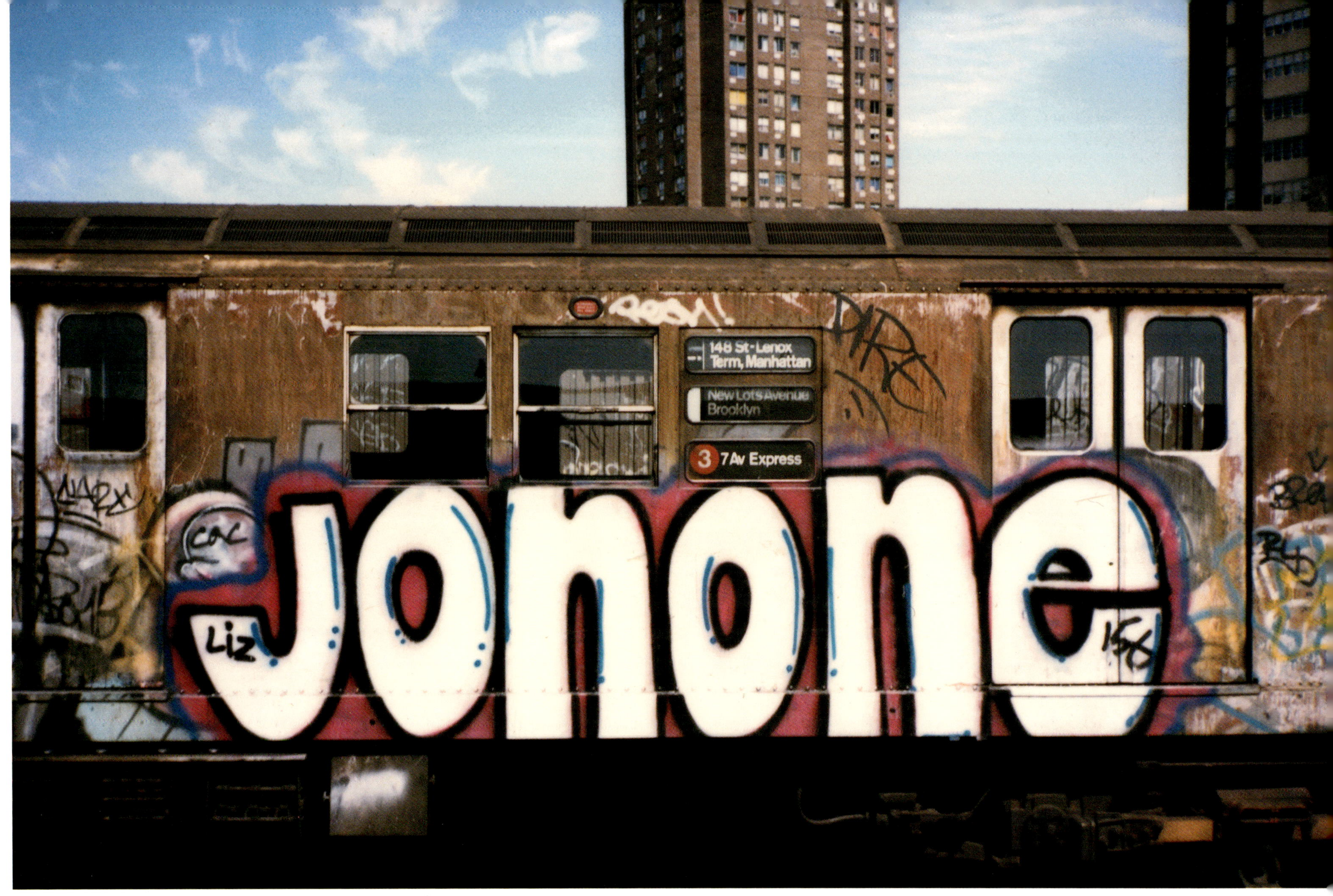

"Jon-one"

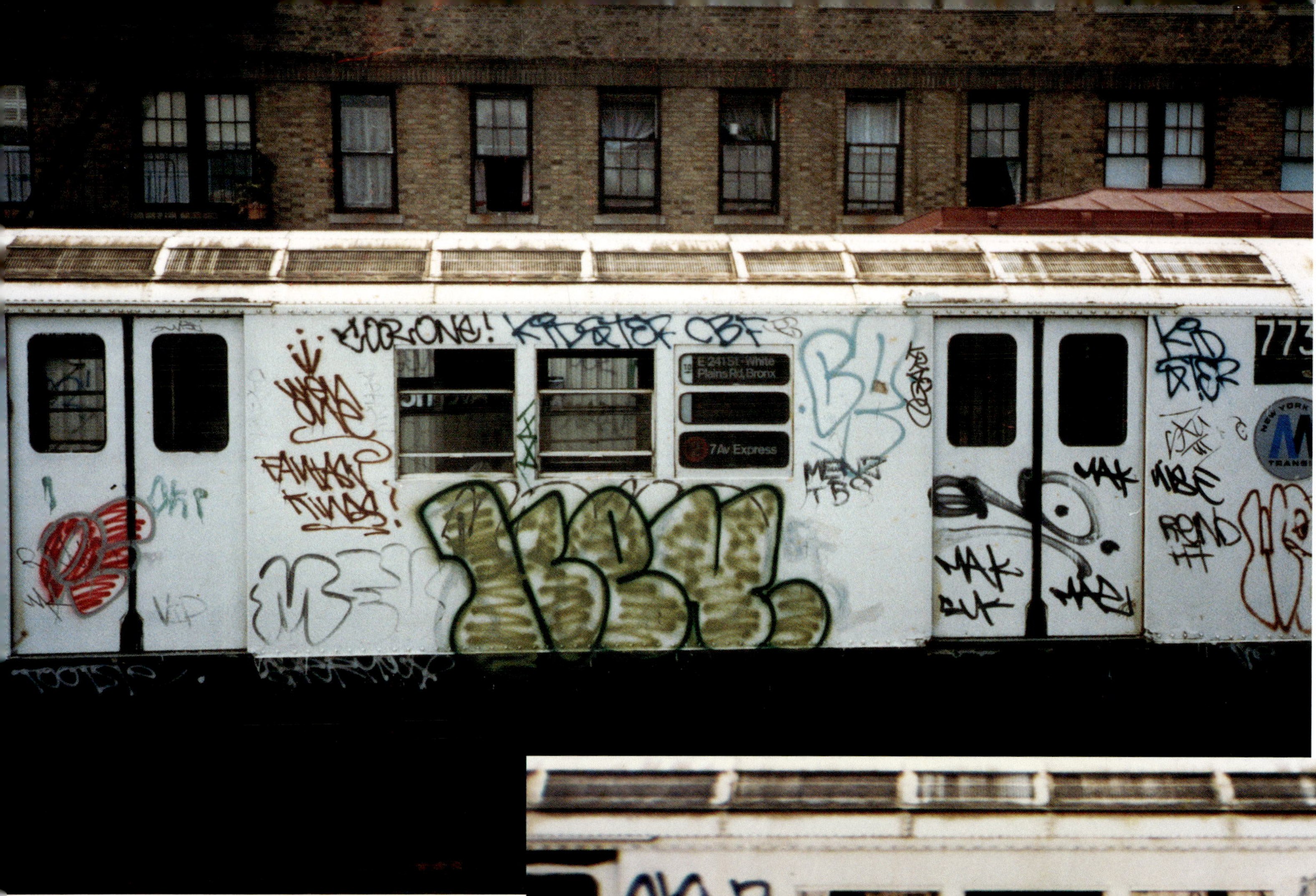

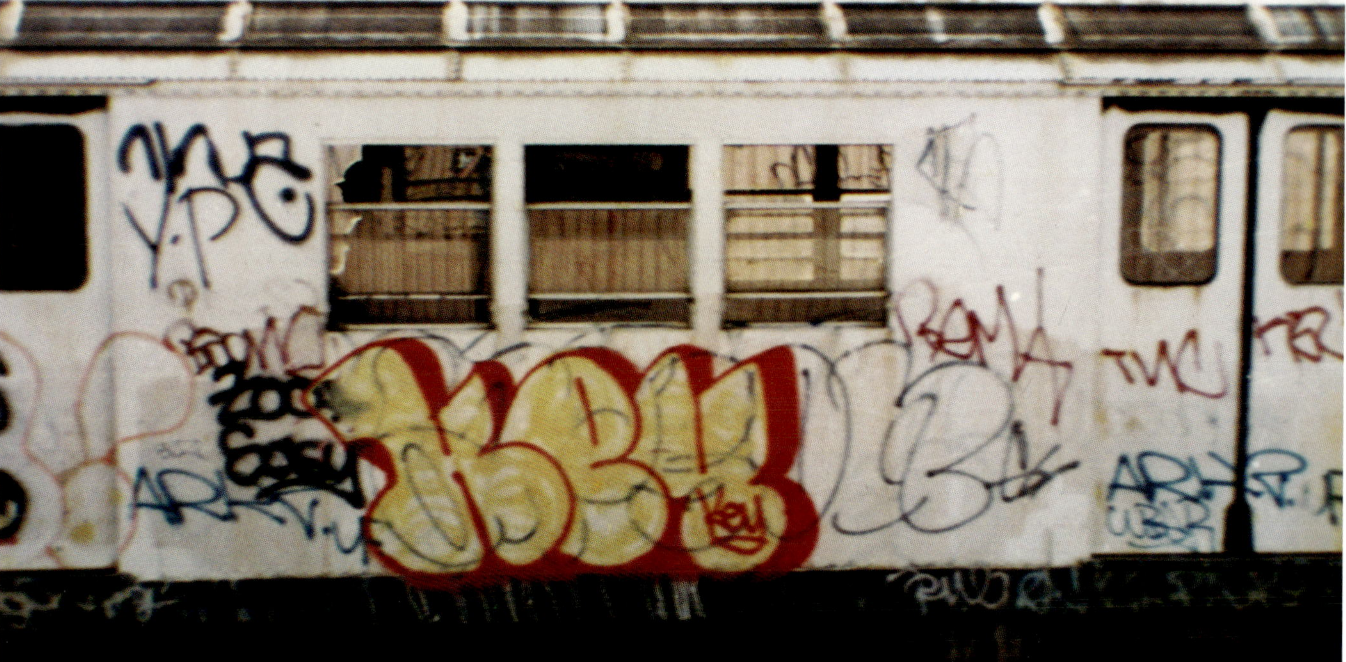

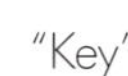

"Key"

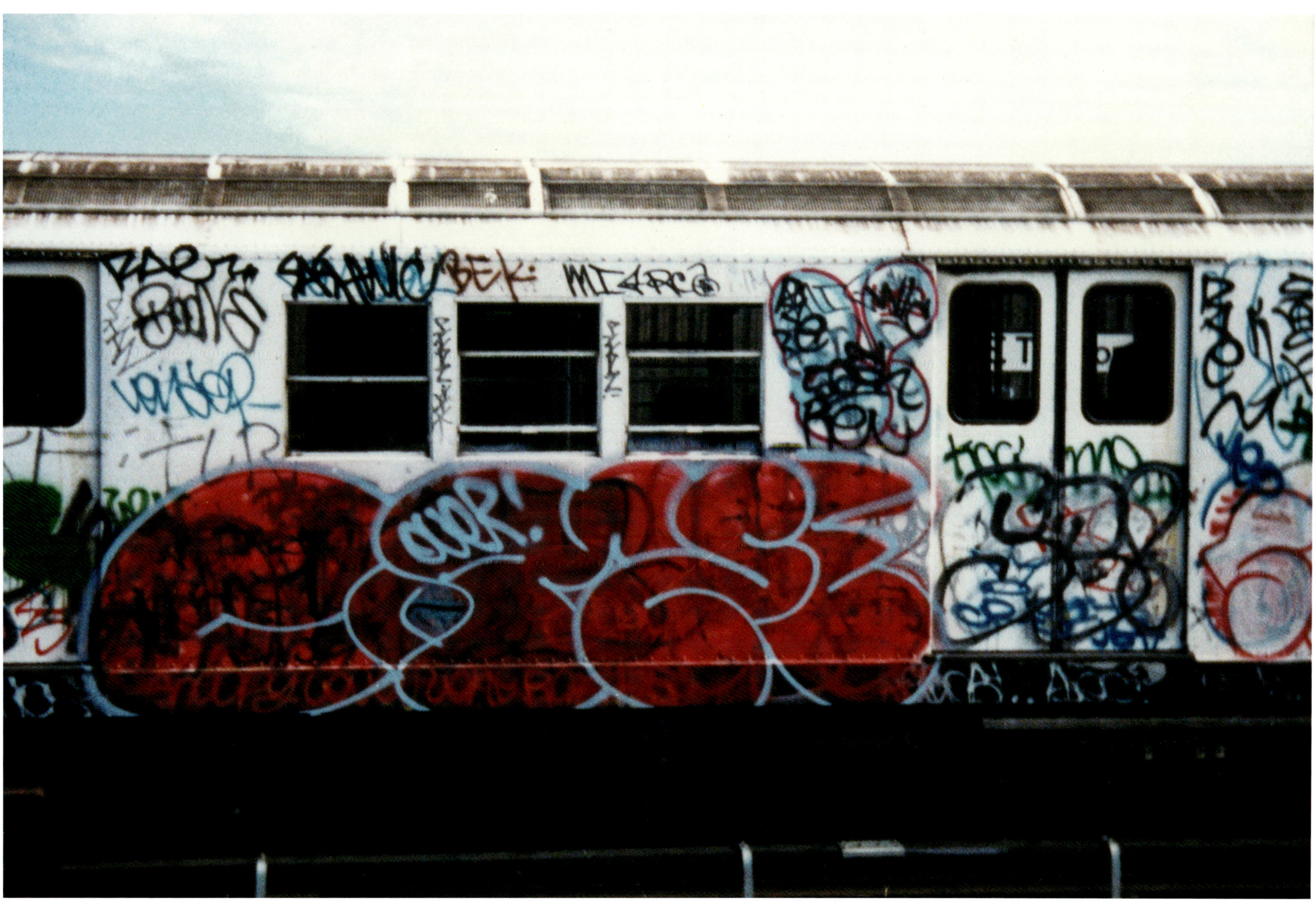

"Comet"

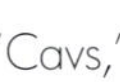

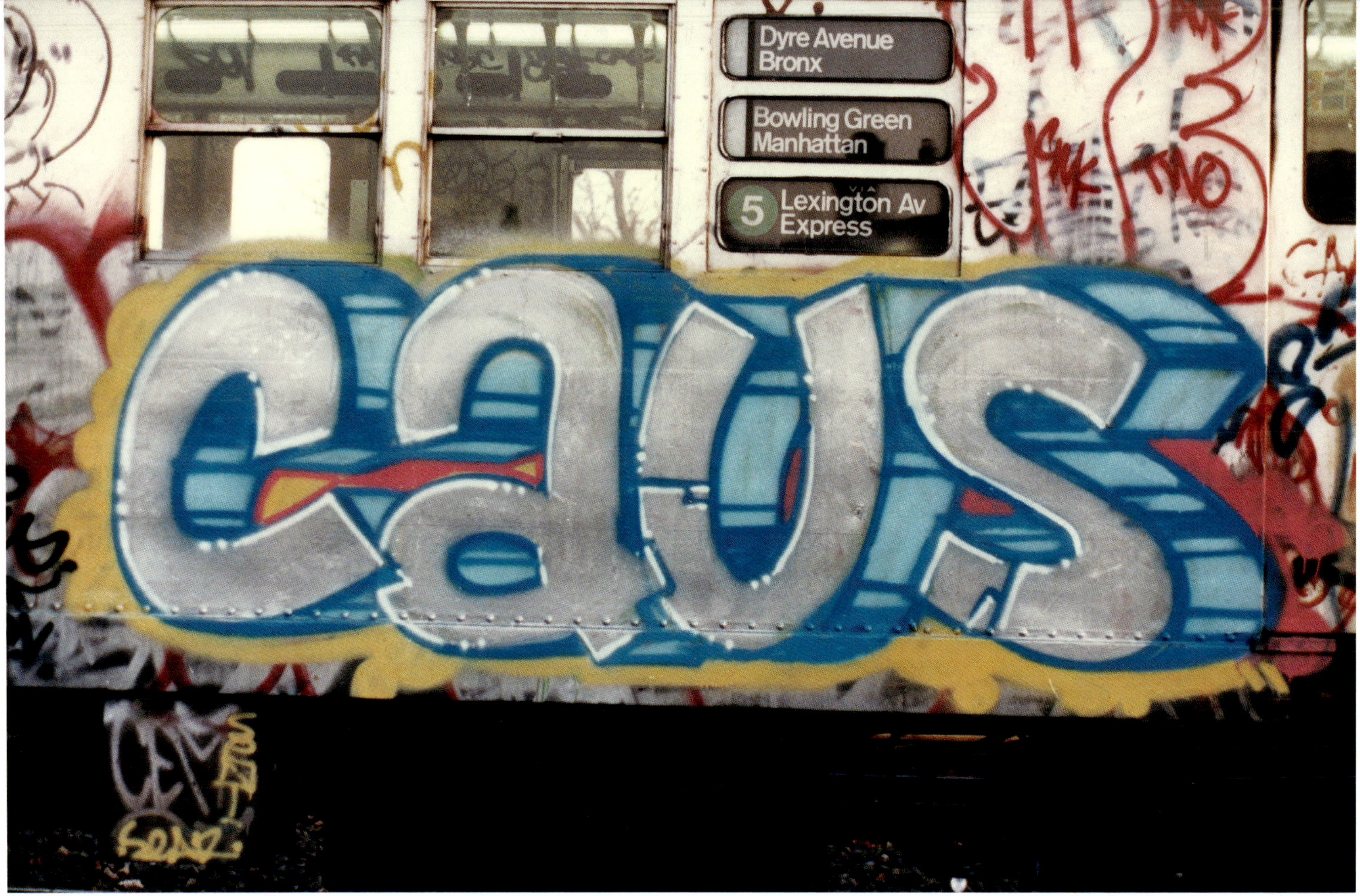

"Cavs,"

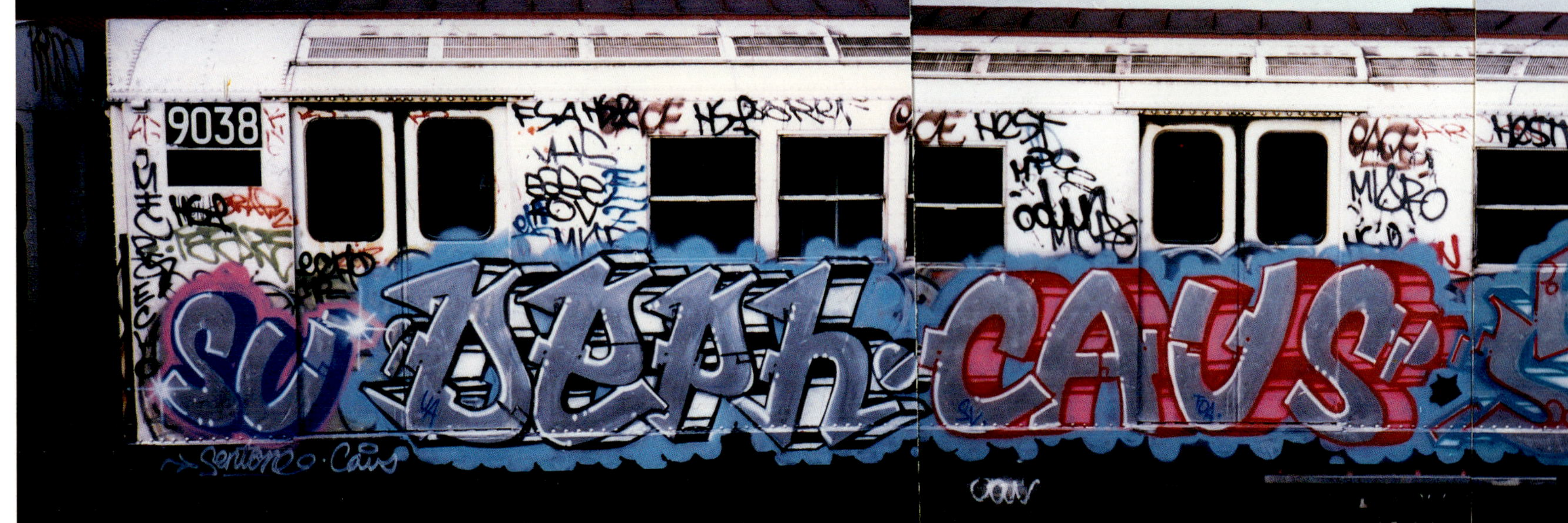

"Deph," "Cavs" & "Sent"

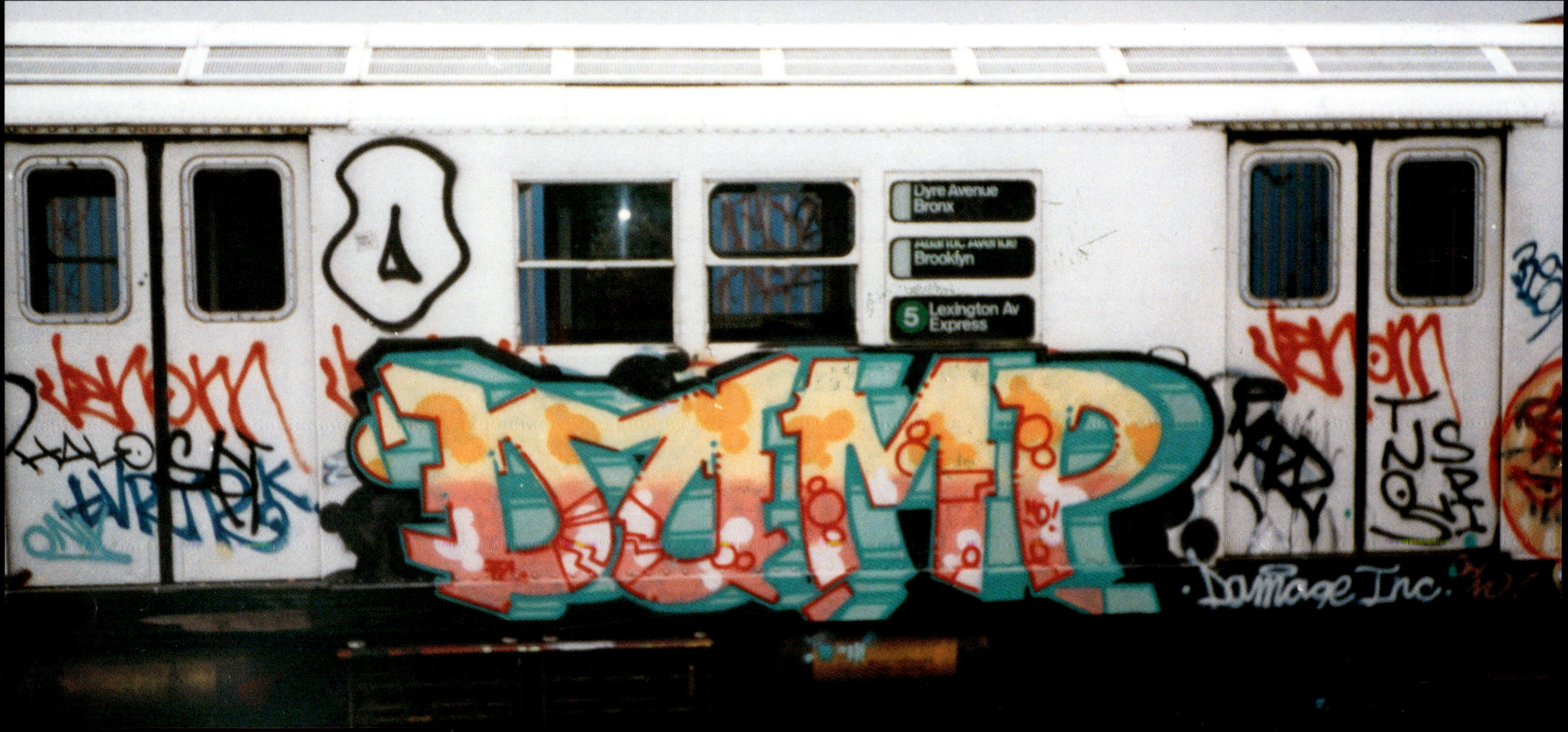

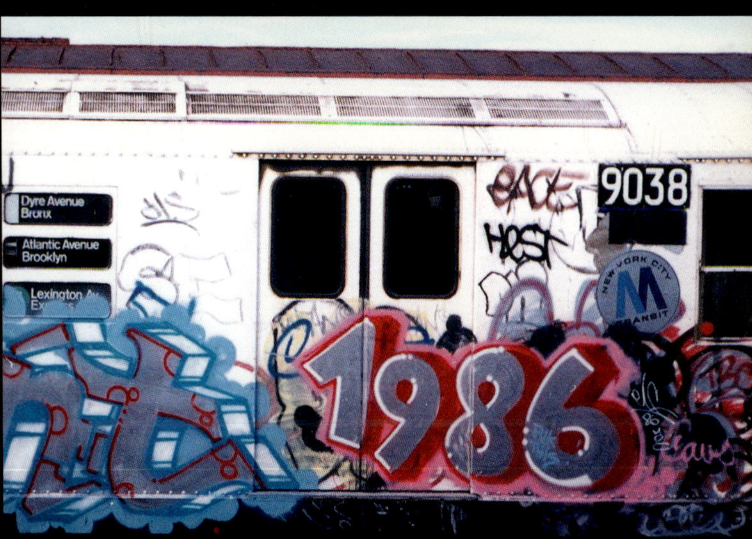

"Damp"

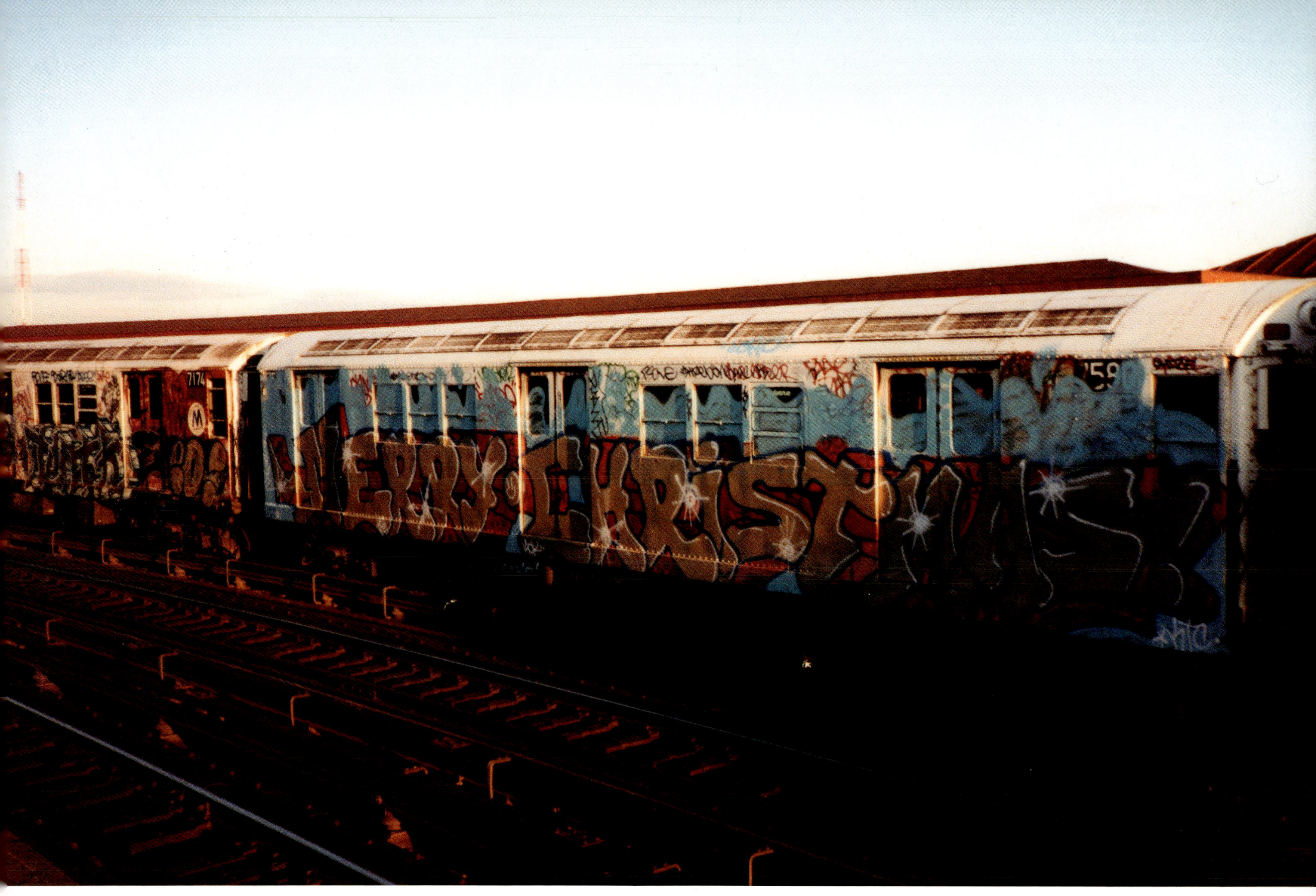

"Merry Christmas," by Echo

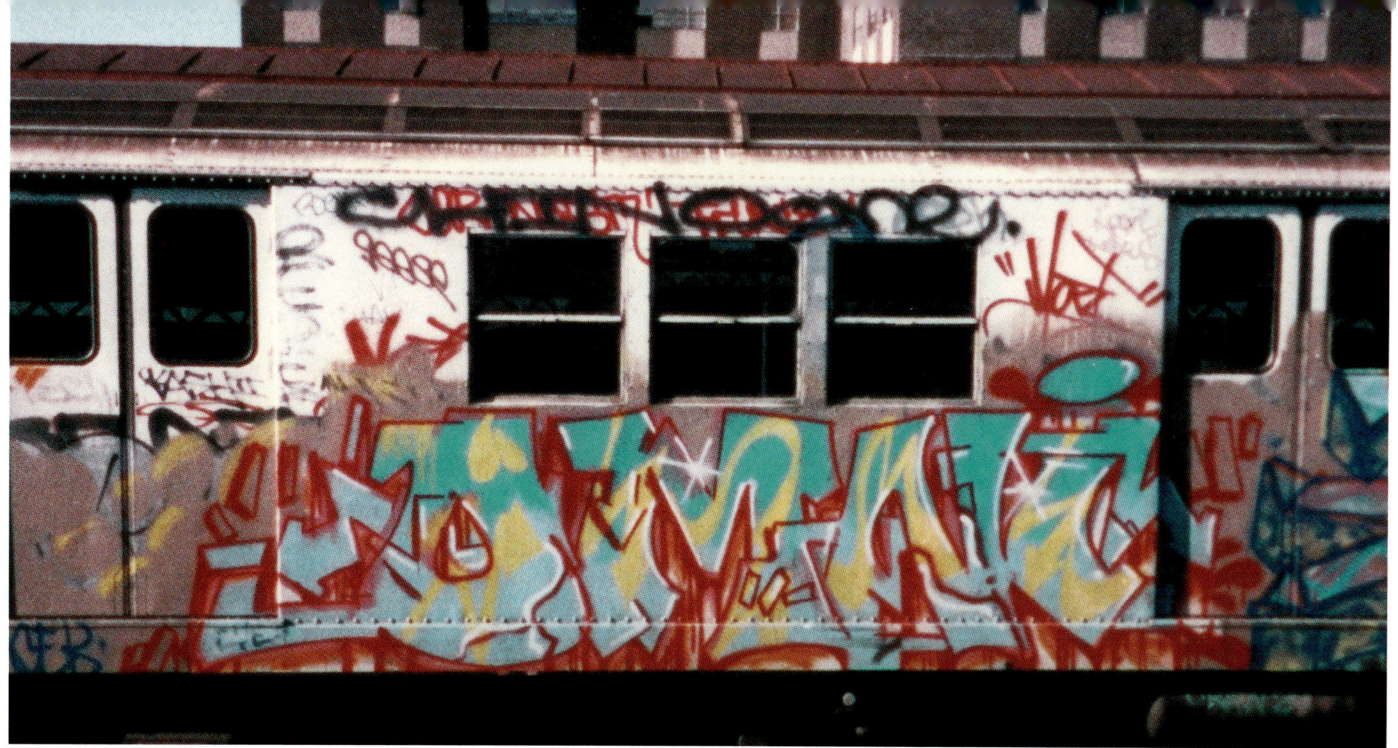

"Omni"

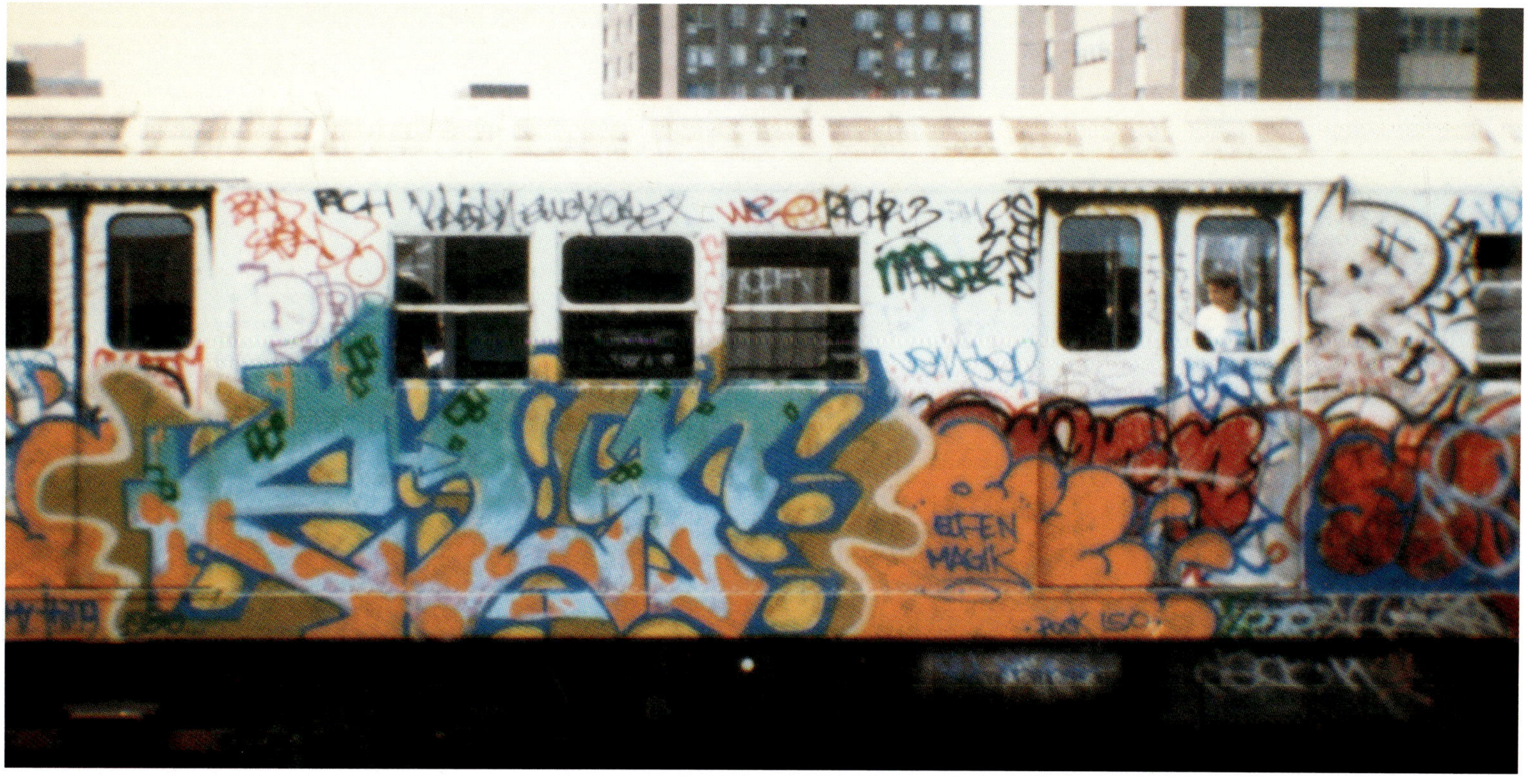

"Elf" (RIP)

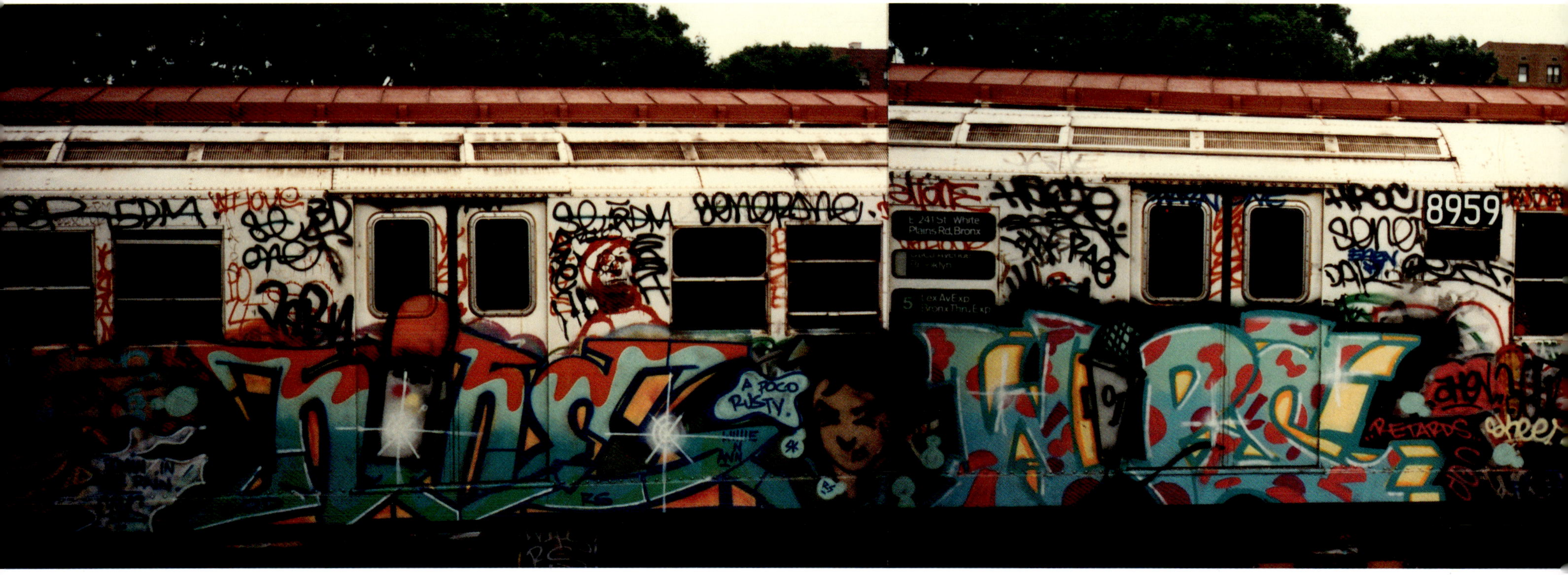

"Nine" & "Wips"

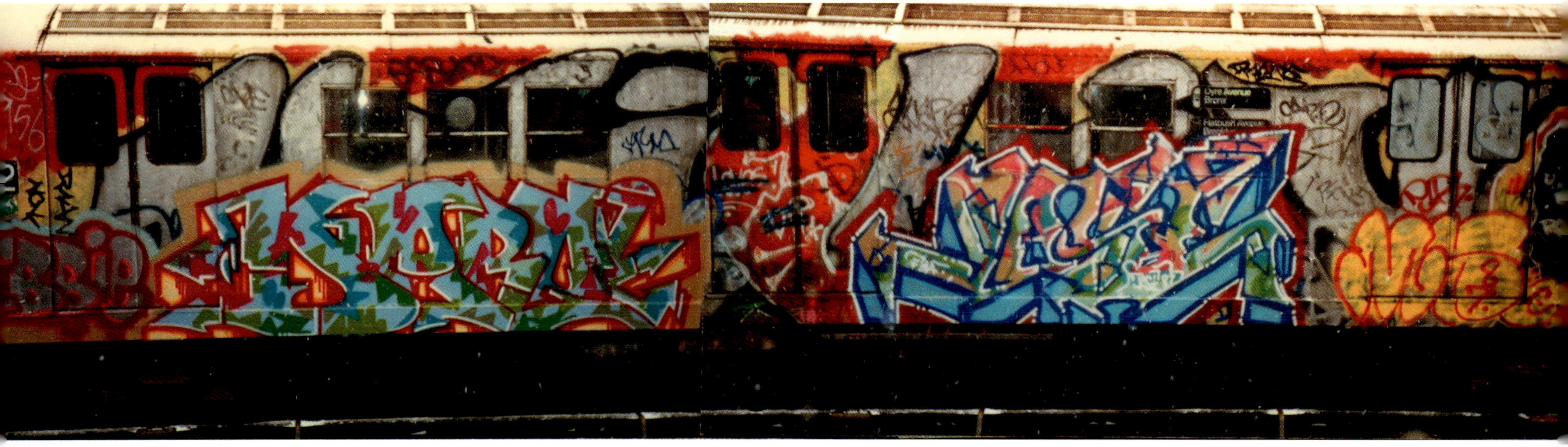

"Dero" & "Jase"

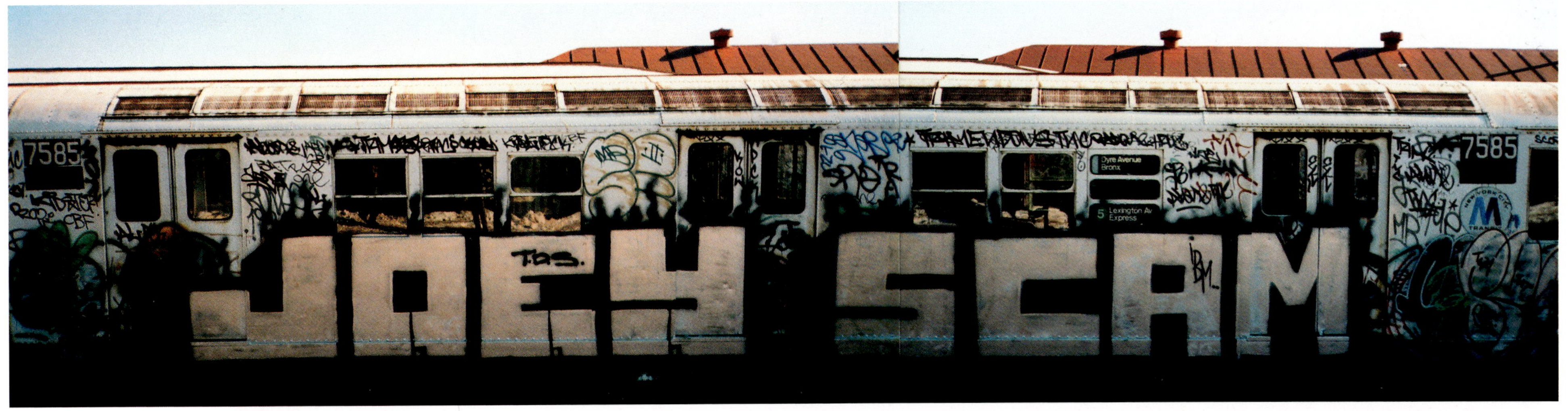

"Joey" & "Scam"

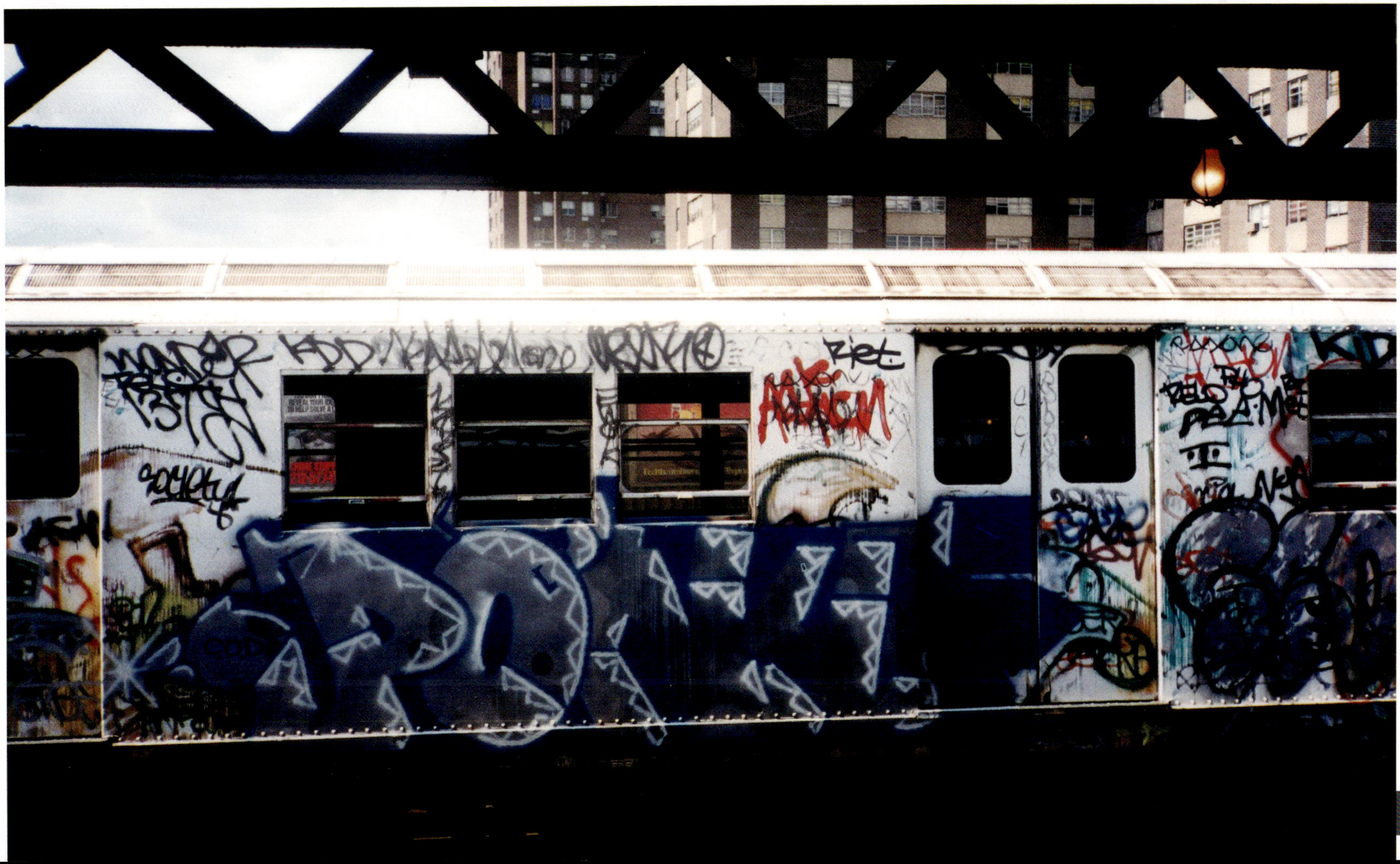

"Pony"

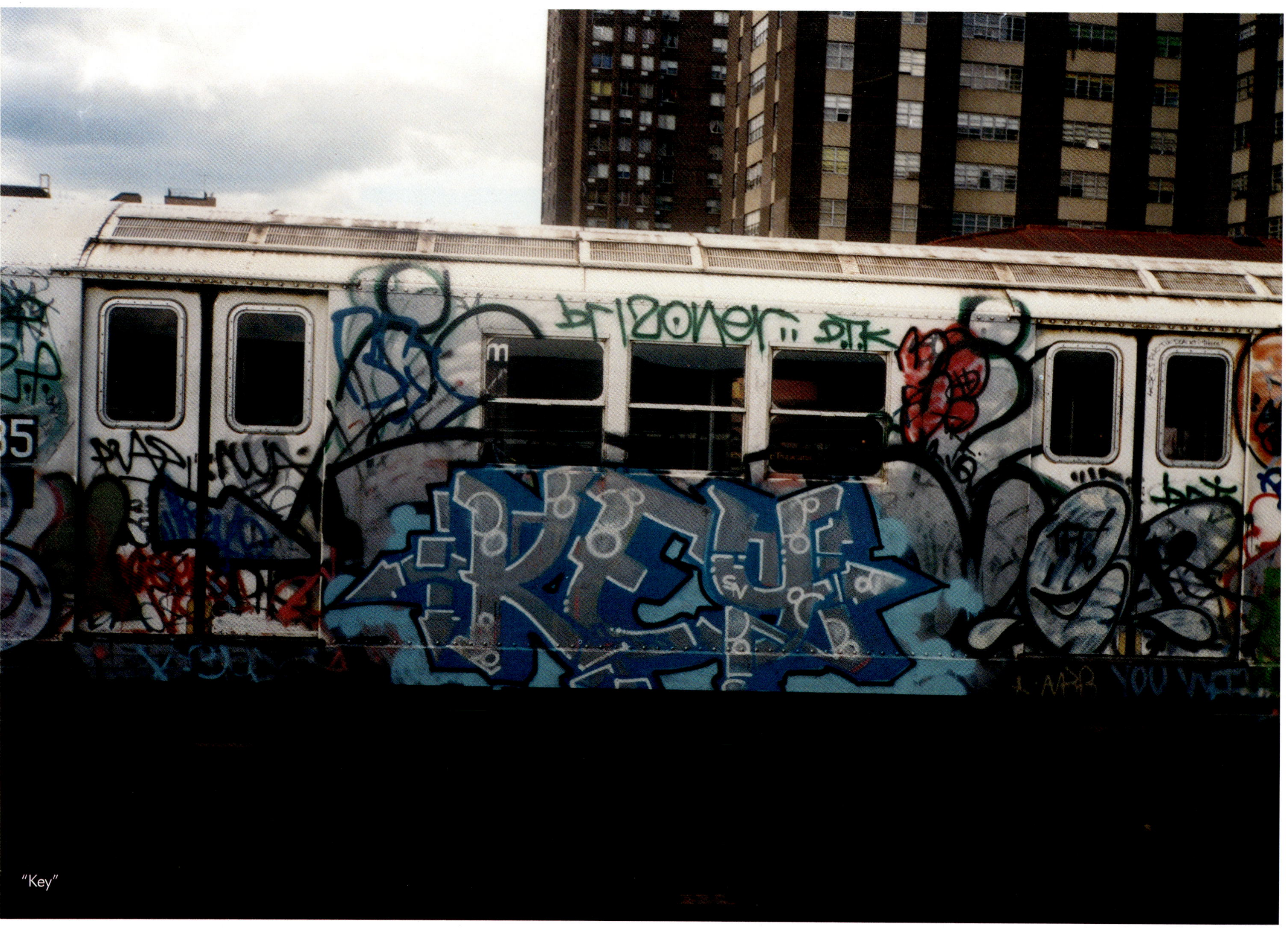

"Key"

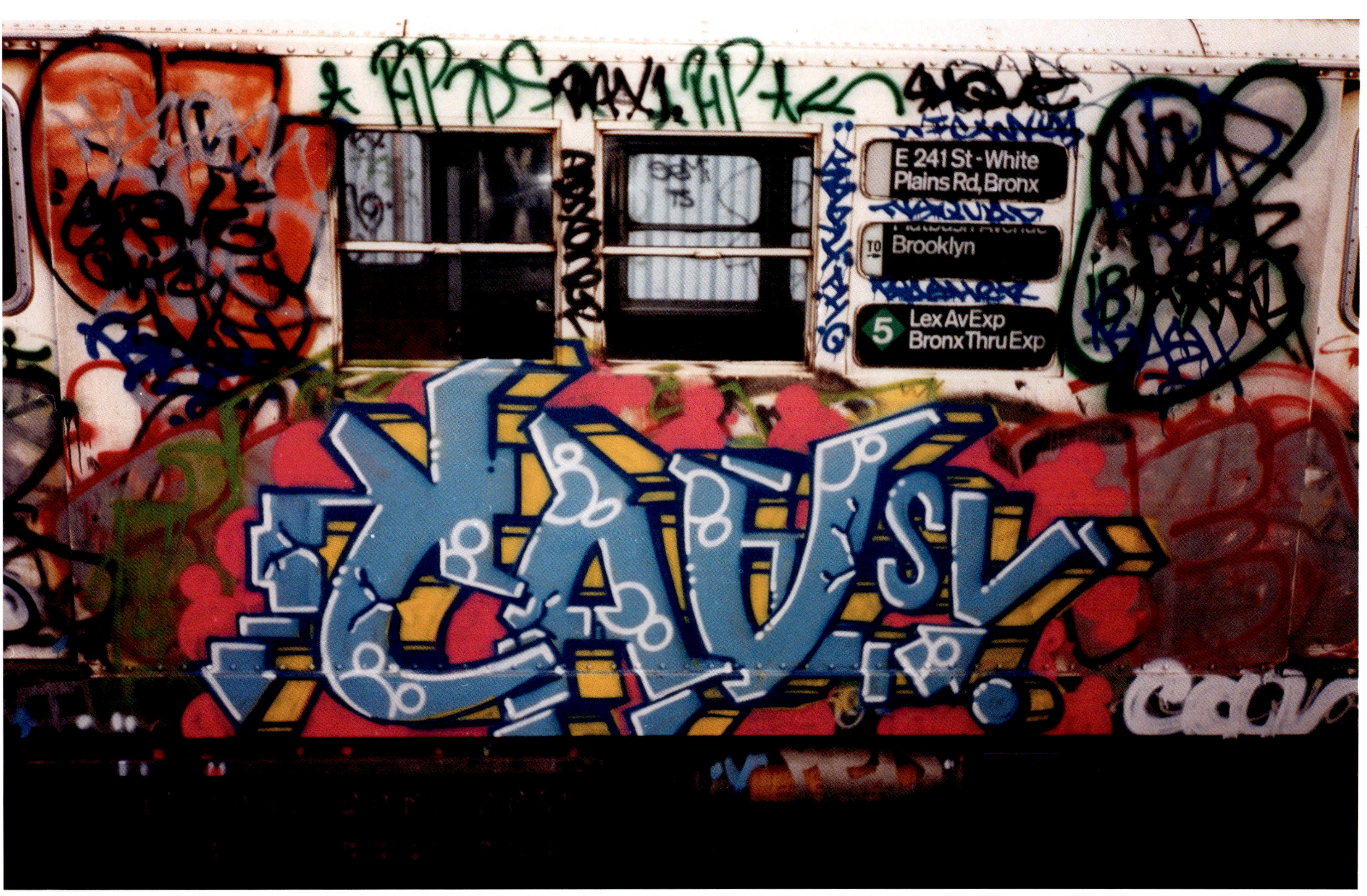

"Cav," by Sento, 1987

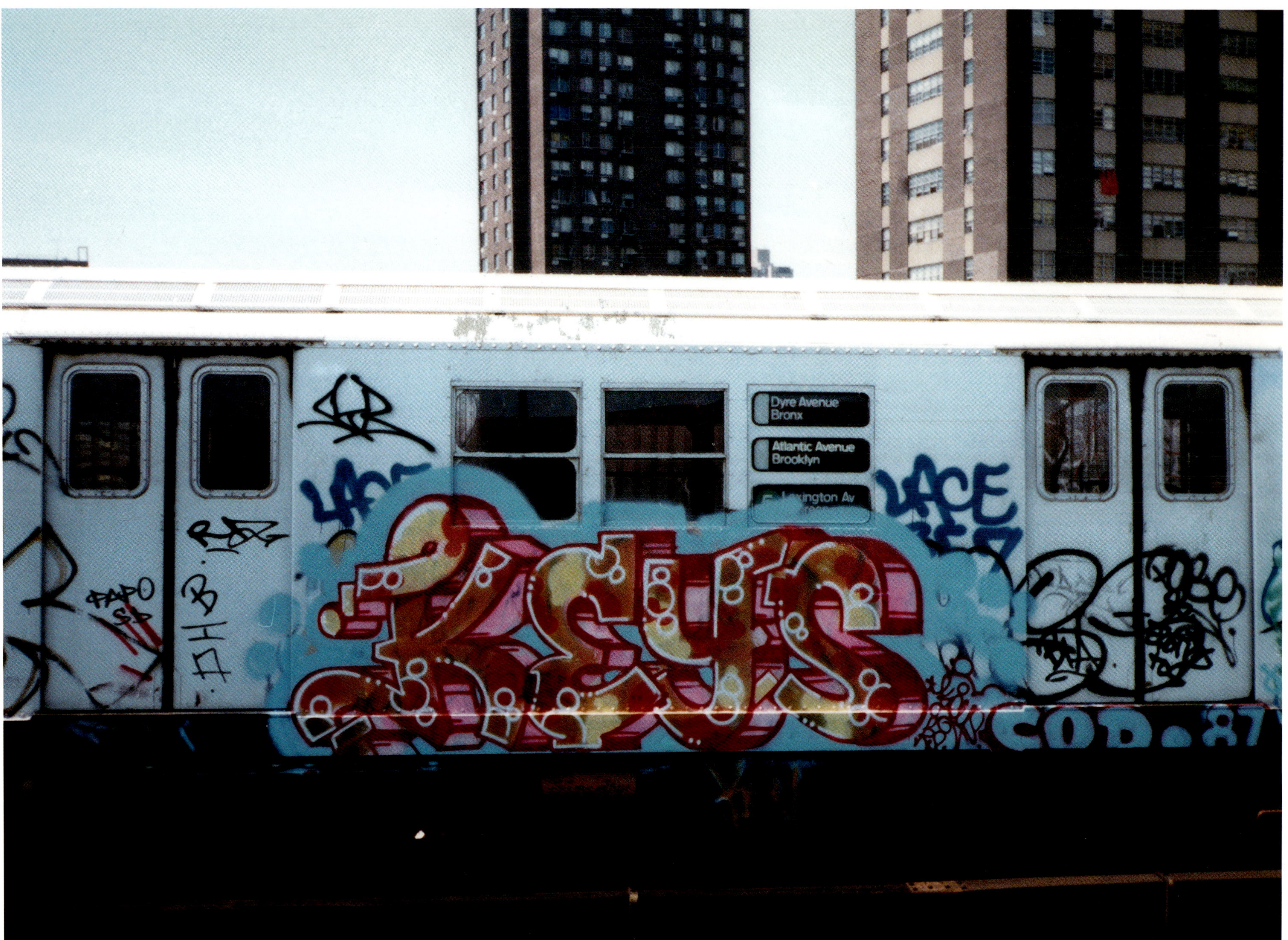

"Keys"

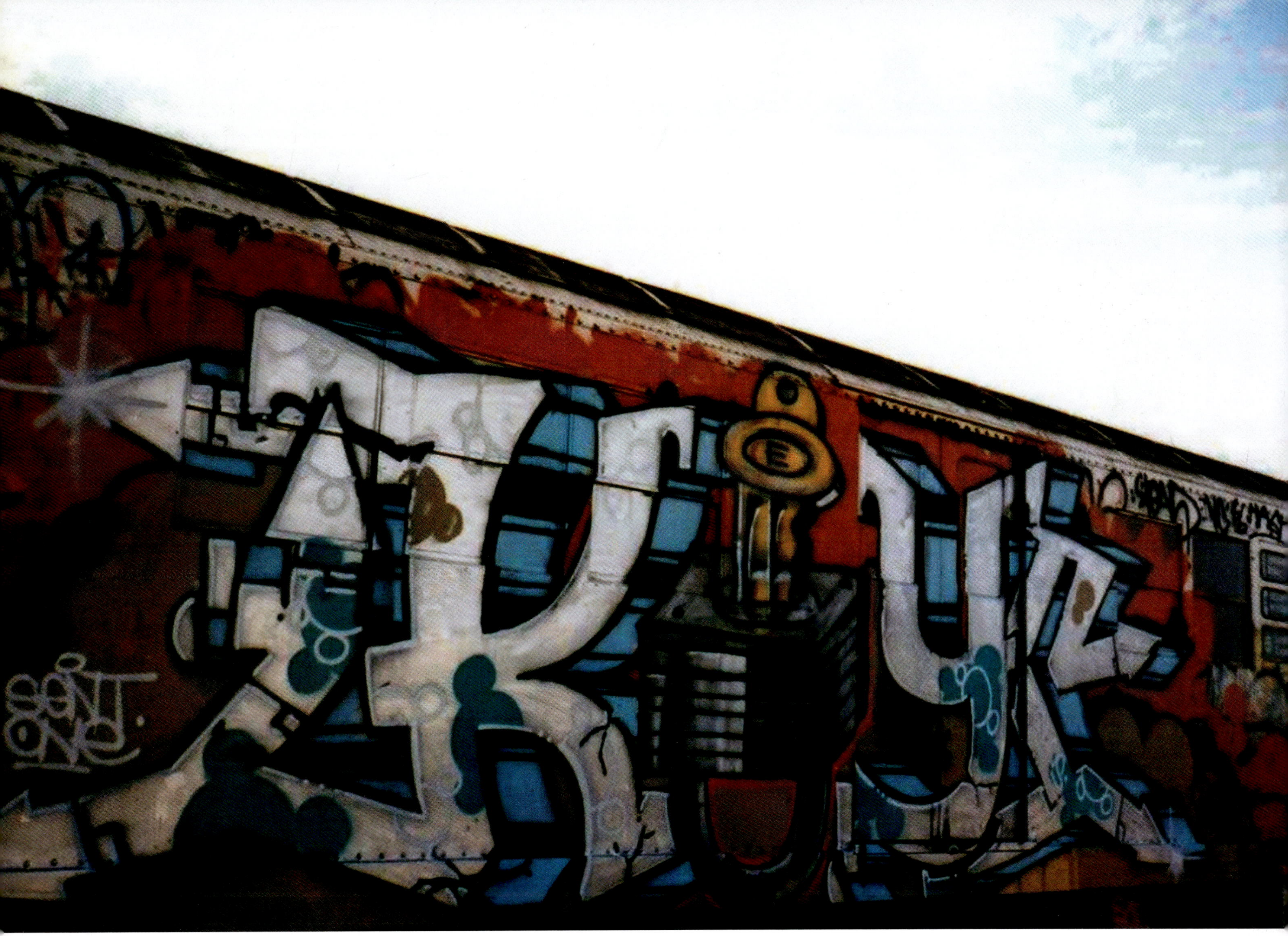

"Key"

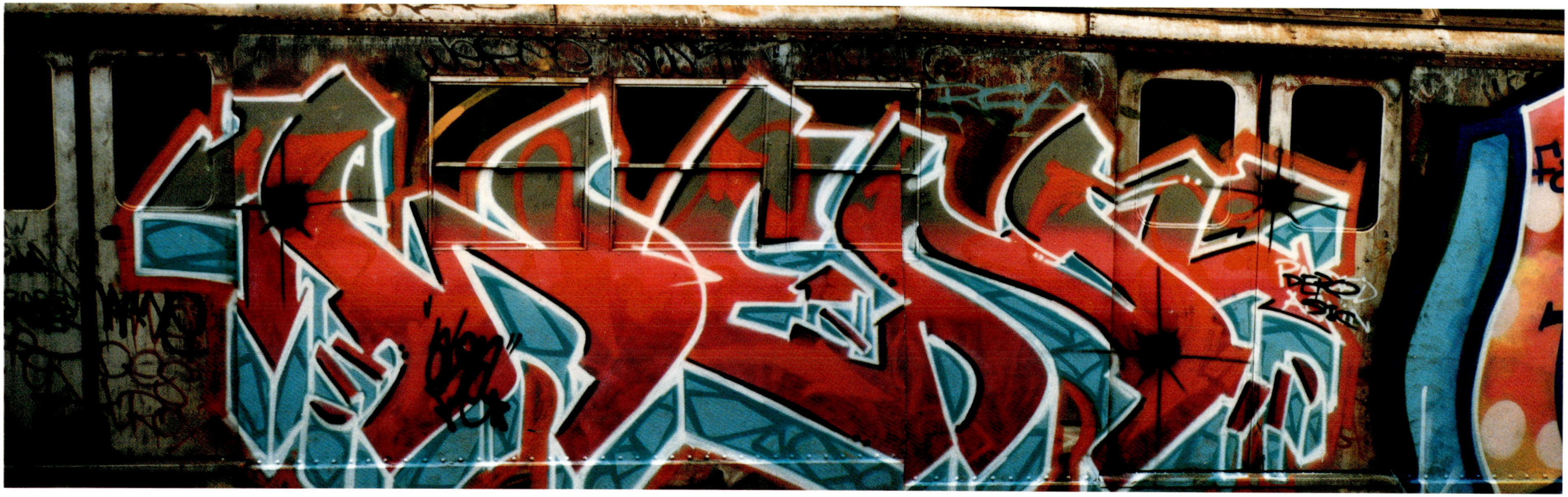

"Wen"

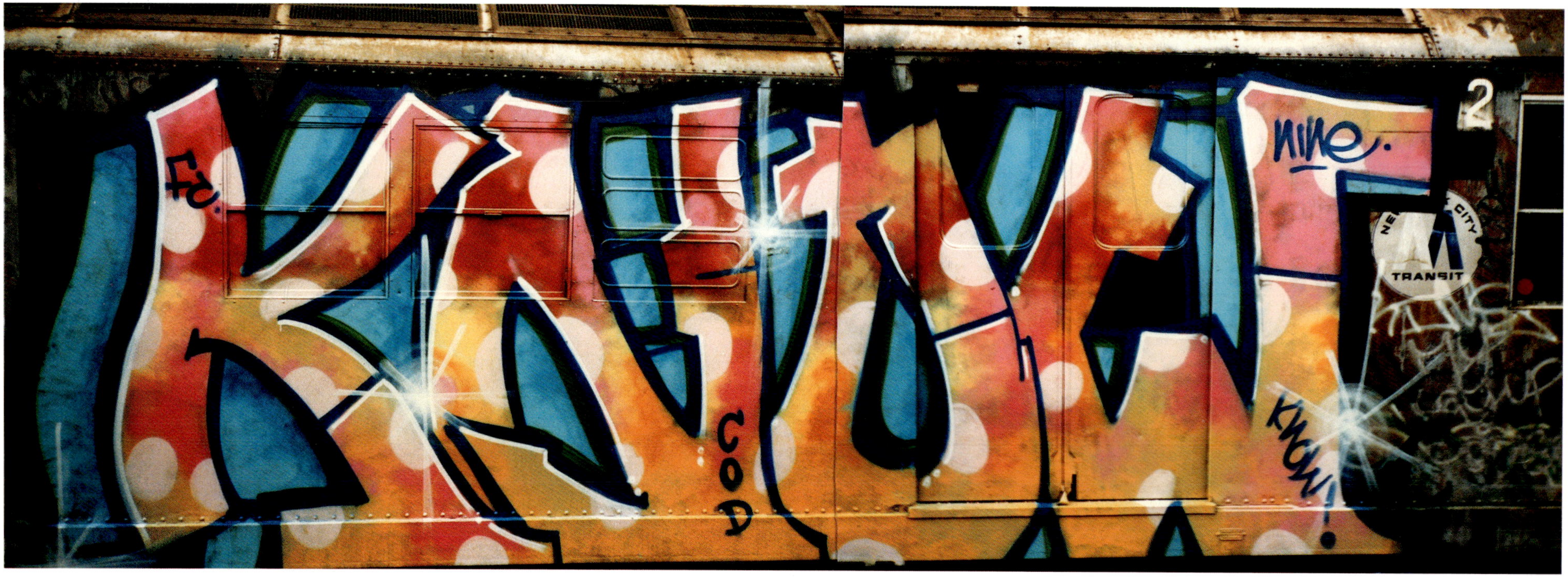

"Know"

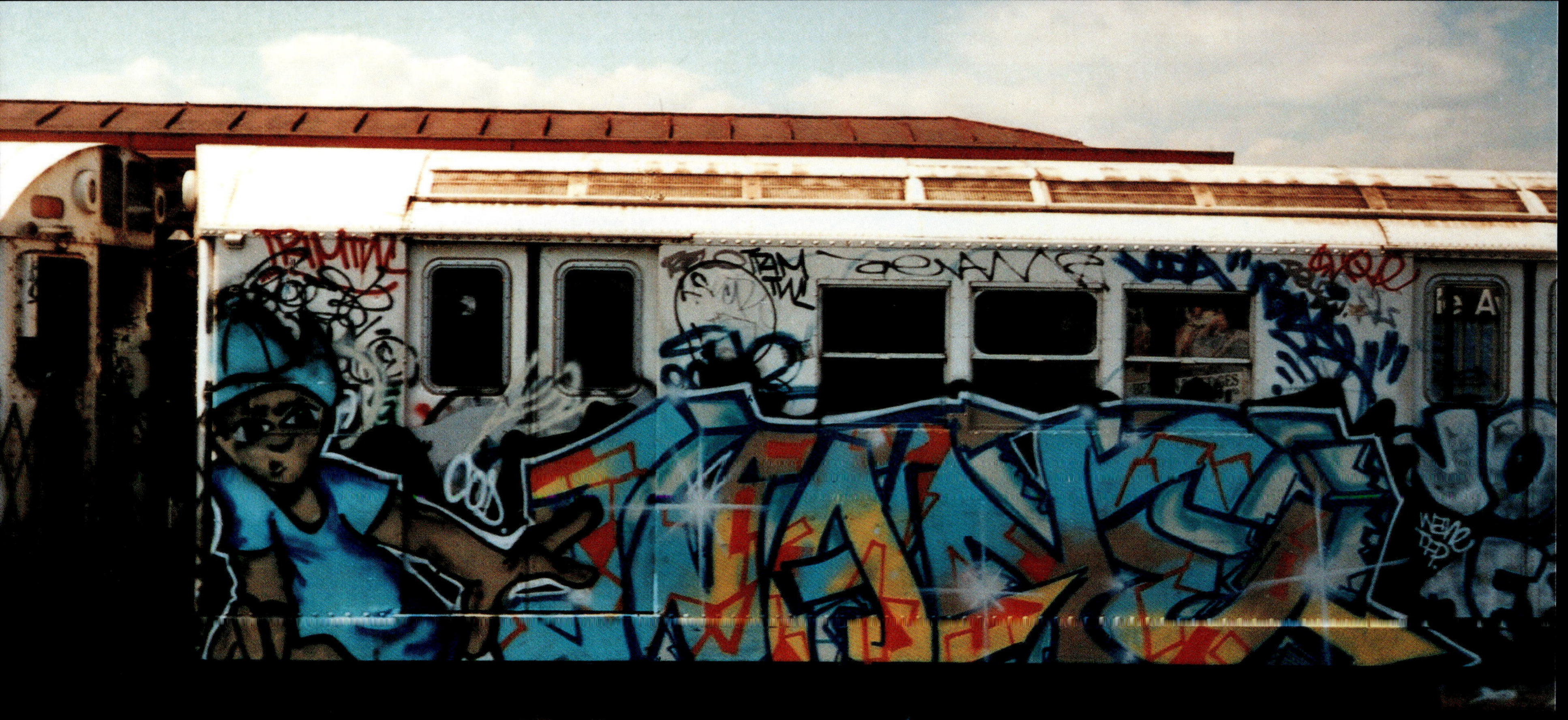

"Wane"

Cav and Key were two of the first writers in the eighties that were documenting subway art by taking photos. They were spending hours on subway platforms. Meeting up with other artists to trade pictures. Similar to a baseball fanatic trading their baseball cards.

–Wane

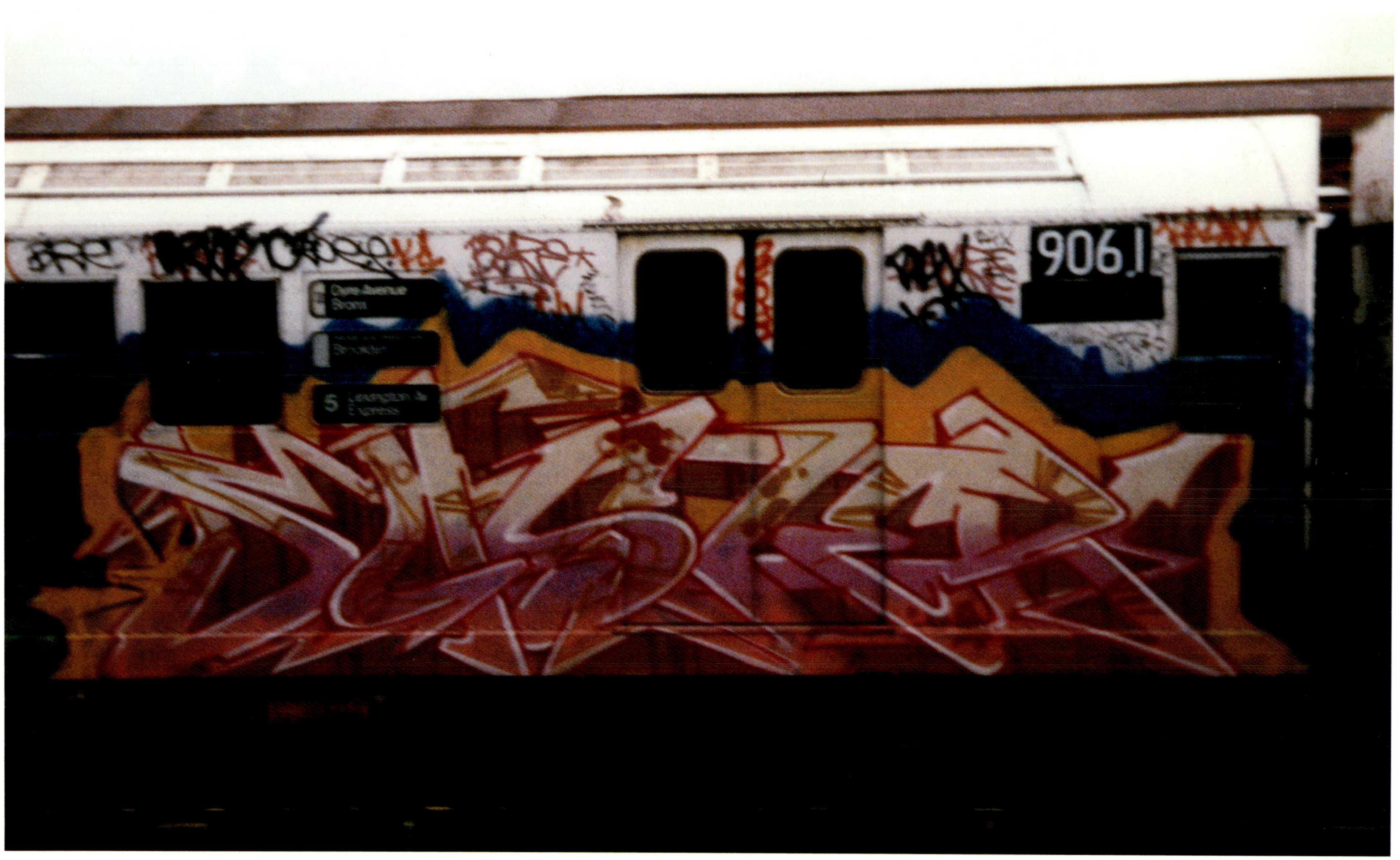

"Duster"

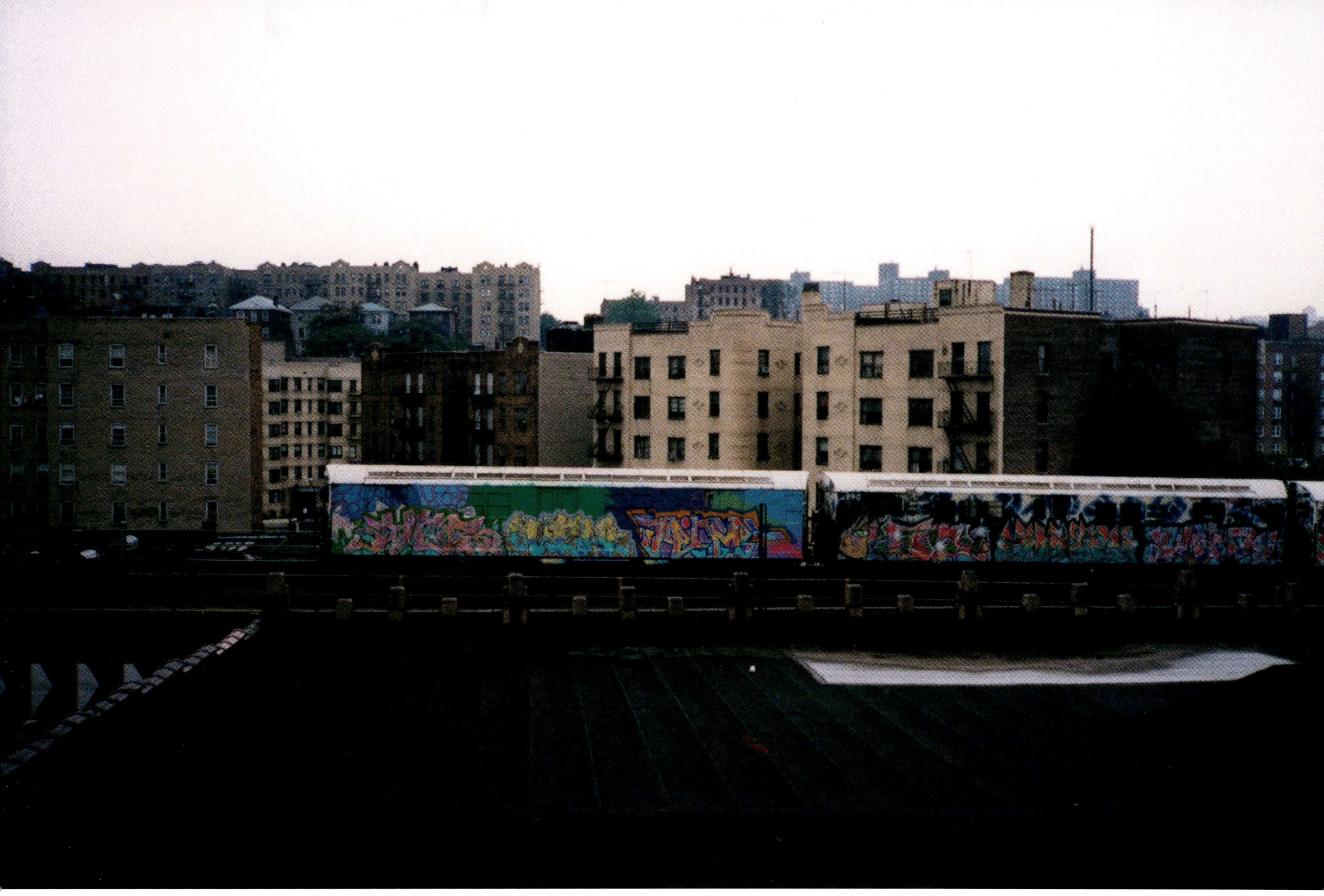

"Web," "Ven" & "Him"

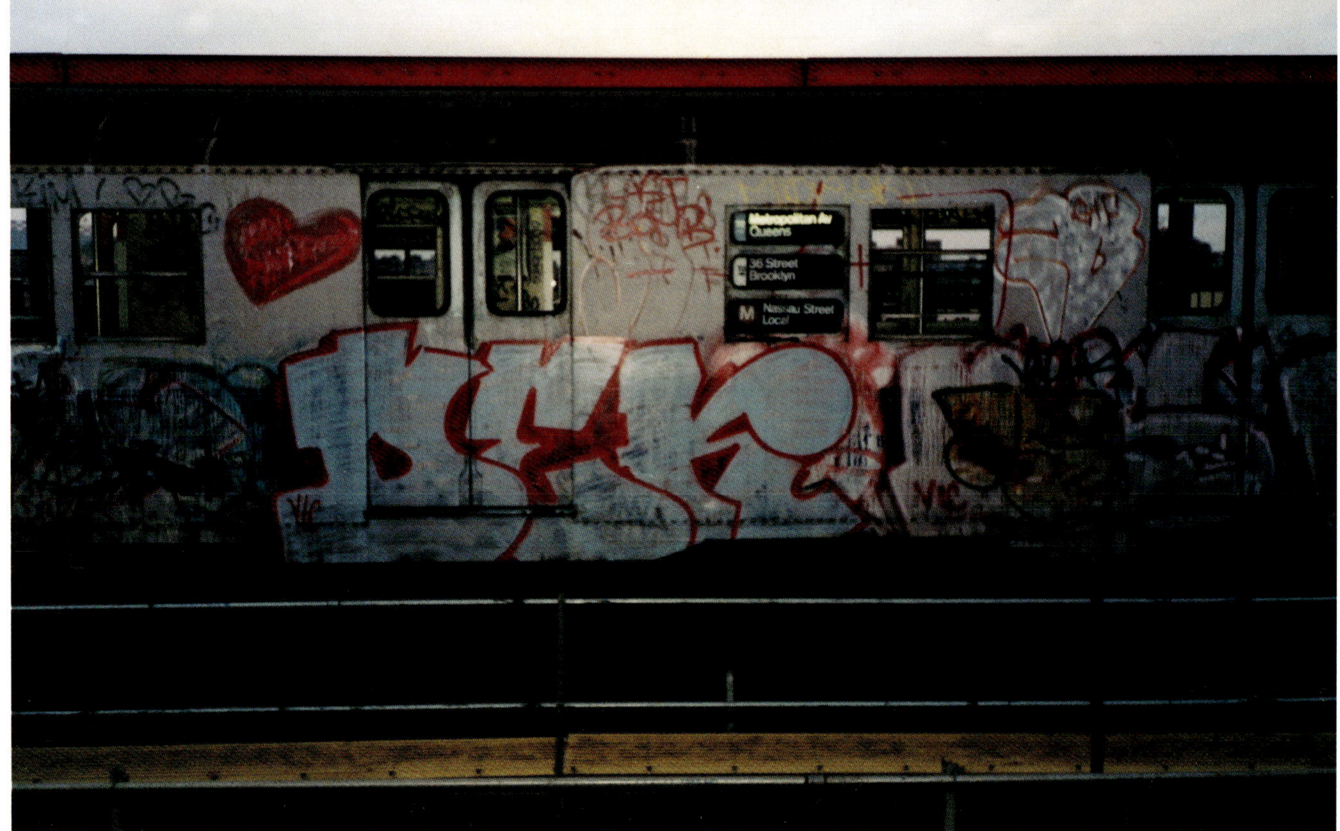

"Dek," 1987

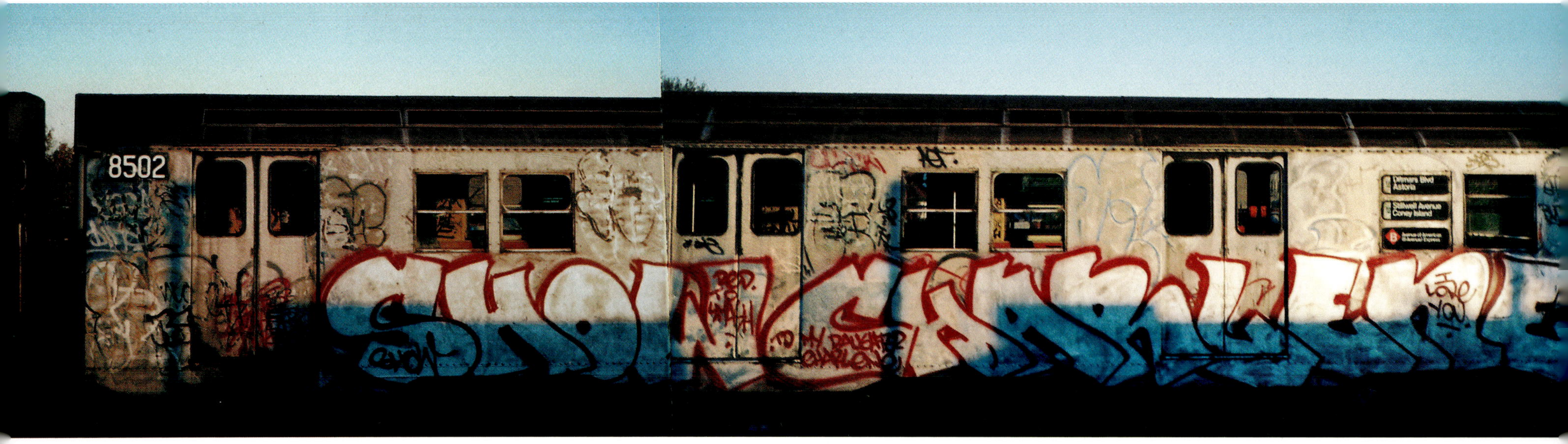

"Show & Charlene," by Show (RIP)

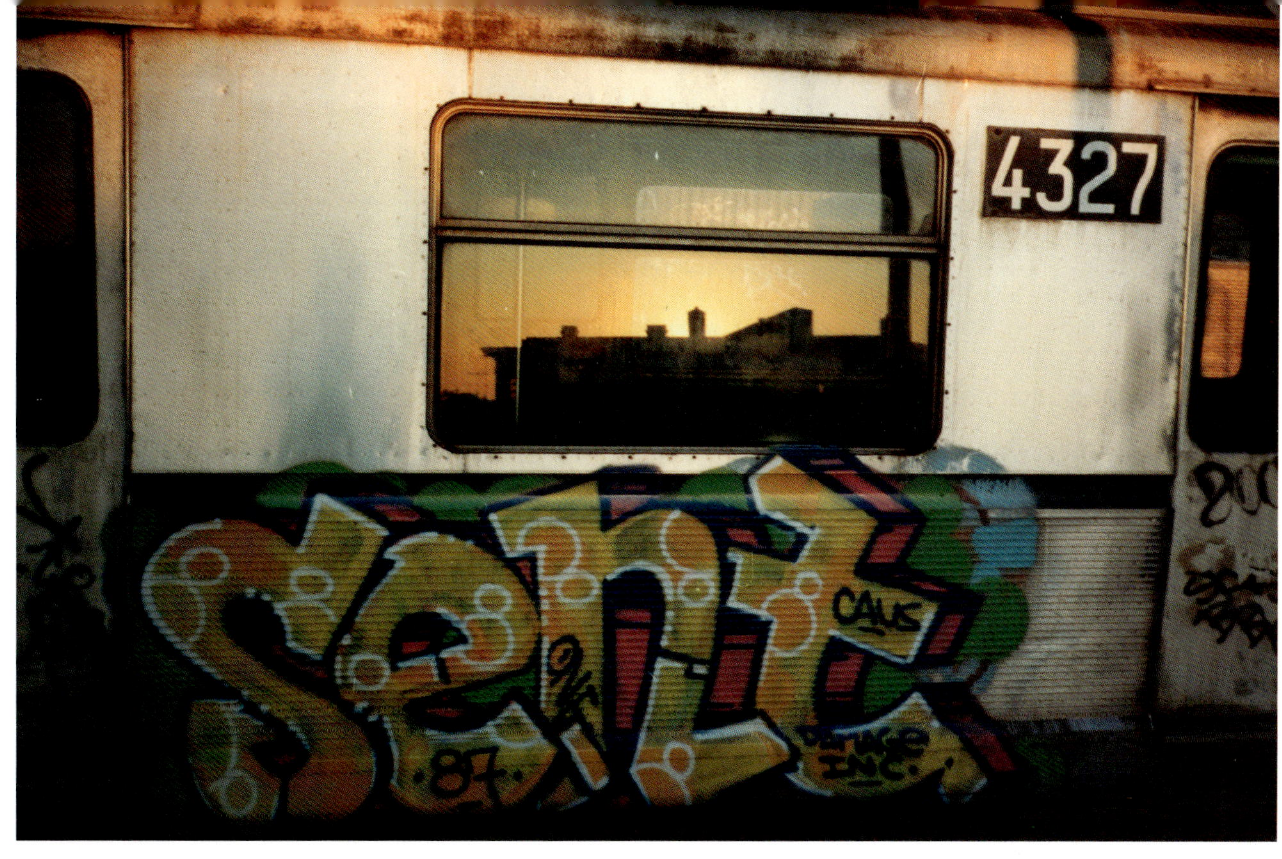

"Sent," 1987

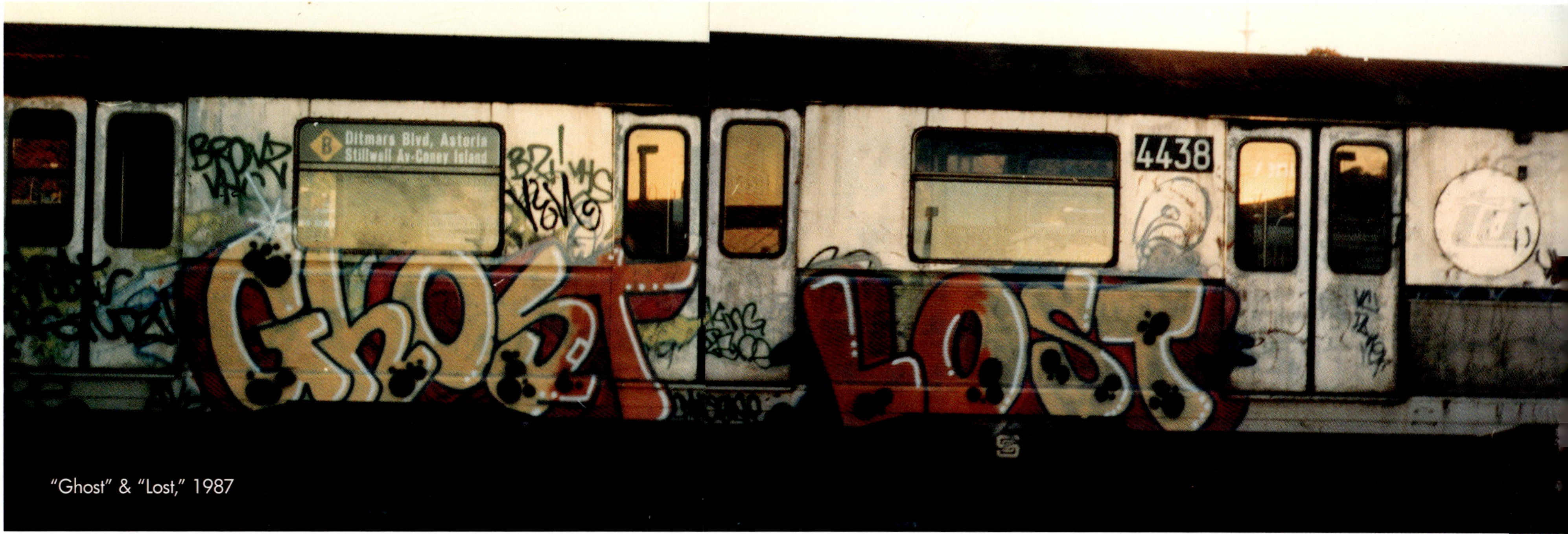

"Ghost" & "Lost," 1987

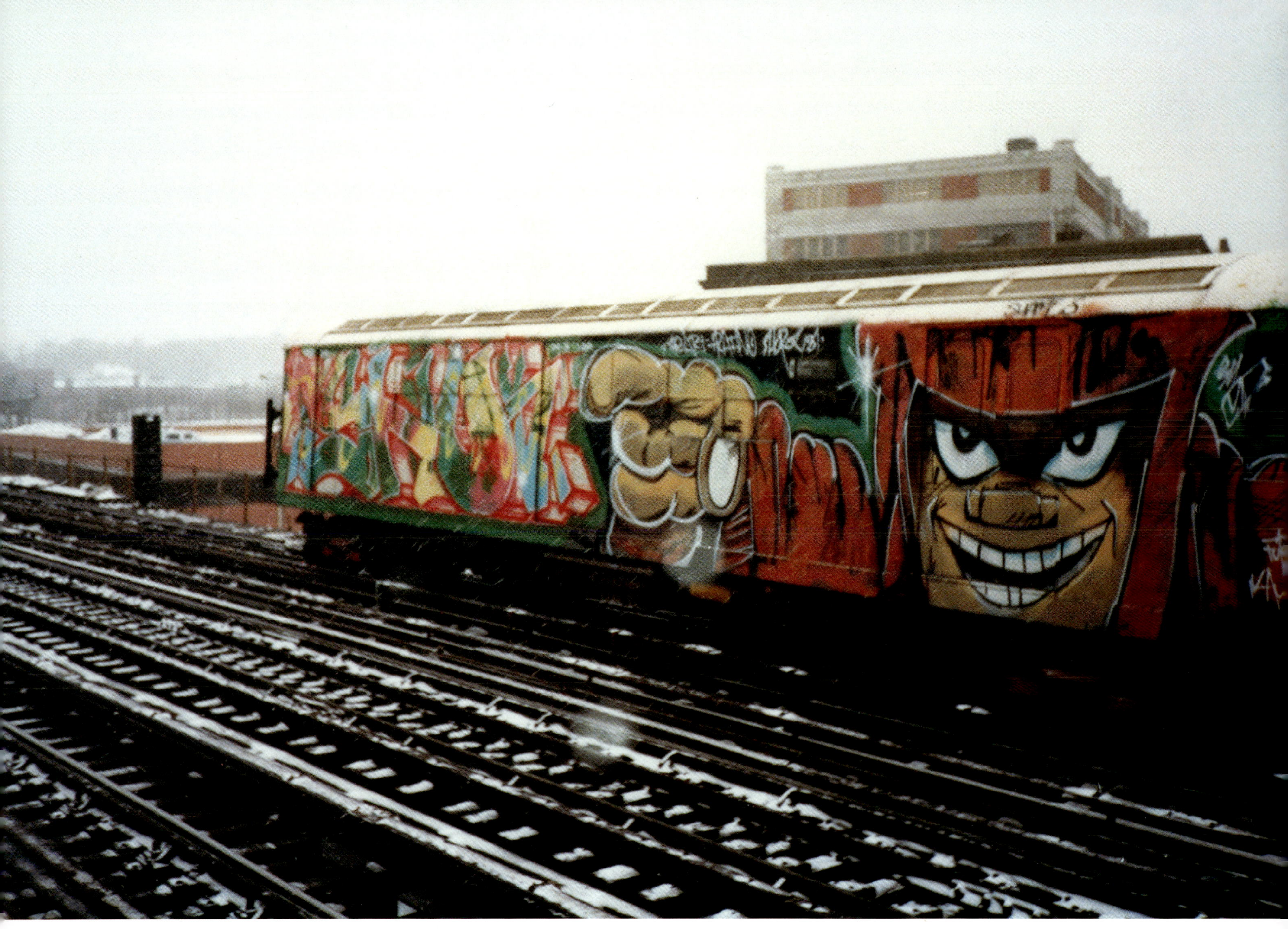

"Sho"

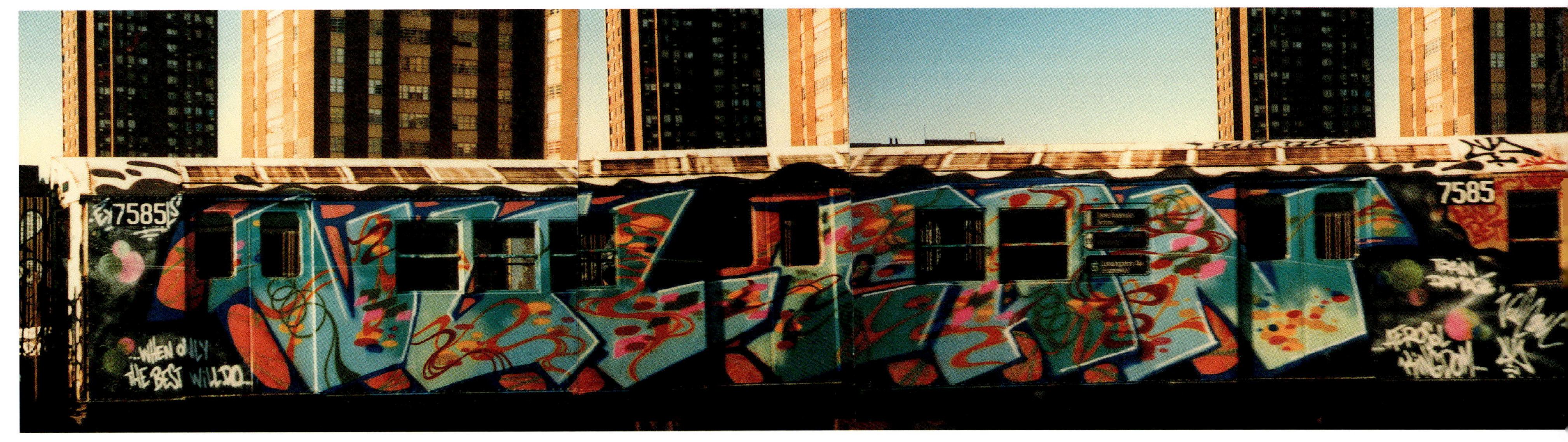

"Vulcan," 1987

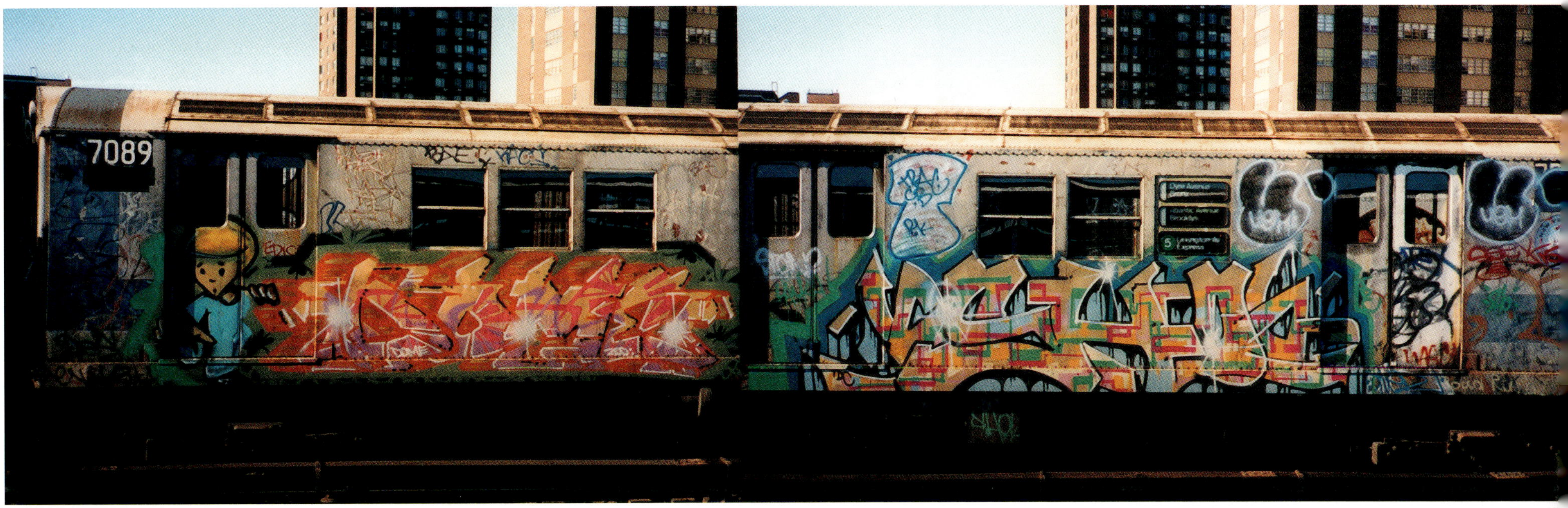

"Dome" & "Sho"

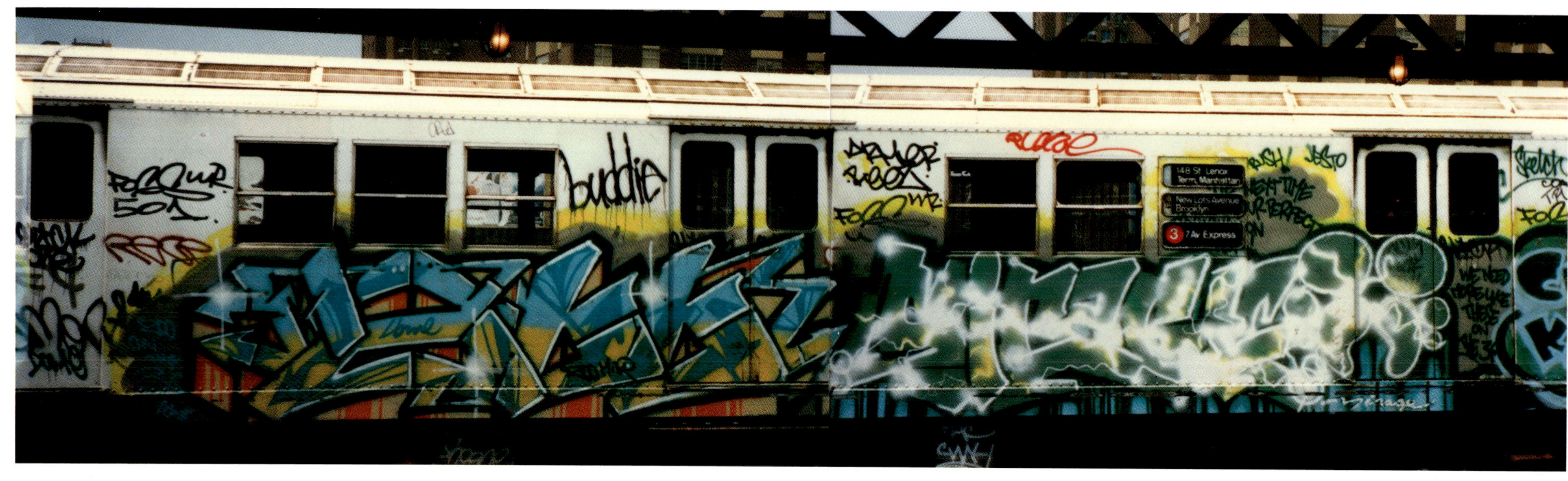

"Zoo" & "Mirage" (RIP)

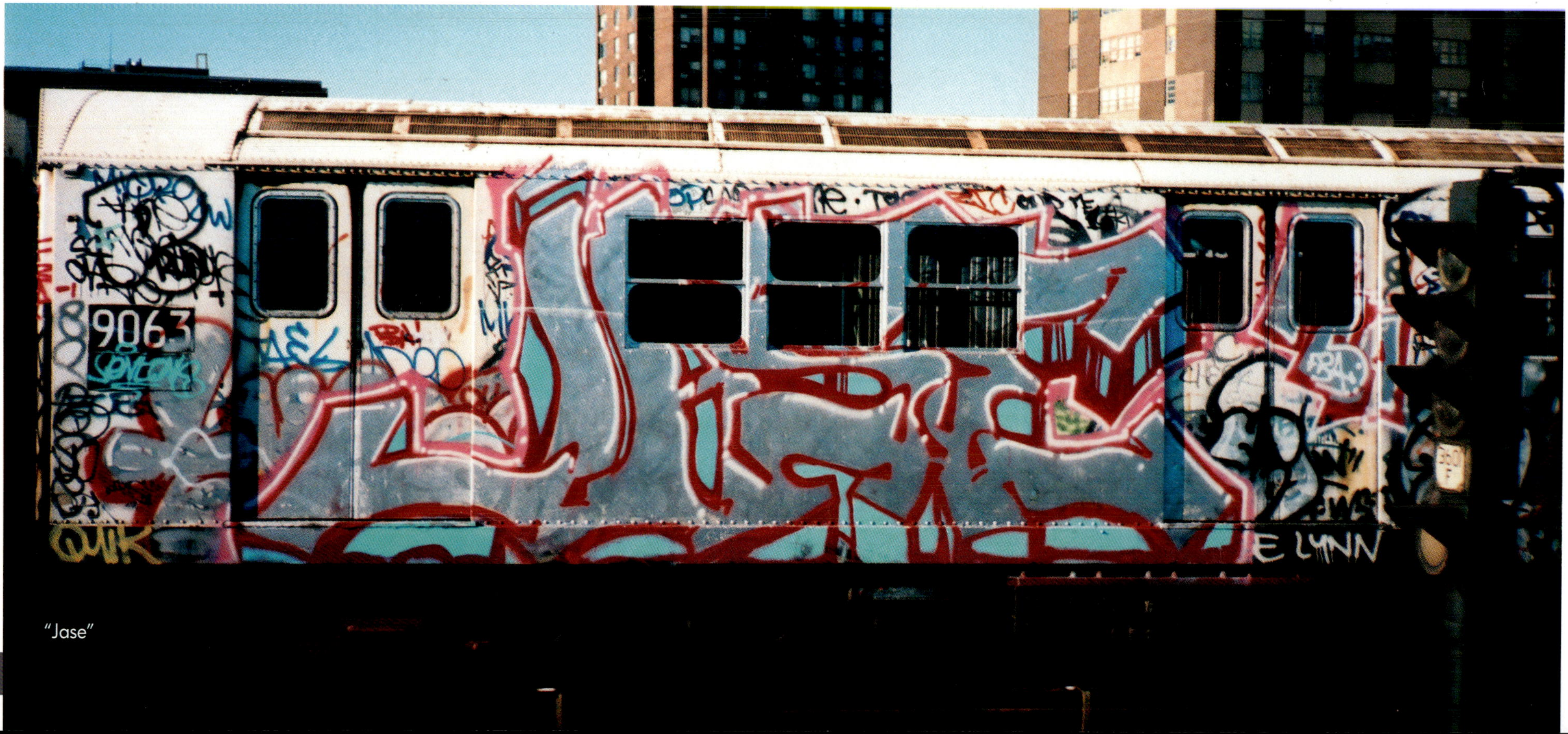

"Jase"

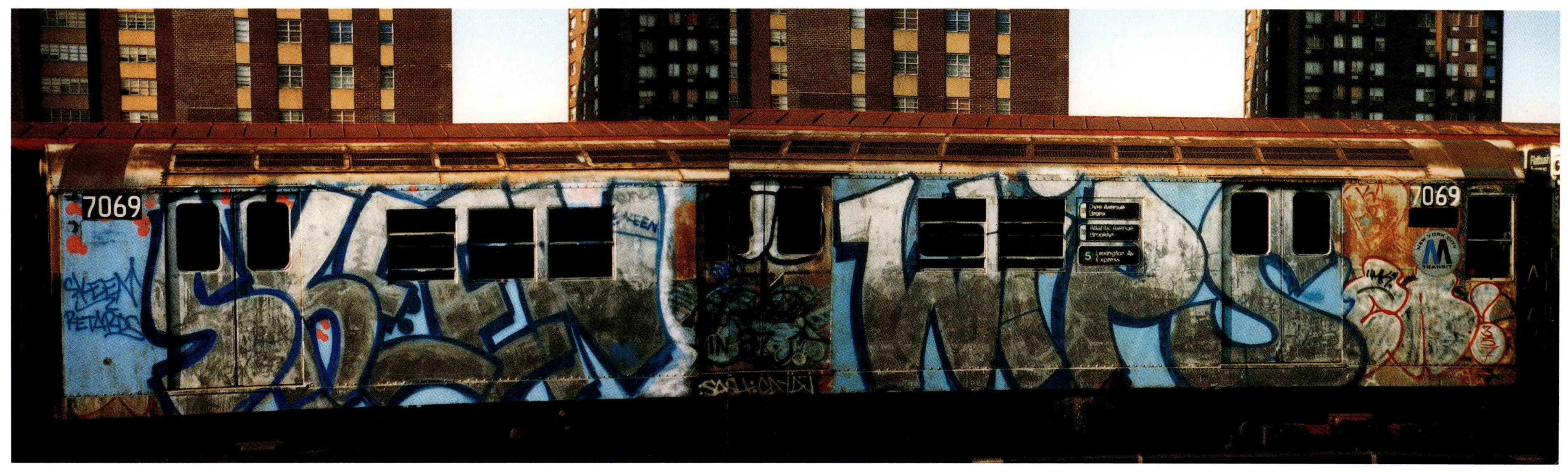

"Skeen" & "Wips"

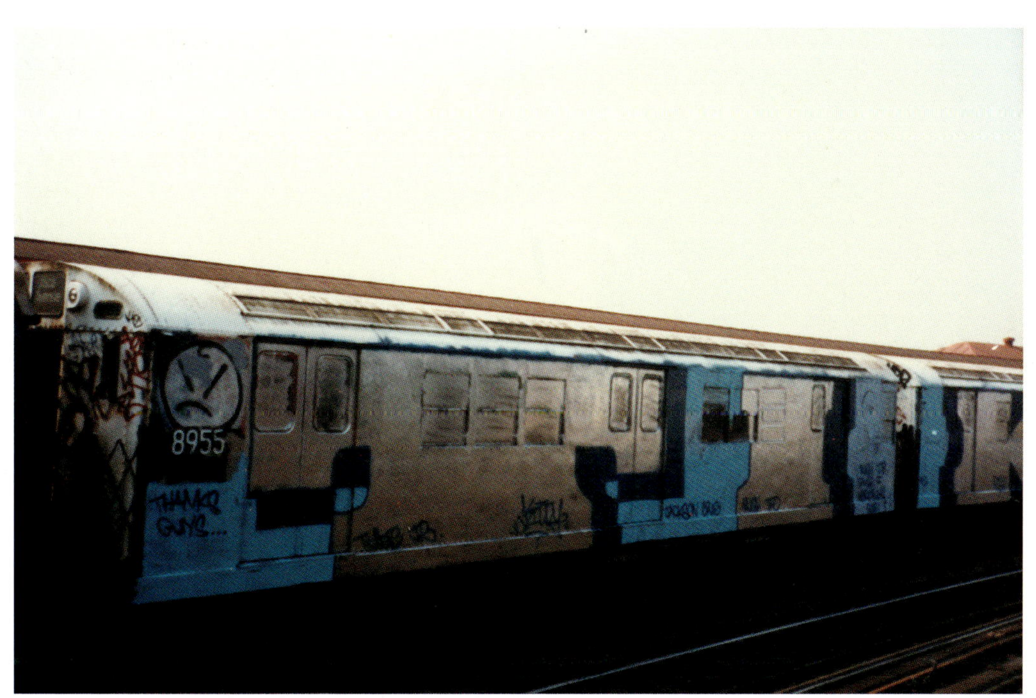

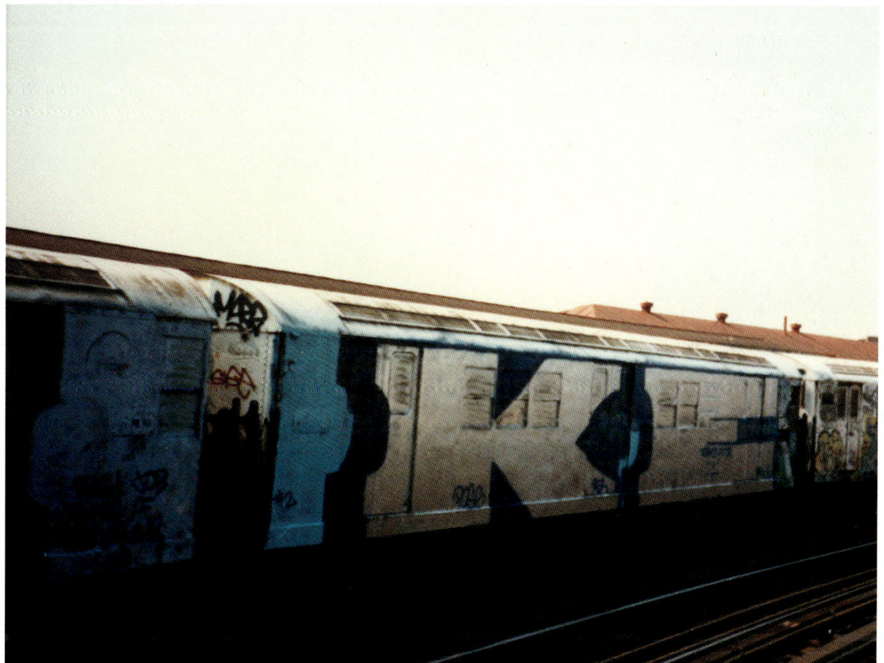

"Tike" married couple, 1987

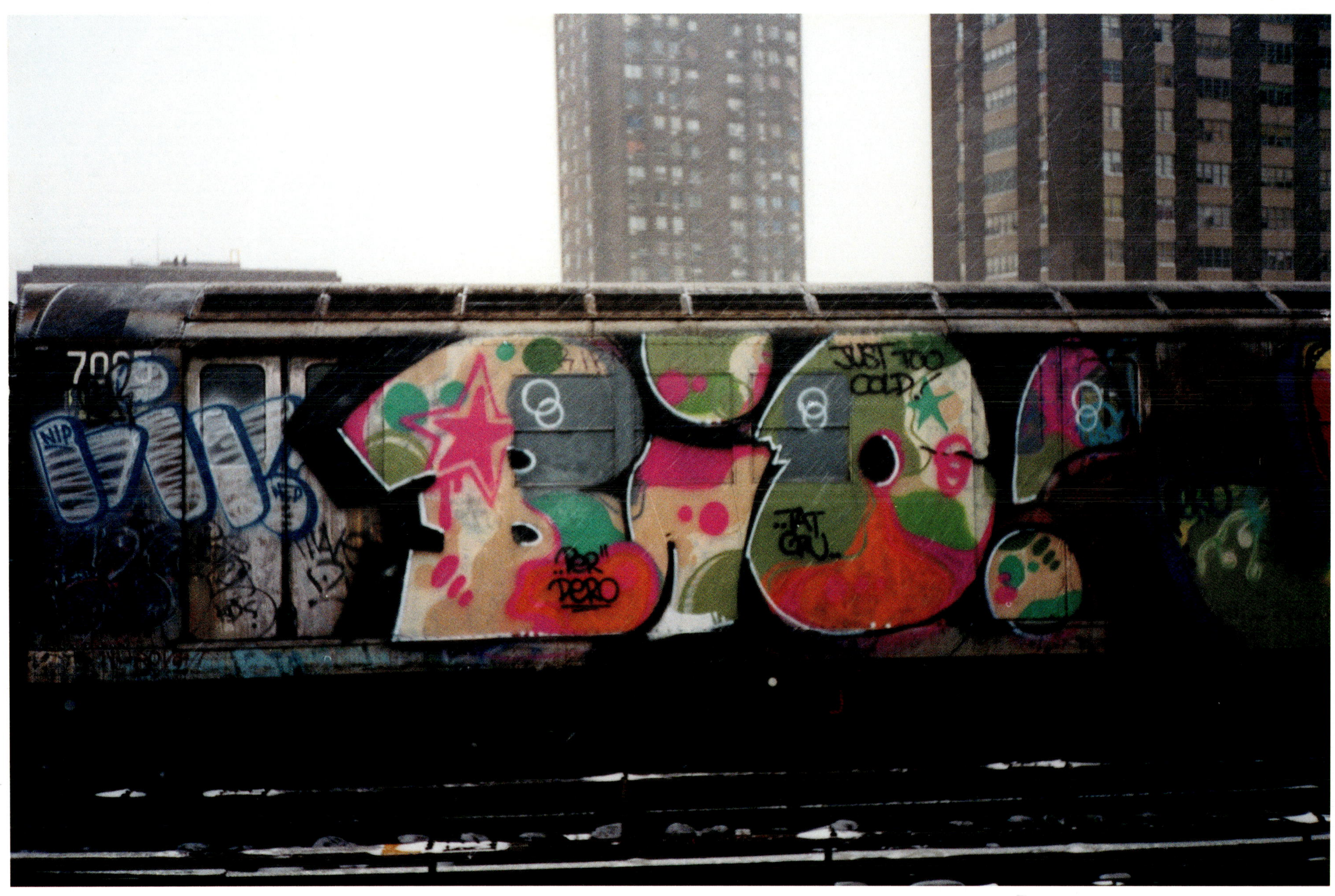

"Bio"

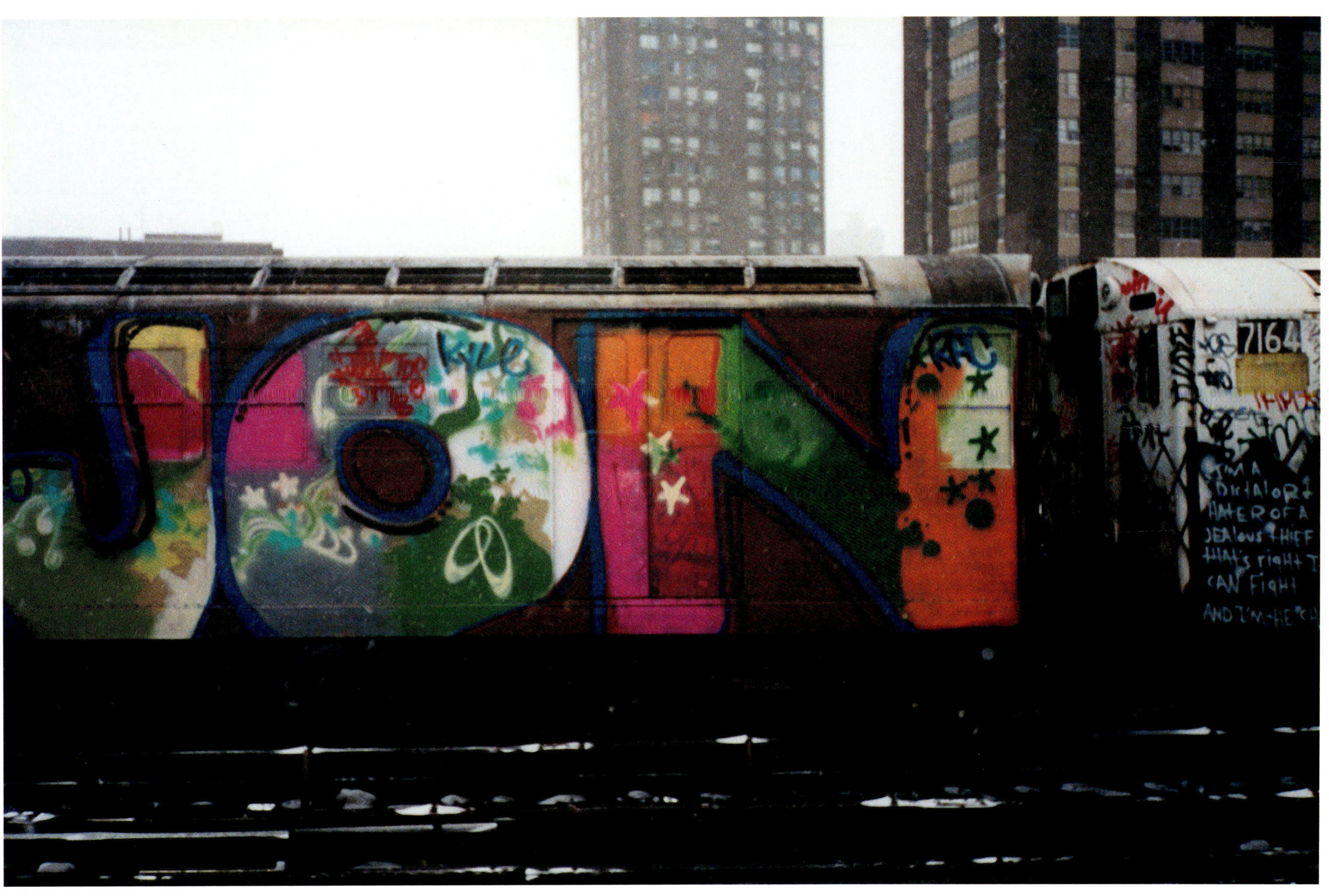

"Jon"

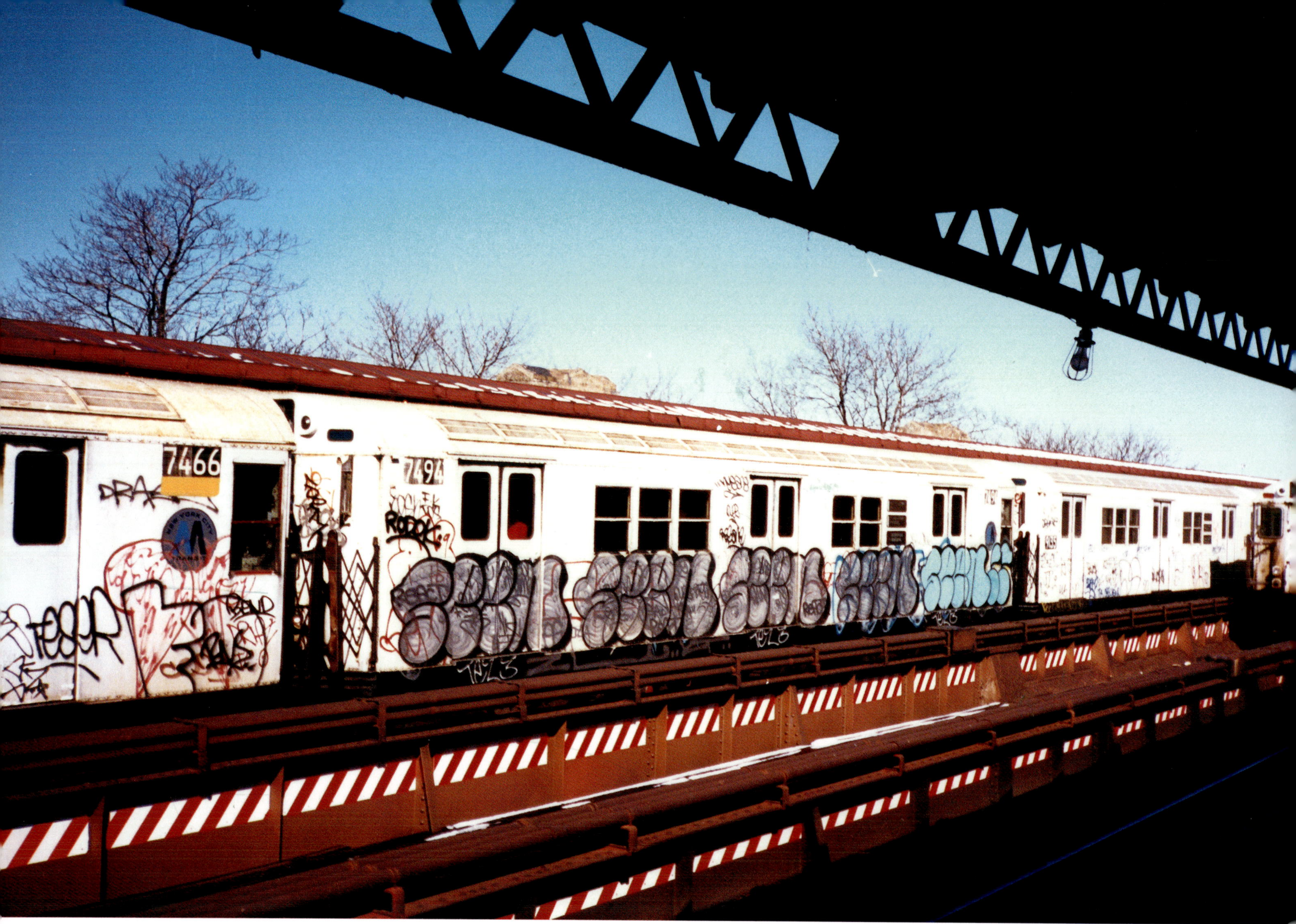

"Seen"

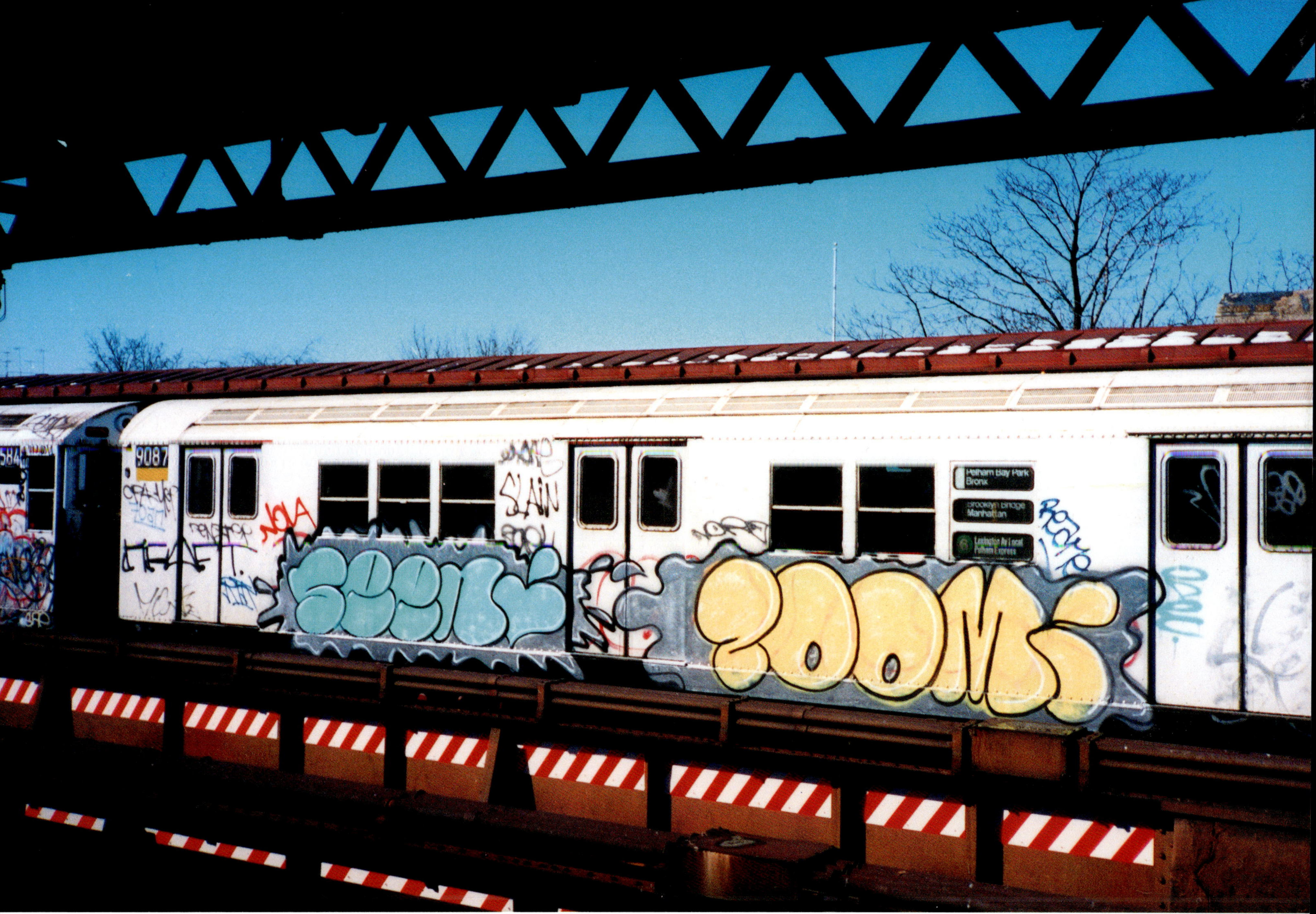

"Seen" & "Zoom" (RIP)

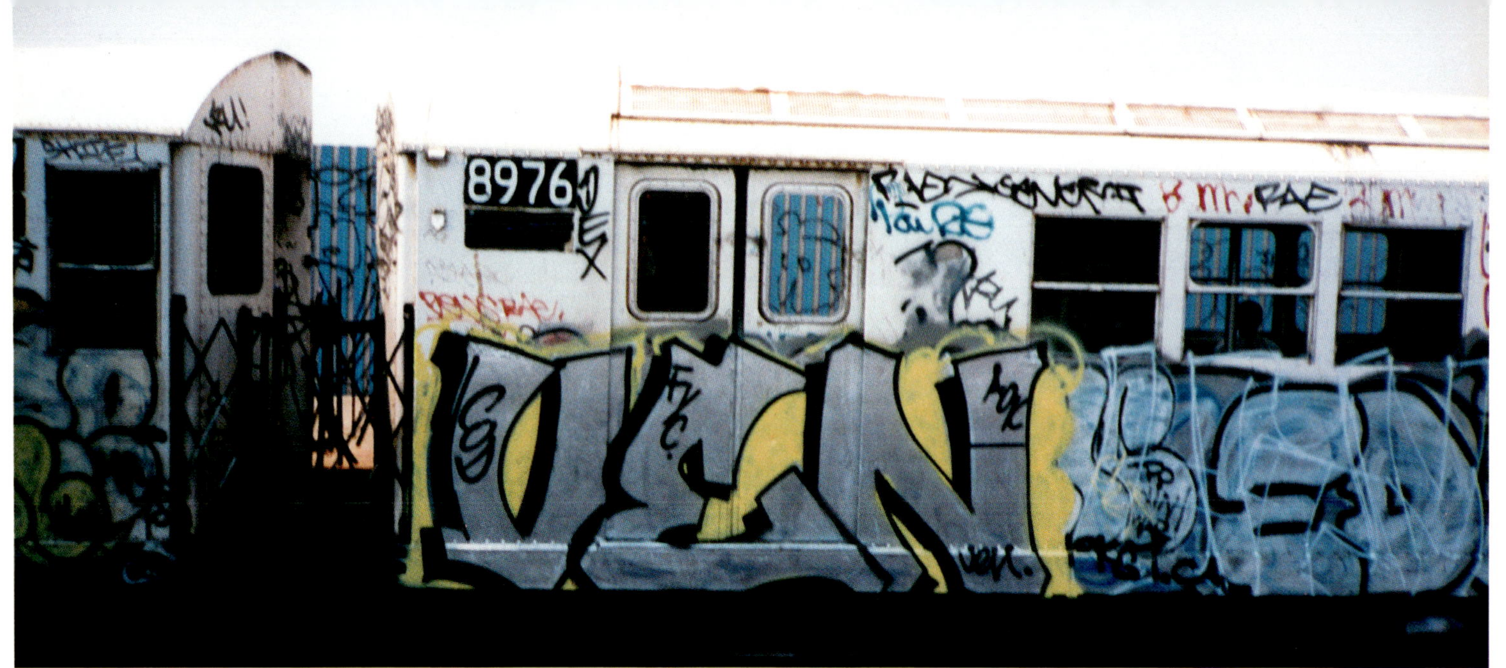

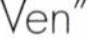

"Ven"

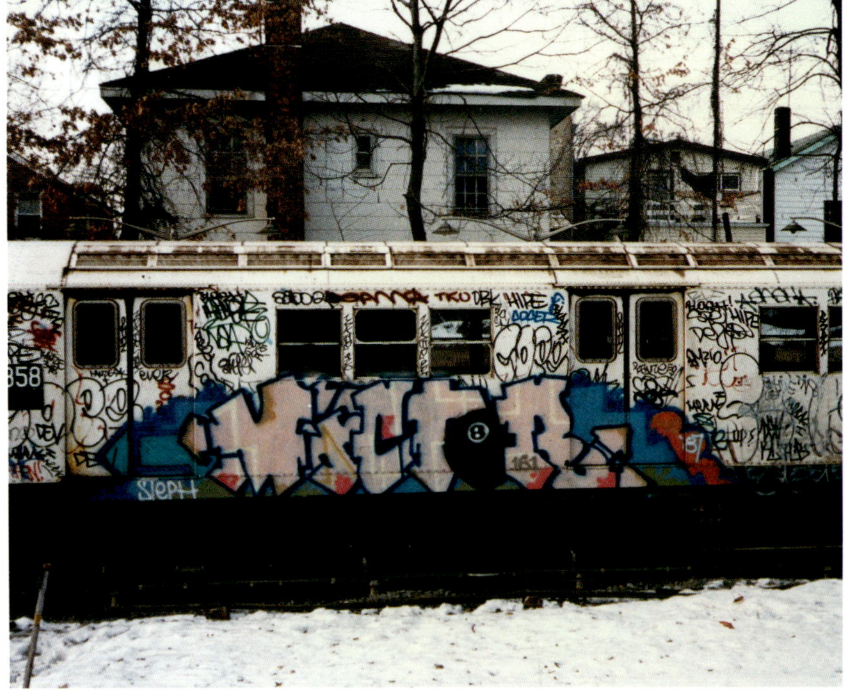

"Victor161"

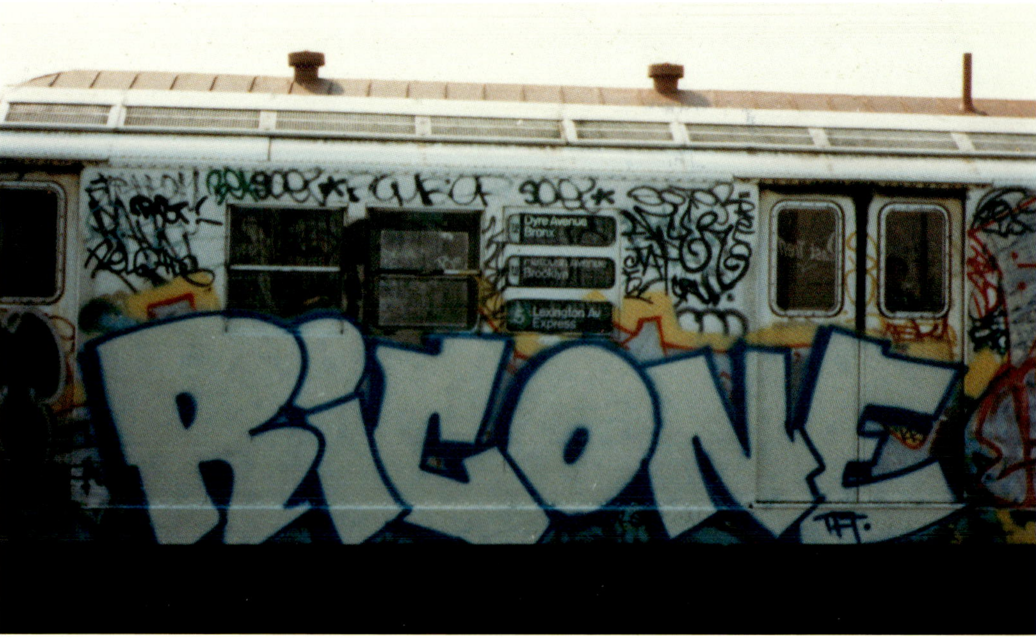

"Ric-One"

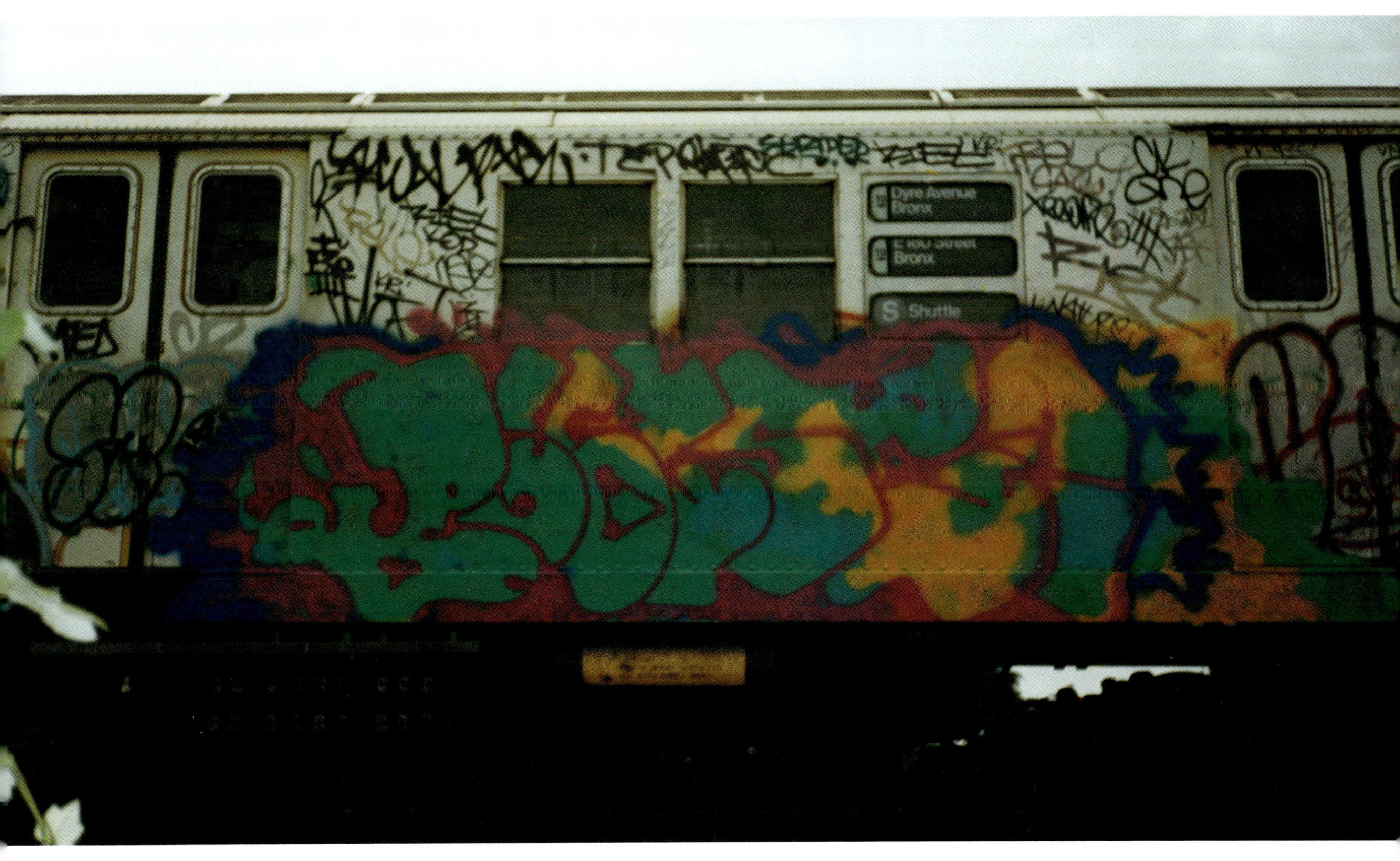

"Phase2," 1987

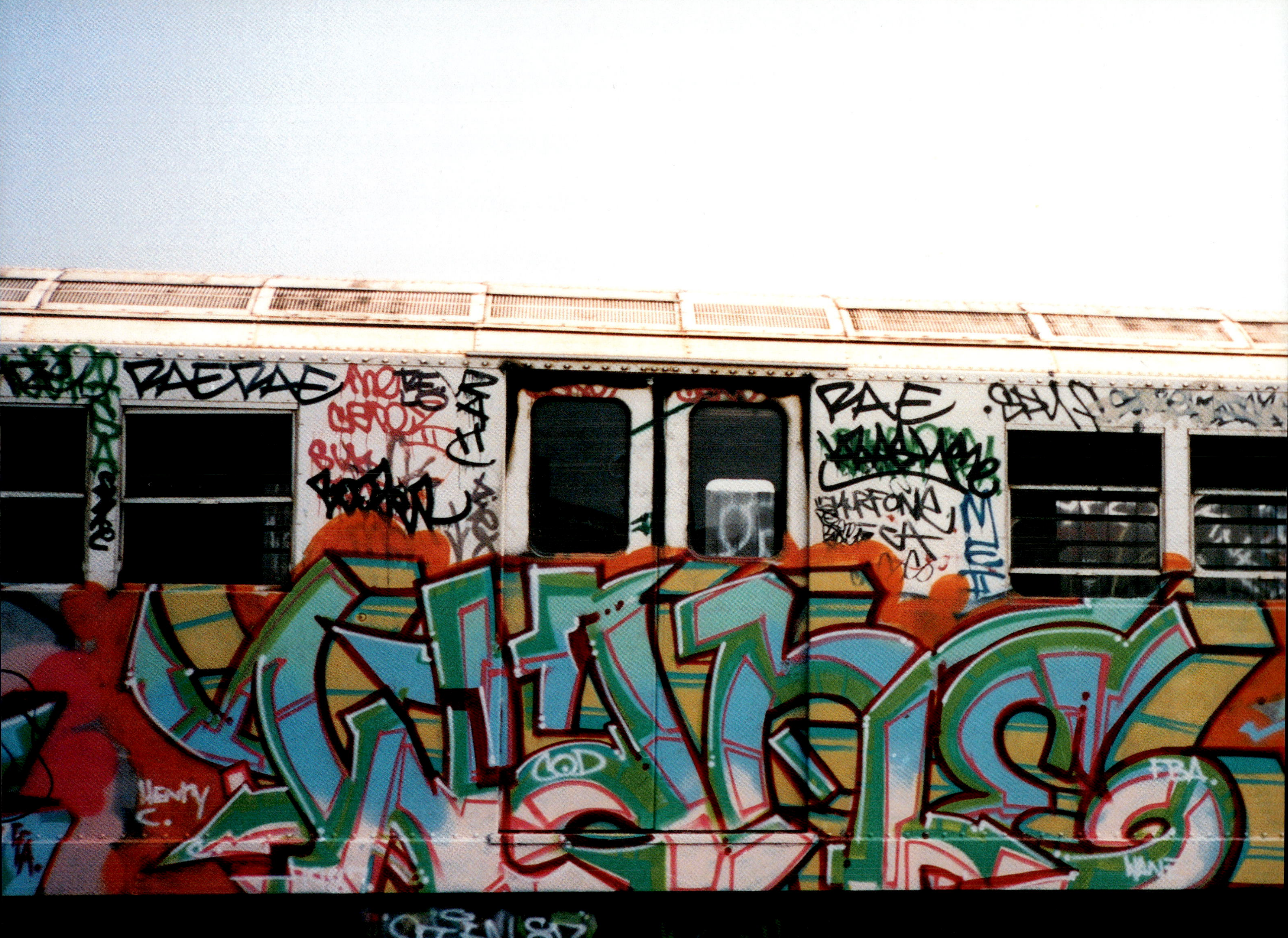

"Wane"

Dyre Avenue
Bronx
Atlantic Avenue
Brooklyn
5 Lexington Av
Express
7535

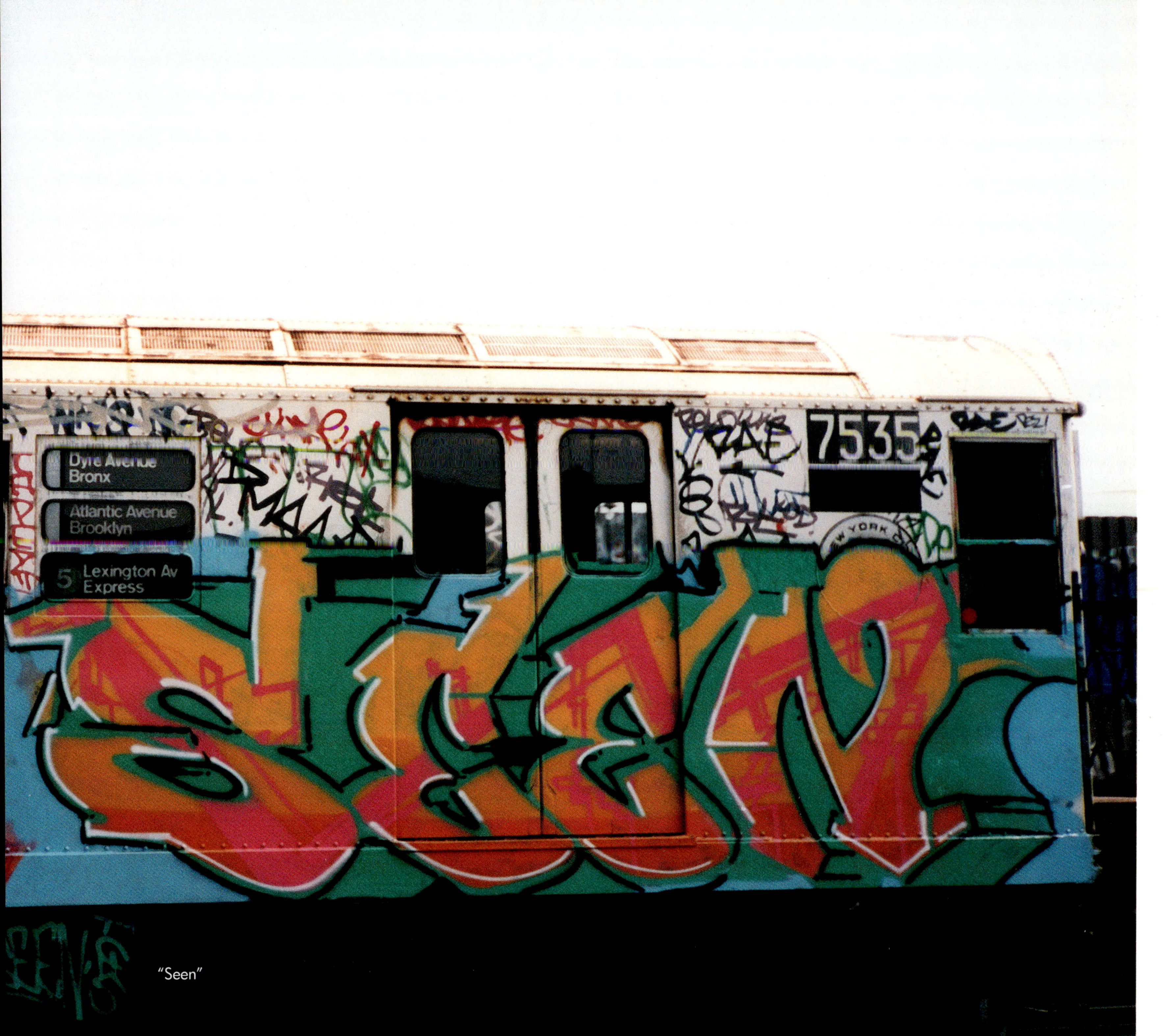

"Seen"

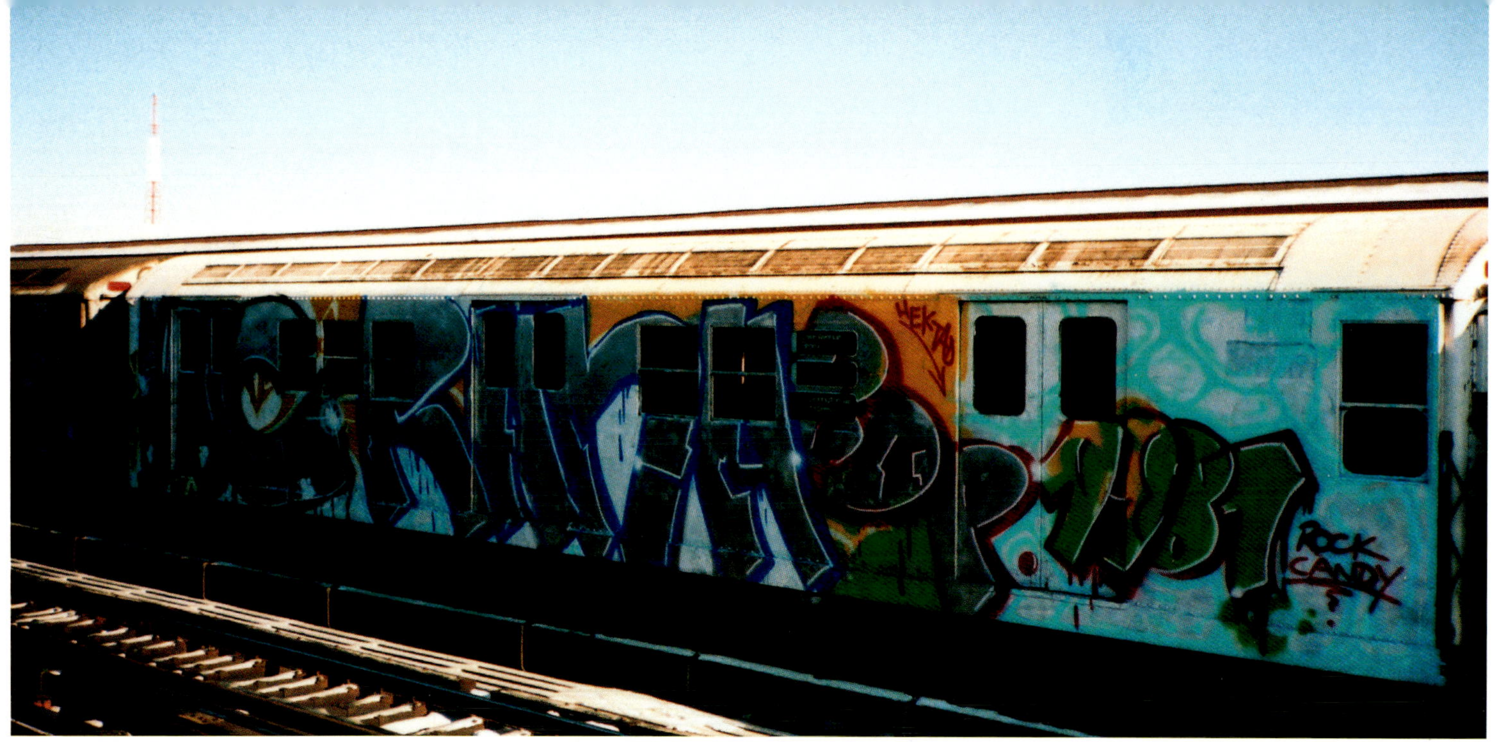

"Vic" & "Rana"

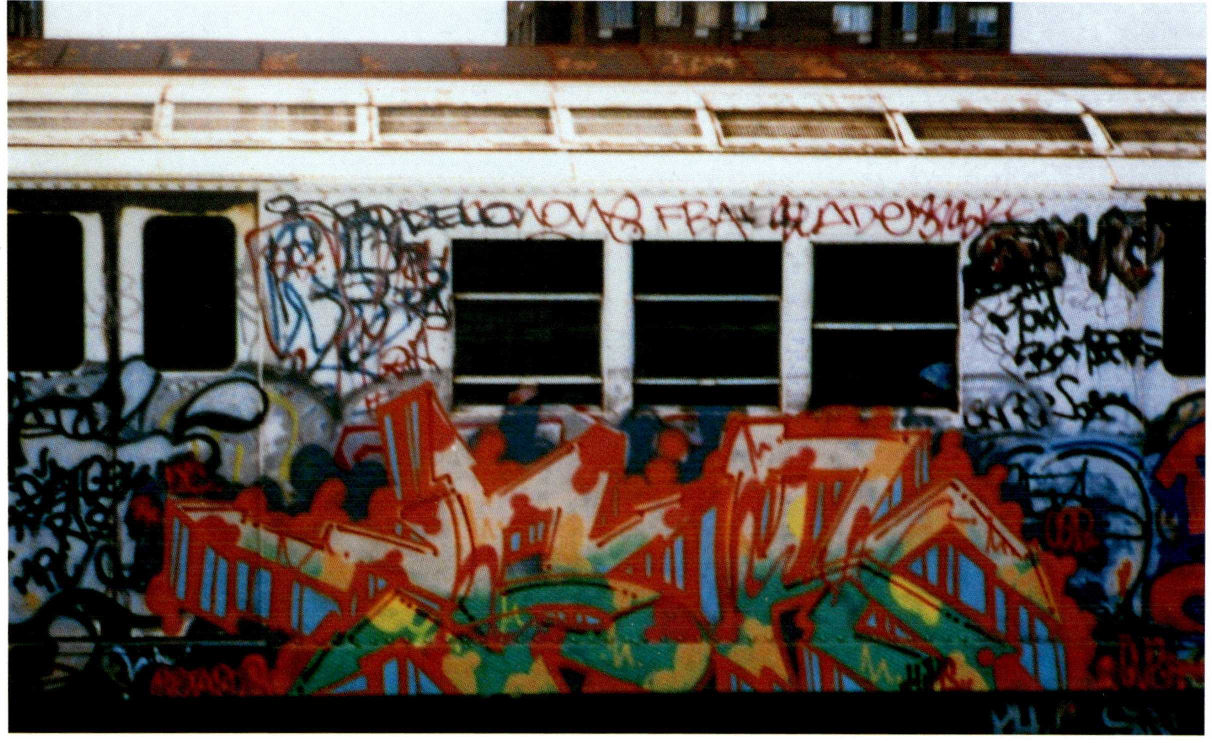

"Sk," by Skeen

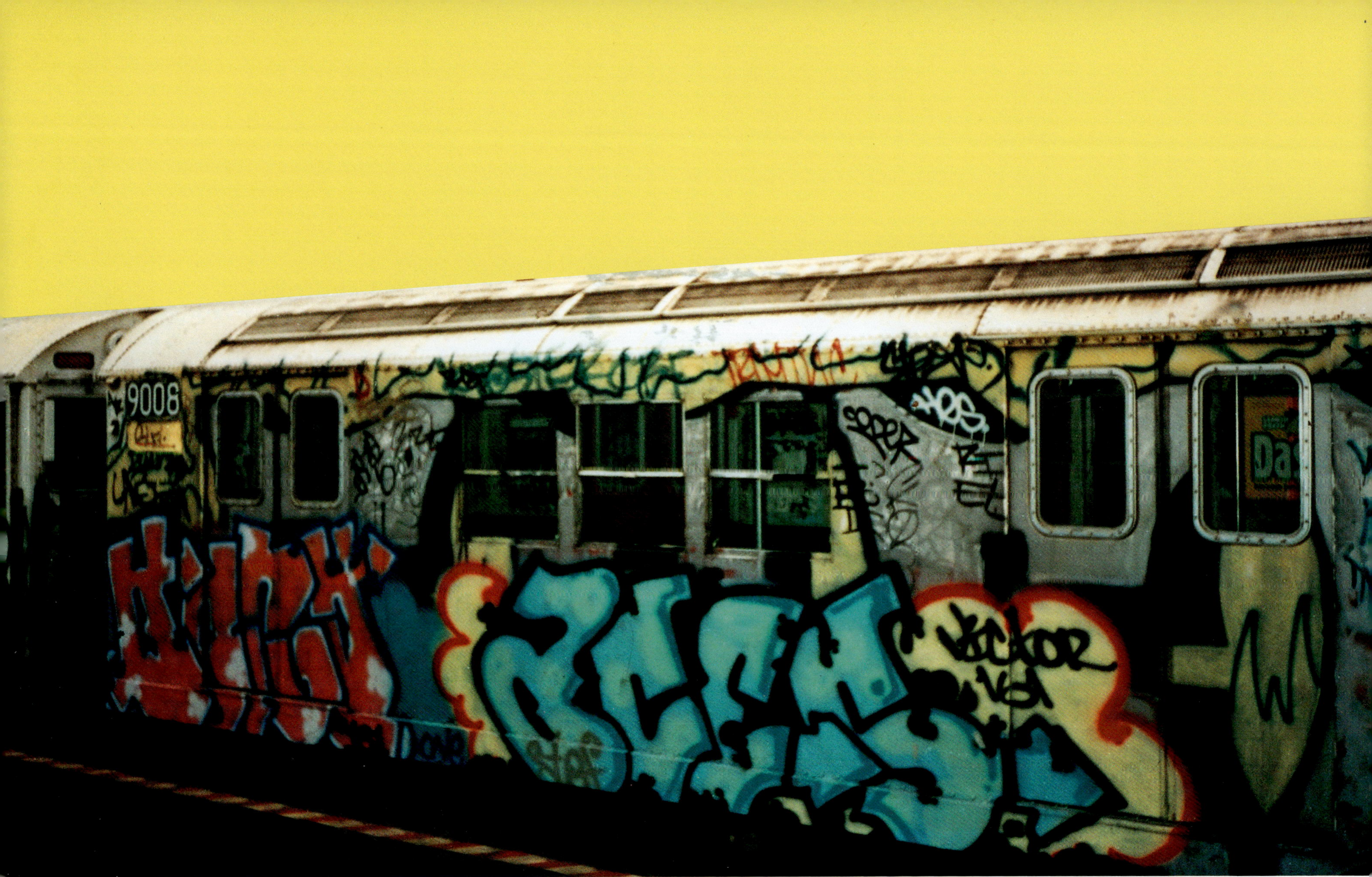

"Bond" & "Aces"

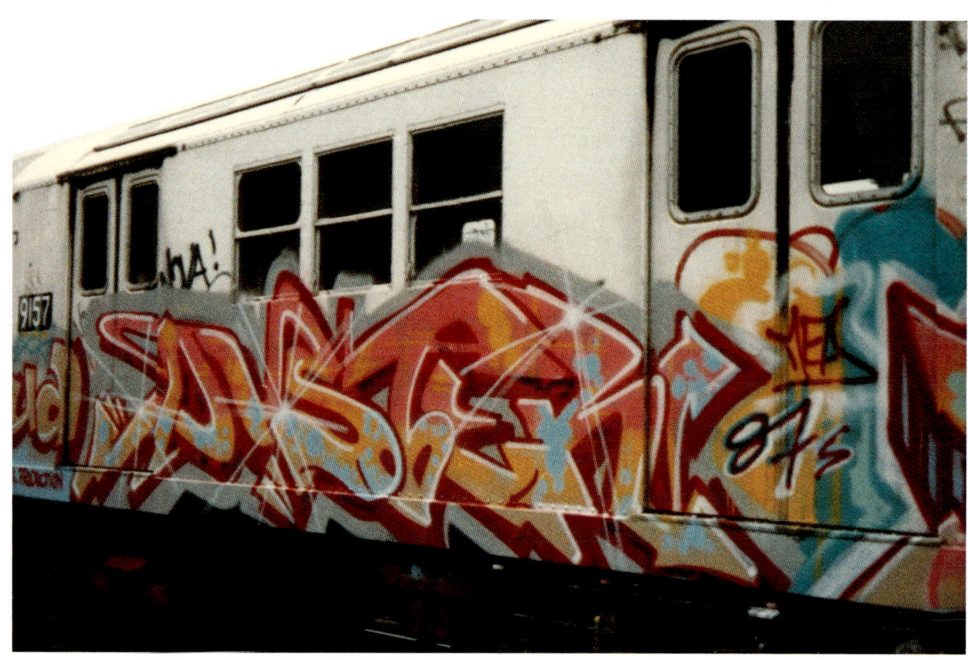

"Duster"

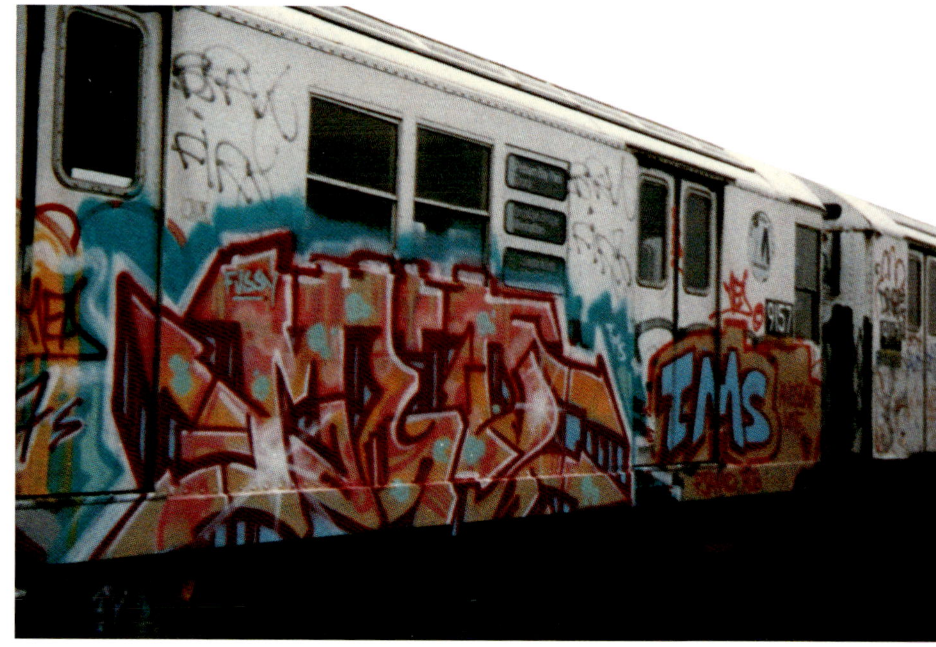

"Med"

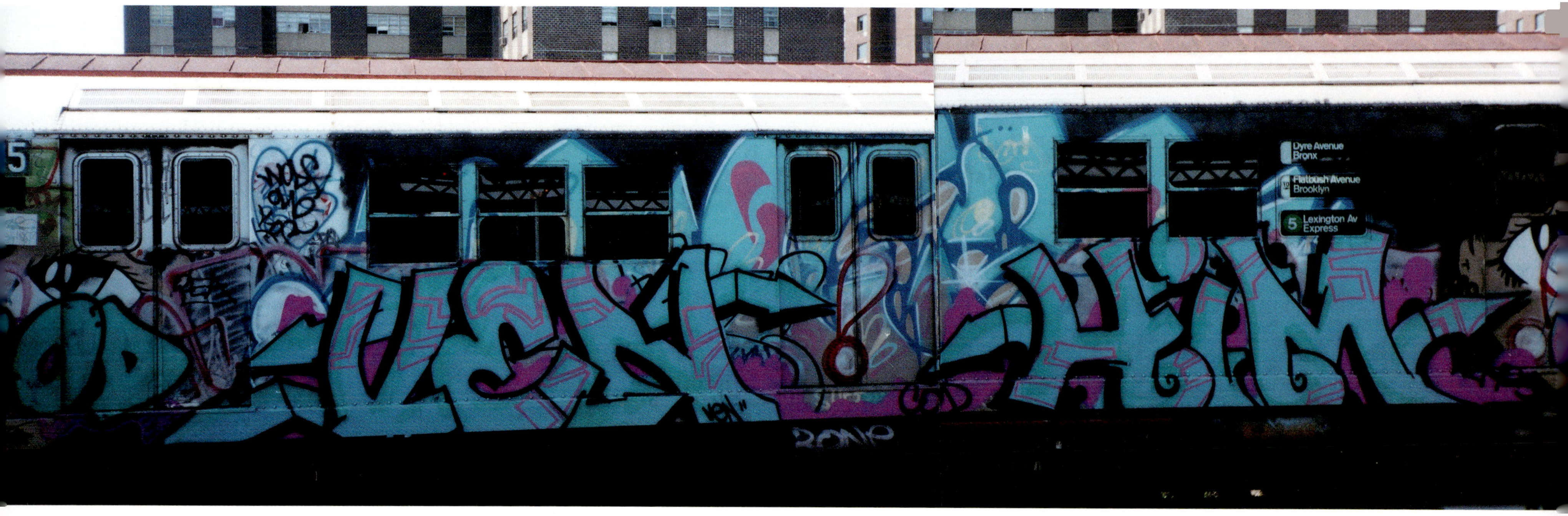

"Ven" & "Him"

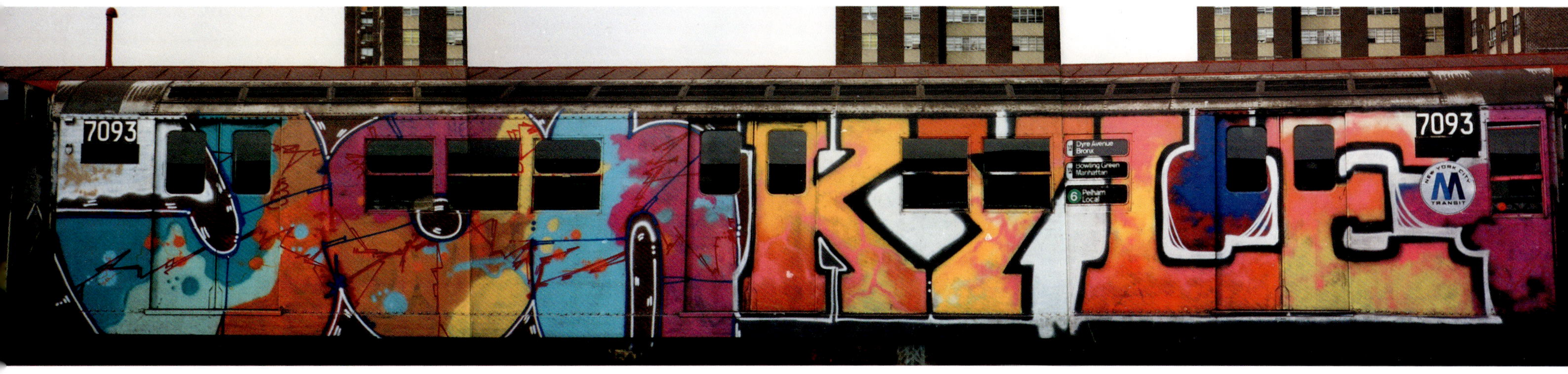

"Jon" & "Kyle"

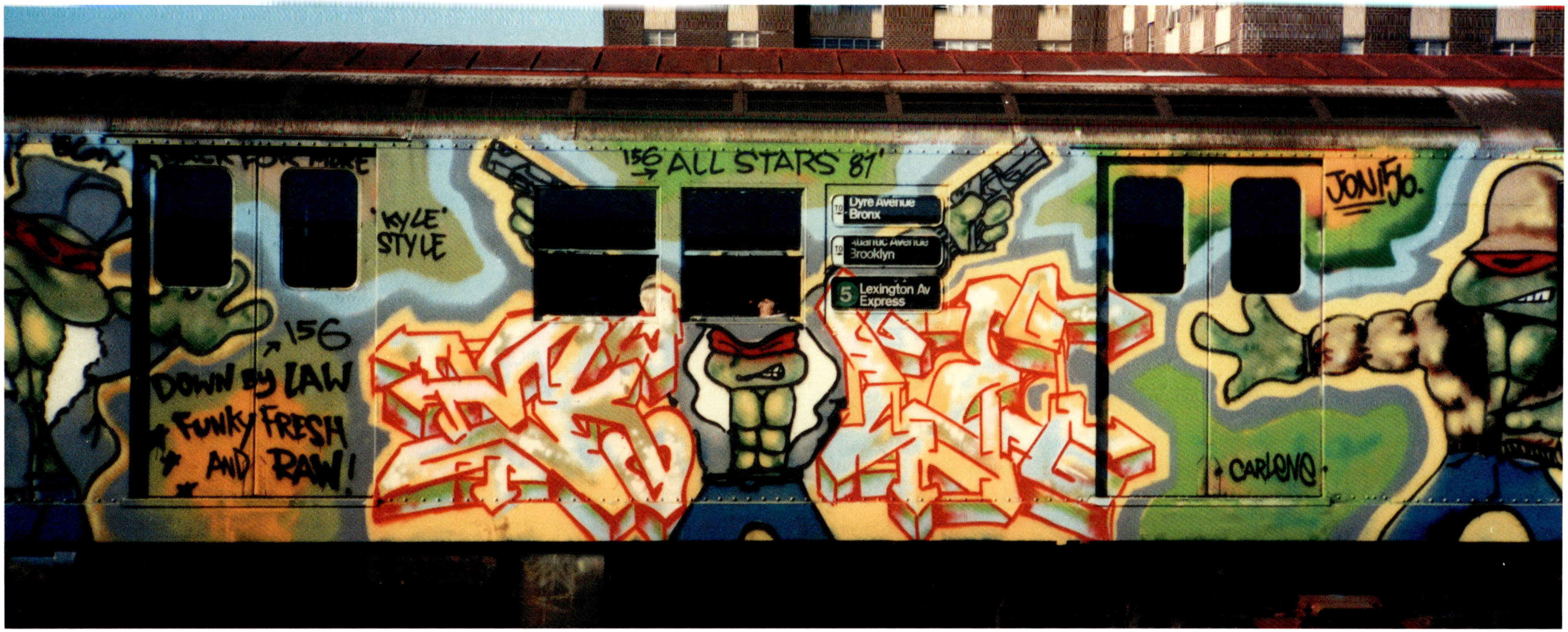

"Kyle"

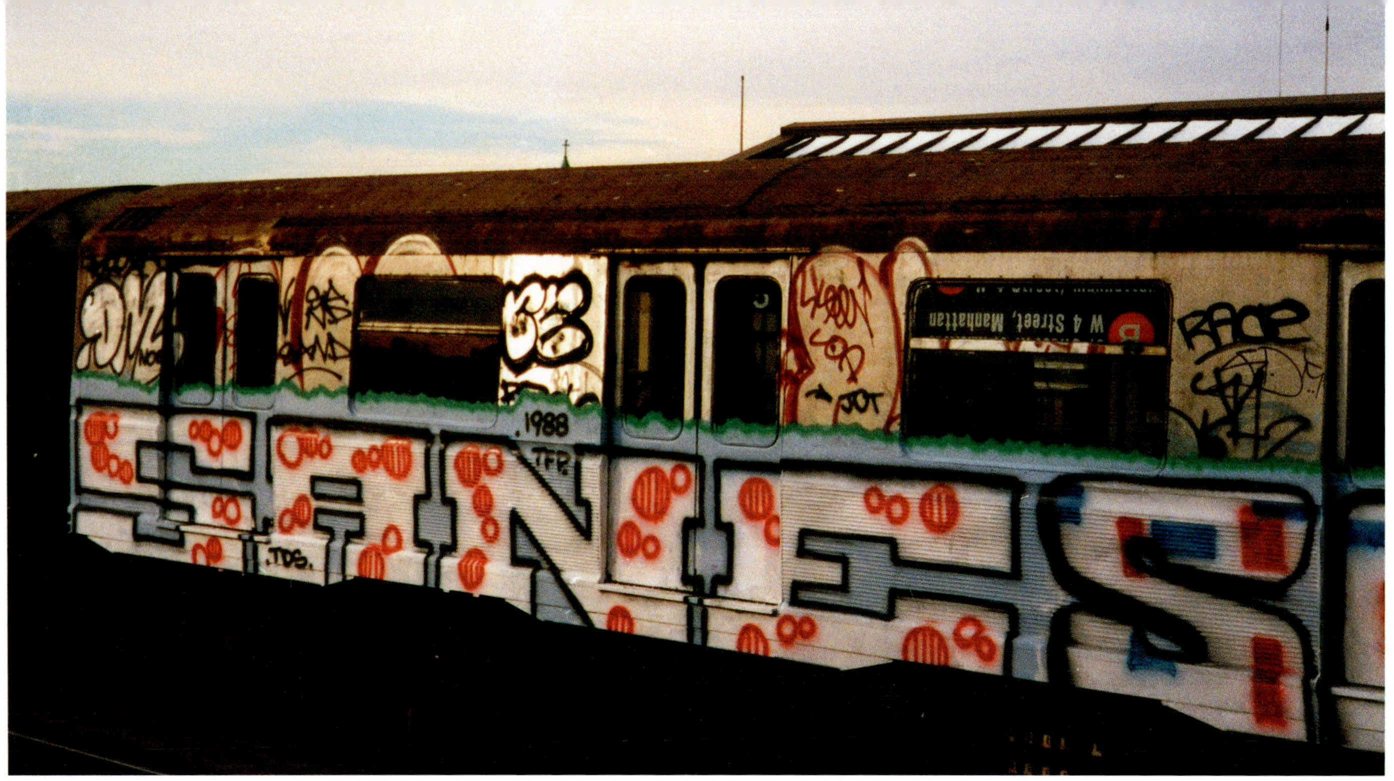

"Sane" (RIP)

"Smith"

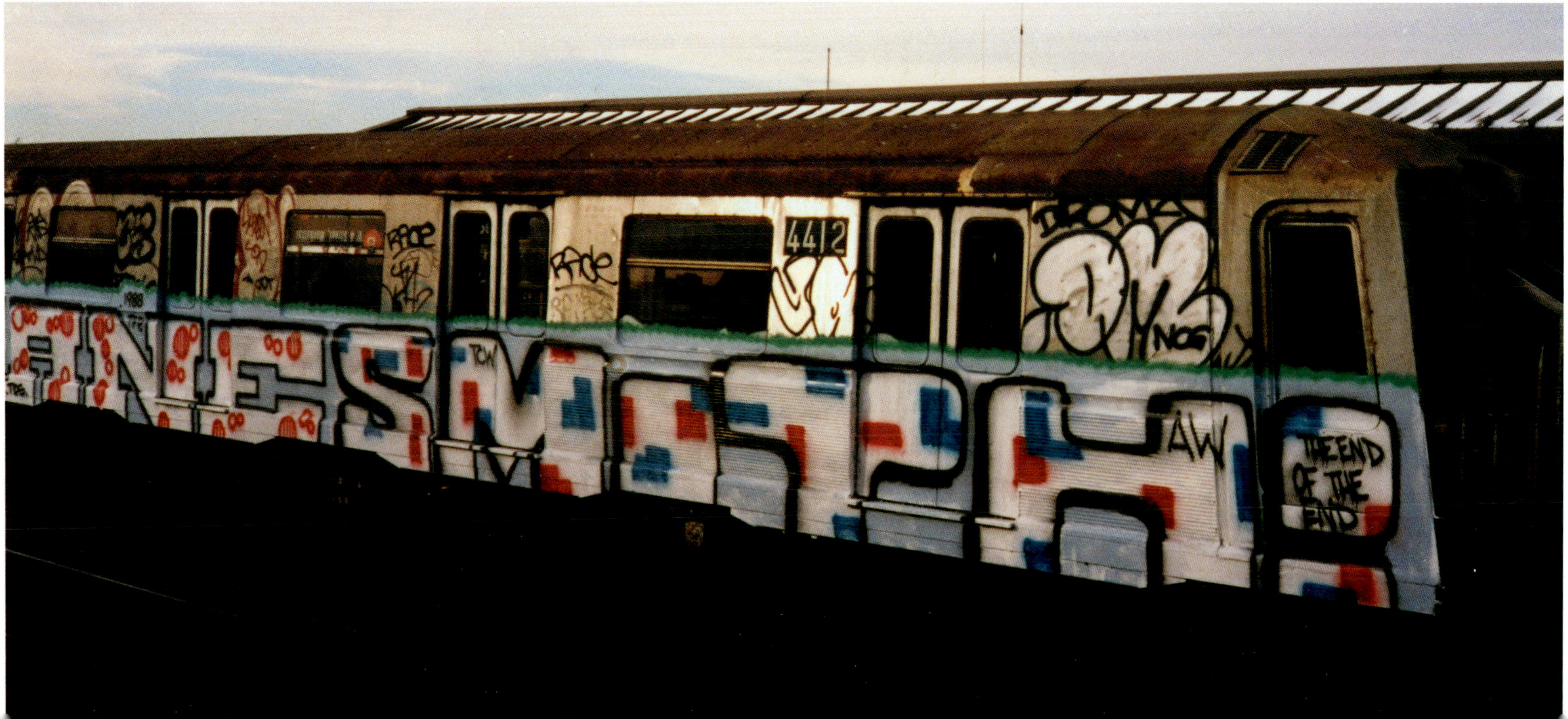

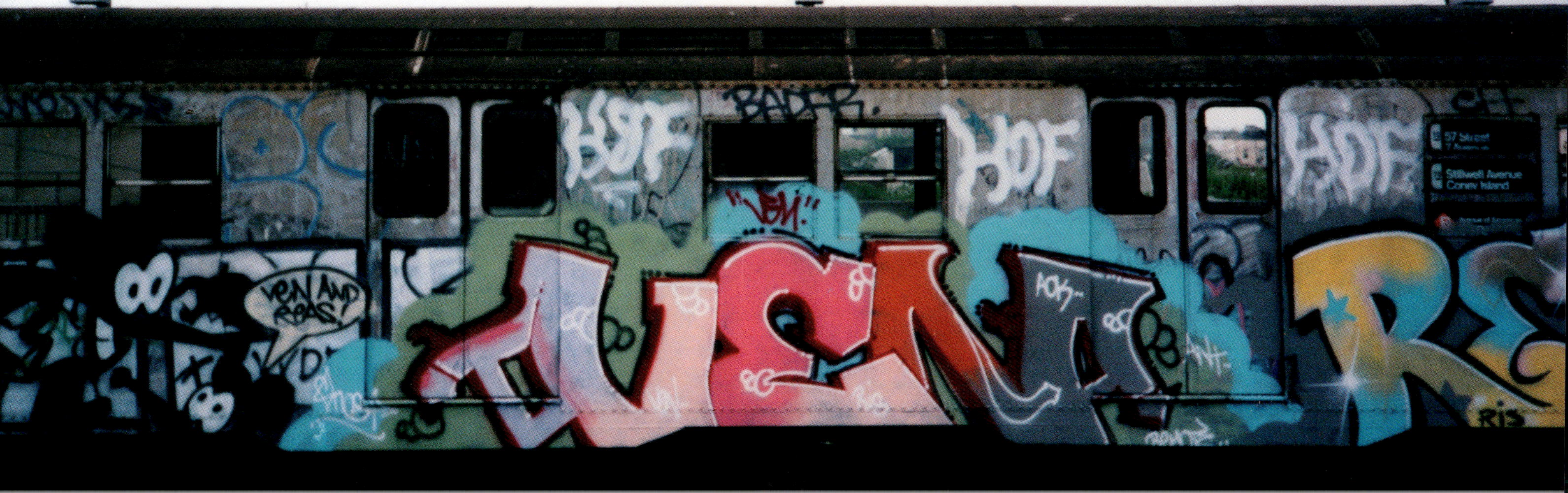

"Ven"

"Reas"

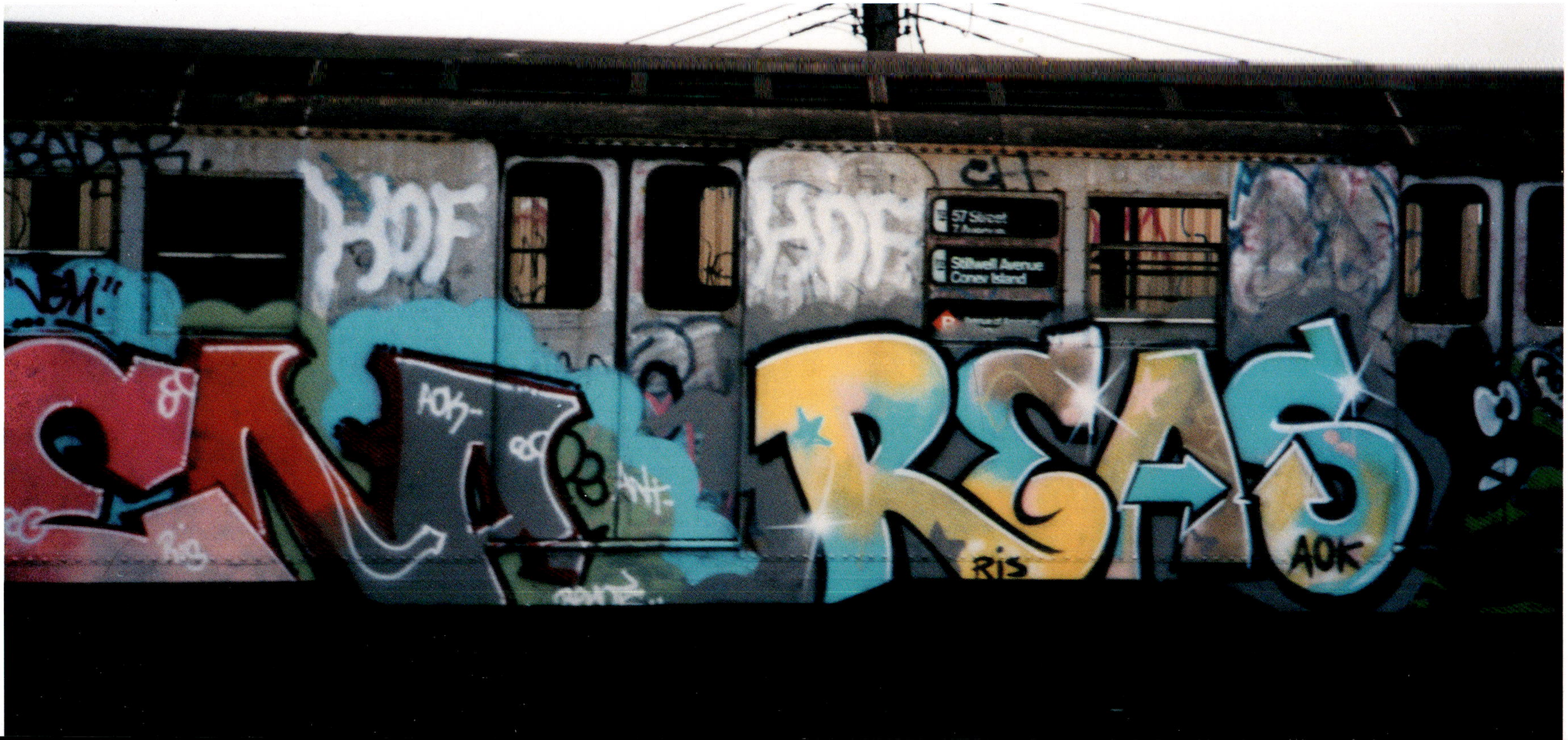

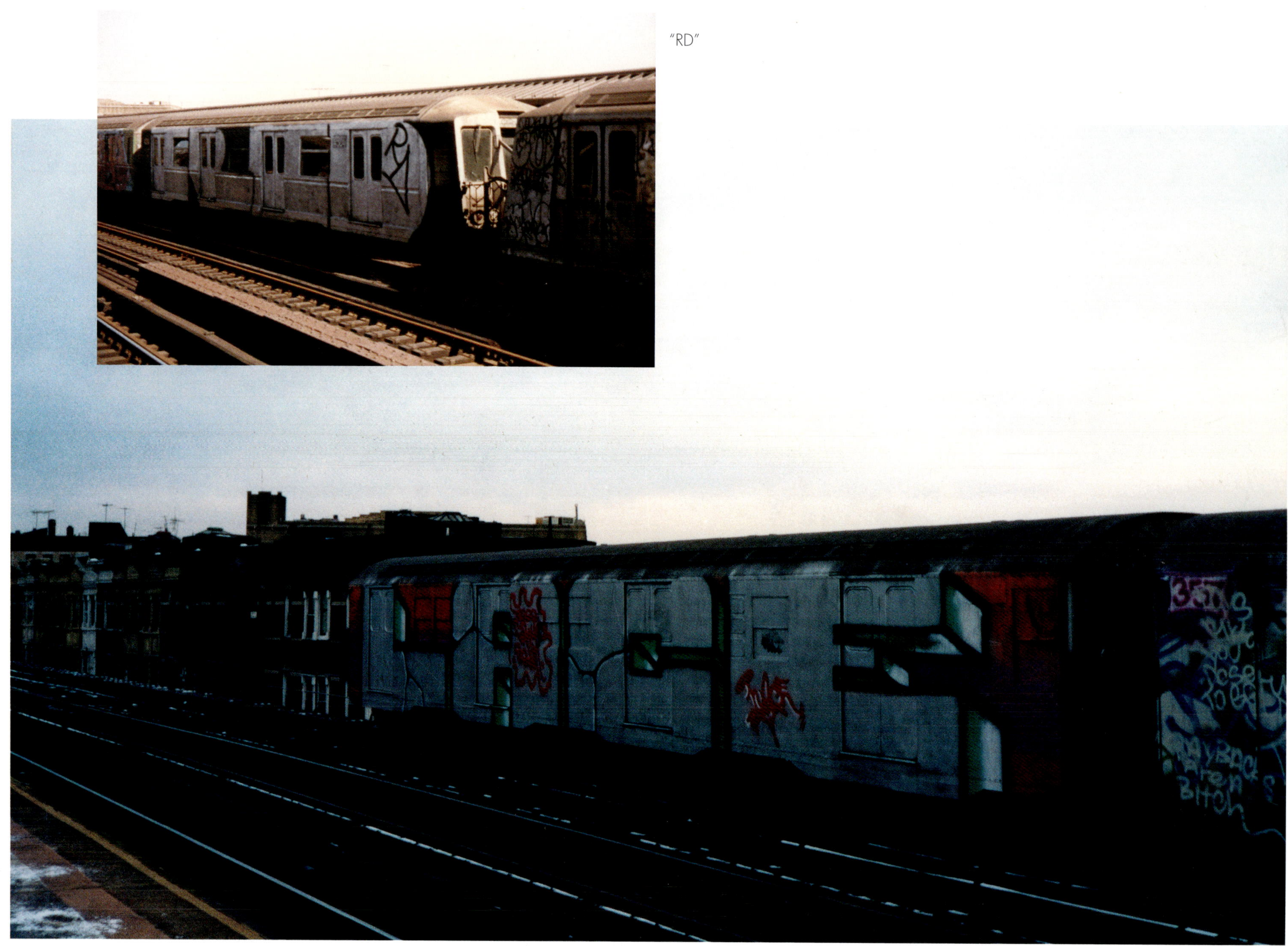

"RD"

"Lace"

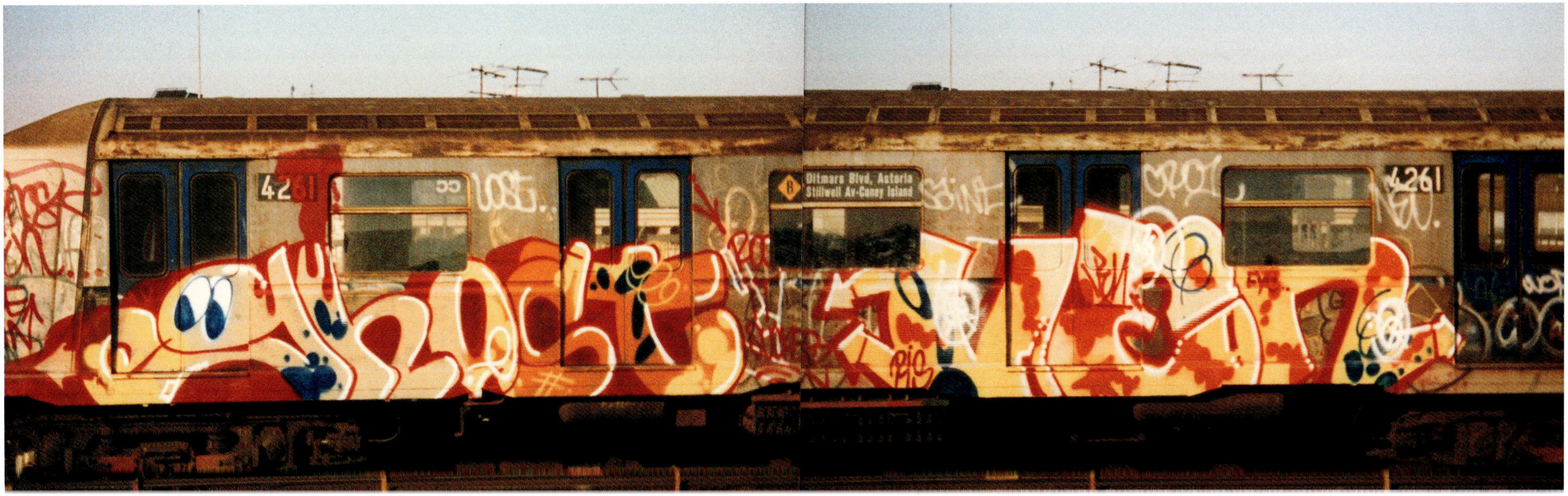

"Ghost" & "Ven"

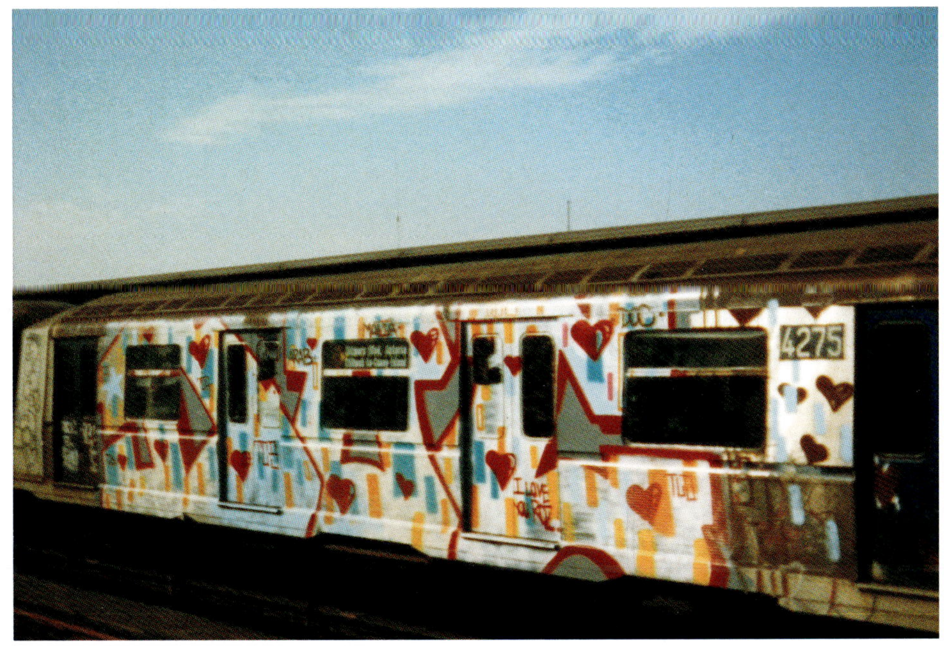

"Doc"

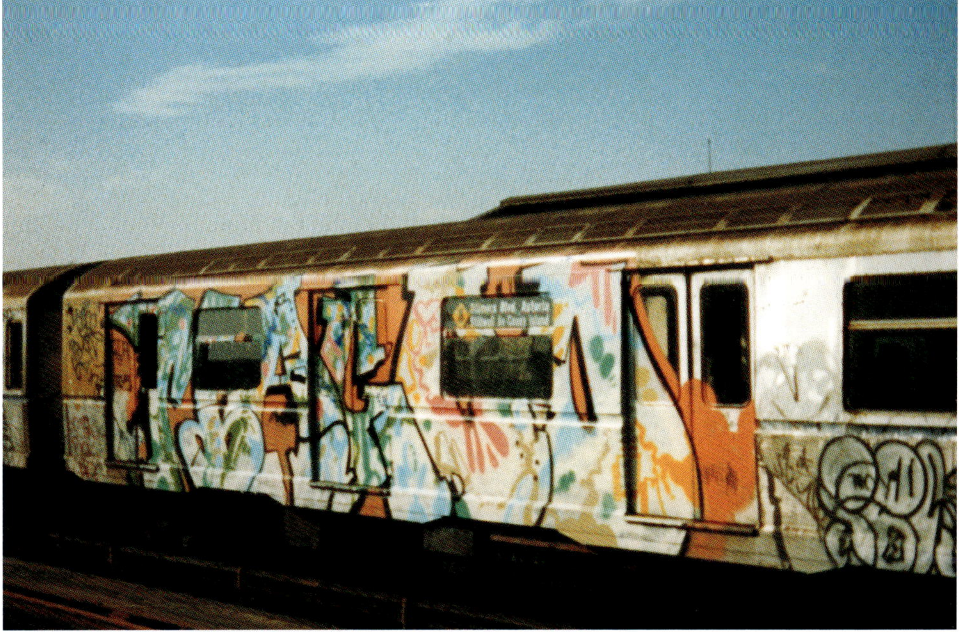

"Magoo"

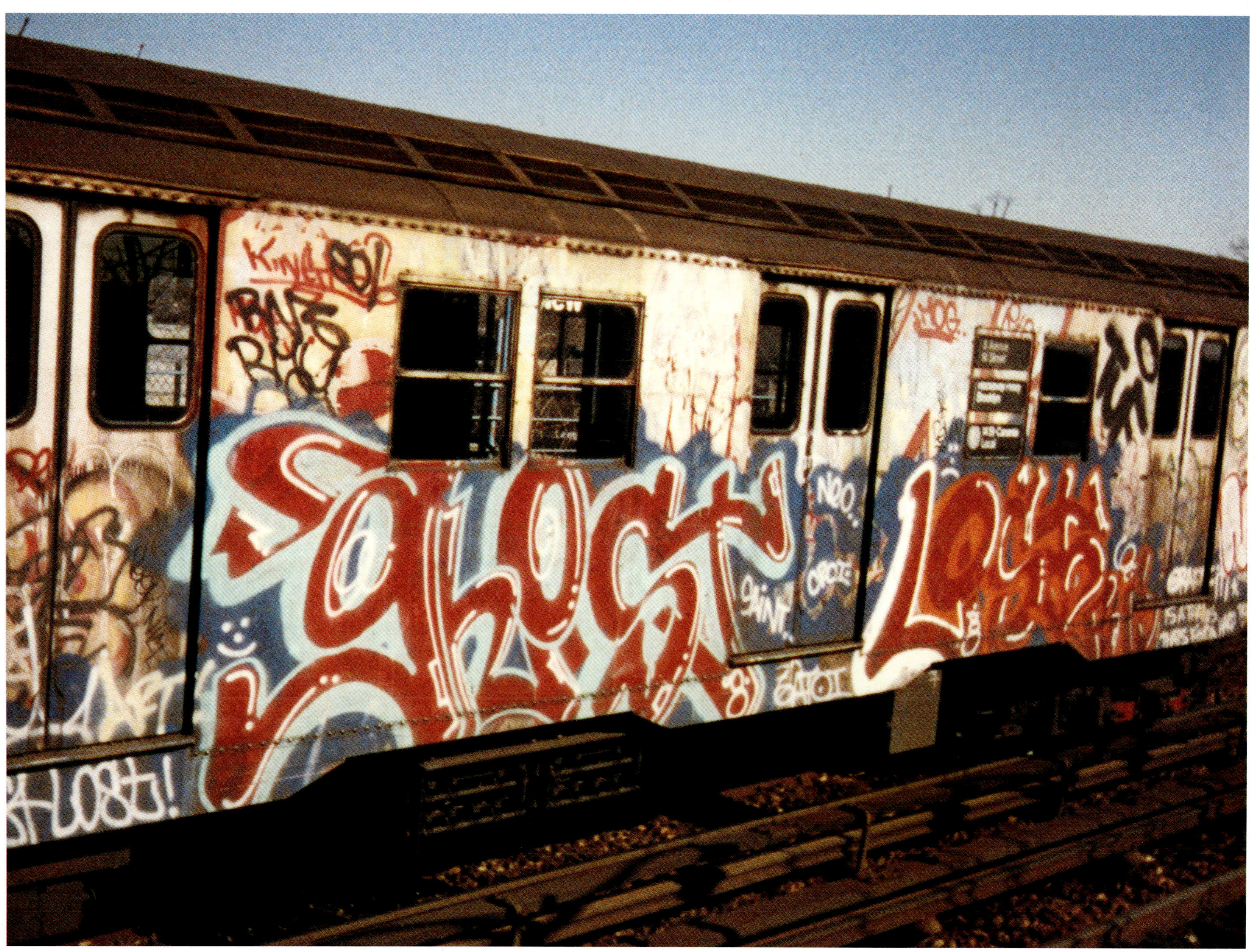

"Ghost" & "Lost"

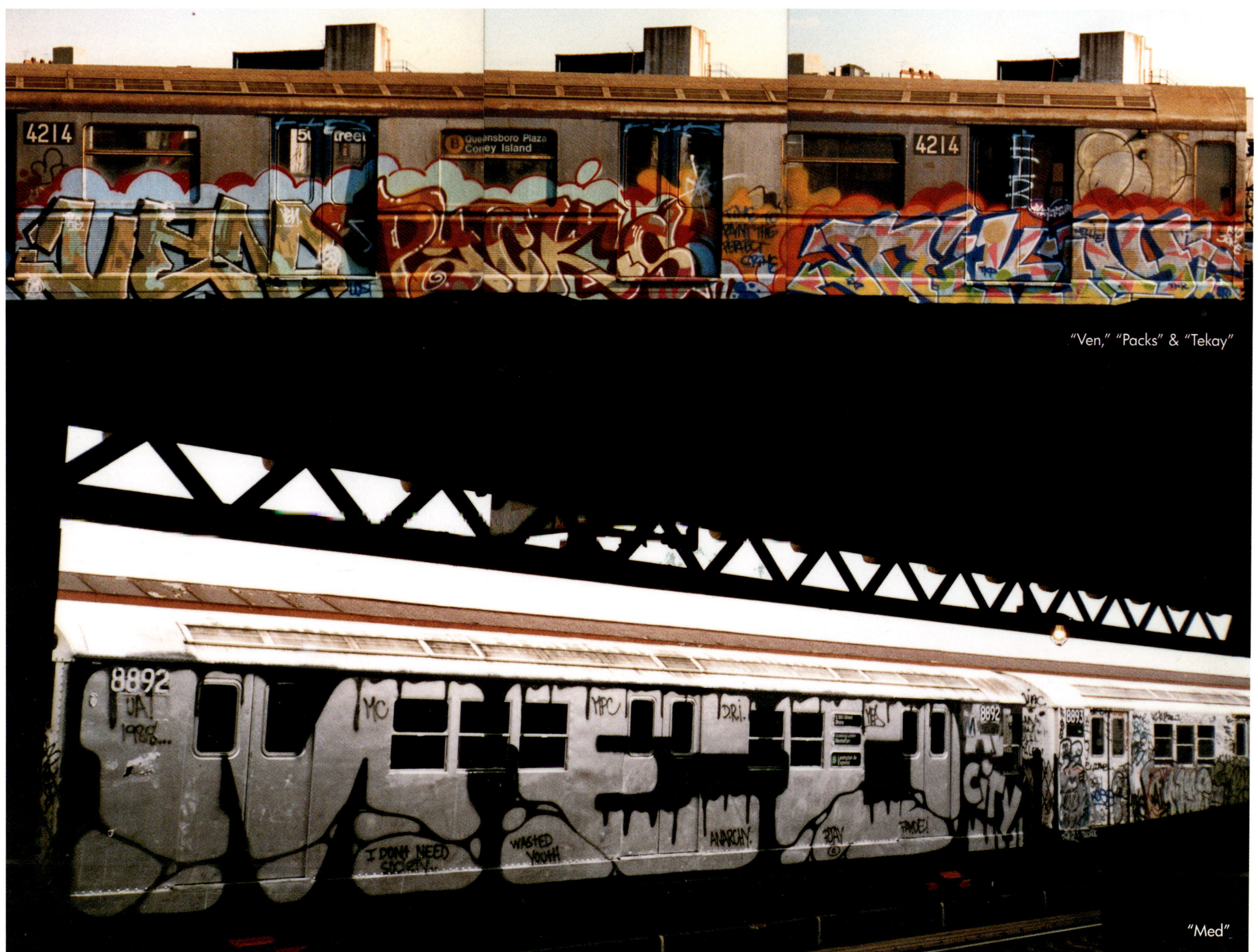

"Ven," "Packs" & "Tekay"

"Med"

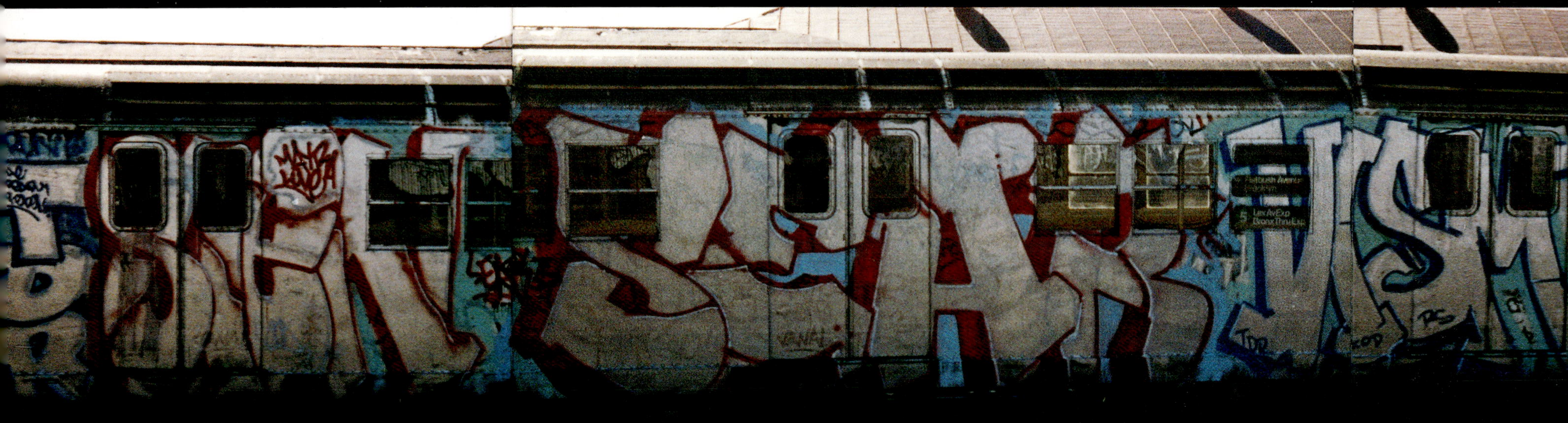

"Sien5," "Sear" & "Vism"

We did this one in Harlem Tunnels on a Sunday morning. Run one MBT (RIP) was with us and had us laughing all the way there, he was like that, always cracking jokes and shit. The lay up was crowded with writers that day. I remember Dero saying Vism and I looked like we were going clubbing cause we used to wear trench coats everywhere back then.

–Sien5

Its not everyday that two brothers write graffiti, even more rare are those that made a real impact on writing. Key and Cavs are the exception to the rule, they tore up the trains and kept writing alive through the last days of the train era. Their contribution to subways and to the beginning of the freight train movement was critical to the development of the trans-continental movement of painting that exists in America today.

–Alan Ket, author

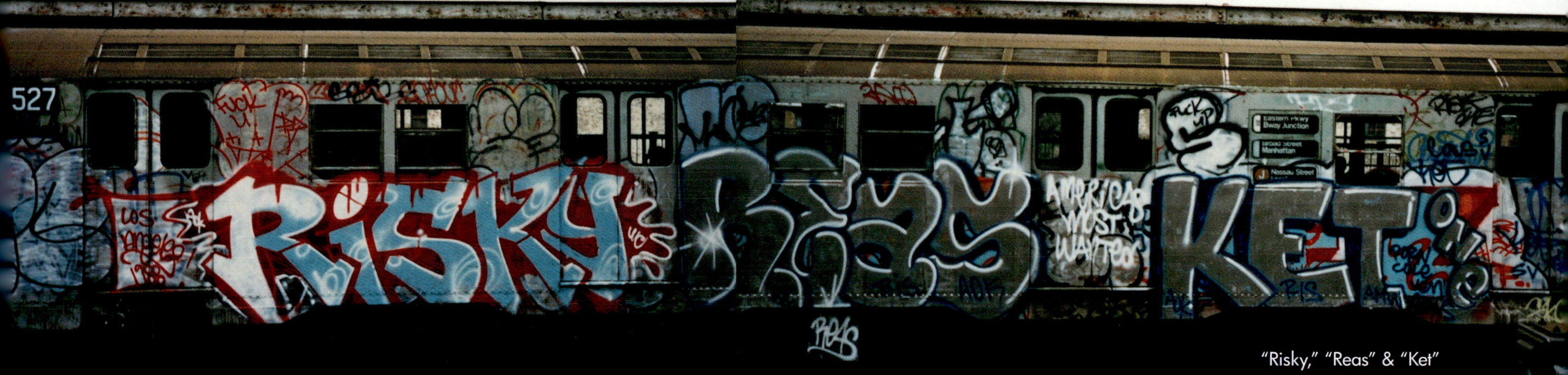

"Risky," "Reas" & "Ket"

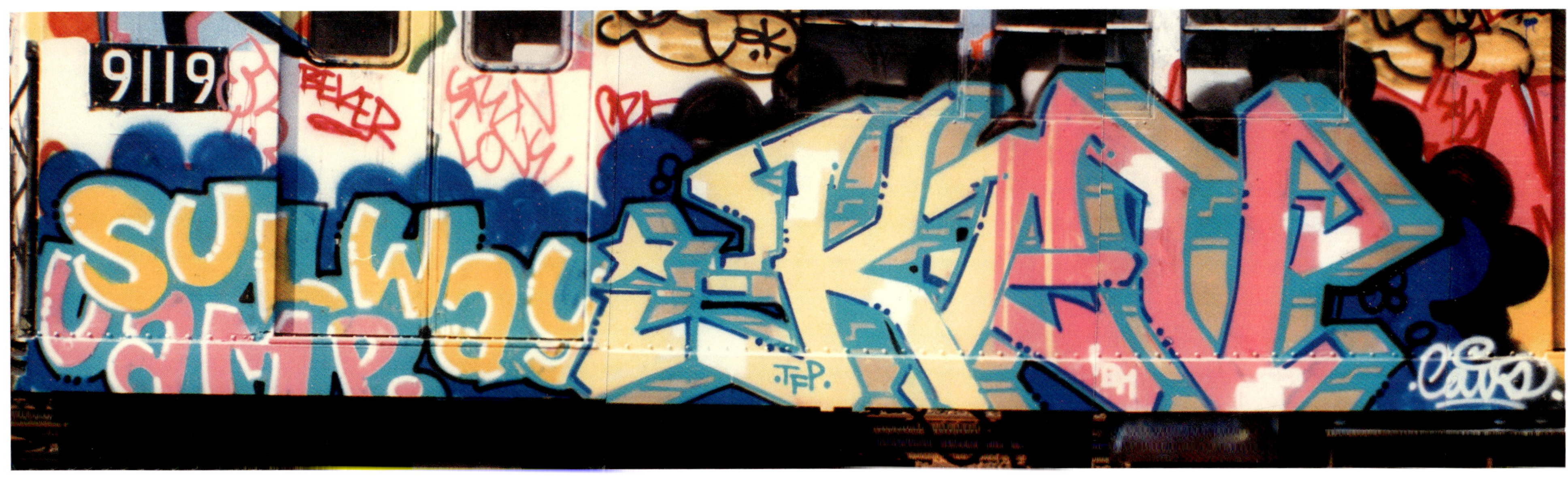

"Kav"

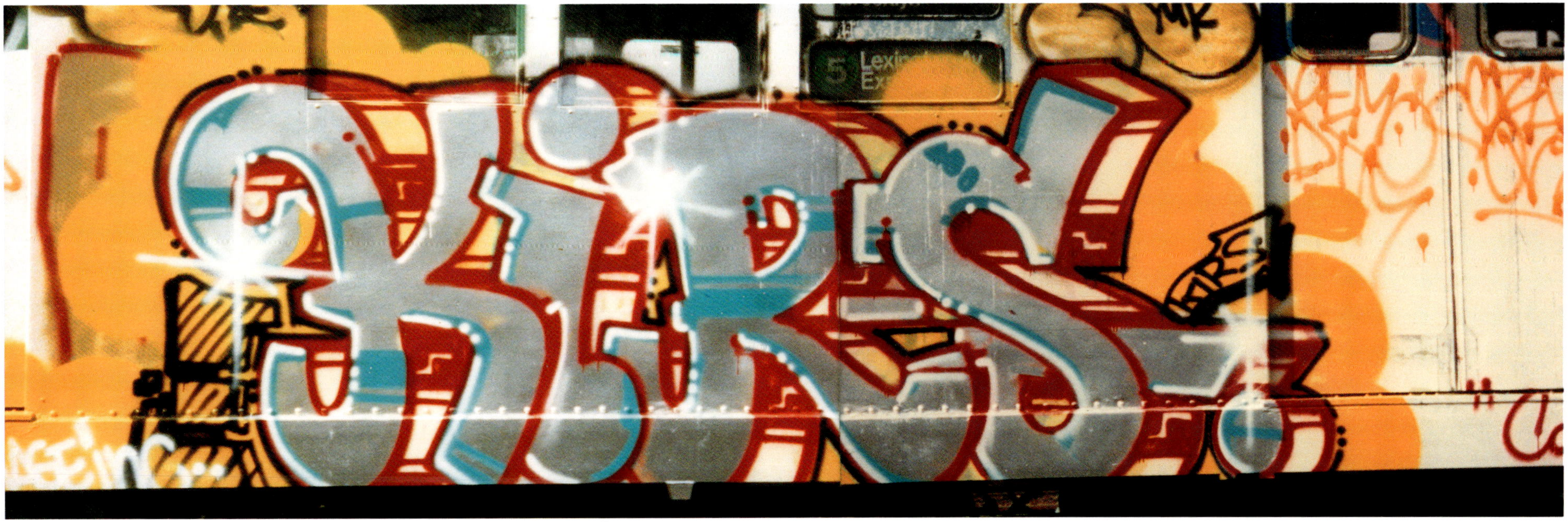

"Kirs"

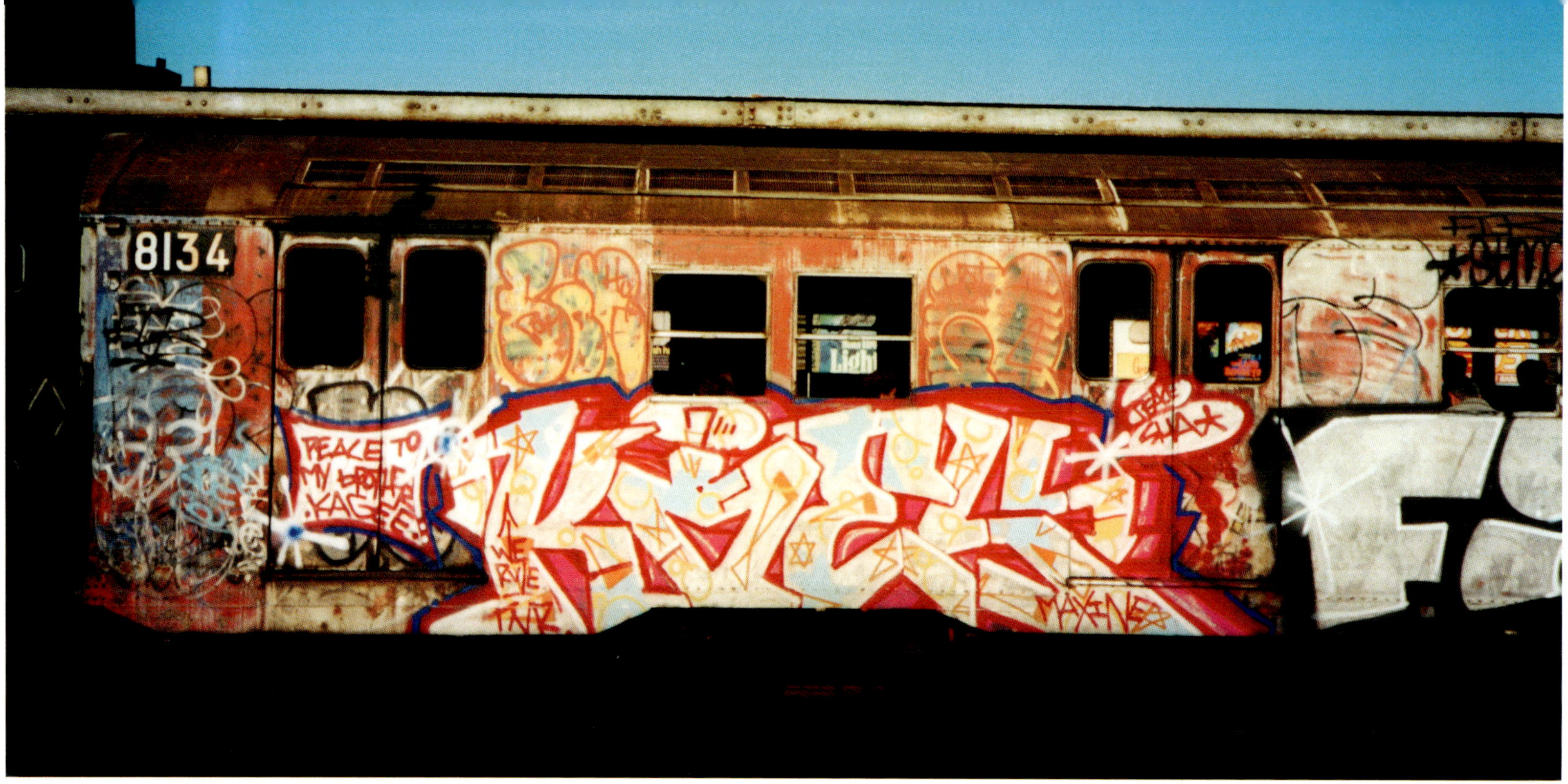

"Kies"

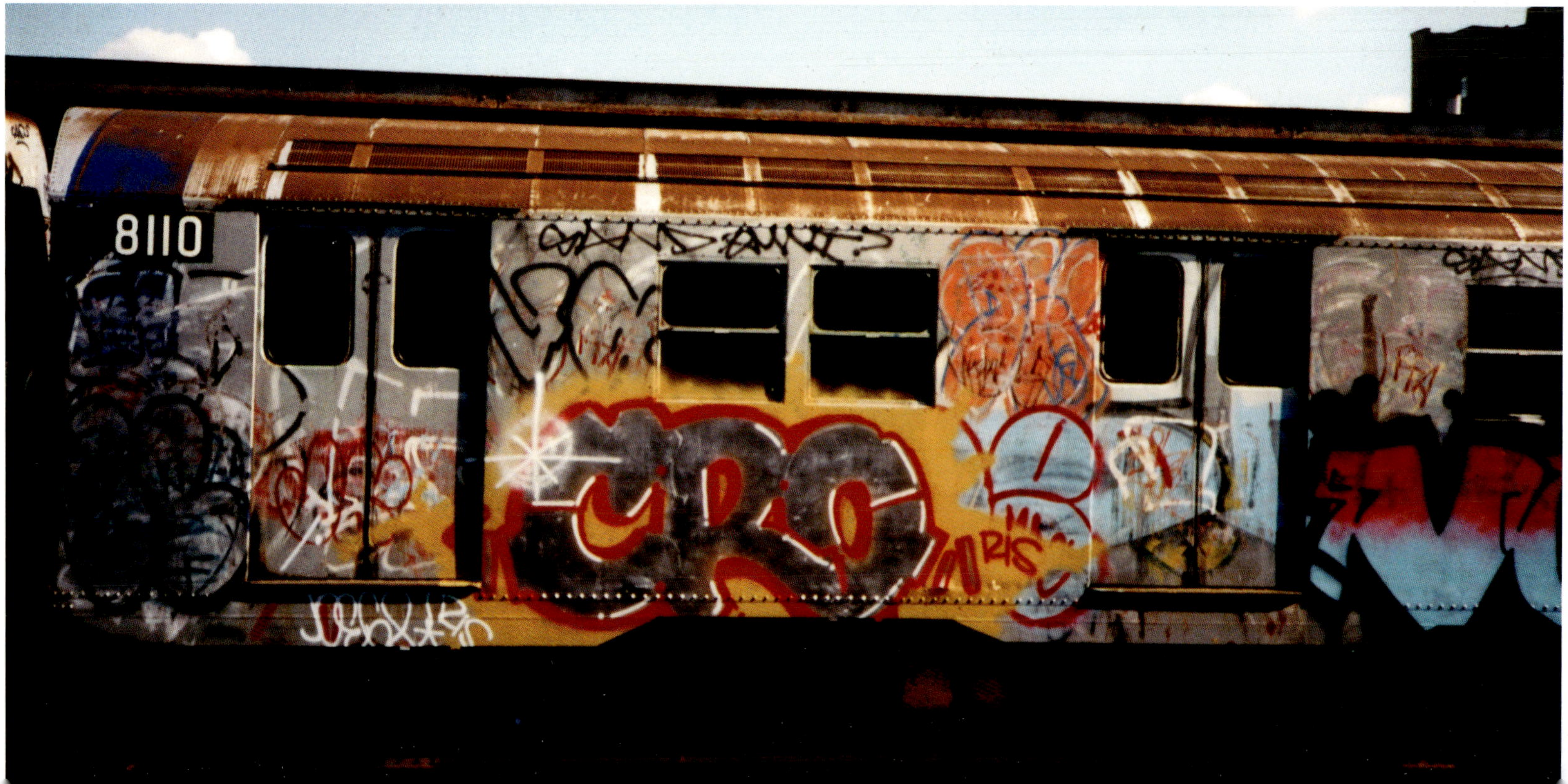

"Cro"

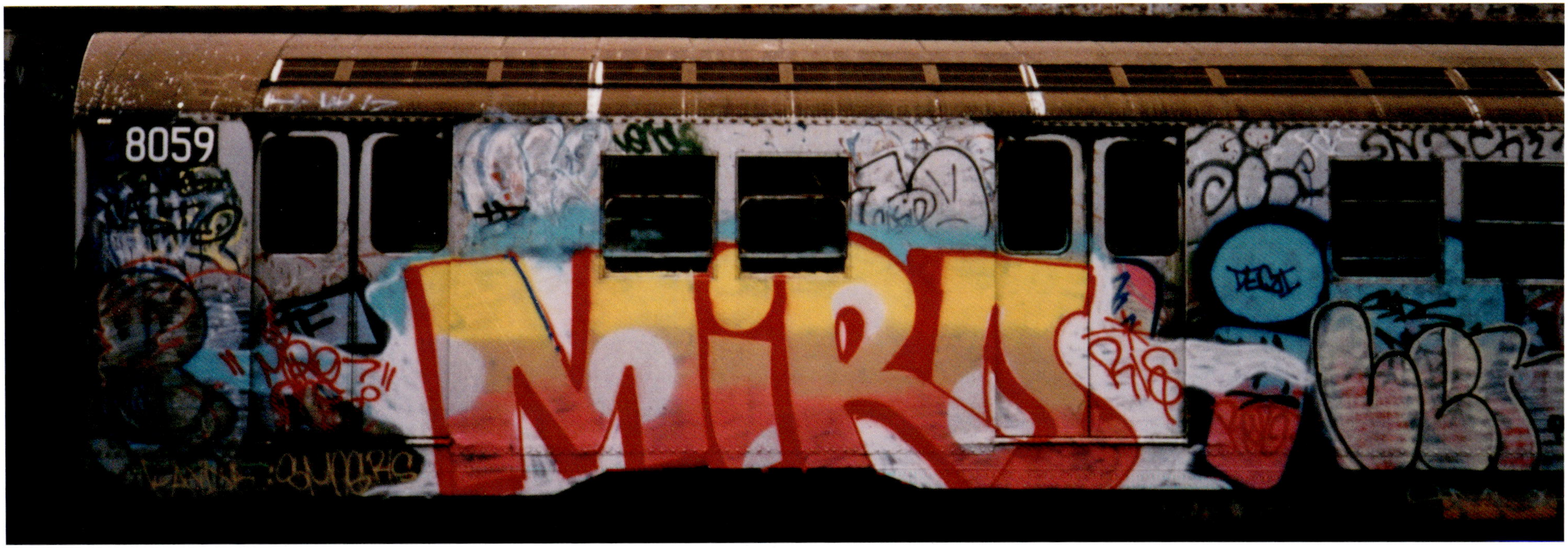

"Miro"

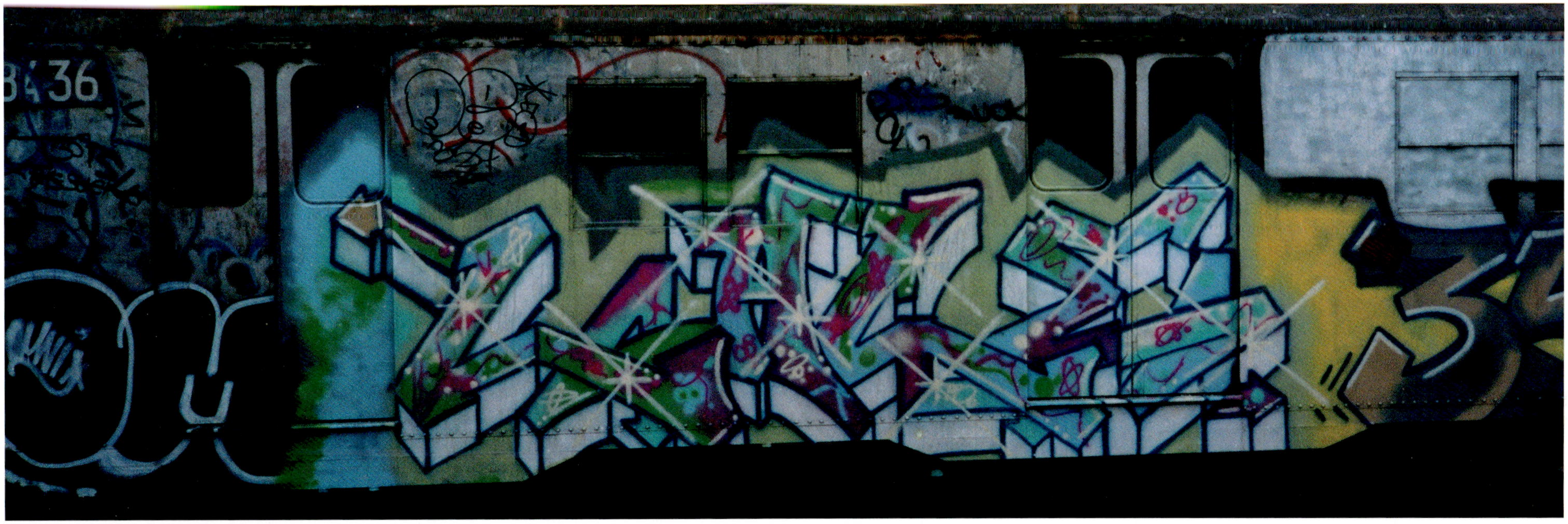

"Lace"

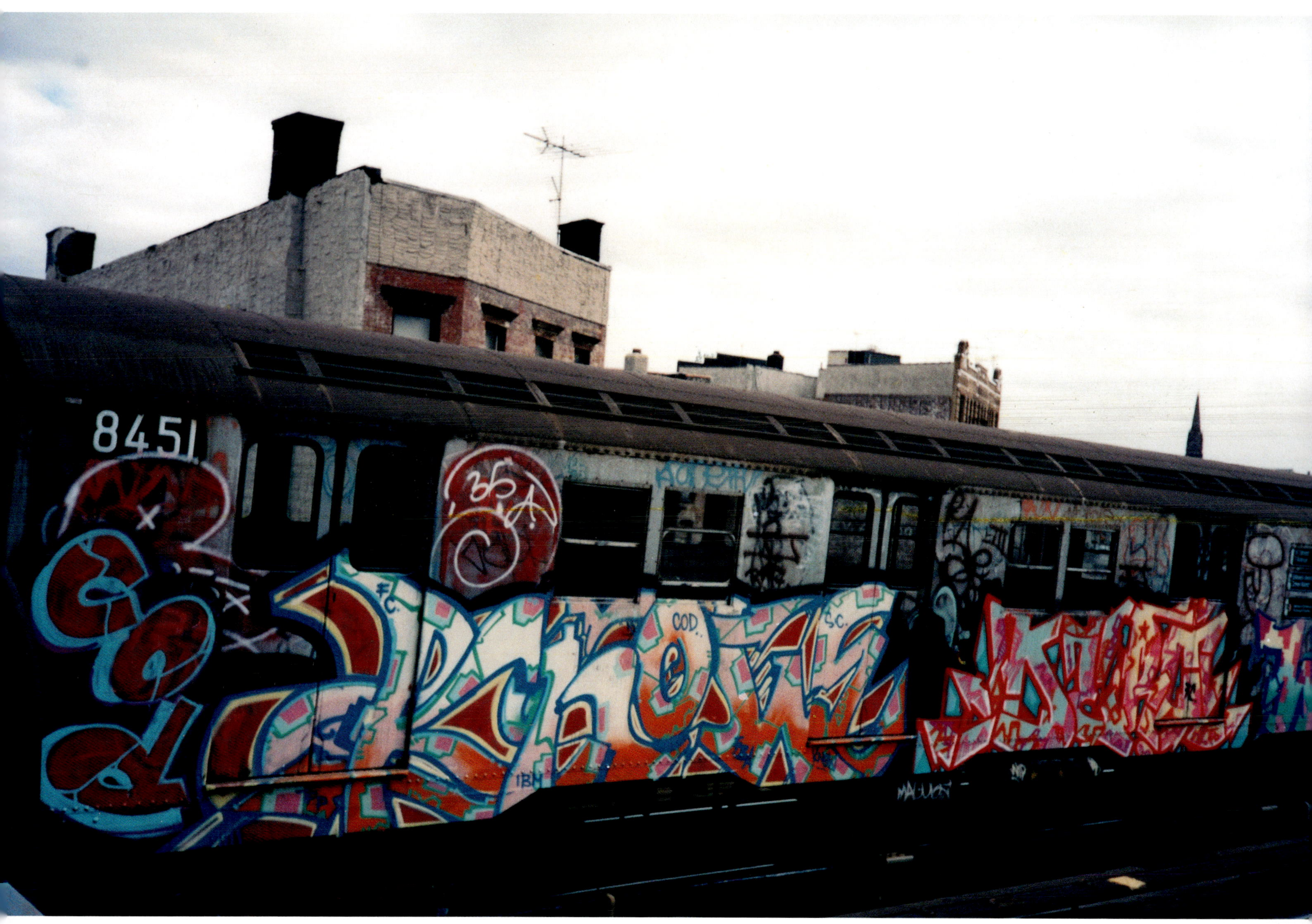

"Know," "Dero" & "Wips"

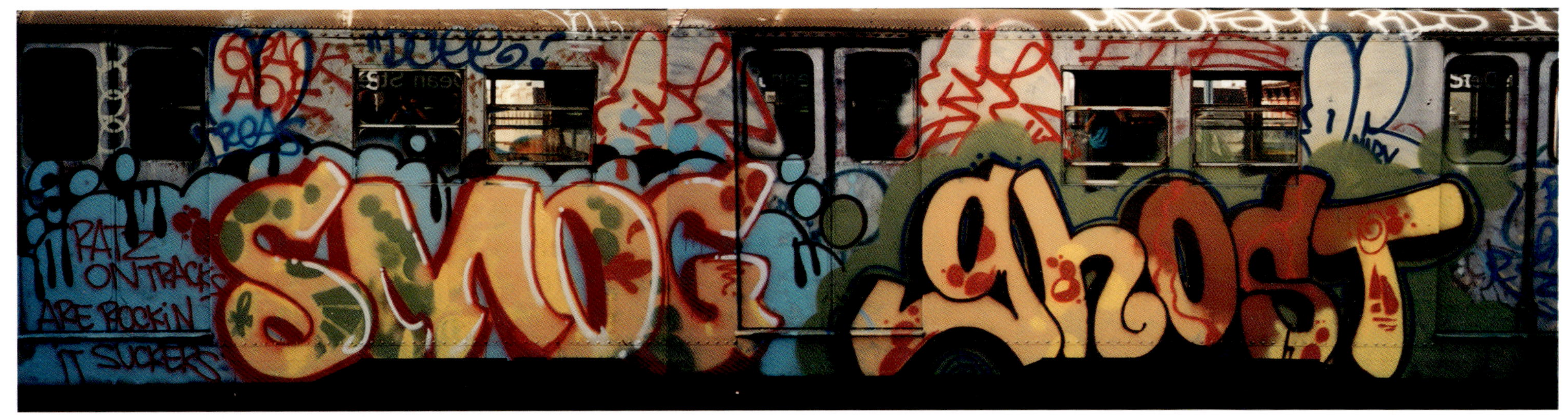

"Smog" & "Ghost"

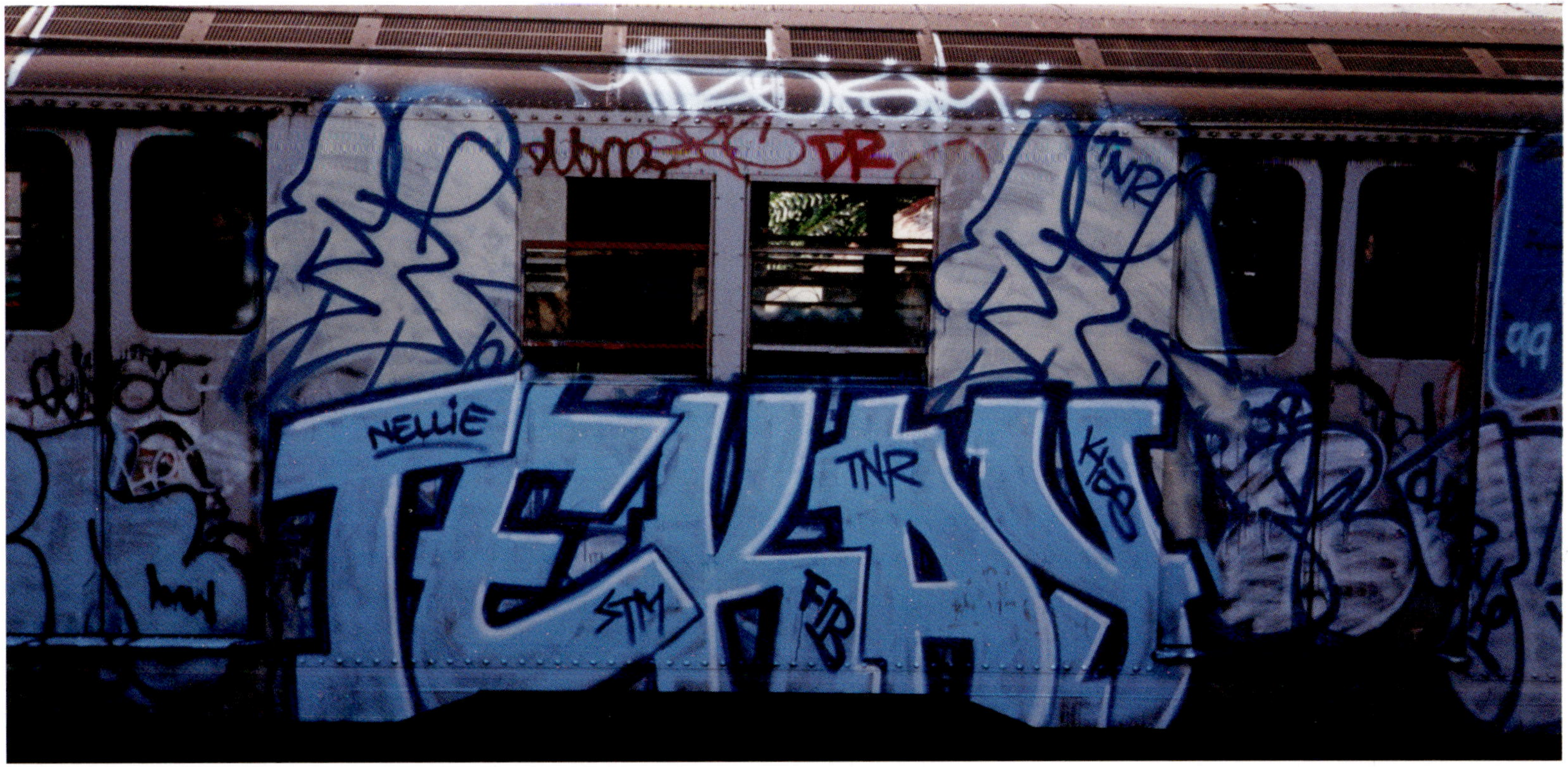

"Tekay"

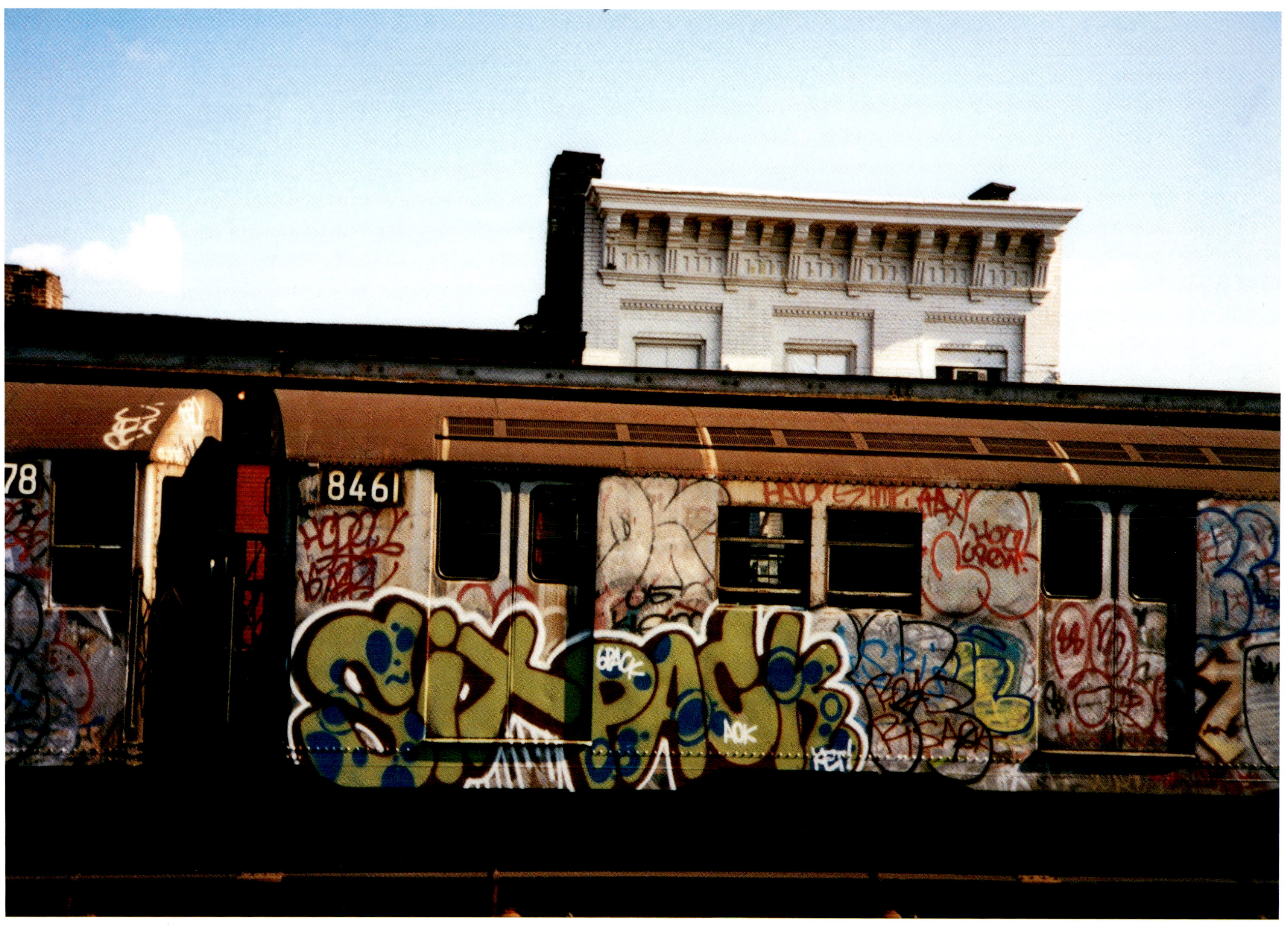

"Six Pack"

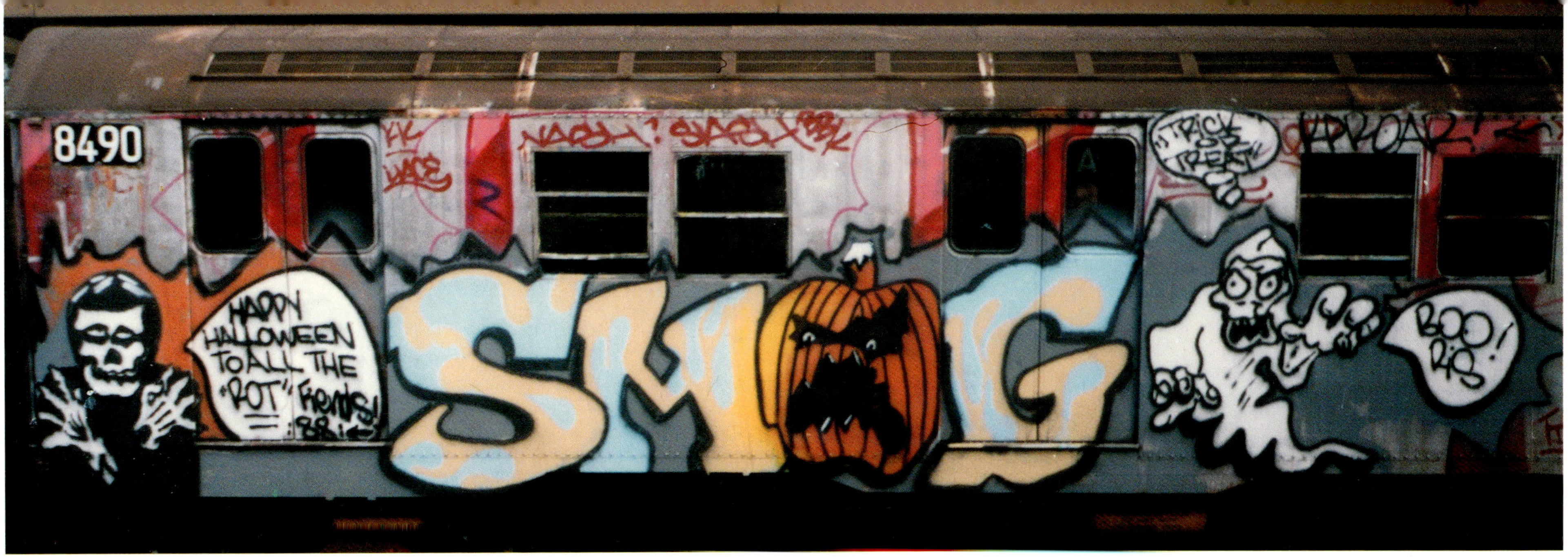

"Smog"

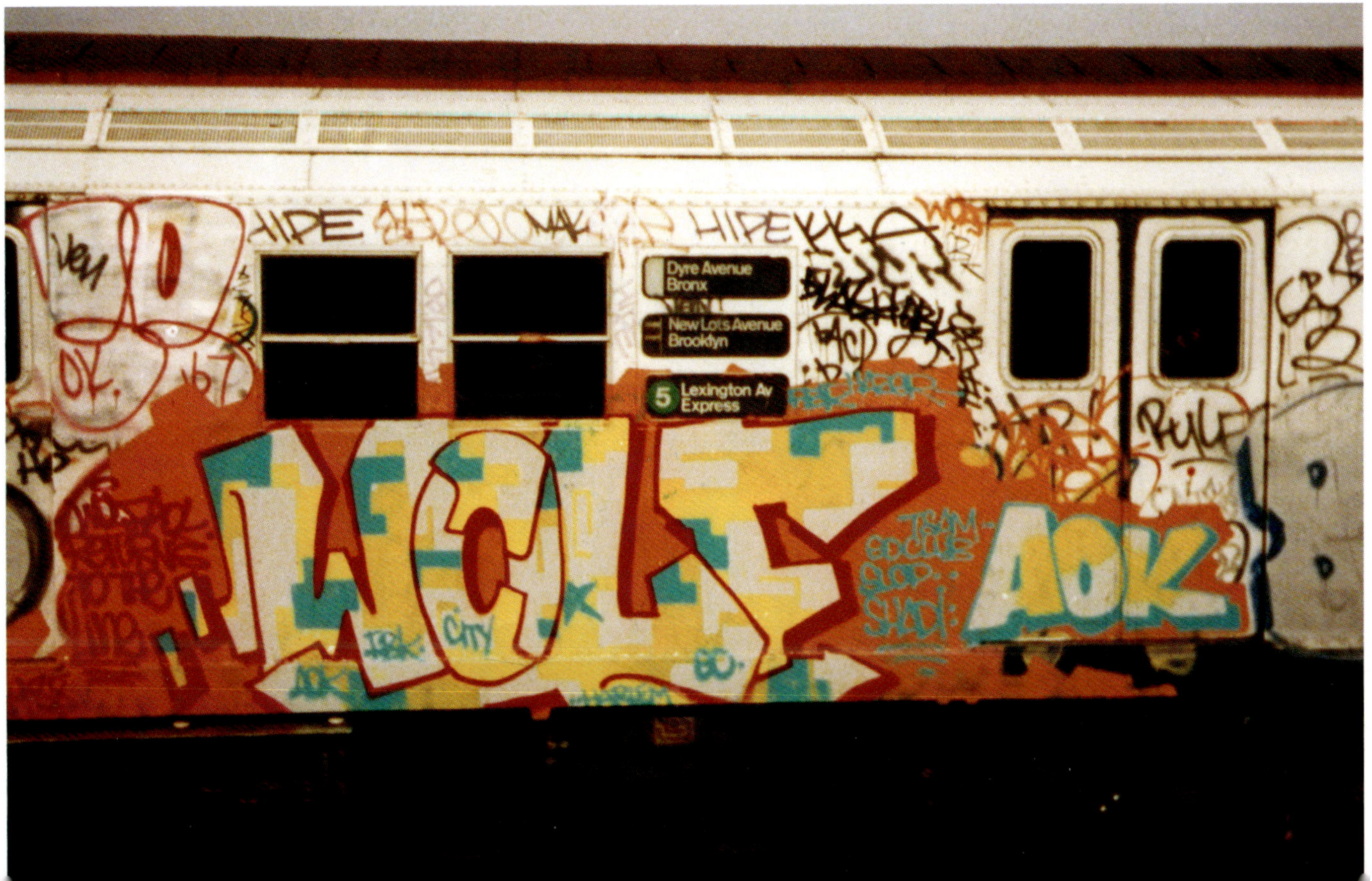

"Wolf"

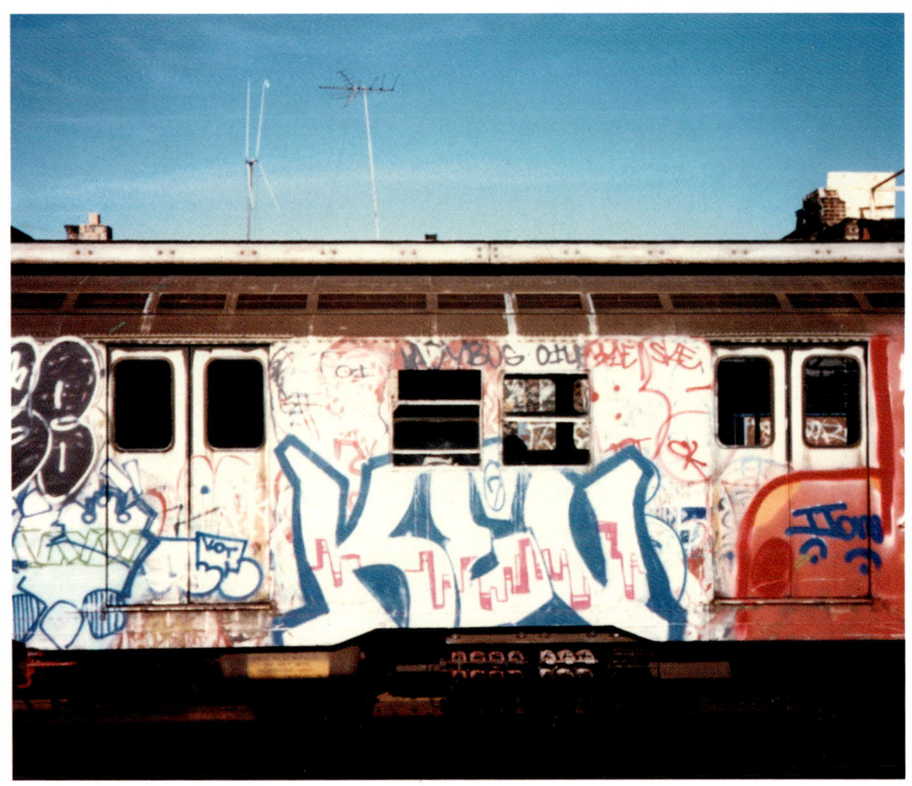

"Kev"

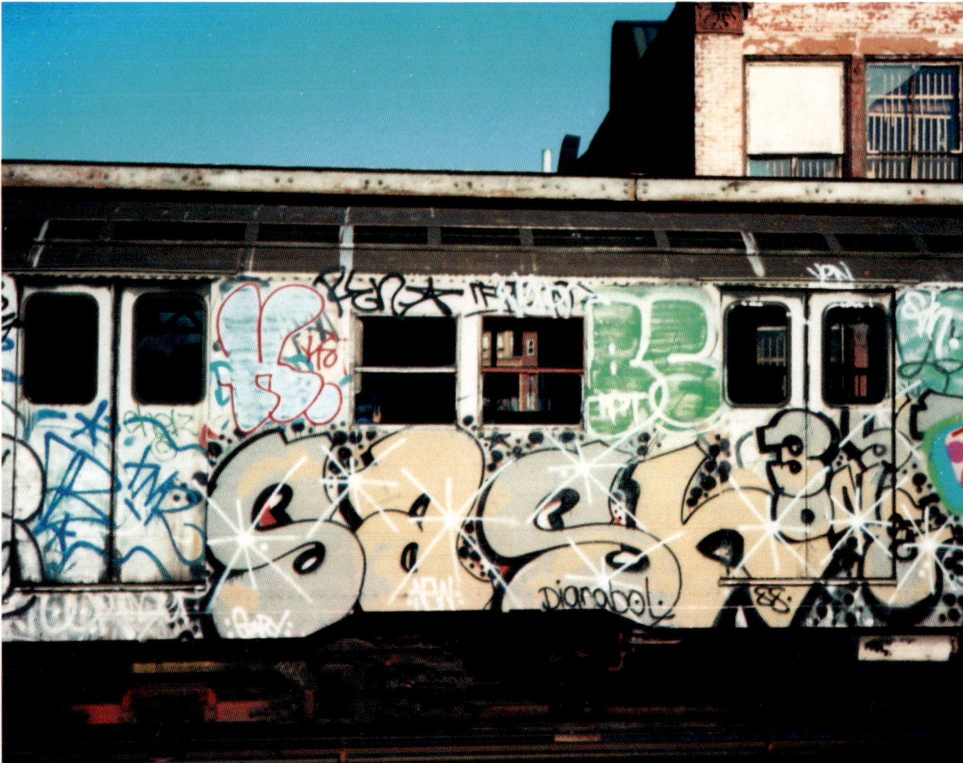

"Sash" (RIP)

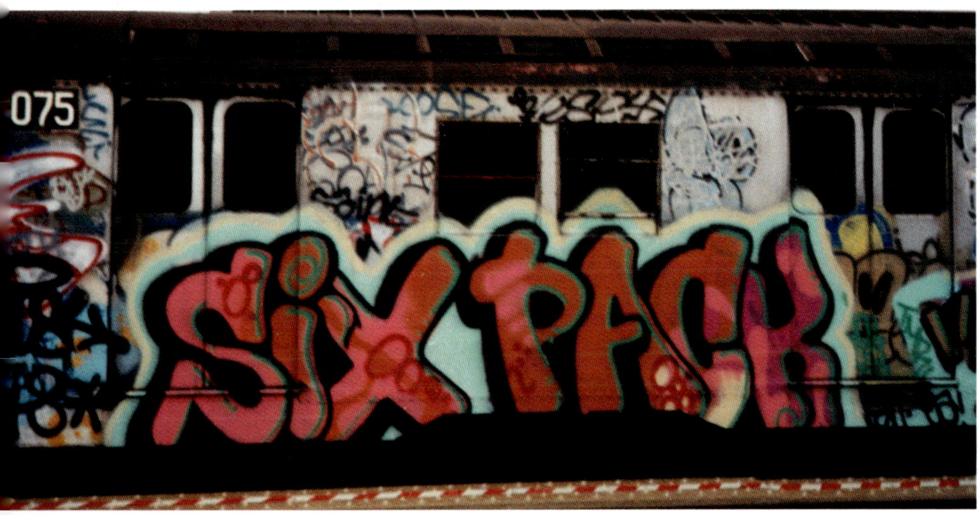

"Six Pack"

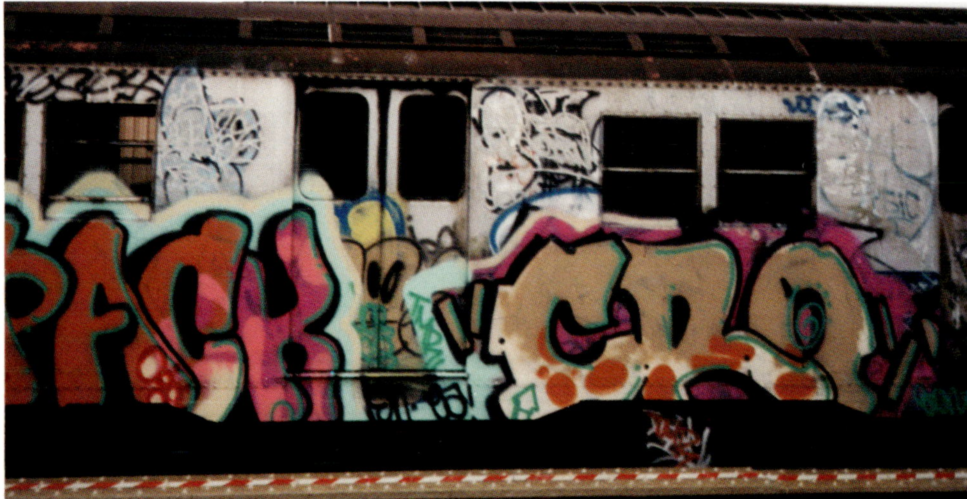

"Cro"

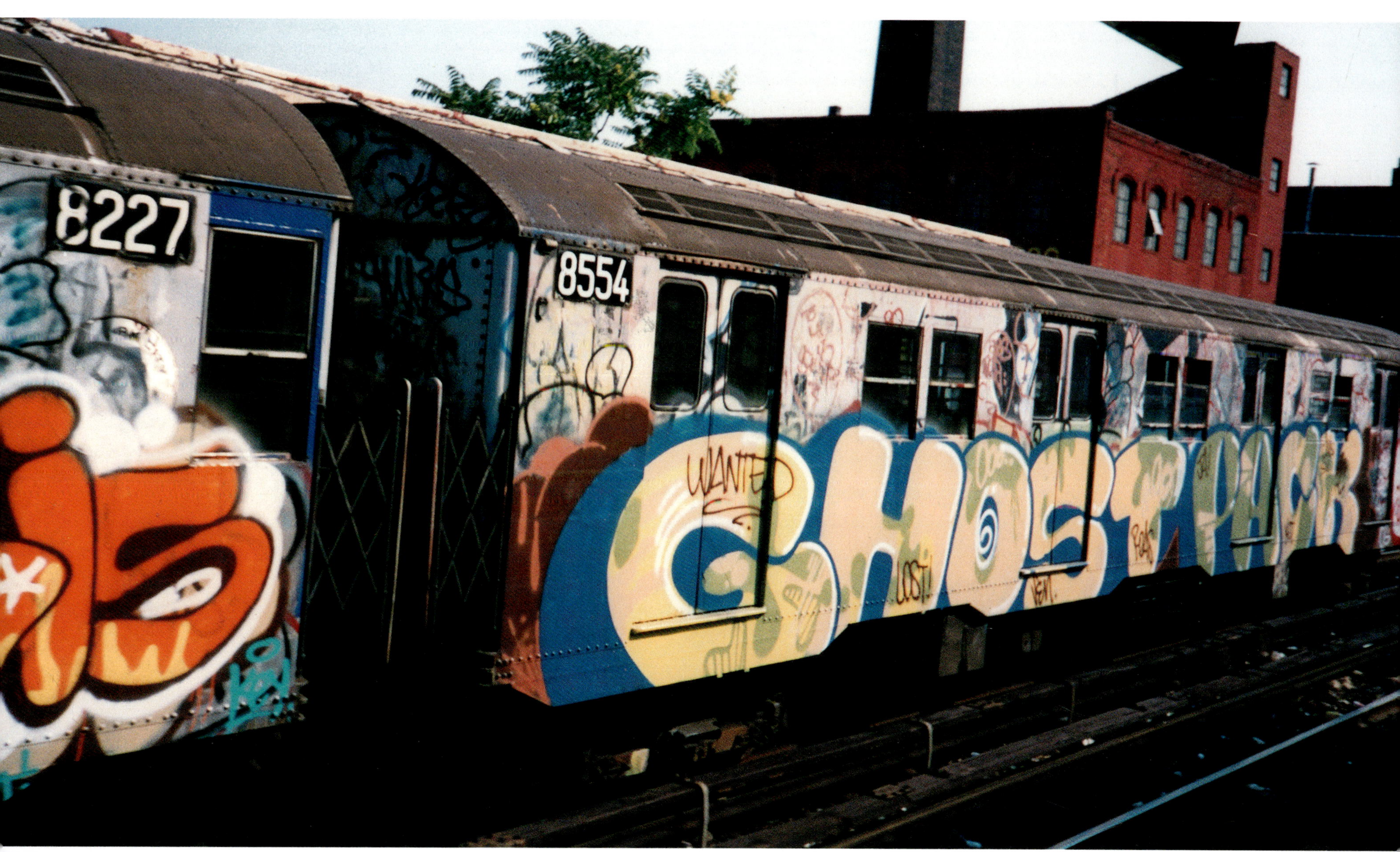

"Ghost, Pack"

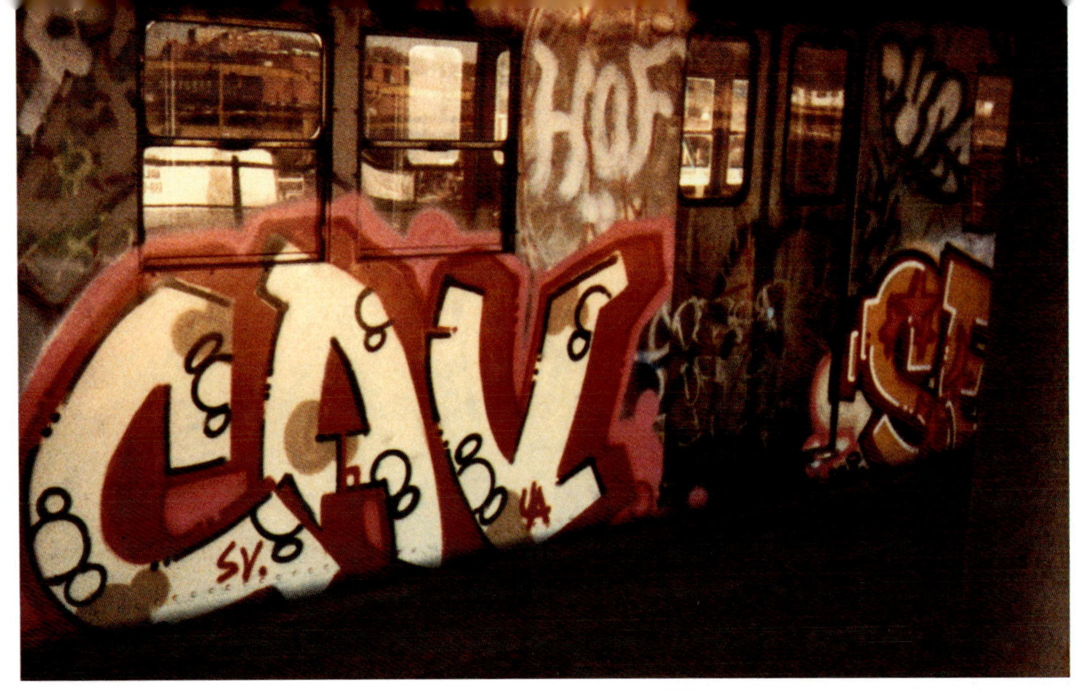

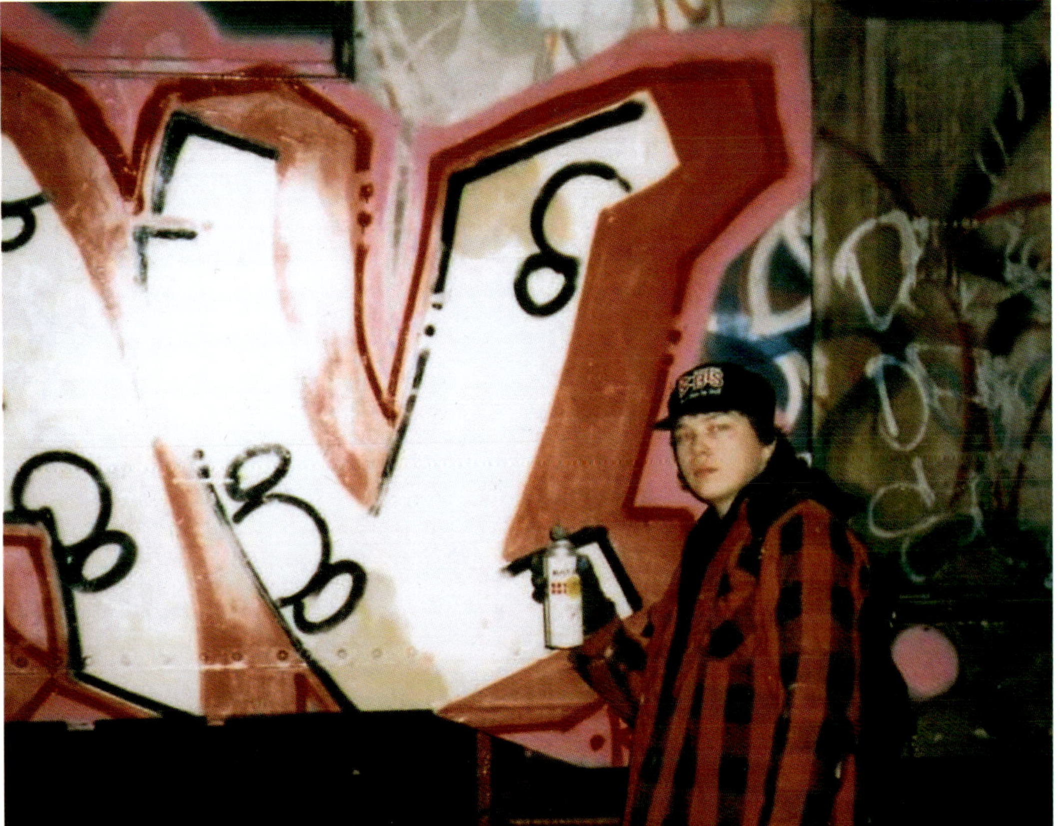

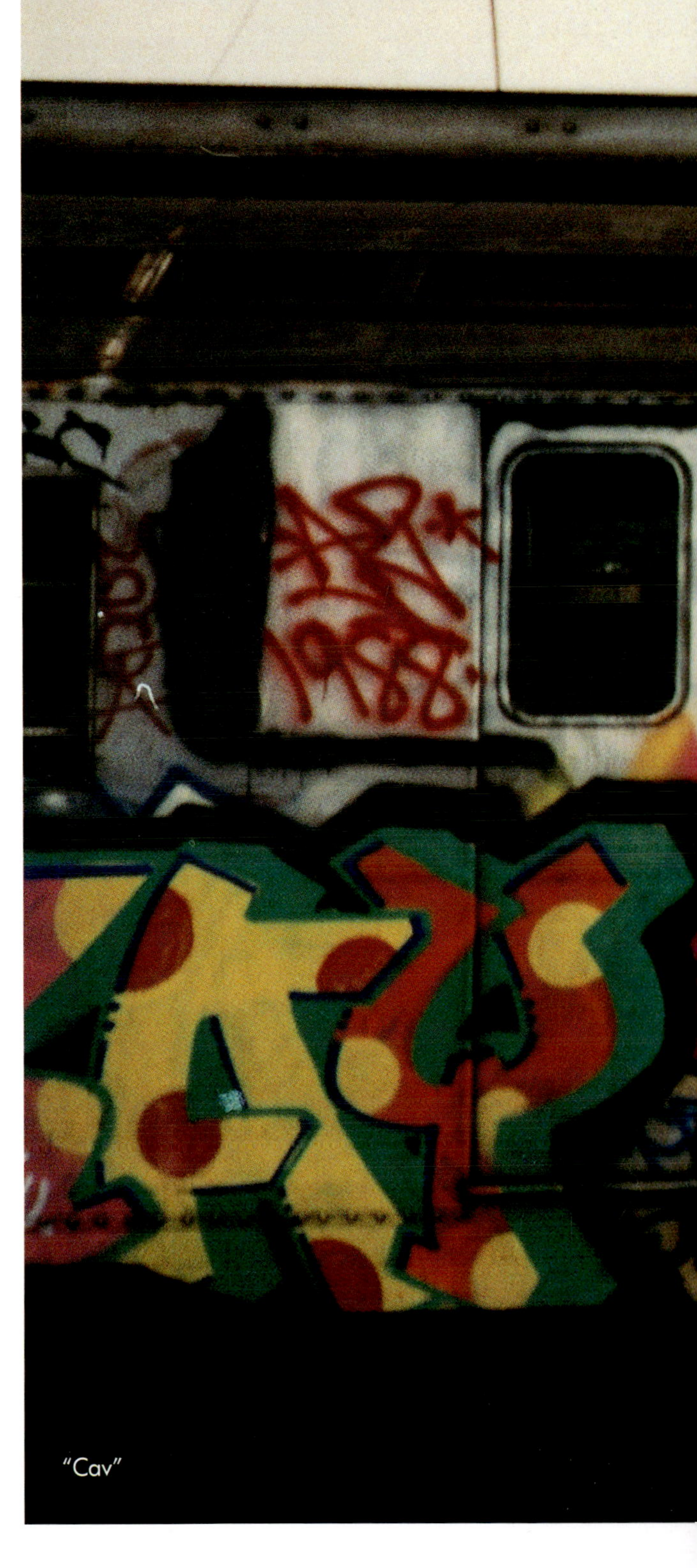

"Cav"

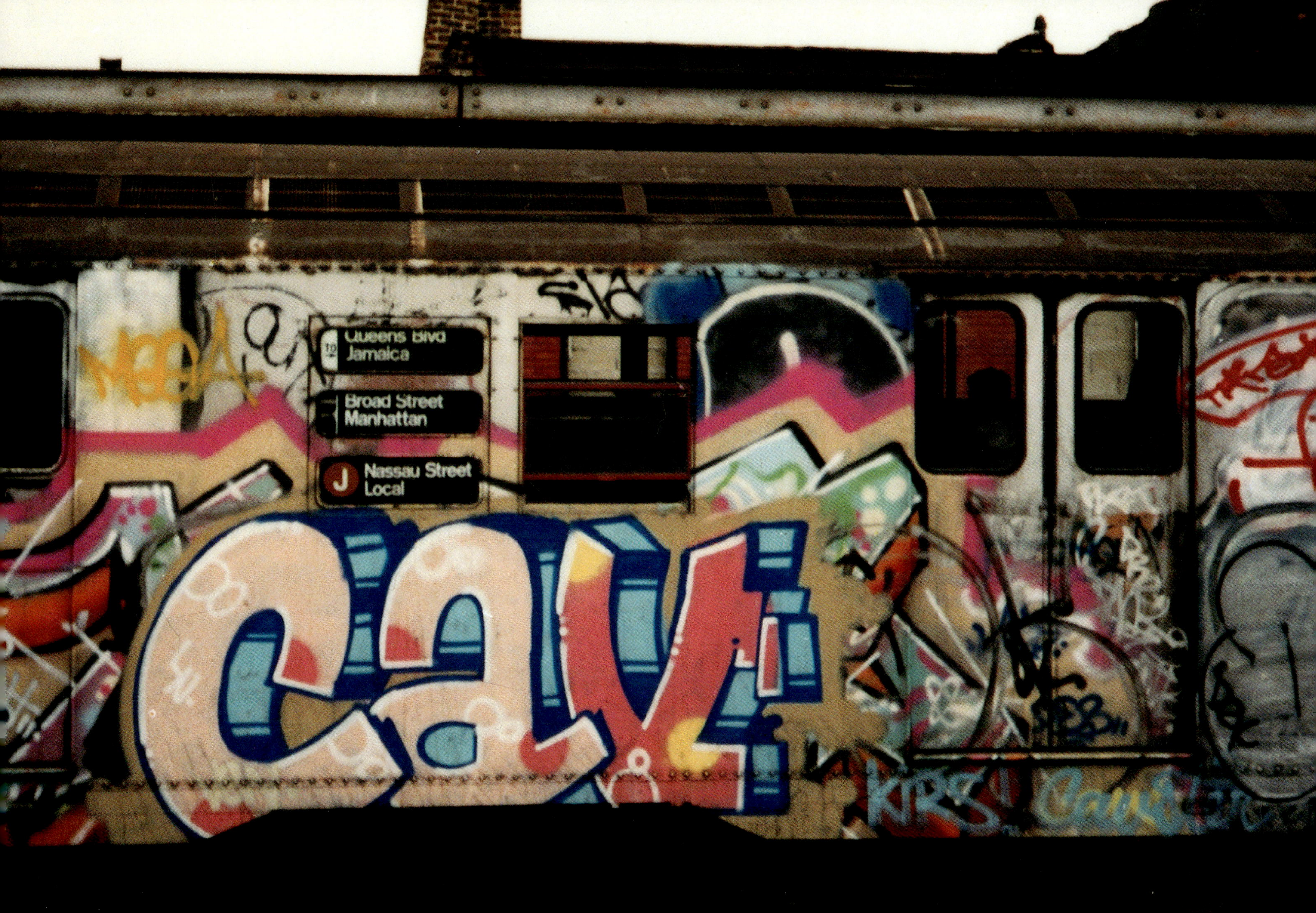
Queens Blvd
Jamaica
Broad Street
Manhattan
J
Nassau Street
Local

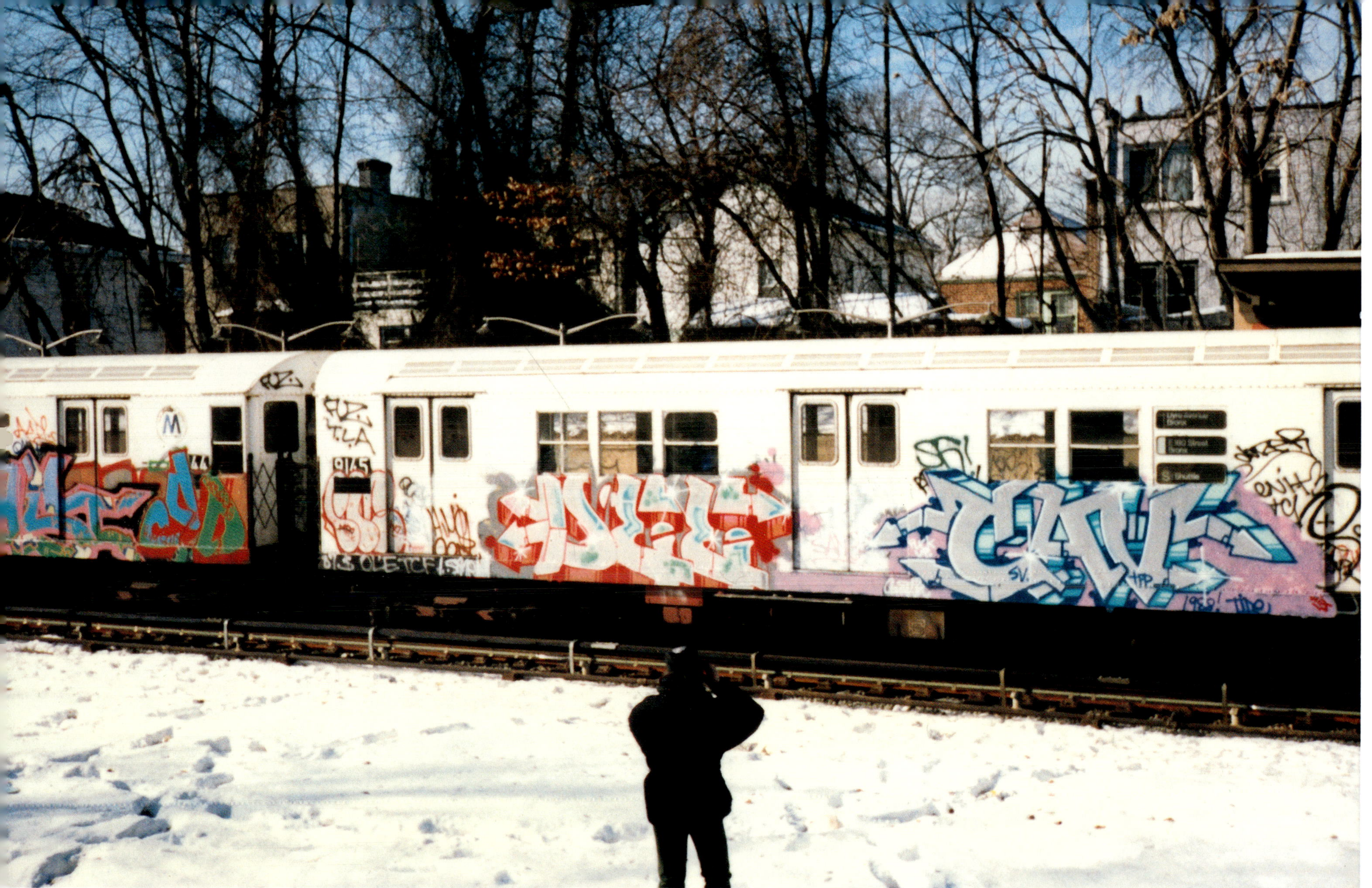

"Dee" & "Cav"

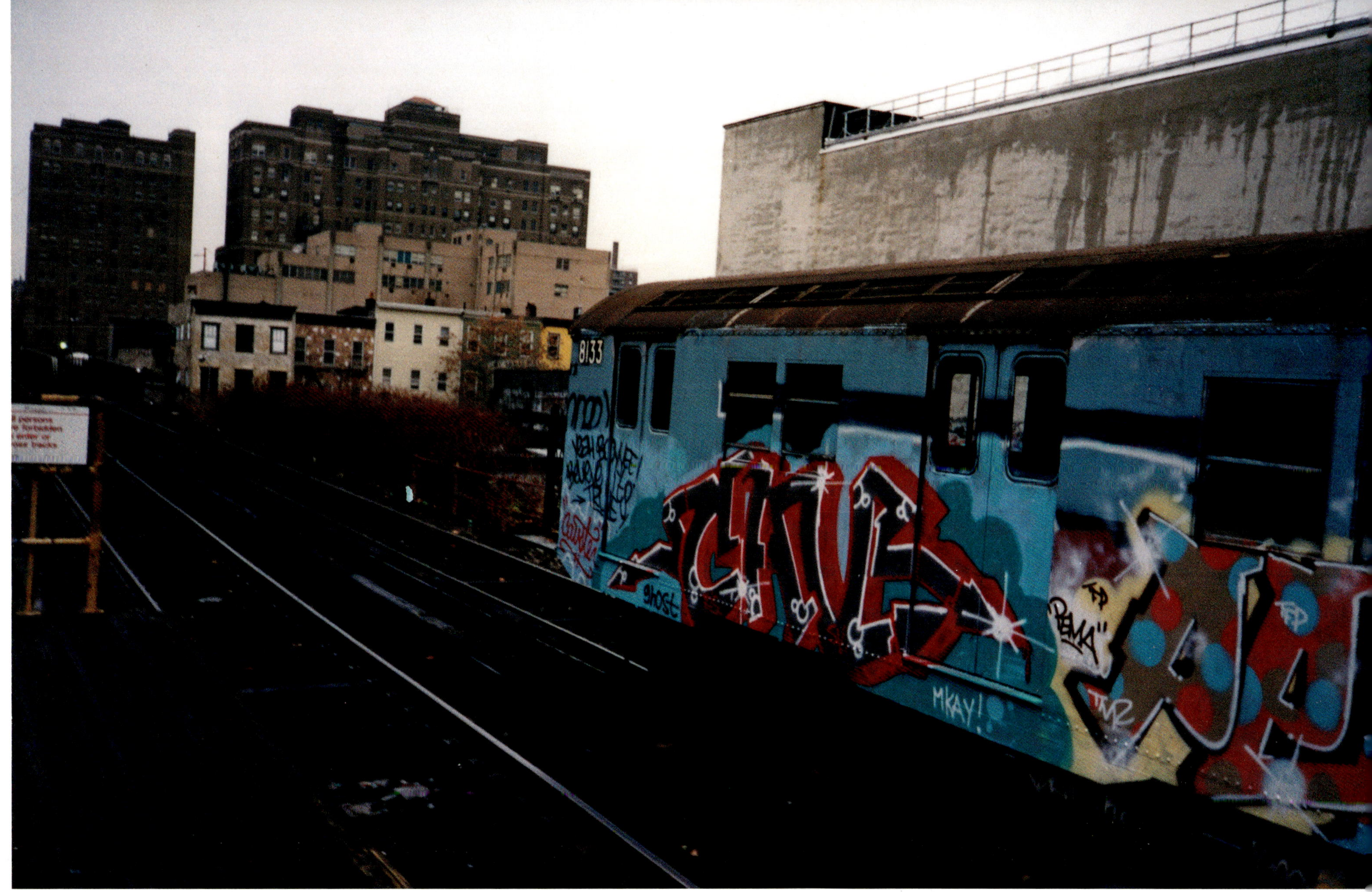

"Cav"

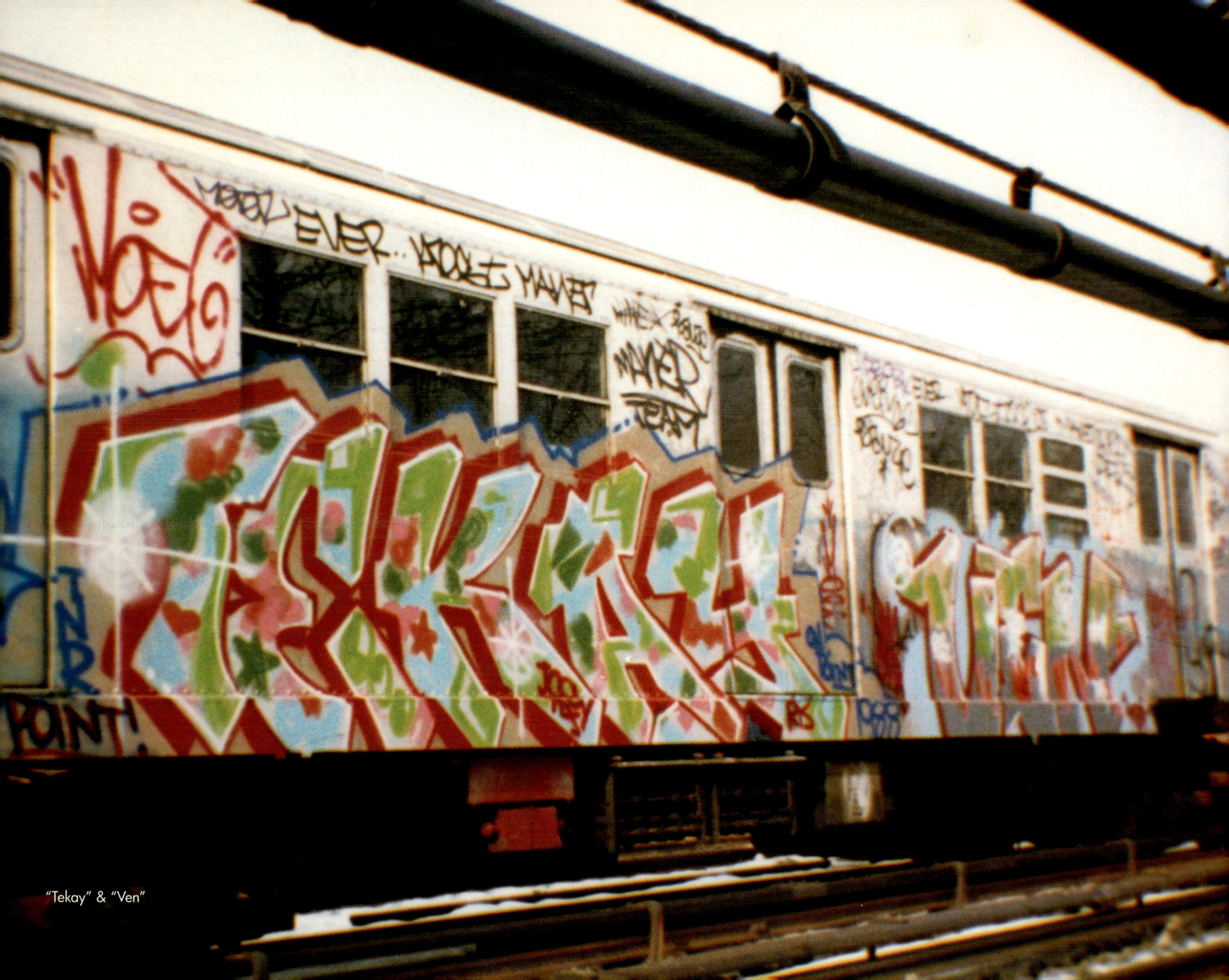

“Tekay” & “Ven”

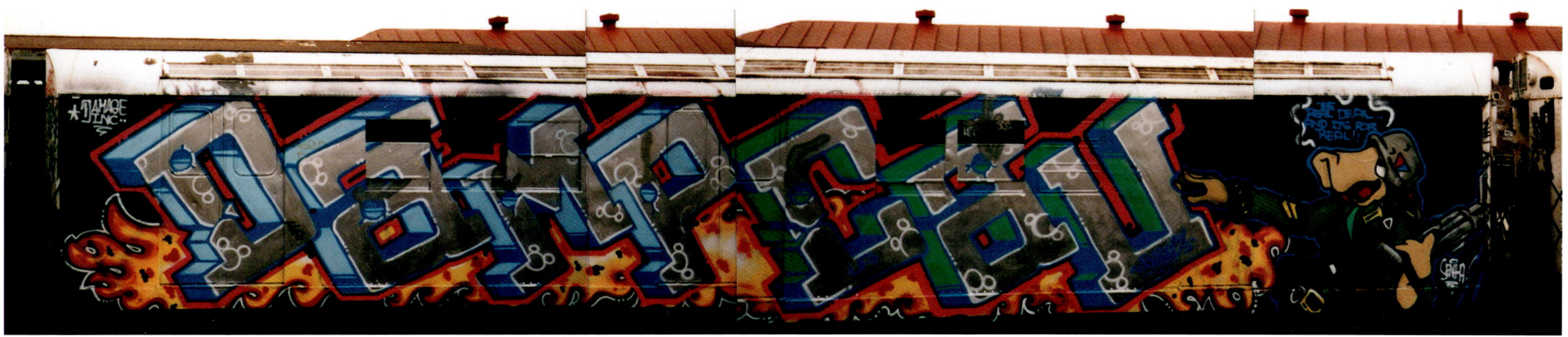

"Damp" & "Cav"

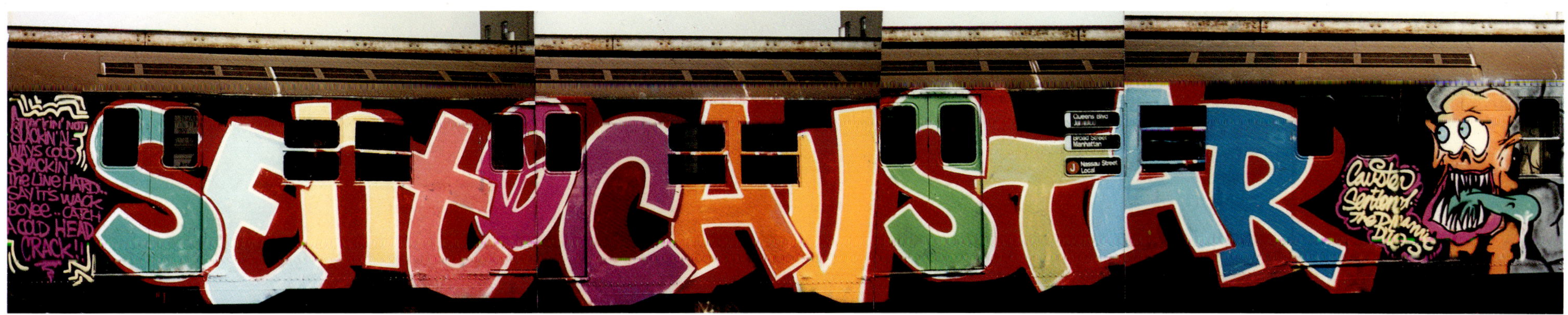

"Sento" & "Cavstar"

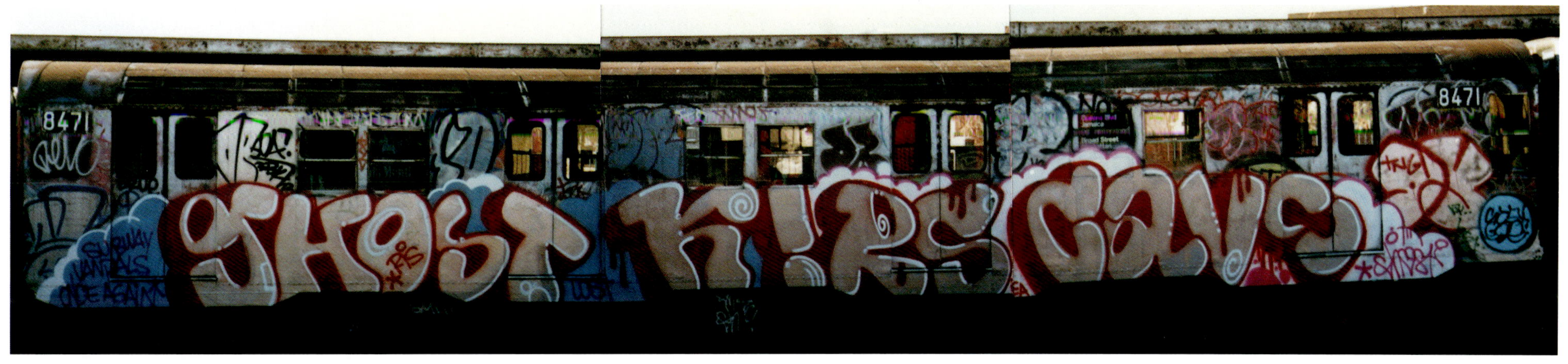

"Ghost," "Kirs" & "Cav"

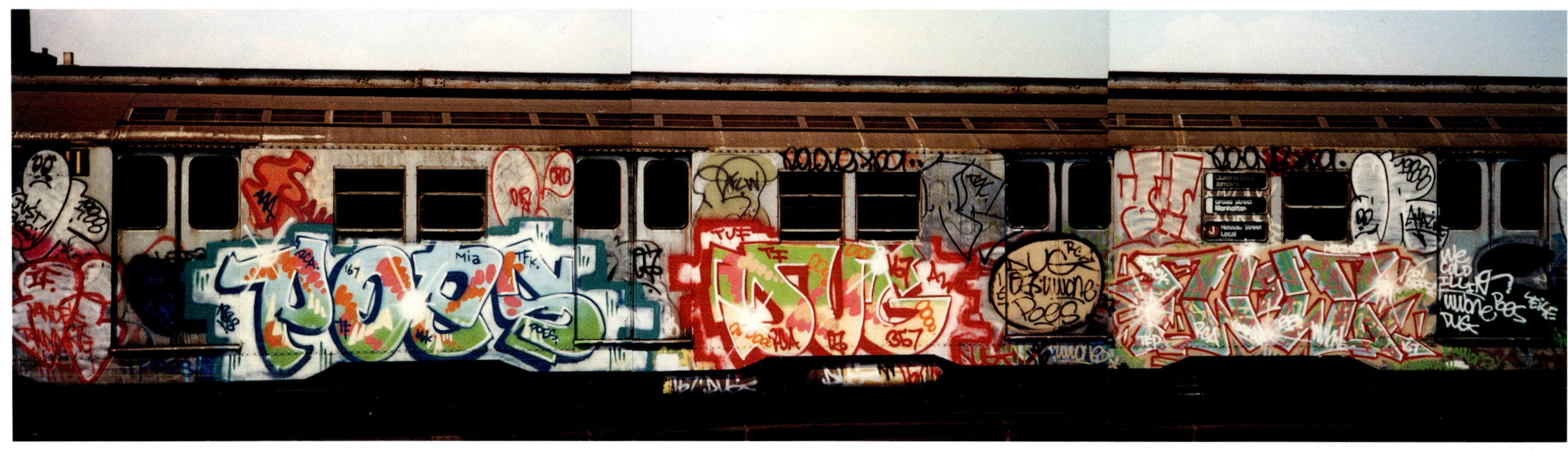

“Poes,” “Dug” & “WW,” by Pema

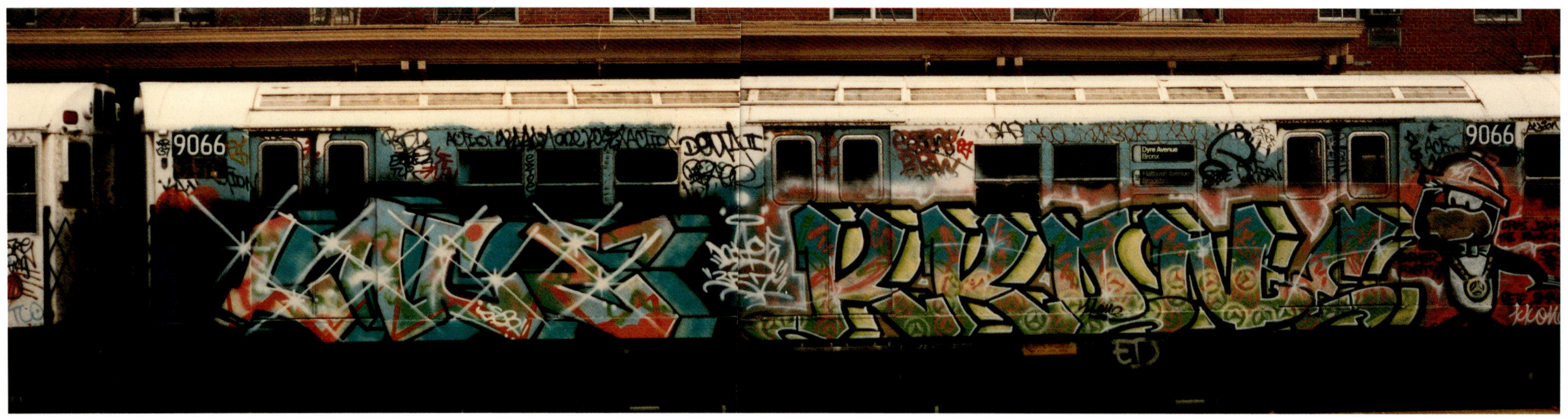

“Lace” & “KK-One”

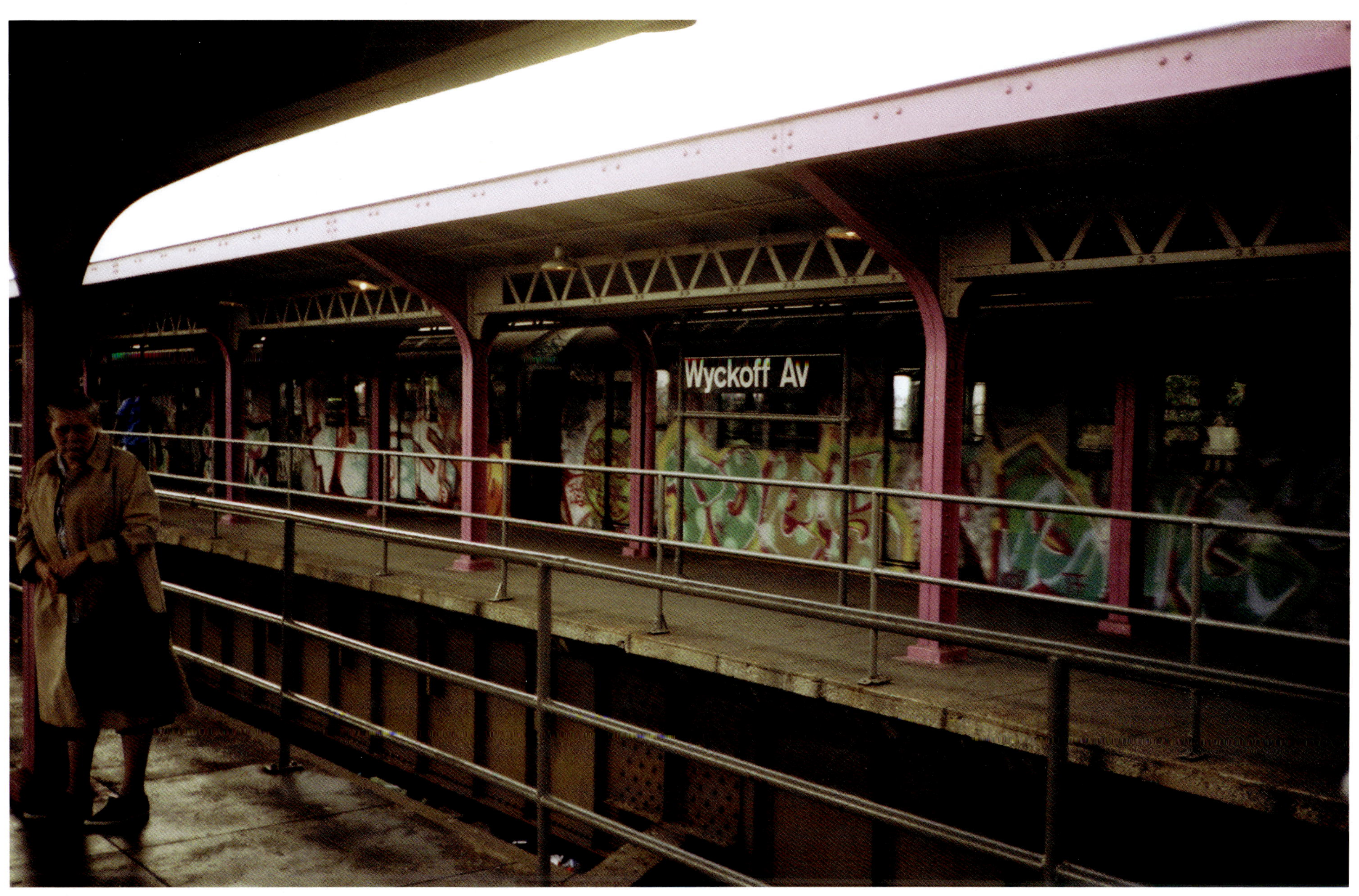

"Poes" & "Duy"

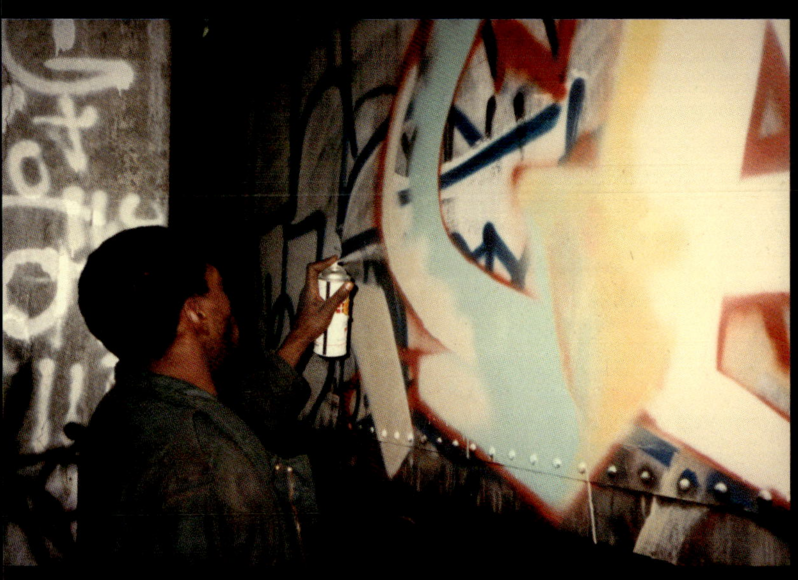

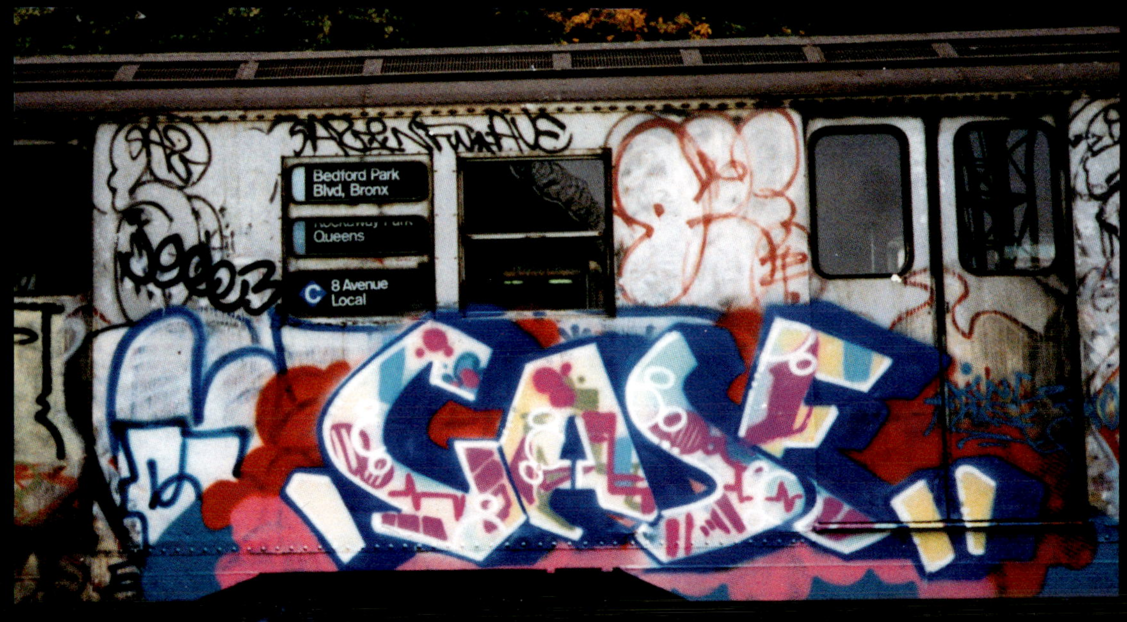

"Case2"

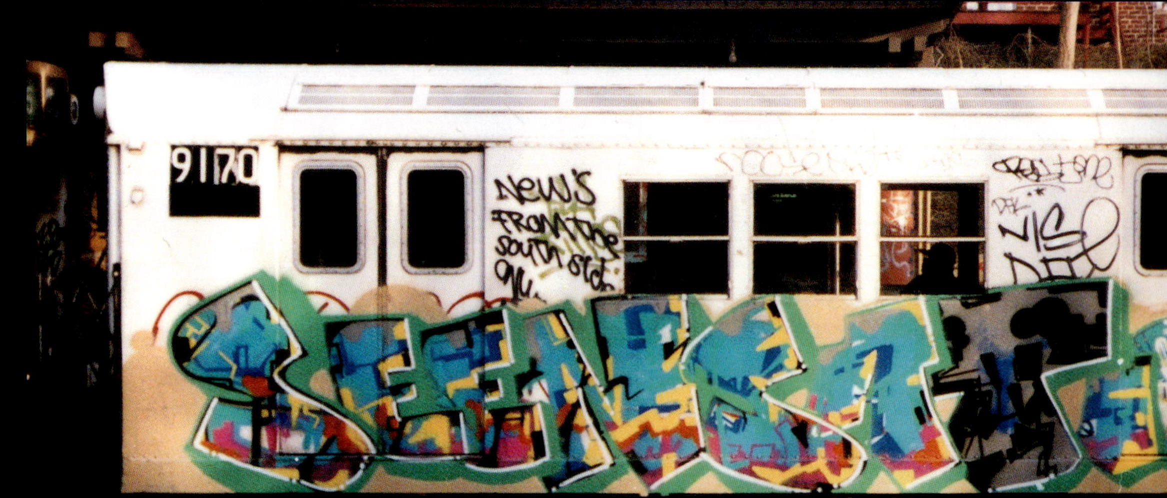

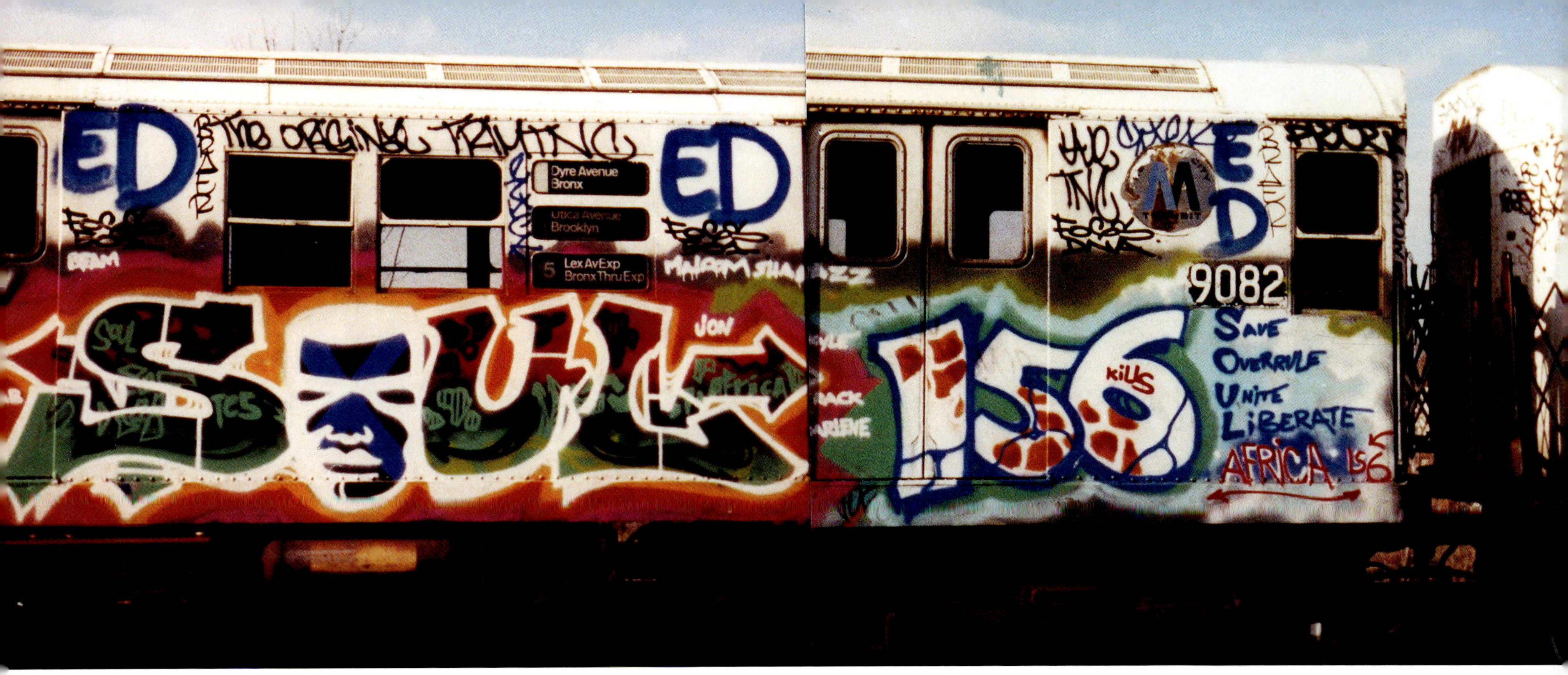

"Soul156"

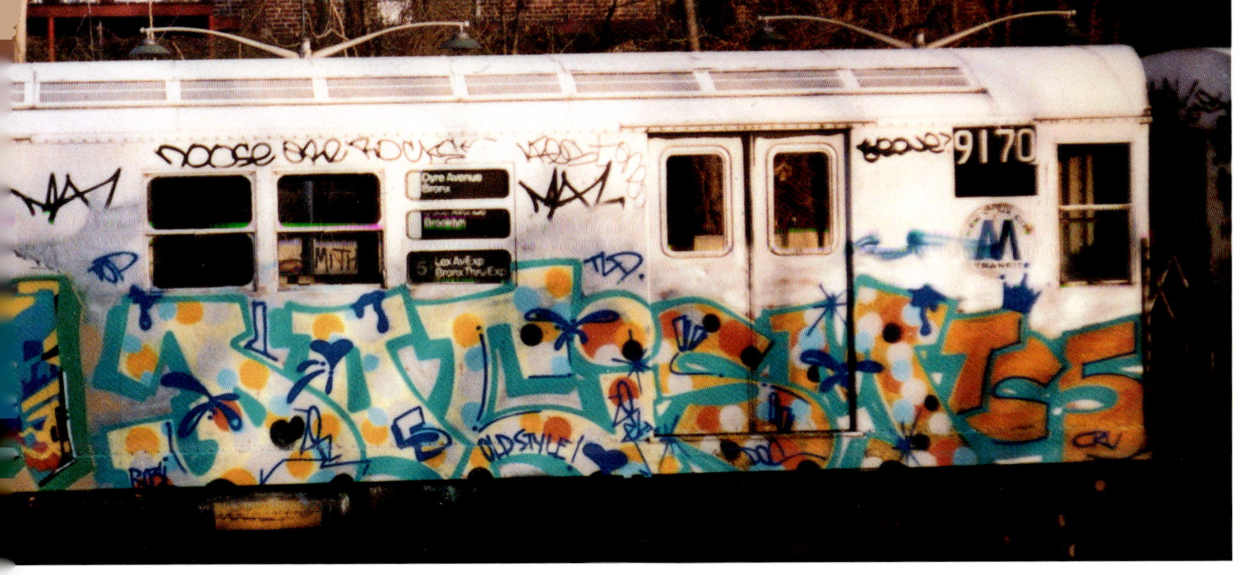

"Seensation" & "Docism"

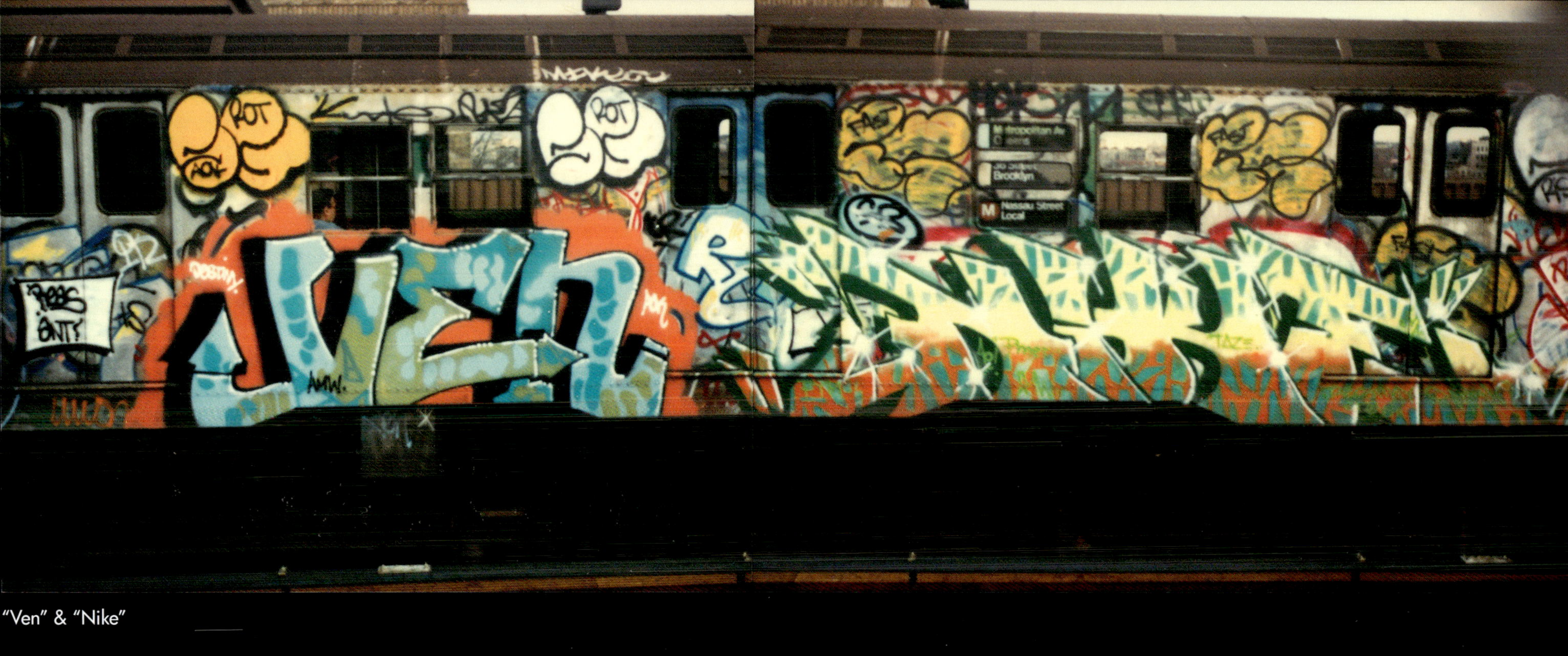

"Ven" & "Nike"

The end of graffiti on trains was near. I started benching at 238th st. Then I went to 180th st and finally Tremont Ave. At this time you could only catch graffiti on trains at rush hour. Cav told me to go out to Brooklyn. I ventured to Marcy Ave and remember sitting there for hours. I was able to catch a glimpse of what was left on the BMTs.

–Maze TMC

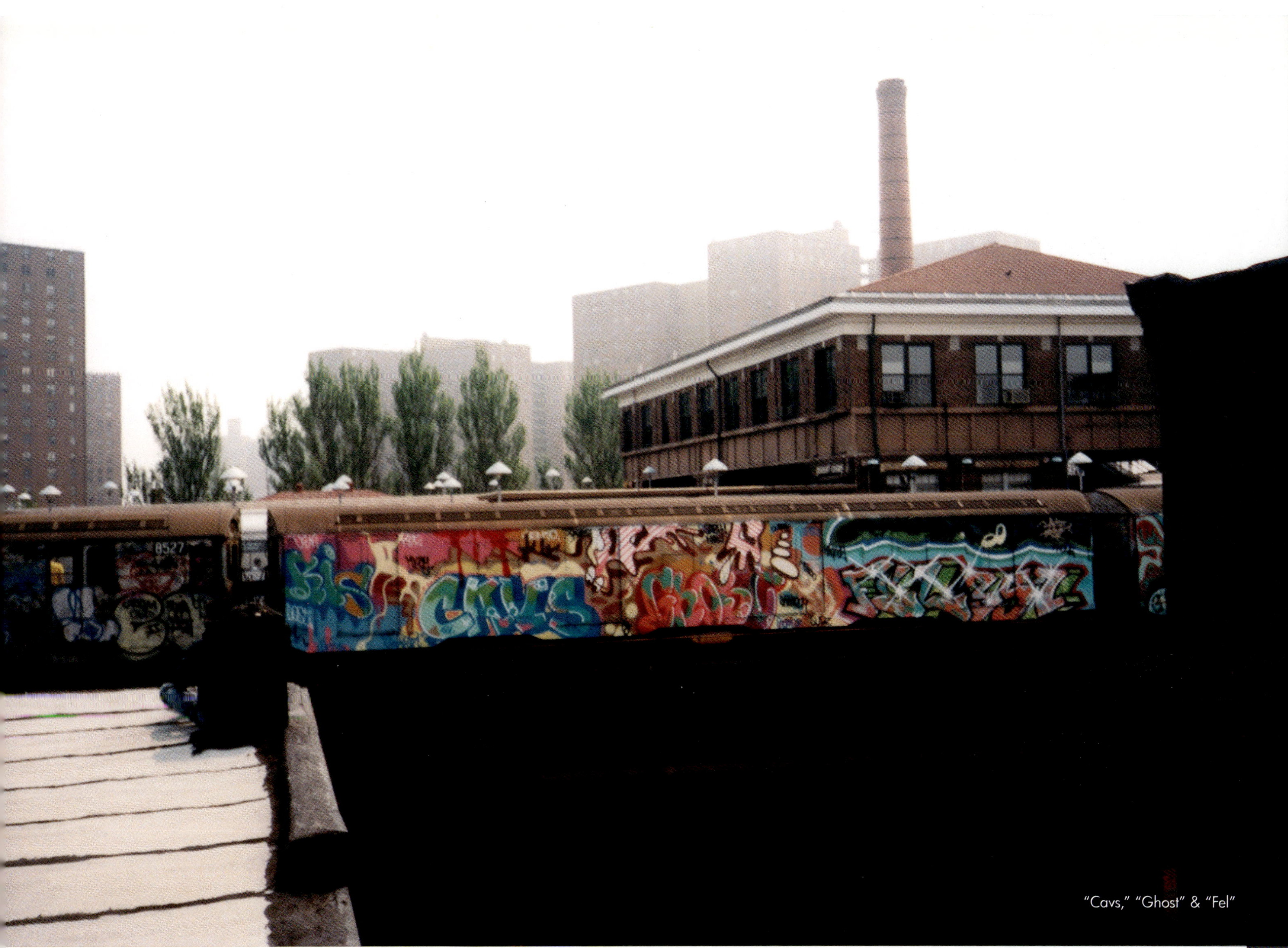

"Cavs," "Ghost" & "Fel"

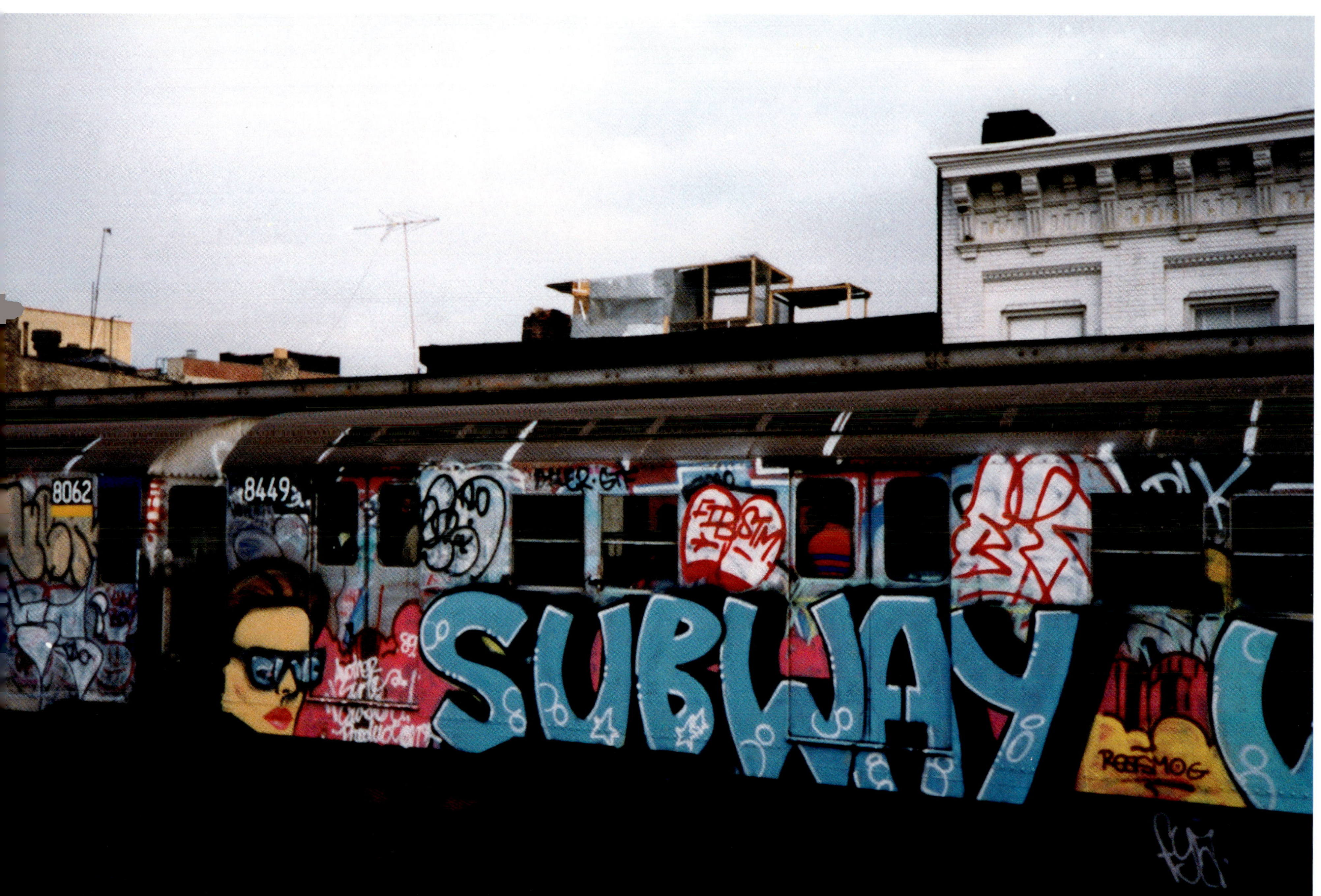

"Subway Vandals," by Sent & Cavs

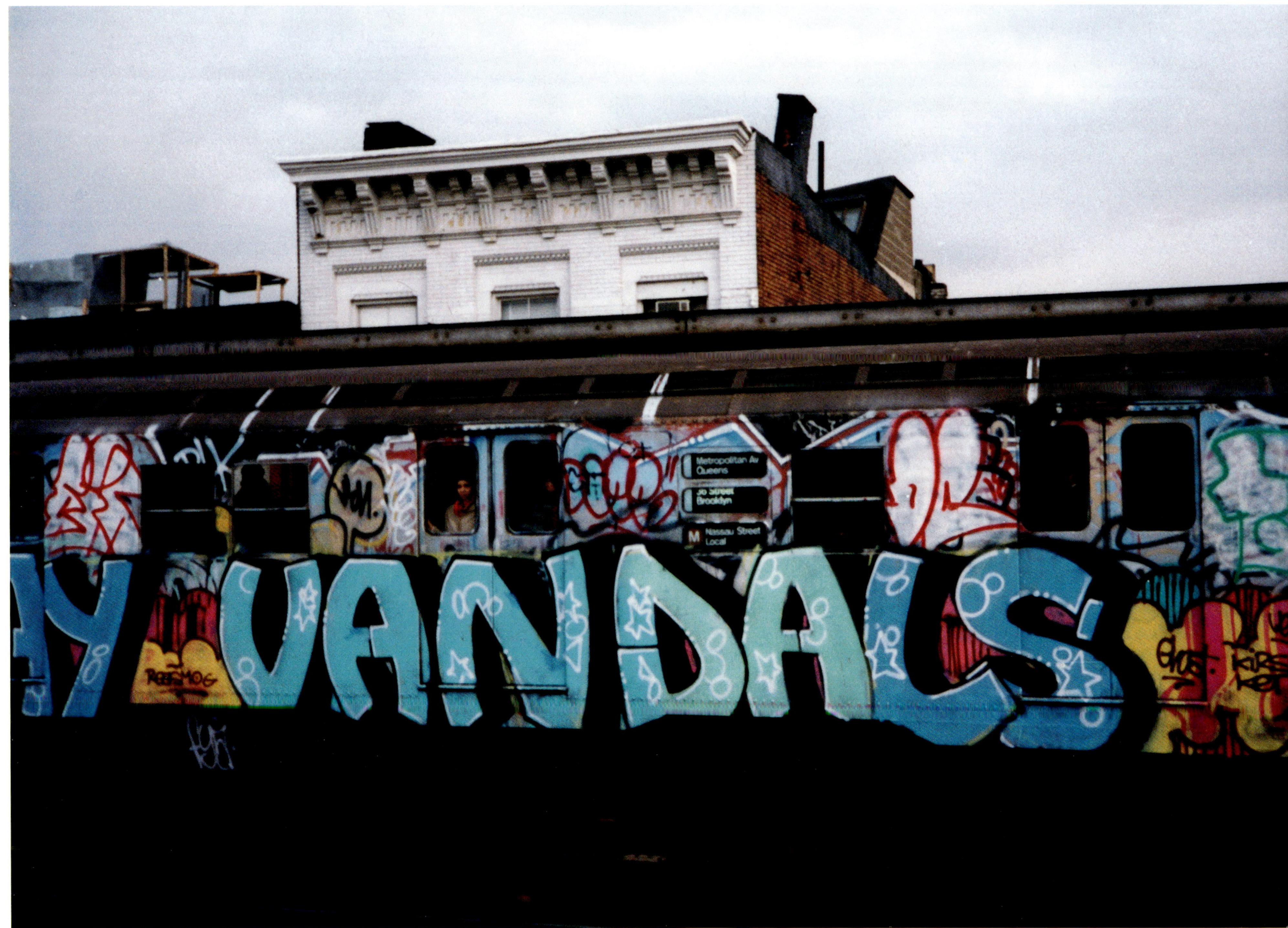
Metropolitan Av
Queens
Brooklyn
M Nassau Street
Local
VANDALS

8 Avenue
14 Street
Rockaway Pkwy
Brooklyn
L
14 St-Canarsie
Local

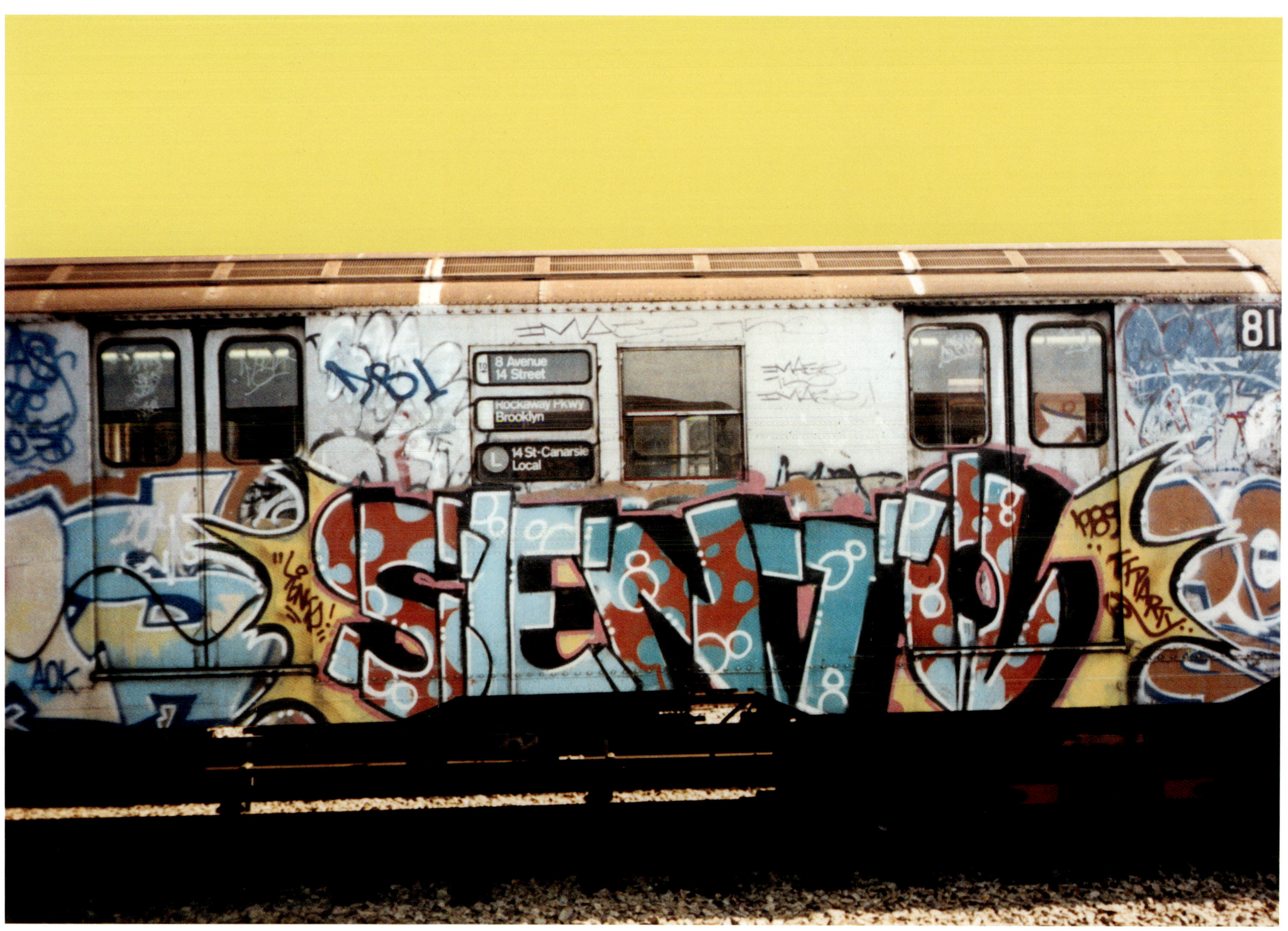

"Sento"

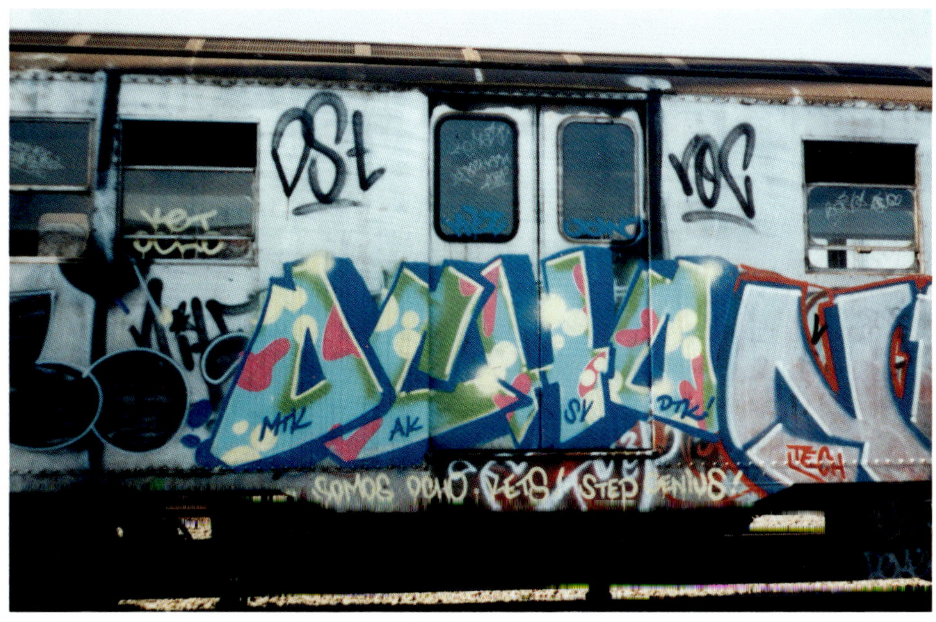

"Ocho"

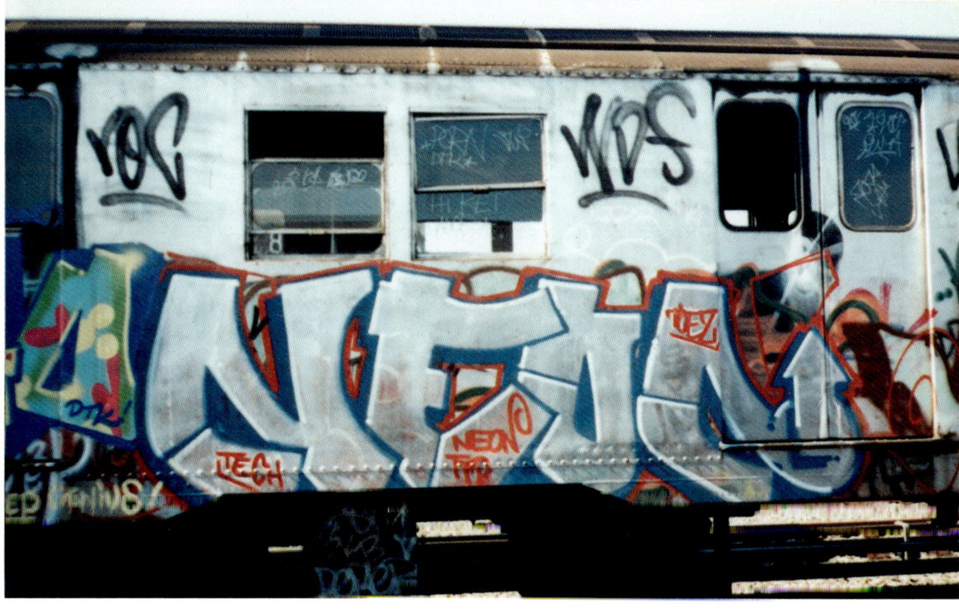

"Neon"

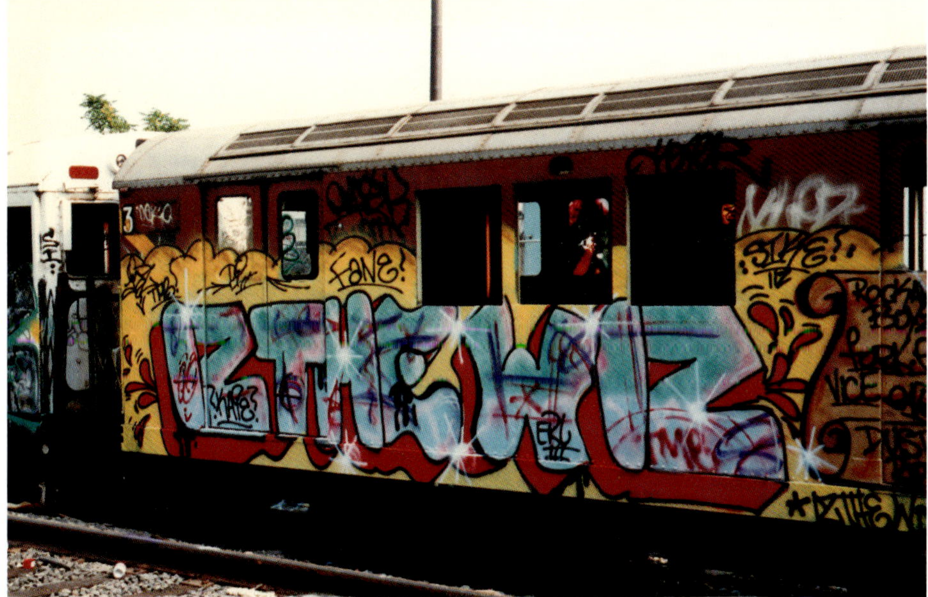

"Iz The Wiz" (RIP)

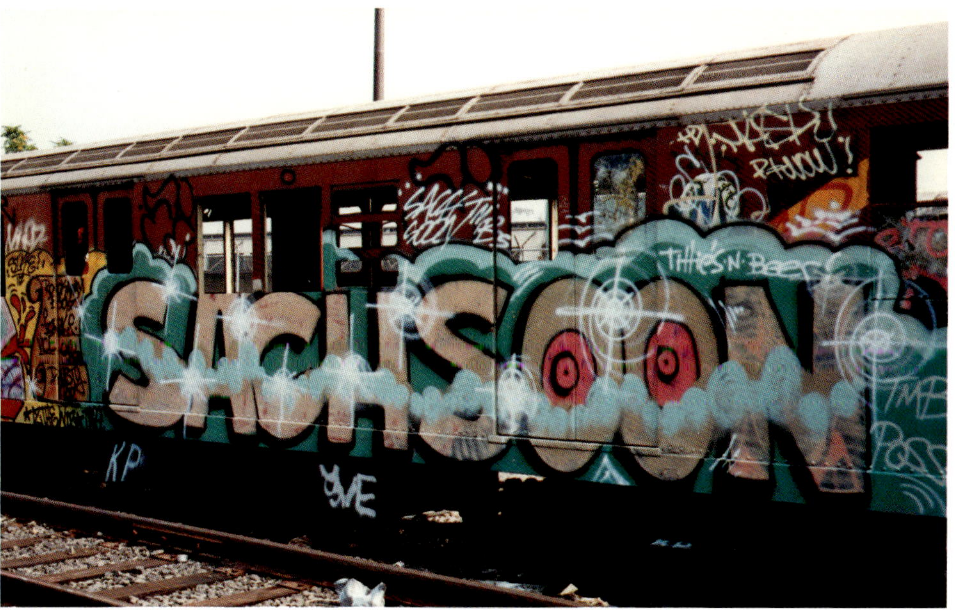

"Sachsoon"

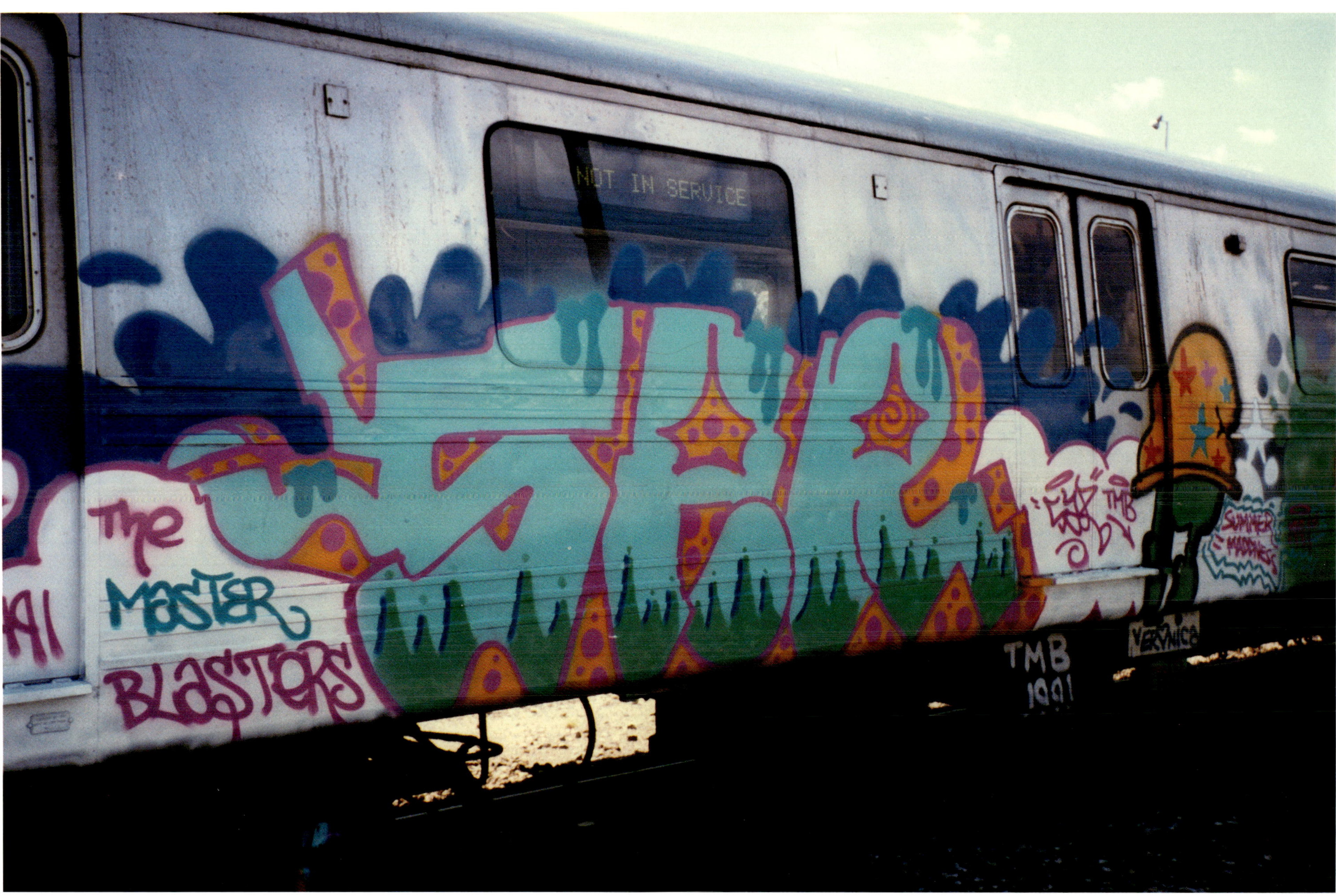

"Sar"

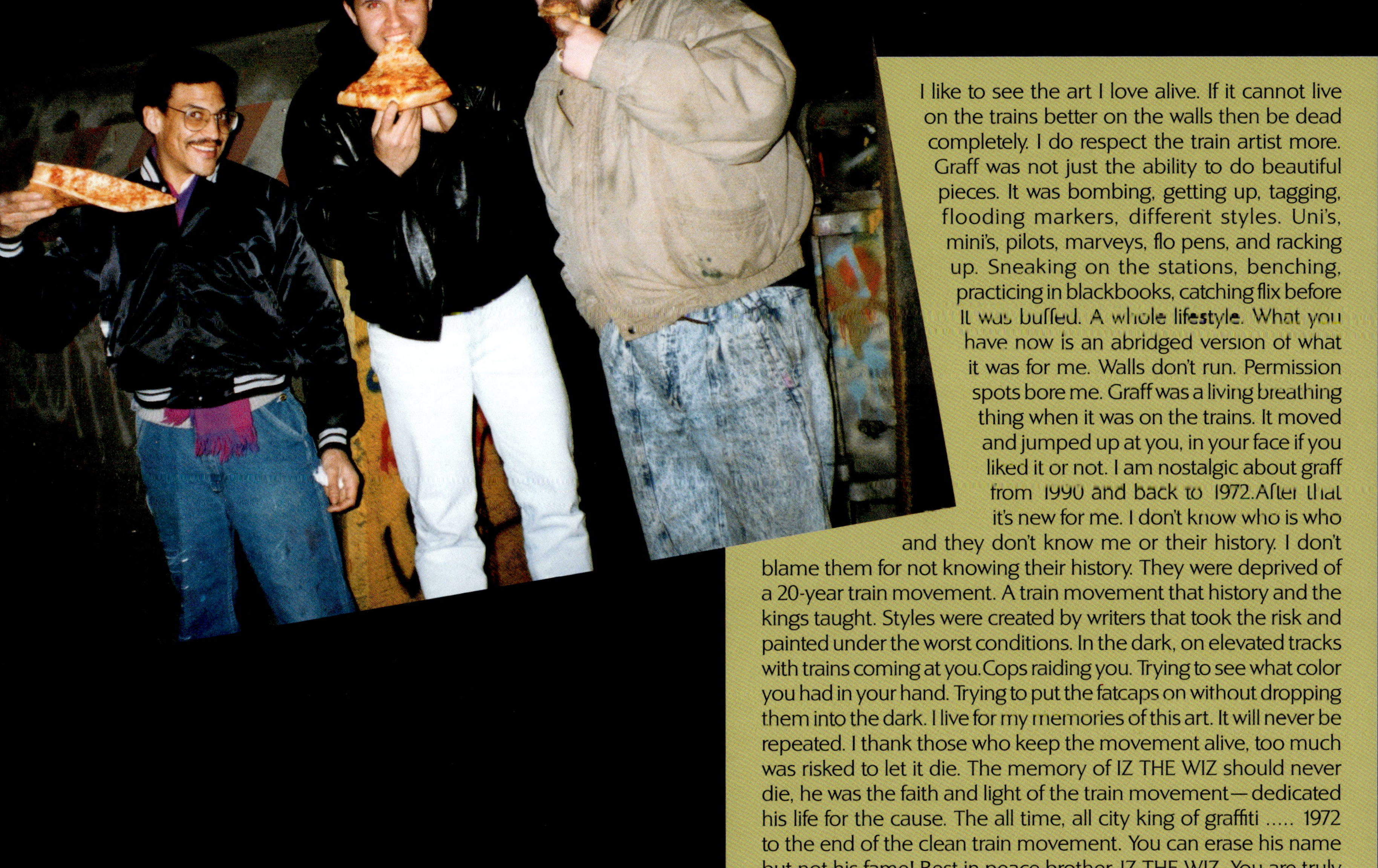

I like to see the art I love alive. If it cannot live on the trains better on the walls then be dead completely. I do respect the train artist more. Graff was not just the ability to do beautiful pieces. It was bombing, getting up, tagging, flooding markers, different styles. Uni's, mini's, pilots, marveys, flo pens, and racking up. Sneaking on the stations, benching, practicing in blackbooks, catching flix before it was buffed. A whole lifestyle. What you have now is an abridged version of what it was for me. Walls don't run. Permission spots bore me. Graff was a living breathing thing when it was on the trains. It moved and jumped up at you, in your face if you liked it or not. I am nostalgic about graff from 1990 and back to 1972. After that it's new for me. I don't know who is who and they don't know me or their history. I don't blame them for not knowing their history. They were deprived of a 20-year train movement. A train movement that history and the kings taught. Styles were created by writers that took the risk and painted under the worst conditions. In the dark, on elevated tracks with trains coming at you. Cops raiding you. Trying to see what color you had in your hand. Trying to put the fatcaps on without dropping them into the dark. I live for my memories of this art. It will never be repeated. I thank those who keep the movement alive, too much was risked to let it die. The memory of IZ THE WIZ should never die, he was the faith and light of the train movement— dedicated his life for the cause. The all time, all city king of graffiti ..... 1972 to the end of the clean train movement. You can erase his name but not his fame! Rest in peace brother, IZ THE WIZ. You are truly missed......

–SAR TMB

Recently, I took a subway ride into Manhattan. I got on at Pelham Parkway station in the Bronx. As I looked around the empty subway platform, fond memories of this station came to mind.

It was in 1974 that this station was my winter playground. While most Bronxites hid inside their homes from the winter chill, my writing partner John 150 and I painted away the winter nights inside the warm subway station. It was the mid-seventies and subway graffiti was everywhere to be found. John and I carefully opened stored bags of spray paint and test fitted fat tops while looking for clean subway cars to paint.

Other writers like Blade and Ajax also came by to paint in the tunnel. We exchanged greetings and talked about how much damage we were doing. John and I roamed the lay up tunnel for hours painting and planning of kinging the line. We never kinged the five line but we managed to pull off lots of whole cars and top to bottom pieces. In any event we got noticed which was what the graffiti culture is all about.

I remember hanging out at Bogart Avenue and drawing outlines for hours while waiting for the sun to go down. The tunnel was very quiet at night. The trains ran at fewer times and we could paint for hours undisturbed.

I painted at Pelham Pkwy station until 1976 when I decided I had enough. These were easier times without video camera surveillance or fingerprinting techniques that are now used to catch writers.

For a brief moment I'm sixteen years old with paint splattered dungarees and a can of spray paint in my hand. No worries or bills to pay. The downtown track clicks, interrupting this thought and I smile as the new silver subway car opens to take me to Manhattan.

–Ale

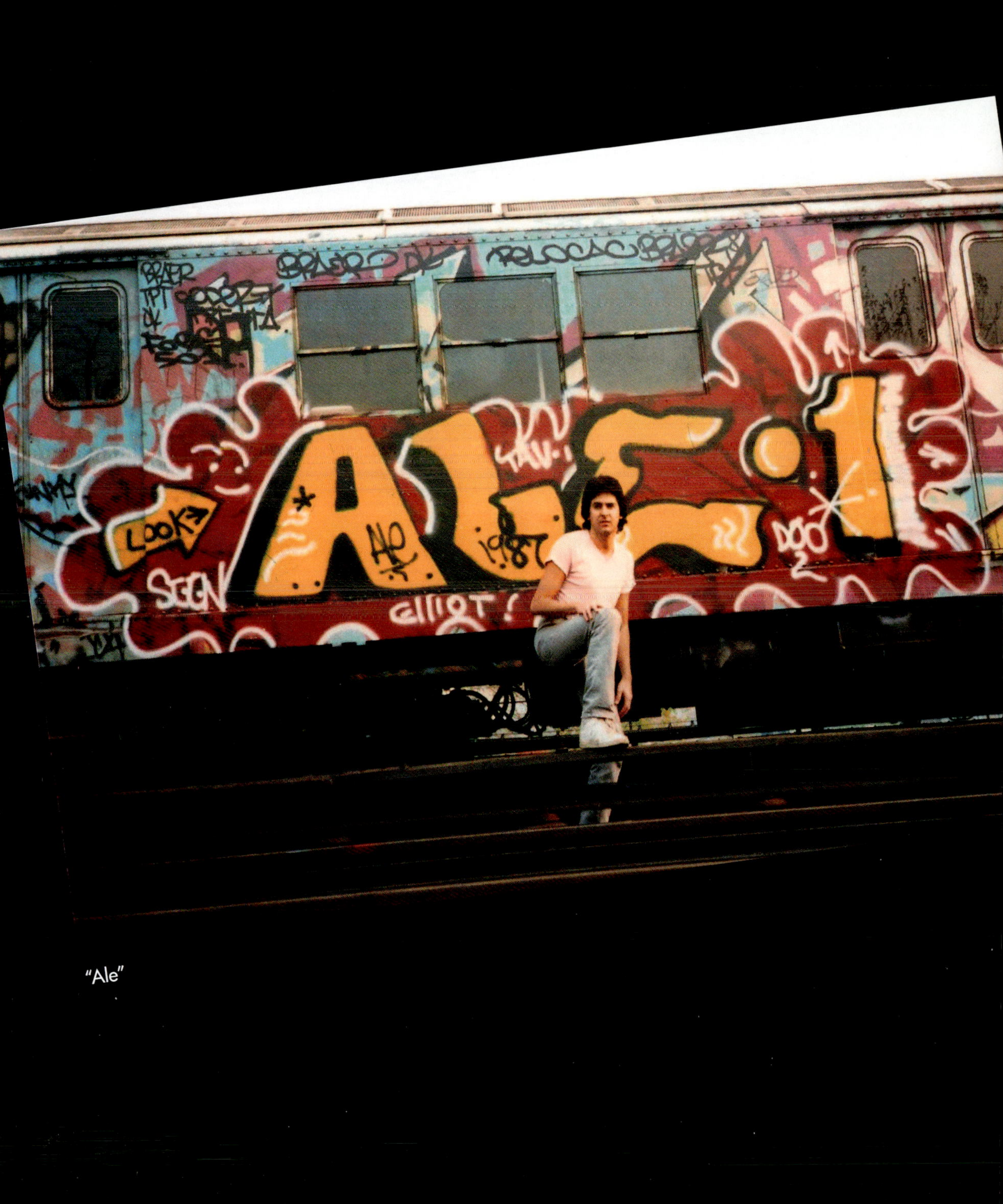

"Ale"

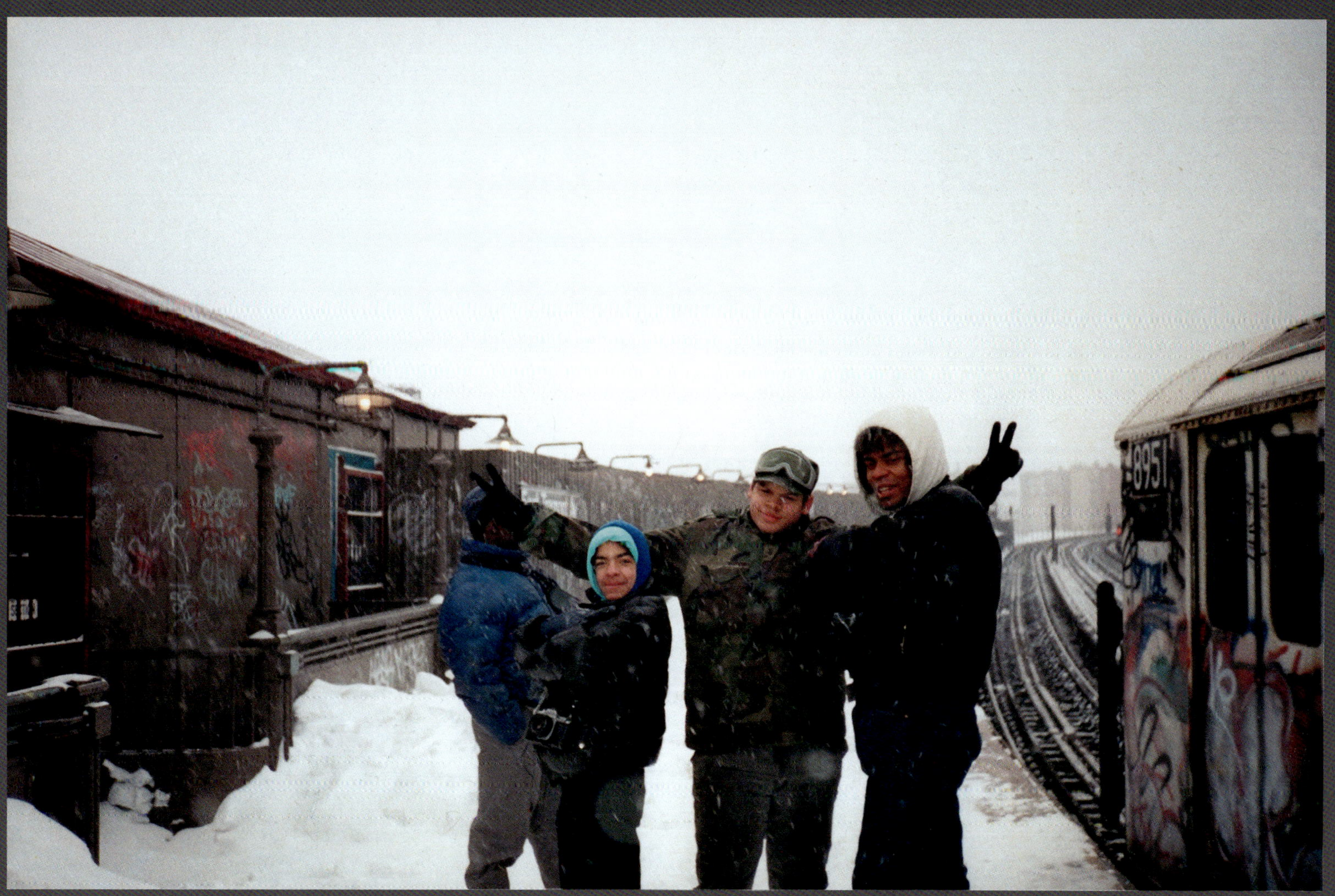
8951

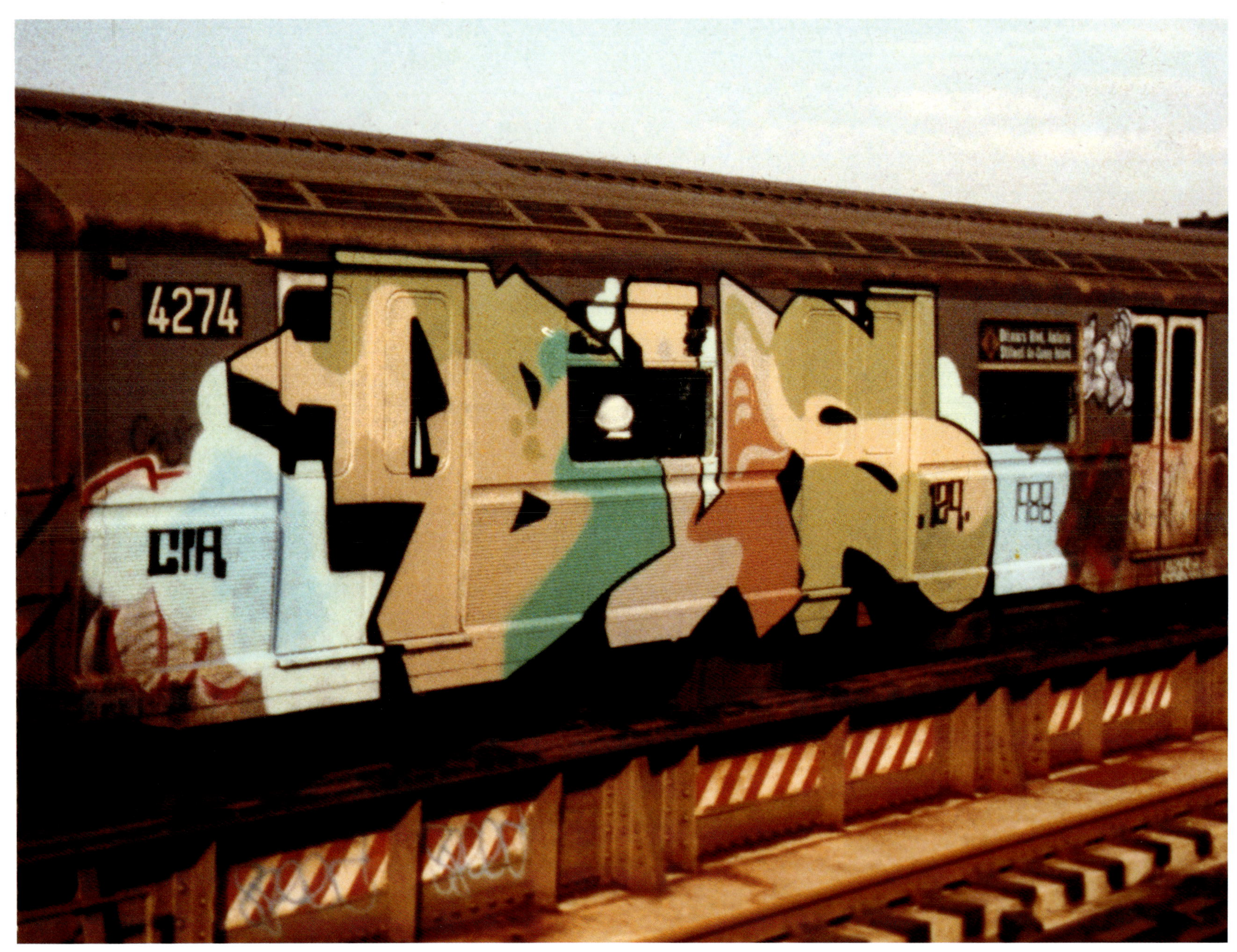

"Bus129," by Dondi (RIP), 1988

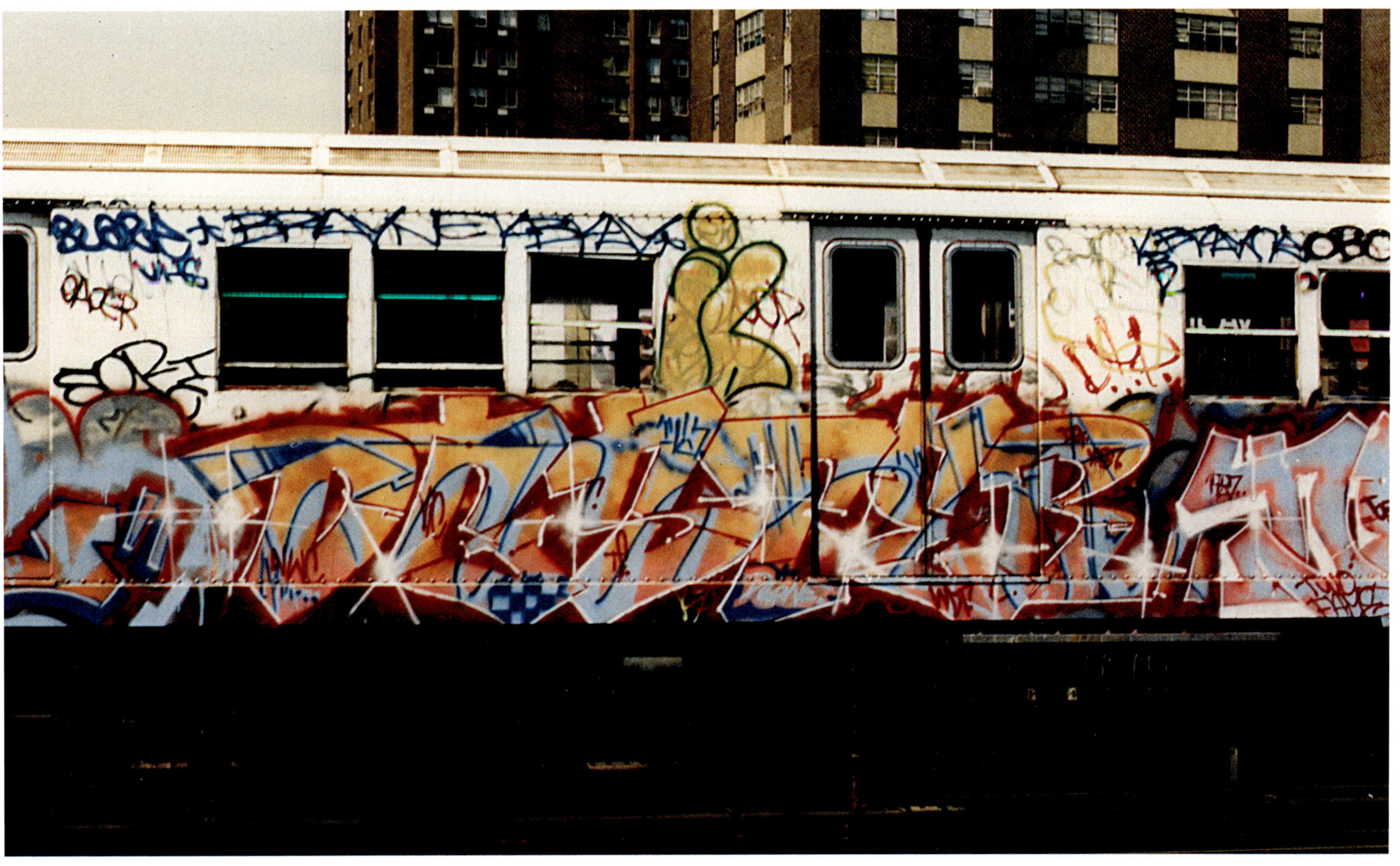

"Dgster," by DG

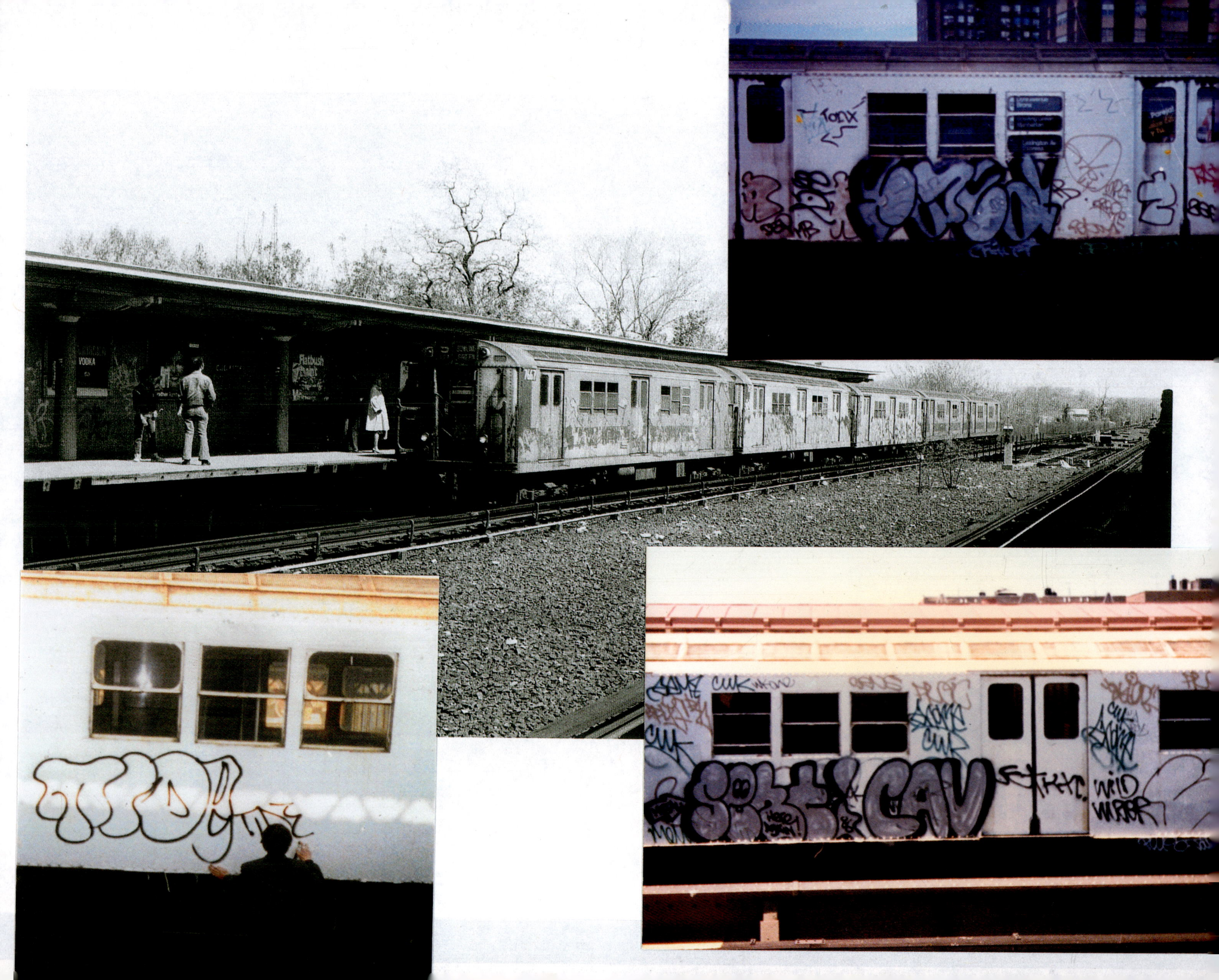
VODKA
Flatbush

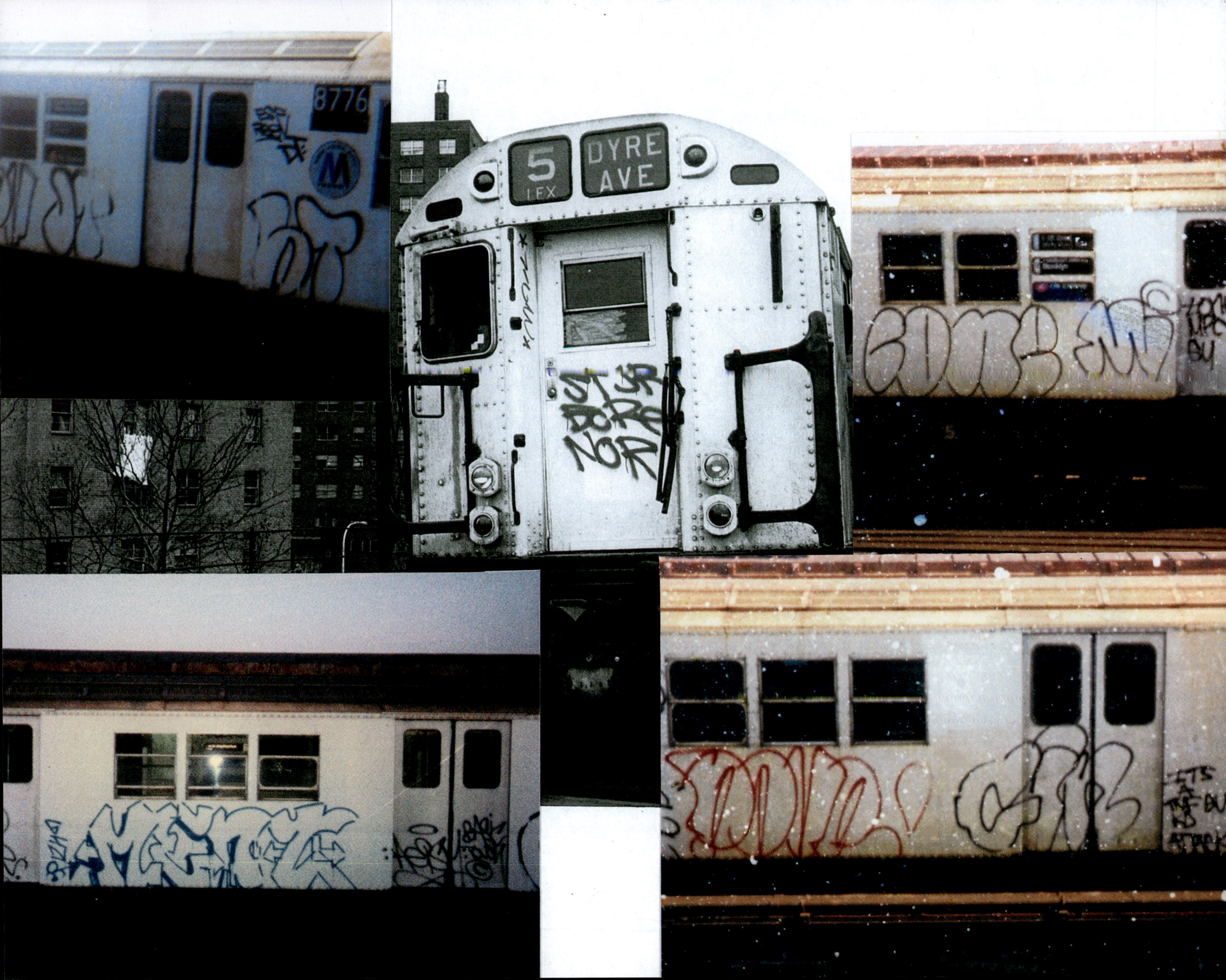
8776
5
LEX
DYRE
AVE

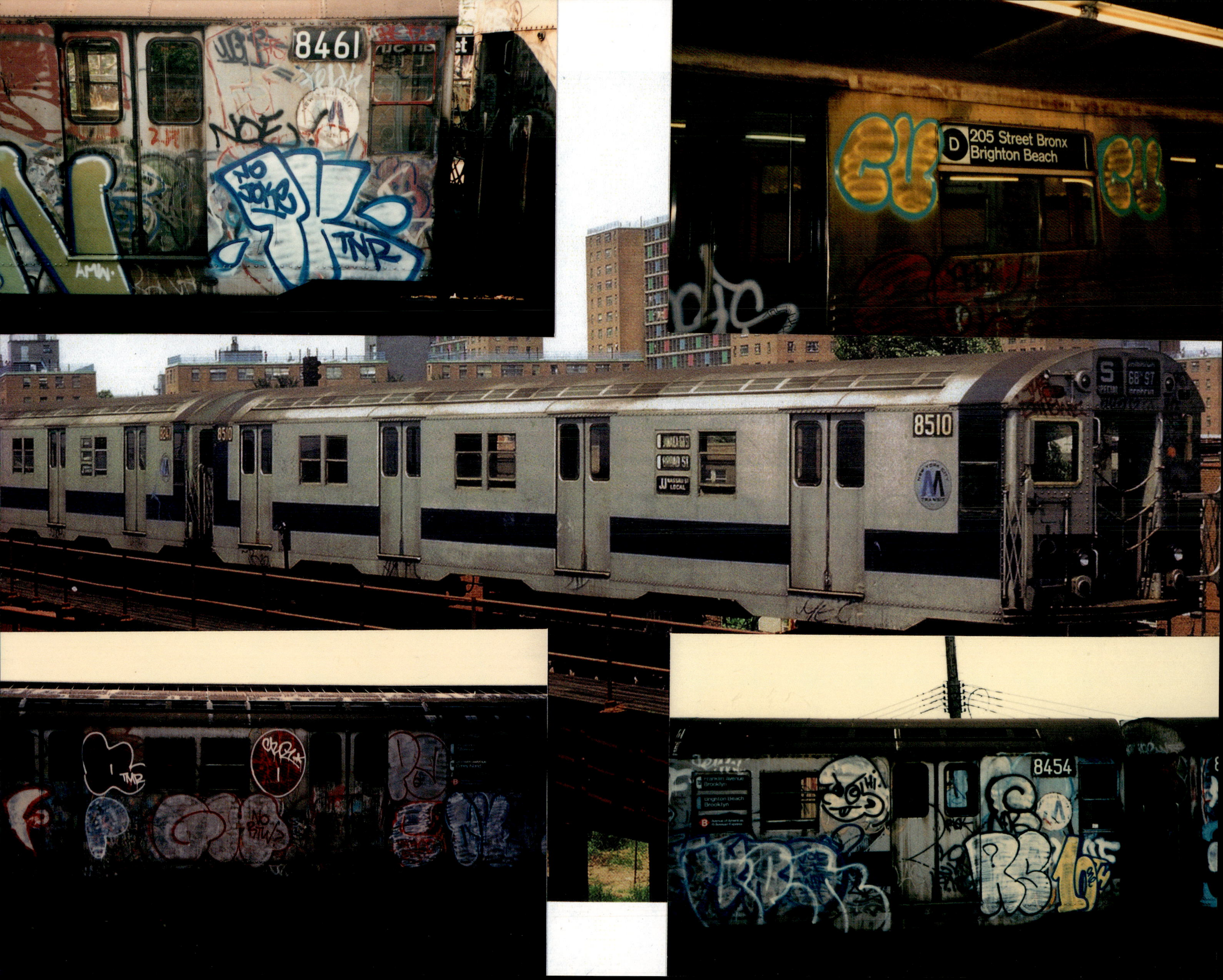
8461
D
205 Street Bronx
Brighton Beach
8510
8454

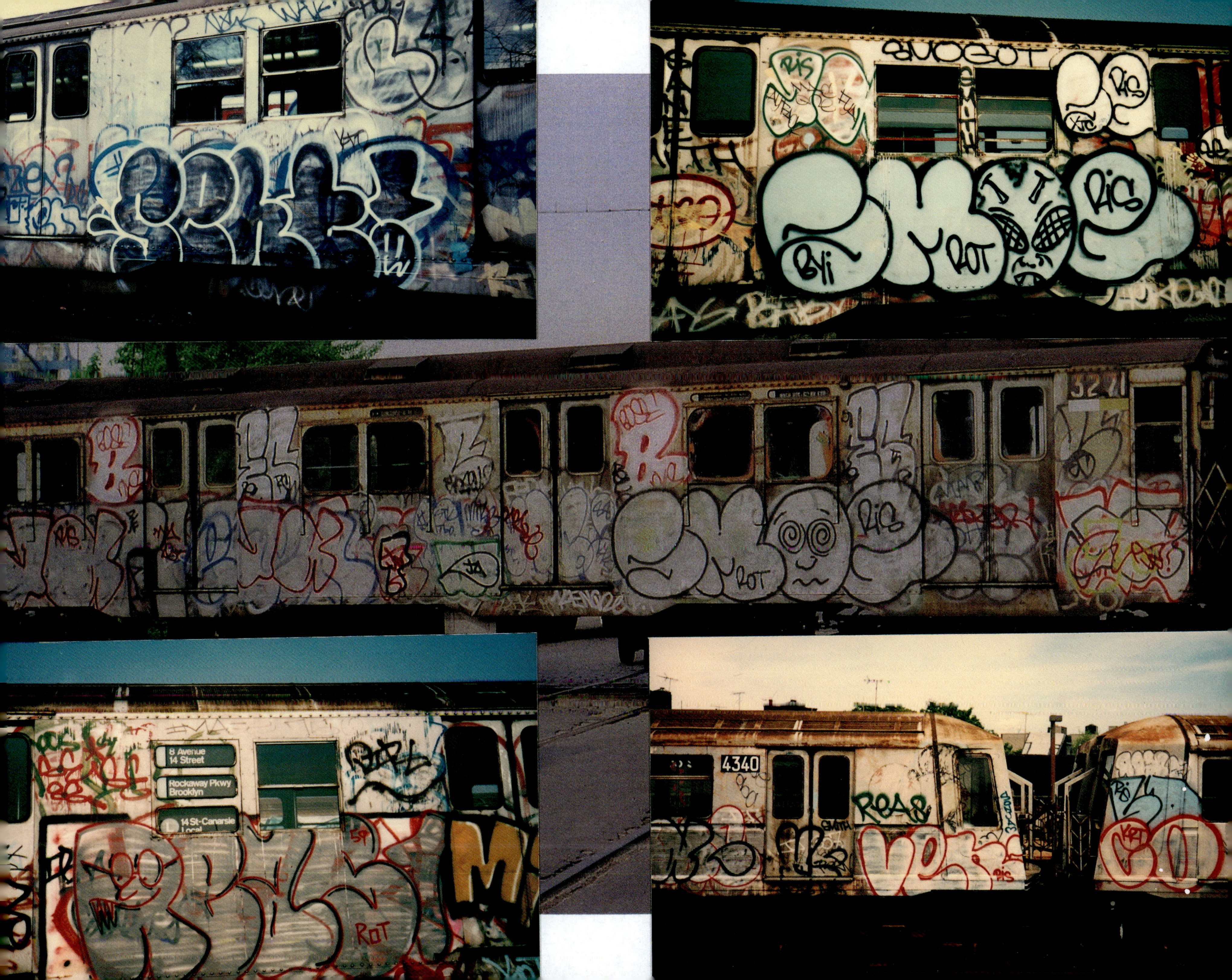
8 Avenue
14 Street
Rockaway Pkwy
Brooklyn
14 St-Canarsie
Local
4340

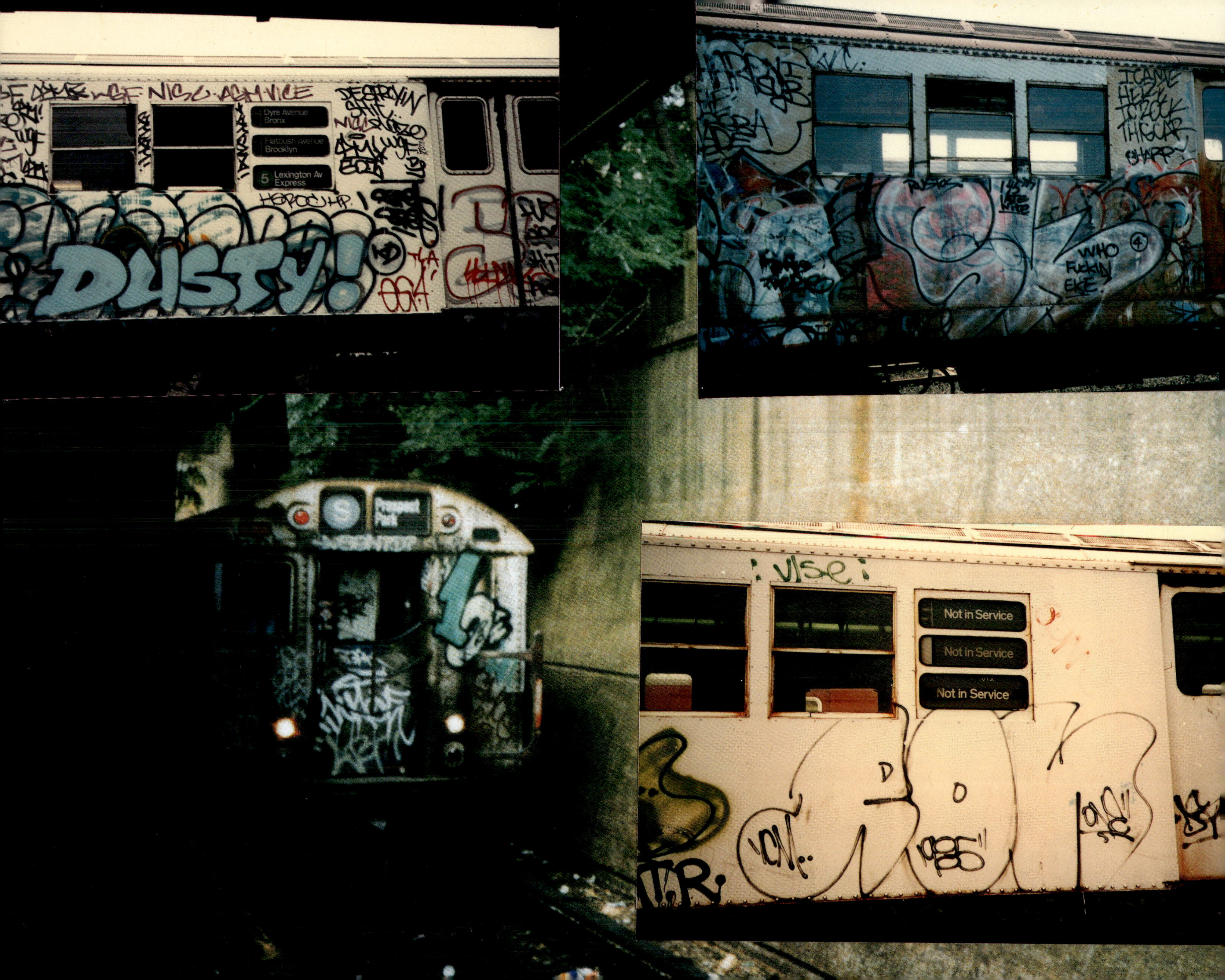

Dyre Avenue Bronx
Flatbush Avenue Brooklyn
5 Lexington Av Express
DUSTY!
S
Prospect Park
Not in Service
Not in Service
VIA
Not in Service

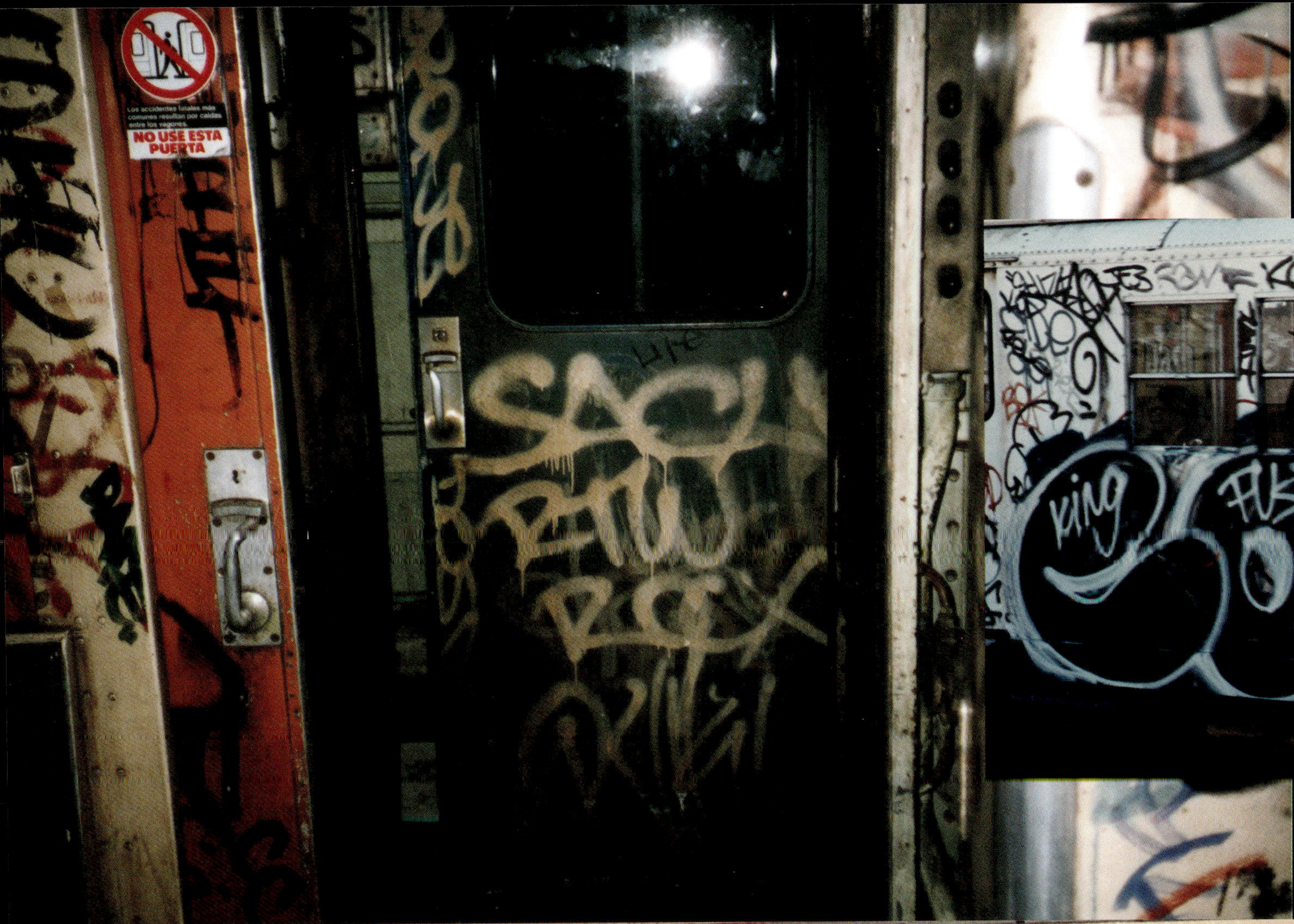

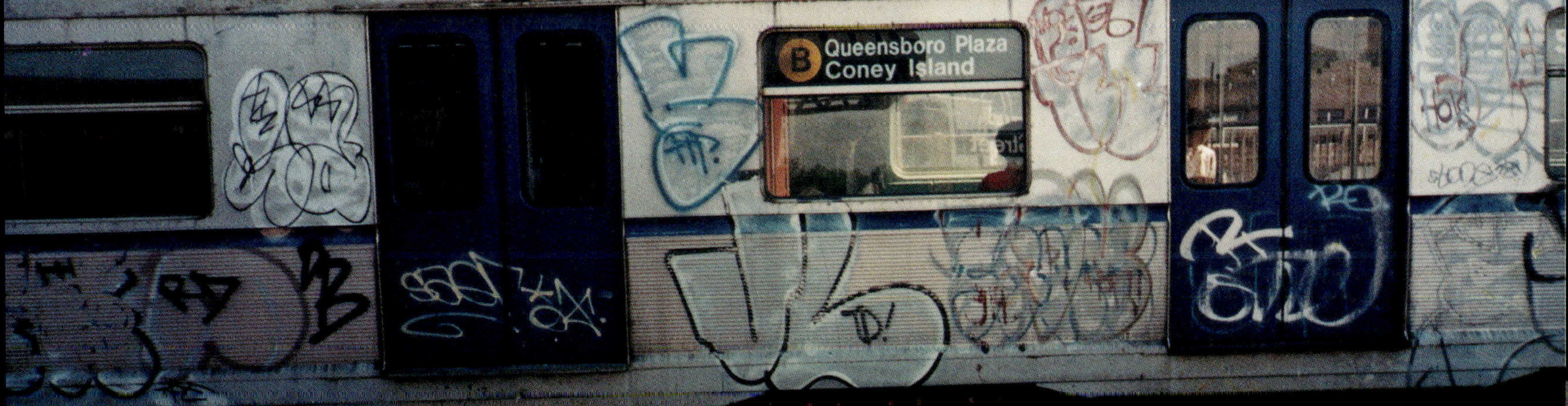
B Queensboro Plaza
Coney Island

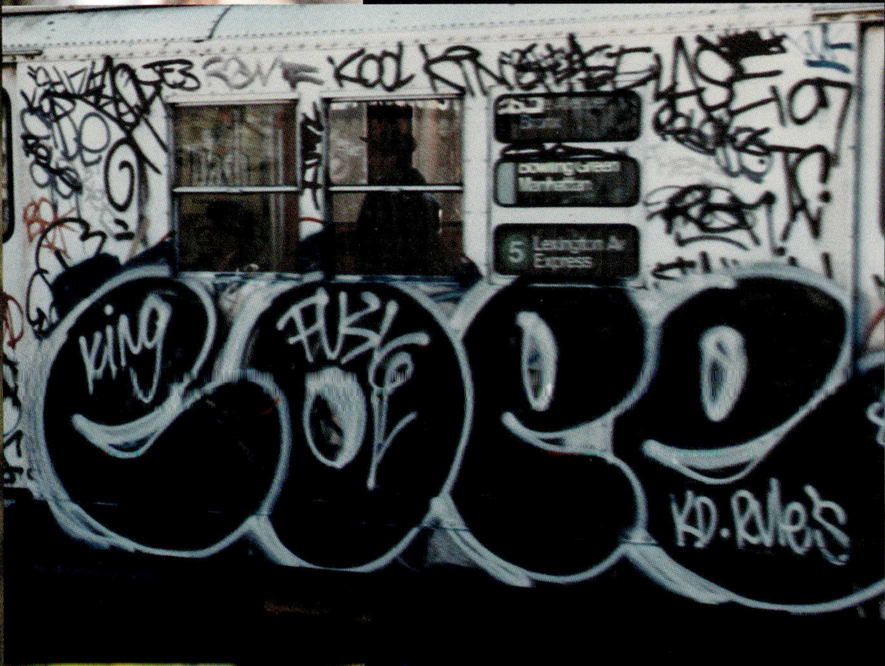

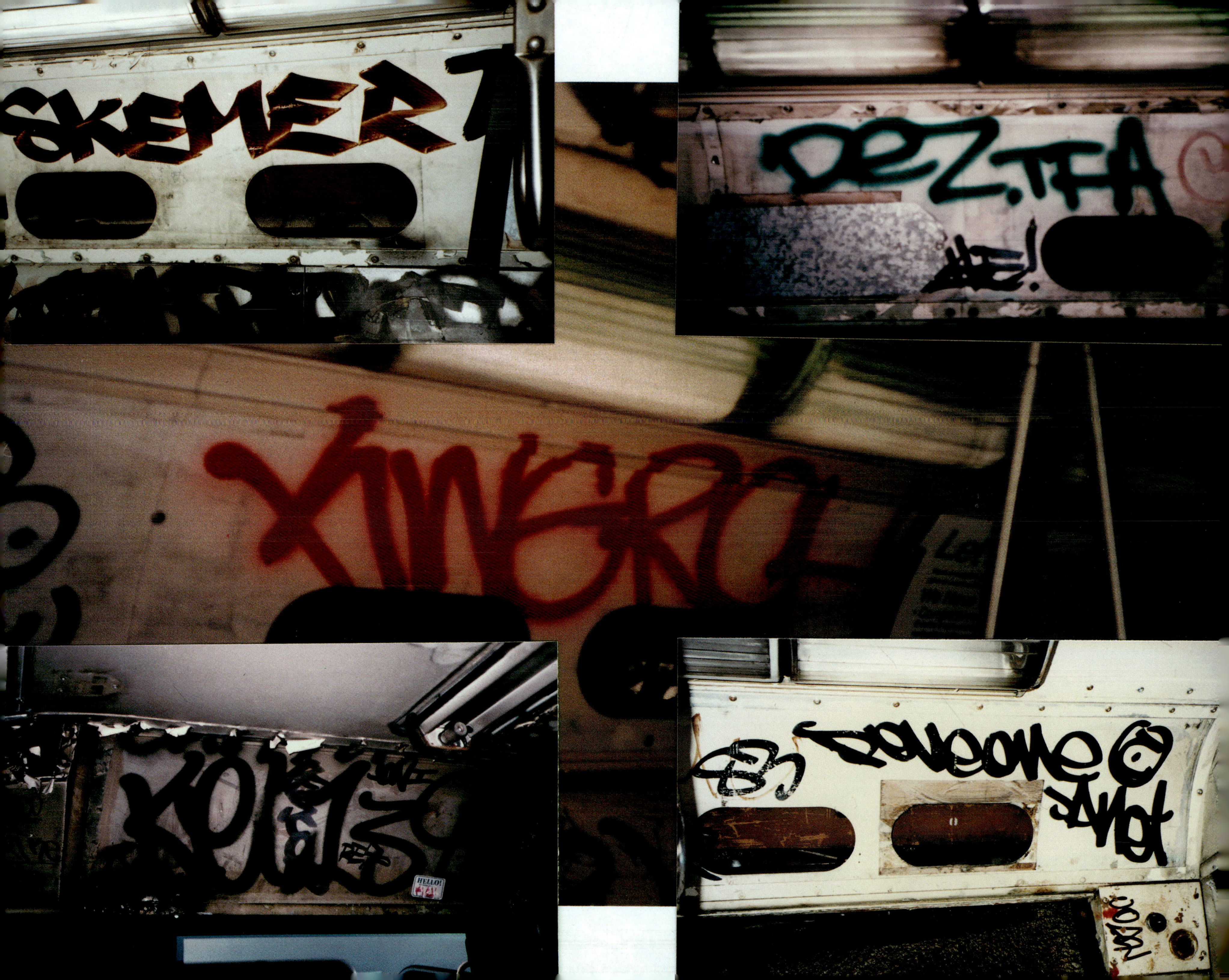
SKEMER
DEZ.TFA

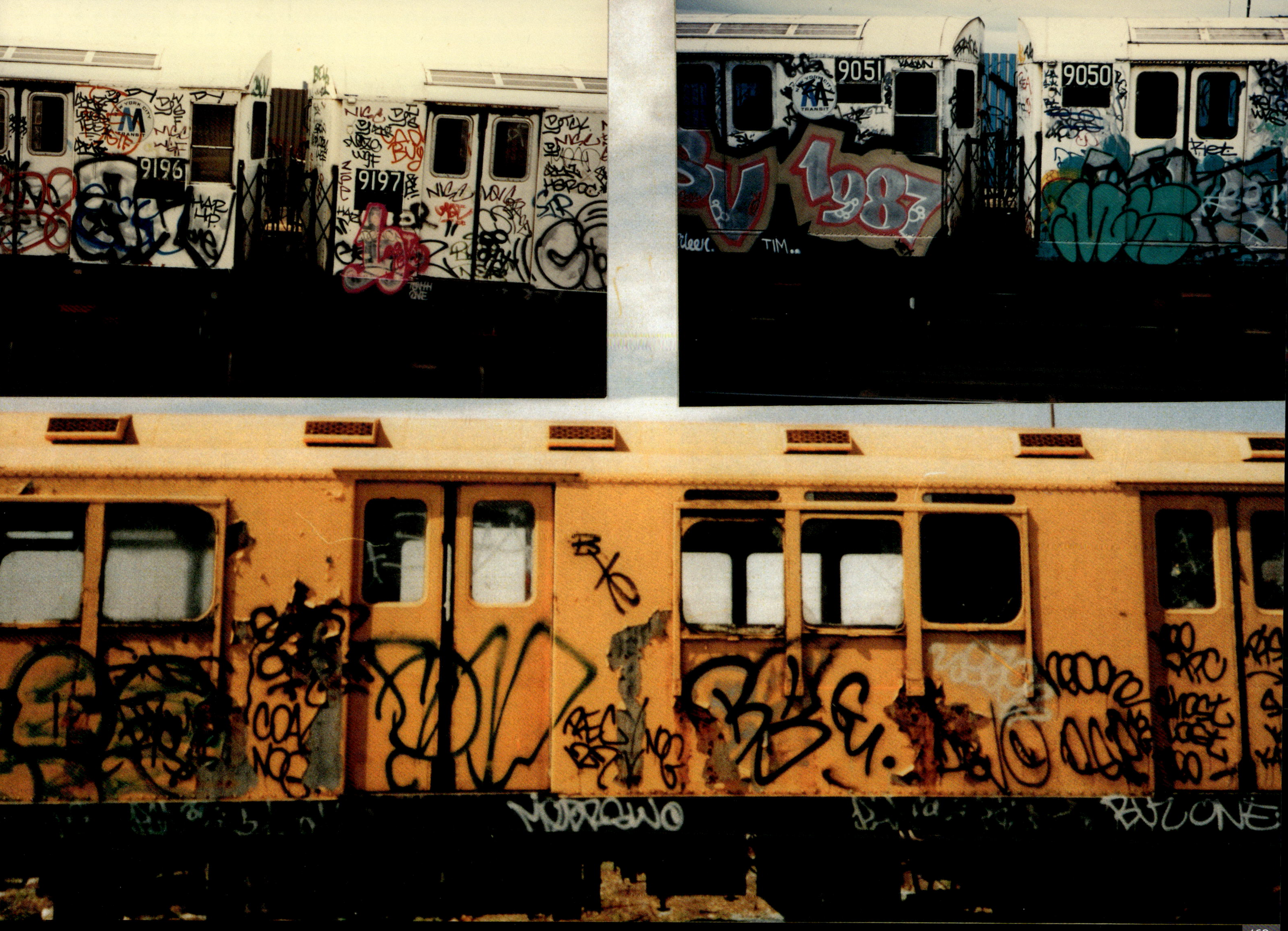
9196
9197
9051
9050

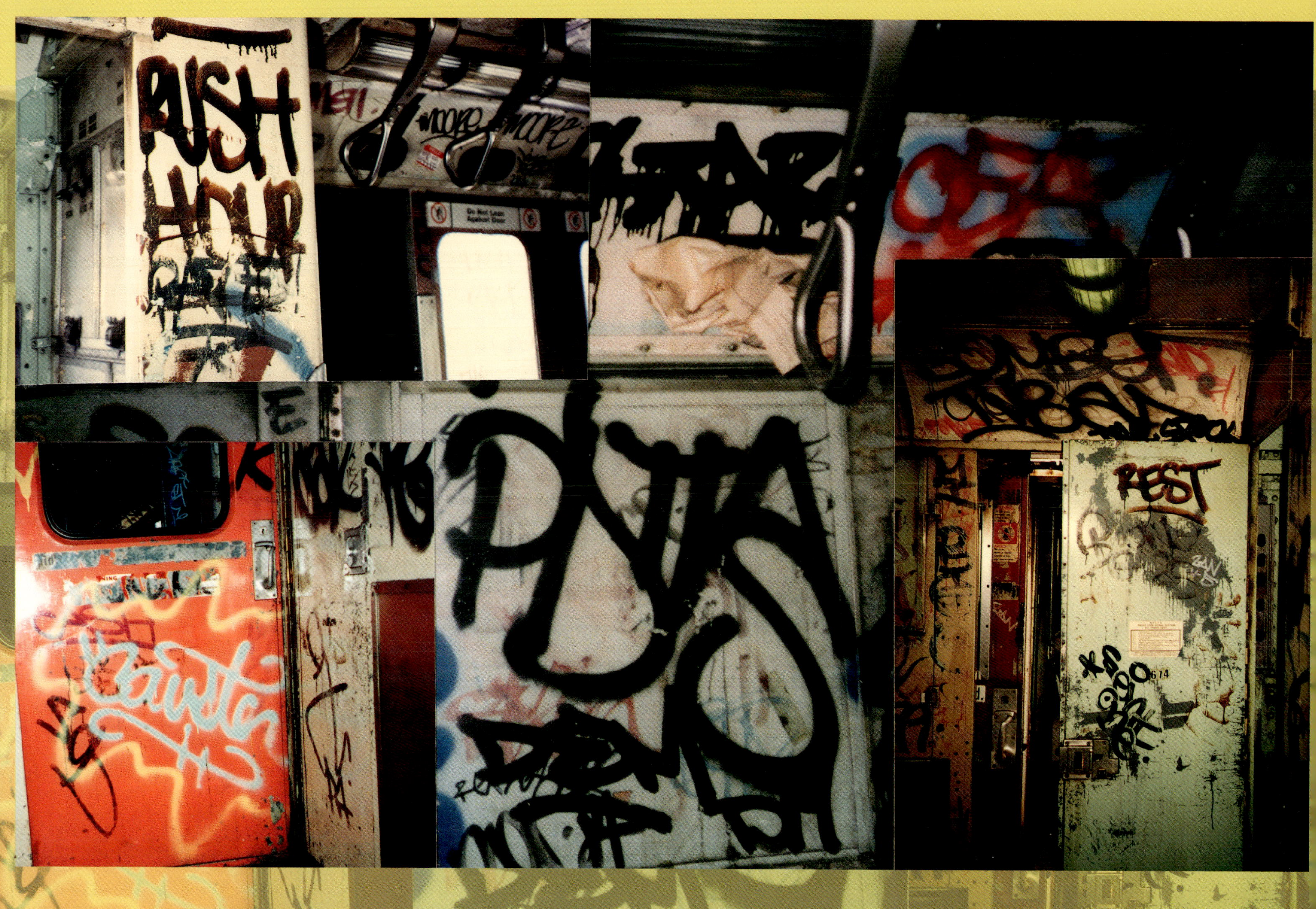
RUSH HOUR
Do Not Lean Against Door
REST

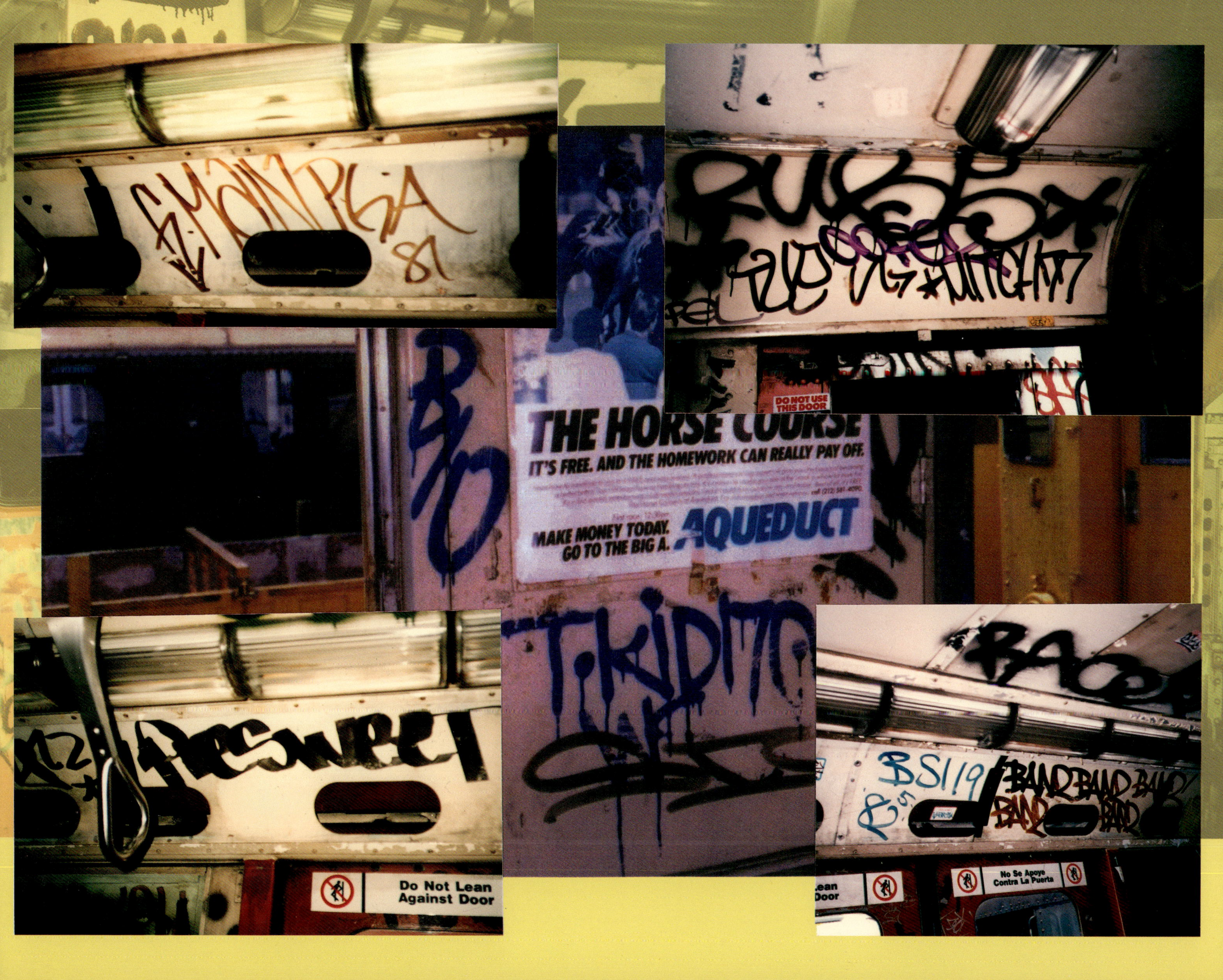
THE HORSE COURSE
IT'S FREE. AND THE HOMEWORK CAN REALLY PAY OFF.
MAKE MONEY TODAY. GO TO THE BIG A.
AQUEDUCT
DO NOT USE THIS DOOR
Do Not Lean Against Door
No Se Apoye Contra La Puerta

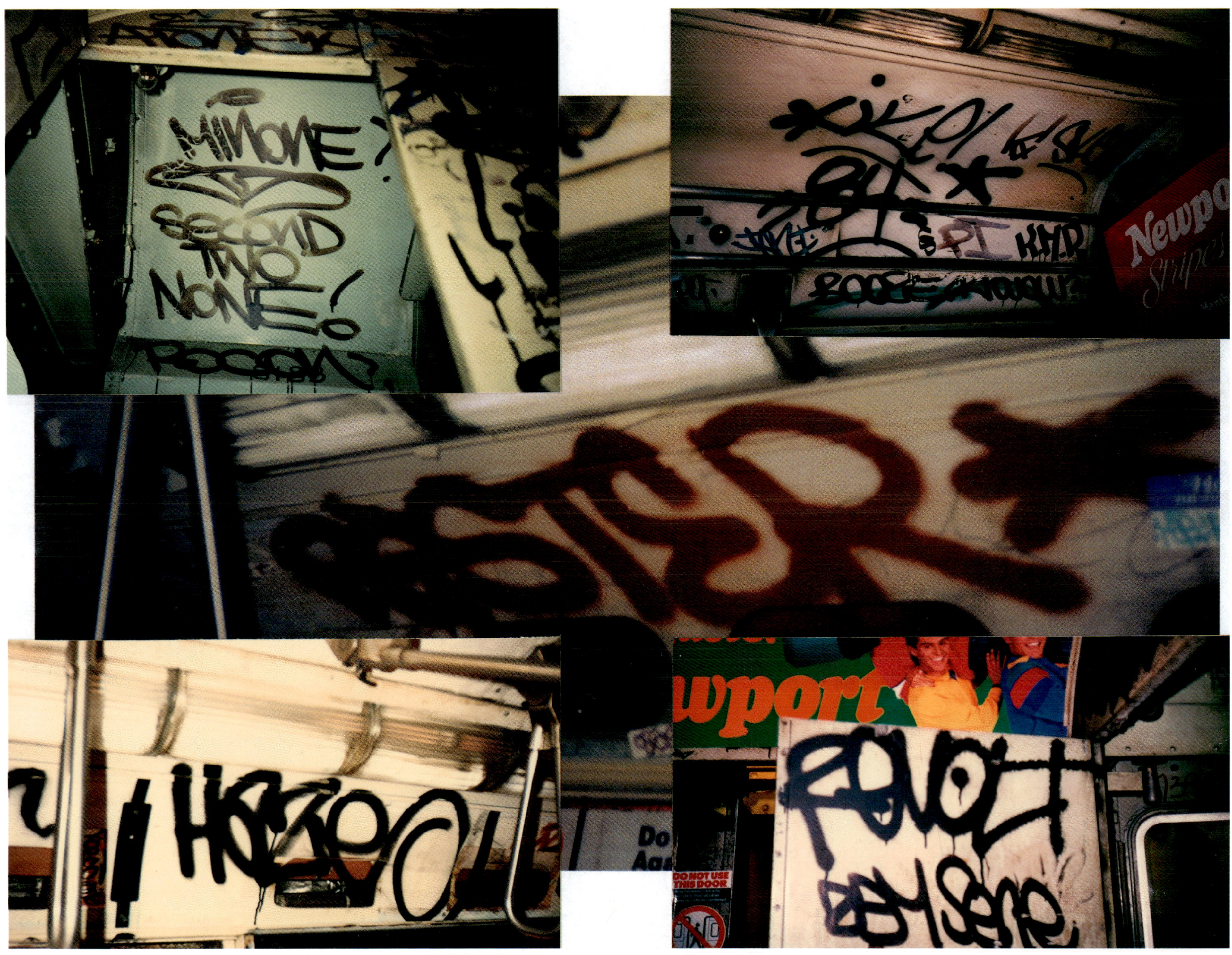
MINONE
SECOND
TWO
NONE
Newport
Stripes
wport
DO NOT USE
THIS DOOR

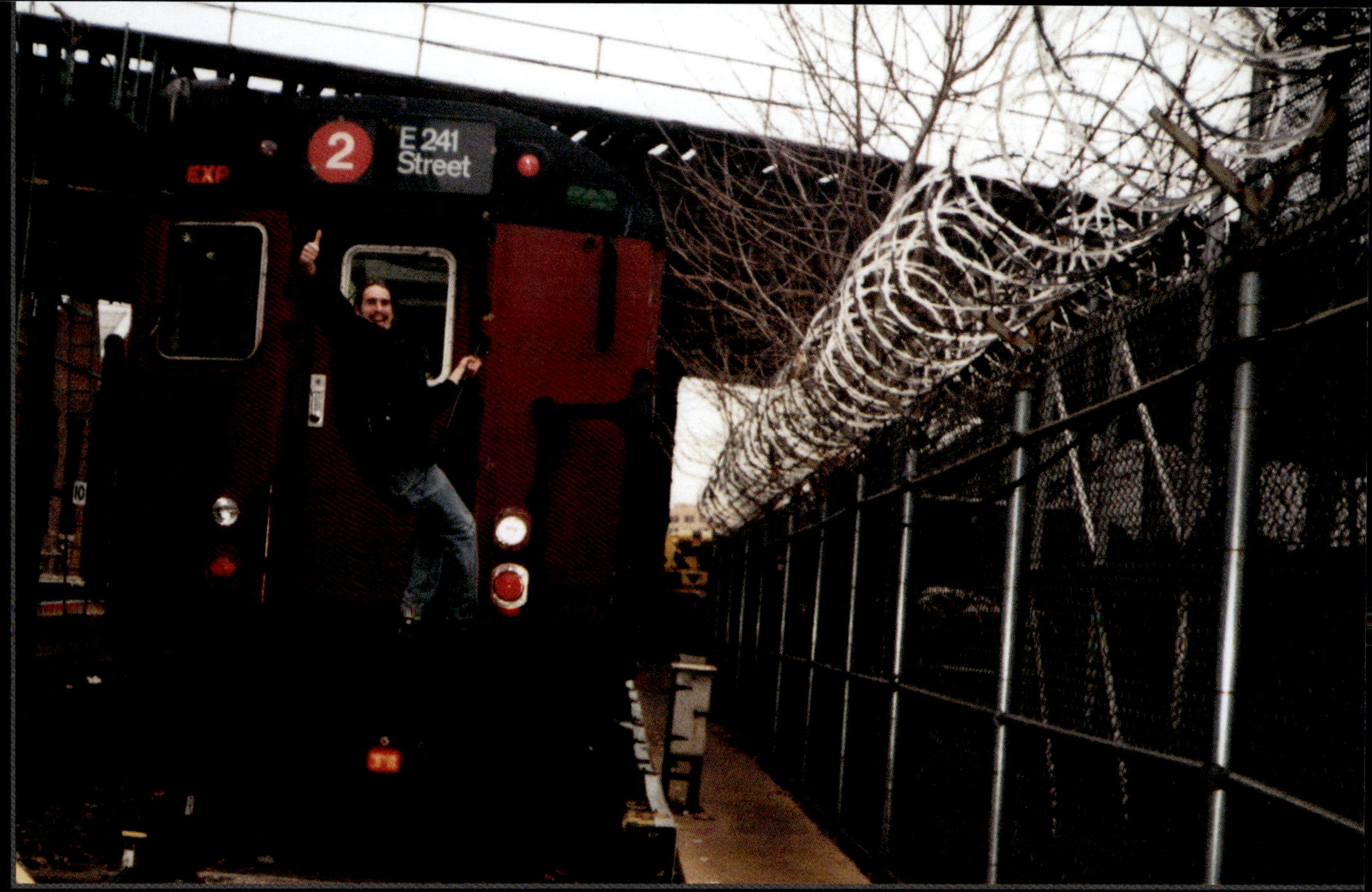

I met Cav for the 1st time back in 1992. I was a young toy with only 3 years of writing under my belt, and in my eyes Cav was a king. I had seen a good amount of his trains, and numerous walls that he did in the Bronx. He was the first real subway writer that I ever had the pleasure of hanging out with. We chilled at his house that night, and he had what seemed like a never ending closet full of subway albums. I remember my head spinning because there was just way too much to take in. Not only because of the photos, but the stories that went along with them. He told me a lot of the sacrifices that he made to get photos back then. Standing in front of a tiny heater all day in the blistering cold while waiting for trains to pull in and out the station. Being chased onto the tracks by neighborhood dudes in Brooklyn who wanted to stomp him out. Getting sucker punched by someone that tried to vic his camera, only for Cav to return with his trusty 2x4 and deliver some street justice. These were just a small fraction of the stories that he had when it came to the 7 years of his life that he dedicated to benching. It became apparent to me that Cav was not only a great writer, but was also an excellent photographer. The photos that he took really speak for themselves. They say that imitation is the greatest form of flattery, and when speaking of his photos there is no better way to put it. His photos have been copied, and bootlegged so many times across the globe by numerous people. Too bad he couldn't collect royalties on all of them. He certainly would have been a millionaire by now.

–Mone One

To my younger brother Kenny Key, thank you for sharing some of your rare classic subway photos. To my childhood friends Joel, aka Blist, and Jeffrey, aka Gin, for influencing me to write Graffiti. The Matilda Avenue/ East 238th street family. The block where it all started. Sento, graffiti mentor. Seen UA, for showing me the ropes. Tod "TL-ONE" Lange (Author), my good friend, thanks for all your help. Thank you to everyone who contributed to *From the Platform*.

To all the graffiti writers in this book. Thanks for the memories: Mione, Iz the Wiz, Quik RTW, Ven, Key, Sar, Ale, Des KTC, Cope2, Zephyr, Blist, Gin, Ghost, Blade, Tkid 170, Wane, Ket, Reas, Zim, Vism, Sien5, Mone, Maze TMC, Vet, LM4.

To all the graffiti writers that are no longer here: Iz the Wiz, Elf KTC, Paws, Mars, Buste, Smiley 149 TED, Elmarko 174, Cliff 159, Dondi, Rook, Billy 167, Caine 1, Sane 182, PG, Shy 147, Zoom, Mirage, Cerism, Siner, Bear 167, Hurst TOP, Stim 1, TO729, Solid TFP, Gary Sash, Rec 127, Sno, Ajax, T rex, Colt MPC, Janet, Rem311, and the list goes on and on. Rest in Peace.

The Author

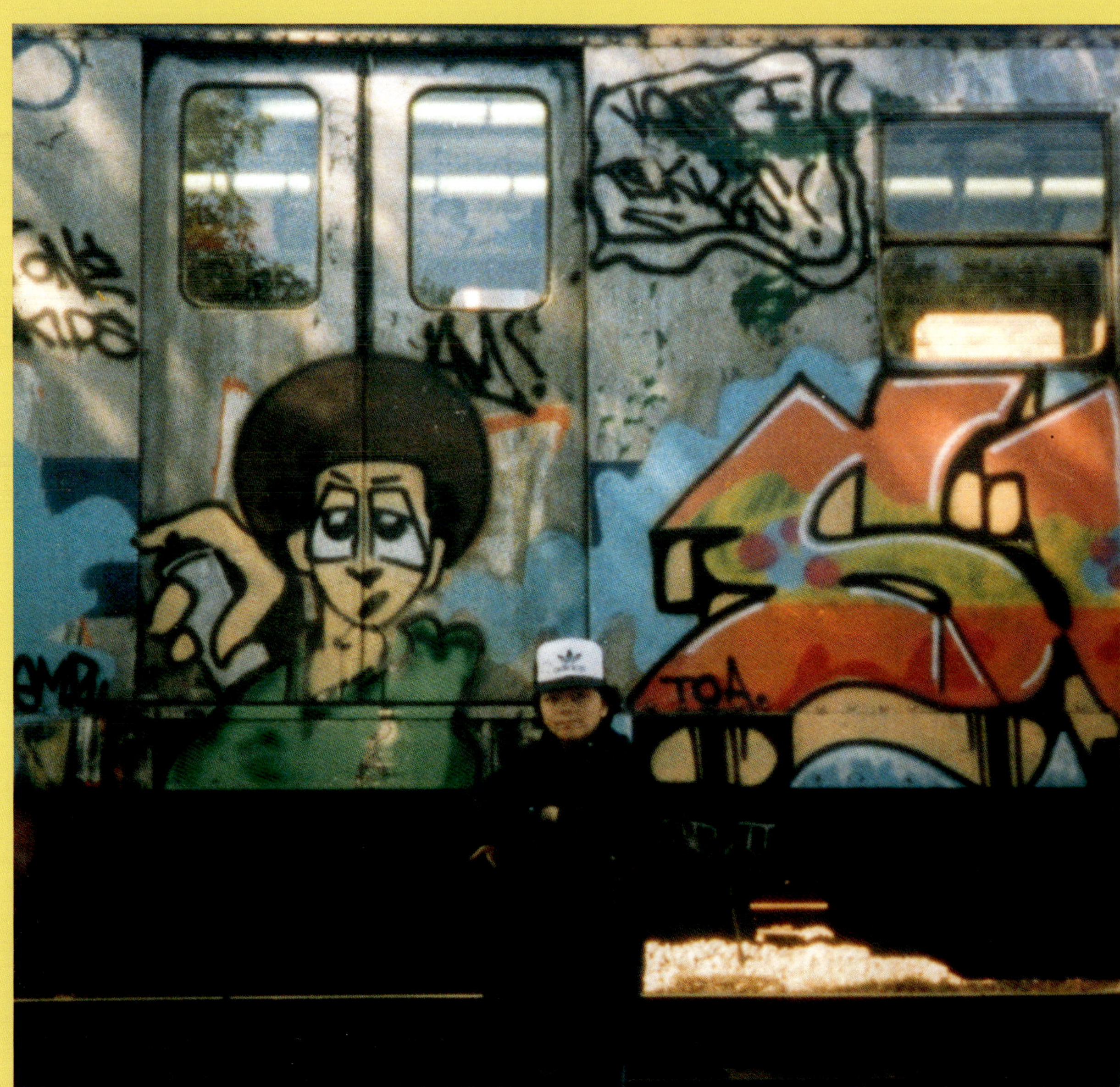

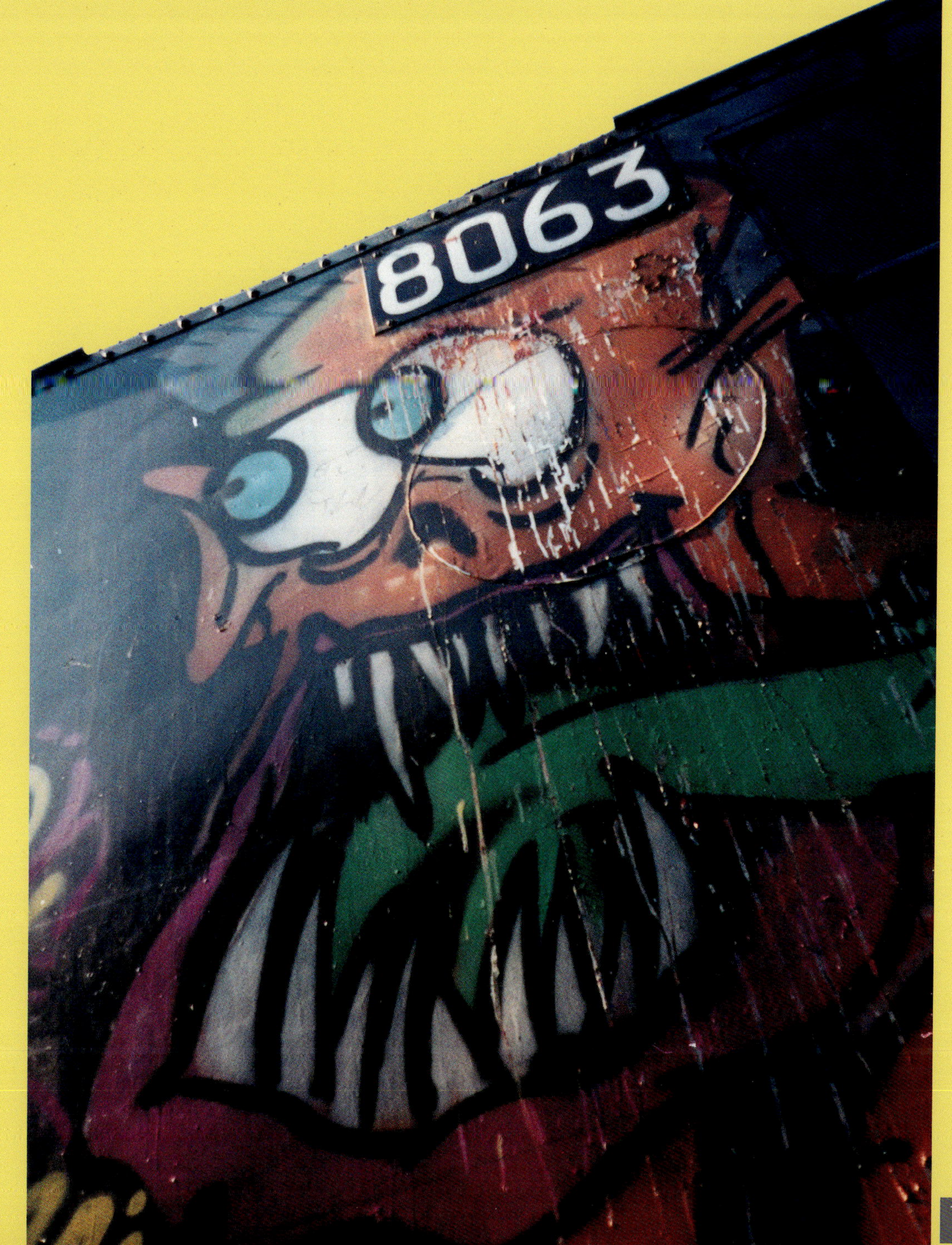

Page 1: Bill Pullman

Page 12: Mione

Page 21: Seen UA (Blade in Action)

Page 73: Quik RTW

Page 78: Reas

Page 147: Poes

Page 156: Sar TMB

Page 158: Ale

Page 161: Poes

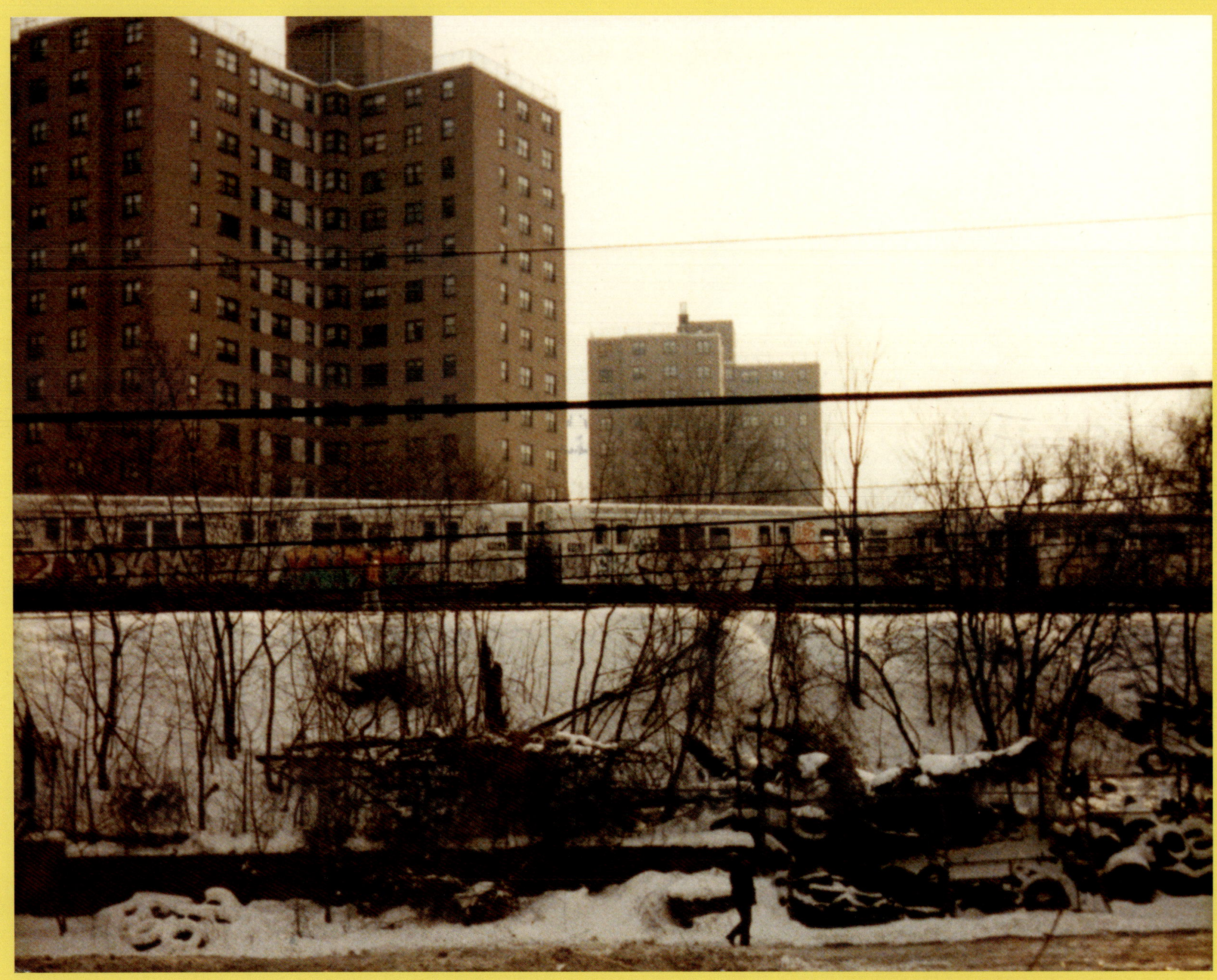

Baychester

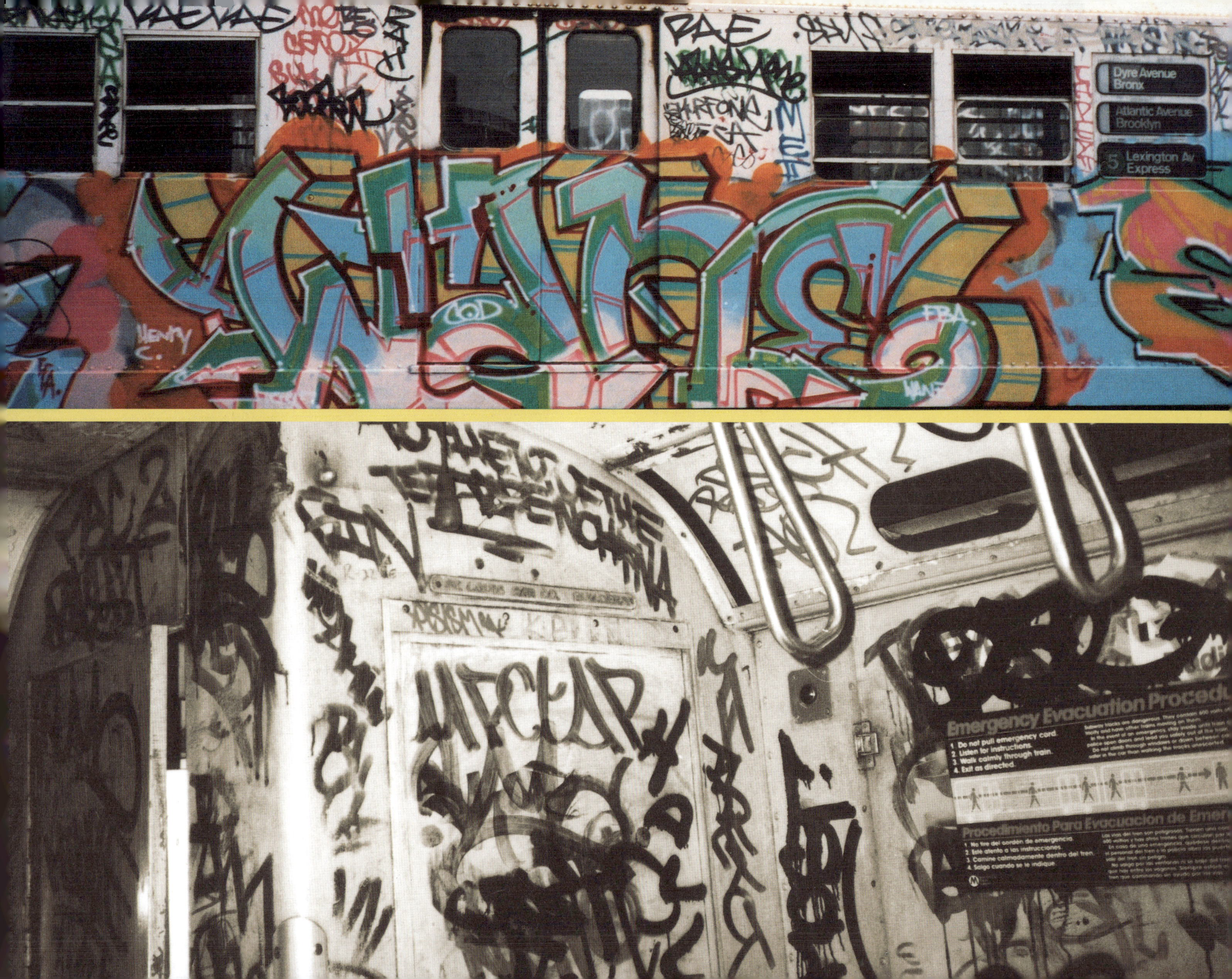
Dyre Avenue Bronx
Atlantic Avenue Brooklyn
5 Lexington Av Express
Emergency Evacuation Procedu
1. Do not pull emergency cord.
2. Listen for instructions.
3. Walk calmly through train.
4. Exit as directed.
Procedimiento Para Evacuacion de Emer
1. No tire del cordón de emergencia.
2. Esté atento a las instrucciones.
3. Camine calmadamente dentro del tren.
4. Salga cuando se le indique.